MW00453340

AT WAR WITH CORRUPTION

ALSO BY MICHAEL J. HIGHTOWER

Inventing Tradition: Cowboy Sports in a Postmodern Age
(Saarbrücken, Germany, 2008)

Frontier Families: The Records and Johnstons in American History
(Oklahoma City, 2010)

The Pattersons: A Novel
(Oklahoma City and Charlottesville, Virginia, 2012)

Banking in Oklahoma before Statehood
(Norman, Oklahoma, 2013)

Banking in Oklahoma, 1907–2000
(Norman, Oklahoma, 2014)

Loyal to Oklahoma: The BancFirst Story
(Oklahoma City and Charlottesville, Virginia, 2015)

*1889: The Boomer Movement, the Land Run,
and Early Oklahoma City*
(Norman, Oklahoma, 2018)

AT WAR WITH CORRUPTION

A Biography of Bill Price, U.S. Attorney for the Western District of Oklahoma

Michael J. Hightower

with a Foreword by Frank Keating

CITIES
PRESS

This book is published with the generous assistance of
Inasmuch Foundation of Oklahoma City, with administrative
support from the Friends of the Oklahoma History Center.

© 2021 Friends of the Oklahoma History Center, Oklahoma City.
All rights reserved.

Published by 2 Cities Press

Distributed by the University of Oklahoma Press
2800 Venture Drive, Norman, OK 73069
To order, contact Longleaf Services, Inc., (800) 848-6224 ext. 1

Cover, text, and book design by Carl Brune

Copyediting by Stephanie Marshall Ward

Cover image courtesy Bill Price

Printed in Canada

ISBN 978-0-9847056-3-4

Library of Congress Control Number: 2021932835

CONTENTS

Foreword

Although Bill Price and I are Oklahomans and attended similar schools (Casady and Cascia Hall, respectively), we grew up in very different cities. Bill's home, Oklahoma City, is at the eastern edge of the western flatlands, and it's the center of state government.

I spent my formative years in the forested hills of Tulsa, which has always branded itself as a businessperson's town. Separated by a scant hundred miles of the Turner Turnpike (aka I–44), the two cities evolved, both historically and culturally, with distinct and not always compatible personalities. Really, Tulsans never felt much kinship with Oklahoma Cityans, and vice versa. It was like we were in different states.

As I was Bill's senior by four years and a resident of the state's second biggest city, there was never much chance that our paths would cross. We did have a couple of near misses: I graduated from Georgetown University the year he showed up as a freshman, and I finished law school at the University of Oklahoma just as he was getting started. When our paths finally crossed, we discovered that we had quite a few things in common, and not only in our choice of educational institutions. First, both of us were devout Catholics. Second, we shared a commitment to bedrock conservative principles that fueled our careers in law and politics. I like to think of us as white-hat guys—toilers in a political landscape where Republicans were rare and not altogether welcome. Republicans only half joked about Democrats spending their Saturday nights hunting us in their headlights. We were fortunate to have mentors like G. T. Blankenship, Henry Bellmon, and Al Snipes to lead a grassroots campaign aimed at turning Oklahoma into a genuine two-party state.

After law school, I joined the FBI and relocated to the West Coast. While Bill was back in Oklahoma honing his skills as a prosecutor, I was investigating bad guys, arresting them, and launching them on their journeys through the legal system. Although Bill and I occupied different positions in law enforcement, we were on the same page when it came to fighting corruption. Governors, judges, legislators— no matter where they stood in the official hierarchy, nobody seemed immune to the temptation to cheat. All we could do was shake our heads in disbelief and then suit up and go to work, determined to do what we could to enforce a level playing field.

By the time I returned to Tulsa to accept a position in the state prosecutor's office, Bill was earning a reputation as a no-nonsense assistant in the U.S. Attorney's Office in Oklahoma City, where he and his colleagues were responsible for enforcing the law in forty of the state's seventy-seven counties. When I was elected to the Oklahoma state House of Representatives and then the state Senate, I found myself (no surprise here!) as a forlorn Republican in a sea of Democrats—a back bencher with little hope of molding legislation to conservative ideology.

About the time I was appointed as U.S. Attorney for the Northern District of Oklahoma, the county commissioner scandal exploded into what became the biggest case of public corruption in U.S. history, and it seized headlines from coast to coast. Hidden in plain sight, commissioners in charge of keeping their counties' roads fixed and bridges safe had been accepting bribes from materials suppliers. Some said unsavory business practices dated back to statehood in 1907, and maybe even before that. Nobody really knows. I came face-to-face with their systemic thievery when I was appointed as the federal government's lead prosecutor in the Northern District. A year later, Bill was appointed to the same position in the Western District, an enormous swath of Oklahoma that dwarfed the eleven counties under my jurisdiction. Although I sent numerous miscreants to jail, the Northern District tally was a mere fraction of the number of county commissioners and materials suppliers that Bill and his assistants put behind bars, through plea agreements and convictions.

I was stunned, and I know Bill was too. Many of the people caught in our crosshairs accepted bribes because, as we were told again and again, "everyone did it." In many cases, the bribes were tiny; in nearly all cases, commissioners were shocked that their time-honored business model had earned them prison sentences when they thought they were just doing their jobs. I felt sorry for some of them, but as the federal government's top representative in northern Oklahoma, I had no choice but to see justice done.

Unlike the Western District, where a tsunami of pleas and convictions kept Bill and his assistants working overtime, the Northern District proved to be less tainted by bribery in county purchasing. In fact, Tulsa County commissioners showed no evidence of wrongdoing. Tulsa lived up to its reputation as a businessperson's town whose elected officials remained true to their oaths of office.

As the U.S. Attorney who bore the brunt of the county commissioner scandal, Bill Price deserves credit for waging a successful war with corruption and, with a nod to the classics, cleaning out the Aegean stable. He was truly at the epicenter, and he handled the challenge with extraordinary skill, integrity, and precision. He would have made a terrific governor or congressman. Denied those opportunities, he reinvented himself as a defense lawyer and, after he retired from public life, spearheaded nonprofit projects that have made Oklahoma a better place to live. Serving with Bill on the Oklahoma Council of Public Affairs gave us a bully pulpit to express our commitment to the cornerstones of conservatism: free enterprise, limited government, individual initiative, and personal responsibility.

Bill's story, from his youthful embrace of conservative values and prosecutions in the U.S. Attorney's Office to his hard-fought political campaigns and volunteering on behalf of disadvantaged youth, needs to be told, both to remind us of where we have been and to inspire us to work toward a brighter future. As a former occupant of the governor's mansion, I can say with some authority that my friend U.S. Congressman Tom Cole, who served as secretary of state during my first term, was right when he called Bill Price the best governor Oklahoma never had.

FRANK KEATING

July 2021

Preface

At War with Corruption began, as many books do, in a conversation between friends. In this case, those friends were the subject of this biography, Bill Price, and Bob Ross, chairman and CEO of Inasmuch Foundation in Oklahoma City. Long before they conceived this book, Bill and Bob belonged to various boards of directors and civic organizations that summoned them to meetings throughout their native state of Oklahoma. To pass their windshield time, Bill regaled his friend with tales of his tenure in the U.S. Attorney's Office in Oklahoma City and his hard-fought political campaigns for governor in 1990 and Congress in 1992. Many of those tales were about the Oklahoma county commissioner scandal of the 1970s and early 1980s, which rocked state governance to its core, spawned the most extensive public corruption case in FBI history, and dominated Bill's fifteen-year tenure as a federal prosecutor. Before he retired from his law career and for many years thereafter, Bill spearheaded philanthropic projects that turned his retirement into something other than retirement, and these, too, became fodder for conversation during their cross-state travels.

There's no telling where they were when Bob posed the inevitable suggestion:

"Bill, you need to write a book!"

That sounded like a good idea. All he needed was a scribe to help put it all together.

Which is why, on a picture-perfect spring day in Virginia, I answered a call from Bob Ross, wondering if I might be interested in writing a biography of the biggest corruption buster in Oklahoma history.

▶ ▶ ▶ ▶

I was, and a few weeks after Ross's call, I traveled to Oklahoma City and went to work. Actually, it didn't seem like work, as most of my early research involved talking to Price and other opinion leaders whose collective efforts since the 1960s helped stymie public and commercial corruption and, in the process, brought a much-needed shine to Oklahoma's tarnished reputation. As I conducted and transcribed their audiotaped interviews and made my first forays into books, articles, and archival collections (that felt more like work), I realized that I had stumbled onto a bigger project than I had anticipated. What had begun as a straightforward biography was morphing into a deeper history that had never been explored, systematically and comprehensively, in book form. Simply put, I was wading into not one, but two narratives: Price's biography, which is historically significant by any standard, and the war with corruption in Oklahoma.

This book, then, chronicles a dual narrative, and it divides rather neatly into three parts. Part I, "Prologue," encompasses the first five chapters. It begins with a scene forever etched into the national consciousness and commemorated most famously in *Far and Away*, the 1992 blockbuster movie starring Tom Cruise and Nicole Kidman: the 1893 run into the Cherokee Outlet, a vast expanse of grasslands that eventually became northern Oklahoma west of the Arkansas River, north of the Oklahoma City metro, and east of the Panhandle. For our purposes, the run's significance lies in the fact that Price's paternal grandparents somehow survived the chaos of that storied day, staked their claim in what became Dewey County near Woodward, and built lives that motivated their descendants to excel in their chosen fields.

But, of course, the backdrop to all that pioneering and homesteading was a pattern of malfeasance dating back to the state's foundation, when "Soonerism" (an inelegant term if there ever was one, but nonetheless descriptive) left its legacy in fraudulent land claims and outright robbery, often accompanied by acts of violence. Hidden in plain sight were abuses aimed at the state's earlier inhabitants, from the theft of Native American land and annihilation of their sovereignty to the Osage murders of the 1920s, which set the standard for perfidy in high places. That juxtaposition of Oklahoma's heroic foundation story and the mayhem and murder that came with it illustrates a theme that pervades this book: the symbiotic relationship between honest and even gallant pursuits and criminality. To borrow an overused metaphor, they are two sides of the same coin whose chemistry has spawned an endless array of corrupt practices and has challenged generations of law enforcement officials and jurists to investigate crimes, delineate what was legal and what was not, and prosecute the offenders.

Weaned on stories of his grandparents' and, later, his parents' grit and ingenuity, Price learned early on the value of honest work, the necessity of education, and the need to serve others as the gateway to a fulfilling life. Those lessons instilled in him a reverence for what became the twin pillars of his personal and professional lives: conservative Republican politics and the law. Throughout his student days at Casady School in northwest Oklahoma City, his undergraduate years at Georgetown University, in Washington, D.C., law school at the University of Oklahoma, and his management of a gubernatorial campaign, Price blended book learning and real-world experience to launch a law career and, at the same time, chart a path to the inner circle of Oklahoma's Republican Party. Part of that real-world experience was the Oklahoma supreme court scandal of 1964–65, a sordid spectacle of bribery and extortion that exploded when Price was a teenager, giving him a glimpse of his future as a federal prosecutor.

Part II, "The Arena," comprises the next five chapters, and it opens with the cloak-and-dagger saga of Governor David Hall's tenure as one of the most corrupt public officials in state history. Beginning on day one of his single term, the ever-smiling governor complemented his inspiring agenda of educational reforms and revenue enhancement with a less inspiring pattern of bribery, extortion, and raids on the public coffers to pay his personal debts. No sooner did Price join U.S. Attorney Bill Burkett's small cadre of assistants, in late 1974, than he was asked to assist in the United States case against Governor Hall, which began just weeks after Hall left office. Hall's trial, conviction, and imprisonment came on the heels of another imbroglio that beefed up Price's resume: that of Oklahoma State Treasurer Leo Winters, whose cozy relationships with state banks came to be known, rather unimaginatively, as the Leo Winters banking scandal.

Famously, Winters's trial ended with his exoneration. Although Price arrived in the U.S. Attorney's Office too late to participate in the prosecution, he was assigned to Winters's brazen (albeit unsuccessful) civil case against Burkett for prosecuting him in the first place, and he spent many hours deposing the wily state treasurer. With experience in two high-profile cases, Price was ready to handle any assignment that Burkett and his successors handed him, which is exactly what he got—in the form of international drug smuggling, interstate shipment heists, tax fraud, and a host of prosecutorial assignments that illuminate the inner workings of a U.S. Attorney's Office.

Then comes the story that inspired this book: the Oklahoma county commissioner scandal. Since territorial days, Oklahoma's populist leanings left counties with lots of latitude and little oversight as they figured out how to pay for improvements and compensate their elected officials. Left to their own devices, county commissioners with a yen for creative financing built independent fiefdoms in which fraud, bribery, and extortion were integral to purchasing road- and bridge-building materials. One county commissioner put it this way: "I've talked to some real old fellows, and they say it's been happening ever since statehood, ever since God made county commissionering [sic]. I just didn't know how it worked until I got into office."

Neither did Price—that is, not until a chance remark at an arson investigation ripped the cover off county commissioners' modus operandi and put him on a trail leading to hundreds of guilty pleas, trials, and jail sentences. In collaboration with FBI and IRS investigations seemingly ripped from a page-turning suspense thriller, Price and his fellow U.S. Attorneys in Tulsa and Muskogee led a no-holds-barred campaign to end corruption in county purchasing and restore public confidence in state governance. As Price explained, in one of dozens of media interviews that made him a household name across Oklahoma and spawned his political ambitions, "When wrongdoing continues, people grow skeptical about law and justice. We prosecuted. We had to send people to prison. That's the only way you can stop a practice." The scandal made it all the way to cartoonist Garry Trudeau's *Doonesbury*, giving the rest of the country a peek into unsavory practices that were by no means unique to Oklahoma but that branded the Sooner State as a crucible of corruption and a risky place to do business. That taint of corruption dissipated as post-Okscam reforms compelled county commissioners to reconsider their business model and embrace, however grudgingly, transparency in materials purchases.

The final five chapters, constituting Part III, "From Whom Much Is Given," begin with Price's seven-year tenure as the first assistant ever elevated to the top job in the U.S. Attorney's Office in the Western District of Oklahoma. Crammed into those years were dozens of county commissioner prosecutions, lawsuits attending the FDIC takeover of Penn Square Bank in Oklahoma City, cesspools of commercial bribery that rivaled the county commissioner scandal in their duplicity, kickbacks in Indian housing, banking swindles, a college president caught with his hands in the till, and cases against drug kingpins that brought Price and his assistants face-to-face with evil on a grand scale. Such was Price's disgust with drug peddlers, who wrecked young people's lives with impunity, that he founded the Oklahoma Alliance Against Drugs (OAAD), a prevention program known nationwide for its effectiveness in saving youth from the scourge of drug and alcohol addiction.

Price capped his career as U.S. Attorney with two successful initiatives that forever changed the imposition of law and order: passage of legislation that brought federal RICO (Racketeer Influenced and Corrupt Organizations) statutes to the state level and laws enabling multicounty grand juries, a long-overdue reform that broadened the scope of state investigations. As former U.S. Attorney for the Northern

District of Oklahoma and, later, two-term governor Frank Keating put it, Oklahoma legislators needed "to muscle up" the attorney general's office. "We have three federal districts here," explained Keating, "and you have a plethora of county grand juries and district attorneys here. So is there anybody who can bring everybody together to attack the problem? That would be the multicounty grand jury."

Yearning to apply his experience as a prosecutor to Oklahoma's highest office, Price tossed his hat in the ring to run for governor in 1990. But before he stepped down as U.S. Attorney, he received a visit from Bob Anthony, a friend since middle school, who had just been elected to the Oklahoma Corporation Commission. New to politics and in need of guidance, Anthony described a conversation with a notorious fixer who seemed all too eager to dispense envelopes stuffed with hundred-dollar bills. Price knew exactly who the fixer was and admonished his old friend to go to the FBI. Anthony did just that and quickly found himself embroiled in the Oklahoma Corporation Commission scandal, a tangle of intrigue that was costing taxpayers millions and branding the state's primary regulatory agency as yet another hotbed of corruption.

While Anthony was getting a crash course from the FBI in undercover surveillance, which resulted in a slew of grand-jury indictments and prosecutions, Price was focusing on his campaign for governor. For polling expertise and campaign strategy, he turned to Tom Cole, then a state senator, whose political consulting business had predated his successful run for, and multiple reelections to, the U.S. Congress. Price's volunteer staff included his wife, Mary, and their three children, Anne, James, and Eileen. Much as Price's caseload in the U.S. Attorney's Office opens a portal into how federal prosecutions worked, his family's odyssey across Oklahoma reads like a primer on grassroots campaigning, from dining on a 7,500-pound cookie to laying wagers in a game of cow patty bingo (more on those later). In her interview, Mary ignored my digital recorder as she read from her campaign diary: "We are enjoying the campaign enormously. Mainly, I am convinced that this is Bill's destiny. He is so good and honest, and genuinely wanting to serve the state. His whole life so far has been dedicated to public service, and his dream has been to run for elective office."

Campaigning might have been his destiny, but winning was not, and Price shook off the letdown of a failed campaign to build a private law practice. But, once again, politics came calling, this time in a race for Congress. When that came to naught, Price bounced back from a second letdown and poured his energy into big-time lawsuits, most notably against group purchasing organizations (GPOs) that were stifling innovations in medical technology and wreaking havoc in healthcare delivery. He complemented his private law practice with managing his family's oil and gas business and promoting a growing number of philanthropic pursuits, including, but not limited to, the Oklahoma State School Board, the Oklahoma School Choice Coalition, Shiloh Camp for disadvantaged children, and Cristo Rey, a Catholic school with campuses nationwide that he helped establish in Oklahoma City to serve low-income students.

Chip Carter served on Price's campaign staff when he ran for Congress. After several years in public relations, he reinvented himself when Price recommended him as president of Cristo Rey Oklahoma City. Carter had been in that position for all of two weeks when I caught up with him in the school's modest building at Oklahoma State University's Oklahoma City campus.

"Few people are familiar with Cristo Rey Oklahoma City," explained Carter, straining to be heard above the hubbub outside his cramped conference room. "So my job in the next several years is to raise our public image within not just the Catholic community, but the overall community." Part of that job was to enlist businesses in offering paid internships to Cristo Rey students, a business model based on public-private partnerships that offered a win-win situation across the country and, with Price's guidance, now promised to do the same in Oklahoma City.

When I asked about his long-range goals, Carter was unequivocal: "I want businesspeople to be able to say to one another, 'We've got a Cristo Rey team. Do you?' And have the other guy say, 'I need to call them.' There's a level of penetration that we need to get to. That's my priority."

For Price, helping Cristo Rey Oklahoma City penetrate the business community was one of many priorities that made his retirement an ongoing process of re-careering.

▶ ▶ ▶ ▶

At the outset, we need a working definition of corruption to provide a broader context for Oklahoma's experiences and Bill Price's prosecutions. I could find none more succinct and straightforward than one offered by Sarah Chayes, a senior associate with the Carnegie Endowment for International Peace whose resume includes reporting for National Public Radio and advising the chairman of the Joint Chiefs of Staff on the international security implications of acute corruption. To discover the causes and effects of corruption on a global scale, she traveled to the world's most renowned kleptocracies before shining her analytical lights on her own country. In her 2020 tour de force, *On Corruption in America*, Chayes cautions us not to look askance at corruption as an aberration or embarrassment best shrugged off with a roll of the eyes. To do so "is to dangerously underestimate its significance. Corruption is not an isolated scandal or even a whole stack of them. Corruption is better understood as the deliberate mode of functioning—the operating system, you might say—of sophisticated, and astonishingly successful, networks."

Even though *At War with Corruption* reveals the darker side of human nature and its appearance throughout Oklahoma history, its intention is not to depress but to uplift and to show what is possible when people of good faith promote legislation and structural reforms in government and then work with like-minded crusaders to make things better. By all accounts, Bill Price did just that. He encountered corruption embedded in an array of sophisticated and successful networks, searched for its underlying causes, and teamed up with law enforcement and elected officials to make fraud less enticing and playing by the rules more rewarding. He would be the first to admit that the job is far from done. He would be the last to throw in the towel and declare the war unwinnable.

Thanks go to Bob Ross and Inasmuch Foundation in Oklahoma City for making this book possible, Dan Provo and the Friends of the Oklahoma History Center for administering the project, attorneys Anne O'Connor and Drew Neville for reading the manuscript to make sure this non-attorney got it mostly right, all the people who shared their experiences in interviews, which constitute my primary sources of both information and inspiration, and Judy Hightower for her consistent good cheer and encouragement. Most of all, I am grateful to Bill and Mary Price and their family for trusting me to tell their story.

If there are errors of omission or commission in the pages to follow, I will surely hear about them. I will just as surely claim them as mine.

MICHAEL J. HIGHTOWER
Oklahoma City and Charlottesville 2021

PART I : *PROLOGUE*

CHAPTER ONE : *Staking a Claim*

For the most part, historians of the early federal period in American history have had little good to say about the Confederation Congress and its rulebook in the Articles of Confederation. Among the shortcomings of that much-maligned and short-lived document were two that might have doomed the American experiment to an abrupt and perhaps bloody end: it did not authorize creation of a standing army and it failed to unite the original thirteen colonies in a comprehensive system of taxation. As the confederation of former colonies teetered on the brink of dissolution and the clamor for a constitutional convention gained traction, delegates overcame their differences to craft what became their most enduring legacy: the Northwest Ordinance of 1787.

The immediate purpose of the ordinance was to create the Northwest Territory, close to the Great Lakes and northwest of the Ohio River, as the United States' first organized region. But its long-term significance was its authorization of an orderly process for regions to attain territorial status as a prerequisite to statehood. Confident that American civilization would one day span the continent, the Confederation Congress guaranteed that the federal government's expansion into the frontier would be democratic in character, orderly in execution and, ideally, free from the corrupting influence of wealthy elites and the perils of partisan bickering.

But then delegates to the Confederation Congress never anticipated Oklahoma.

Convinced that Native Americans were doomed to extinction in a rapidly expanding nation, President Andrew Jackson won congressional approval for the Indian Removal Act of 1830, which sent Southeastern tribes packing to an uncharted wilderness that drifted into history as

3

Indian Territory and, eventually, the state of Oklahoma. Beginning with a trickle of forced migration in the 1830s and continuing through the Indian wars in the immediate post–Civil War period, Indian Territory evolved into a patchwork of displaced tribes. The so-called Five Civilized Tribes (known less condescendingly as the Five Tribes), from the Southeast, occupied eastern and southern regions of the territory, and nomadic tribes from the Great Plains and Rocky Mountains were assigned to reservations in the West. As homesteads and upstart towns transformed America's midsection into an agricultural Mecca and neighboring territories entered the union according to protocols dating back to the Confederation Congress, prospective settlers began to cast covetous eyes on Indian Territory's fertile soil and endless grasslands.

None doubted that Indian Territory's jurisdictional mishmash had to go, and most agreed that God-fearing farmers and townsite developers were entitled to their slice of the public domain. The question was, how could Indian lands, promised to their inhabitants as long as the grasses grew and rivers ran, be opened to non-Indian settlement and included in national networks of business and commerce in such a way that would honor treaty obligations and guarantee (or at least make possible) an equitable distribution of land and resources—equitable, that is, for everyone except Native Americans?

The answer came in a series of land runs and lotteries that branded Oklahoma as utterly unique in its foundation story. Famously, land-run participants who refused play by the rules of settlement and (literally!) jumped the gun before the appointed hour of entry became known as Sooners, thereby bequeathing to future generations of Oklahomans the dubious distinction of living in a state named for cheaters.

That heritage, widely celebrated but only dimly understood and largely forgotten with the passage of time, forms a fitting introduction to a book about corruption in Oklahoma and Bill Price's crusade to do something about it.

▶ ▶ ▶ ▶

The run of 1893 into the Cherokee Outlet unleashed a torrent of disputes over land ownership and exacerbated tensions between settlers and Native American tribes that had occupied the region for generations. COURTESY OKLAHOMA HISTORICAL SOCIETY.

No tribe in Indian Territory was more concerned with the disposition of their lands than the Cherokees, whose vast reservation in the northeastern corner of the territory was complemented by a seven-million-acre swath of prime grazing land to the west known as the Cherokee Outlet. Its opening to non-Indian settlement on September 16, 1893, became Indian Territory's fourth and largest land run, and economic pressures, poor planning, and inadequate policing resulted in a nightmare of chaos and contested claims. The pell-mell dash across the prairie on that storied day left numerous people wounded, some fatally, when their horses stumbled and wagons upended; many who survived the maelstrom died that night from heatstroke. Those hoping for a more orderly entry into the Cherokee Outlet boarded trains, only to face armed gangs aiming to get a jump on the competition. Some bailed out en route and suffered grievous injuries when they hit the ground and watched the train chug on without them. Many who made it to their claims unscathed were quickly confronted by rival claimants, armed to the teeth and prepared to impose their own rules of settlement.[1]

Sadly, most participants risked their lives for nothing. In keeping with the inexorable law of economics, the demand for land outstripped the supply. James L. Brown was an attorney who arrived at Oklahoma Station—later dubbed, rather unimaginatively, Oklahoma City, and then comprising little more than a depot and a few crude buildings—the day after the run of April 22, 1889, an affair that opened central Indian Territory to non-Indian settlement and rivaled the run into the Cherokee Outlet in its disorder and long-lasting confusion. The good news was that Brown and other attorneys throughout Indian Territory found steady employment in their chosen profession. "There was much contention over the possession of, and the right to make homestead entries upon, public lands and town lots, as there were so many more claimants for the land than there were quarter sections and lots opened to settlement," wrote Brown in a 1909 retrospective. "All the foregoing led to contention and disputes to such an extent that it was simply confusion confounded, and opened wide the doors for men to swear at each other in the land office with a vengeance. Large numbers of men bound themselves together in groups to swear each other through; innocent men were sworn into the penitentiary or sworn out of their lands or lots."[2] Prescient observers caught a whiff of Oklahoma's future, as Sooners and people in positions of power—often one and the same—secured the best homesteads and town lots. Not for the first time and certainly not the last, Lady Luck smiled on the favored few at the expense of the many.

As a postscript to the run of '93, the chaos endured long after the dust settled. Towns were overbuilt, rivalries raged, and farmers went broke on land never meant for the plow. Untold thousands abandoned their homesteads and town lots and drifted from the pages of history. There were, of course, success stories of thriving businesses, generosity, and even gallantry during and after the run. Yet both the economy and the land it depended on were unforgiving, and even those who secured productive homesteads and choice lots in town learned that opportunities were limited in a nation where runaway industrialization was redefining the meaning of opportunity.

▶ ▶ ▶ ▶

Somewhere in the melee of September 16, 1893 were Bill Price's paternal grandparents, Joel Scott and Reila (née Reynolds) Price. Joel and his descendants were often asked if they were related to Major General Sterling Price, who had served as the governor of Missouri from 1853 to 1857. Although he originally opposed secession, Price fought for the Confederacy in various trans-Mississippi theaters. Bill certainly thought he was a descendant of the famed officer. As proof of his family's lineage, a photo of the general, decked out in his martial regalia, had been circulated through generations of Prices as a prized heirloom.

Although Bill never knew his grandfather, his grandmother lived to the age of ninety-nine, and he grew up listening to tales of her and Joel clattering into the Cherokee Outlet in a covered wagon and staking a claim to a 160-acre homestead near Oakwood in what later became Dewey County, Oklahoma. As a newlywed of eighteen, Reila's post-run challenges were compounded by a husband who had lost a leg cutting lumber somewhere along their westward trek from southwestern Missouri to Kansas and on to Indian Territory. In the absence of trees, the couple made do with a sod house, dubbed in plains vernacular as a "soddie," until they could afford a more suitable dwelling for a family that mushroomed to include eight children.

Price's paternal grandparents, Joel and Reila, joined the land run into the Cherokee Outlet. Posing for a photo at the family's homestead in Oakwood, Oklahoma, are Joel (left, seated), Reila (right, seated), Bill's father, Joel Scott (center, standing), and Joel Scott's six siblings. COURTESY BILL PRICE.

Oakwood survived into the late twentieth century, but just barely. On their way to visit the family farm, Joel Scott occasionally pulled off the highway to show his son the ruins of the house where he was raised. Nearby, abandoned buildings on Main Street told the story of a town that never lived up to its founders' expectations. Decades later, Bill would have opportunities to reflect on those detours, and the tales his father spun, when legal cases drew him back to his roots in northwest Oklahoma.[3]

"Can you imagine coming in on the run of 1893, then in a sod house, and having only one leg, and making a living for your family that way?" asked Bill rhetorically. "I imagine my grandmother, raising eight kids on the prairie, one of whom died young. She was ninety-nine when she died..." He paused to ponder the grit and determination that saw his grandparents through blizzards, prairie squalls, dust storms, droughts, and whatever else Mother Nature had in store for the pioneers of '93.

Reila's favorite tale comes from the birth of a son shortly after she and Joel moved into their soddie. As Reila told the story, the baby was small enough to fit in a teacup, and the couple assumed he was not long for this world. With no access to medical care and precious little exposure to literature of any kind, Reila sometimes visited a nearby community (most likely Oakwood) with a building containing enough books and magazines to pass for a library. She was fascinated to read about a contraption in Kansas City, called an incubator, that sustained life through a combination of heat and oxygen. She promptly returned home and put her premature baby in a crib beneath a cloth-covered table, surrounded him with plants, pushed the table as close to the fireplace as she dared, and stoked the fire with whatever flammable material she could find.

"She created her own incubator!" declared Price, clearly impressed with his grandmother's ingenuity. The child survived and is remembered not only as Bill's great uncle, but also as testimony to one woman's refusal to let nature take its course.

Bill's grandparents on his mother's side were Kincheloes. He never knew his maternal grandfather, John Allison, a pharmaceutical salesman with a photographic memory and an aptitude for math, who set off for college at the tender age of fifteen or sixteen and proceeded, at age unknown, to go broke in an oil deal. Bill did get to know his maternal grandmother, Laura, better known to her brood as Ni-Ni. Due to her late husband's unwise investments, she lived in modest circumstances. As Laura's house was only a block from Bill's childhood home in Oklahoma City, his parents could keep an eye on her and offer help when needed. More to the point, Bill could learn about his ancestry and watch *Perry Mason* on television as he and his grandmother sat on her bed and devoured ice cream. As a type-two diabetic, that was perhaps not the most appropriate item for her diet, but no matter—she enjoyed her grandson's company and the opportunity to share her stories with a receptive listener. Bill, who acquired his lifelong penchant for ice cream at an early age, was hooked on both family stories and legal dramas playing out on the screen.

"That may have inspired me to become an attorney," he said matter-of-factly.

Laura's upbringing at Scott Lawn, a former plantation in western Tennessee, gave her lifelong bragging rights as a Southern belle with deep cultural roots in the Old Confederacy. Between *Perry Mason* and bowls of ice cream, Bill and his grandmother enjoyed arguing about politics, as he acquired his allegiance to the Republican Party about the same time as he learned to like ice cream, and she was a self-confessed dyed-in-the-wool yellow-dog Democrat. "She was very prejudiced against Republicans," explained Bill, "because those were the people who burned her family's barn! It went back to the Civil War!" Such was Laura's distaste for Republicans that she skipped the presidential election in 1960; she couldn't vote for Richard Nixon because he was a Republican and, in keeping with the prejudices of her time, couldn't vote for John Kennedy because he was a Catholic. In an irony that made Bill smile, he never wavered from the Republican Party, converted from Presbyterianism to his wife's Catholicism, and raised his three children in the Catholic faith. "She would roll over in her grave today to know that most of her family, including myself, are Catholic Republicans," said Bill with a laugh.

During Bill's formative years, his parents sometimes took him to visit his Kincheloe relatives in Forrest City, Arkansas, just west of the Tennessee line. Seemingly related to just about everybody in town, Bill spent his days playing kick-the-can with his cousins and exploiting the perks of being part of his family. That included going to movies for free and cajoling drug store clerks into giving him candy. On occasion, Bill's Southern sojourns were extended, when his parents deposited him in New Orleans to visit Richard W. Freeman and his family. Freeman, who had married into the Price family, owned Coca-Cola dealerships throughout southern Louisiana and served on Delta Airlines' board of directors. He was named chairman of the board in January 1955 and remained in that position until November 1, 1965. Such was Freeman's success in business—and, no doubt, sizeable contributions to his alma mater—that Tulane University's business school was named for him.

More important than kick-the-can, free movies and candy, and hobnobbing with New Orleans' glitterati were the cultural lessons that the youngster from Oklahoma picked up from his exposure to Southern culture—lessons that would accrue to his benefit in his career as a lawyer and opinion leader in state politics.

"Southern culture is all *who you're related to*," explained Bill. "Oklahoma culture is *who you are*—it's on the merits of who you are."

"How do you account for that difference?" I asked as I glanced at my recorder to make sure the red light was lit.

"I don't know," said Bill.

I knew that wasn't true, and I waited for him to gather his thoughts about the differences between his ancestral South and his native state.

"I guess it's because of the newness, the fact that everybody is new," said Bill finally. "If you have roots that go back hundreds of years, then you're more likely to be *based on ancestry*. If you go back just one or two generations, *you can't be based on ancestry*."[4] Price then expressed a lifelong belief that people should be judged not by their race or ancestry but, as Martin Luther King said, by the content of their character.

▶ ▶ ▶ ▶

Joel and Reila's youngest son and Bill's father, named Joel Scott after his father, was born at the family's homestead in Dewey County in 1902, just nine years after the run into the Cherokee Outlet and five years before Oklahoma and Indian territories joined to become the forty-sixth state: Oklahoma. As Oakwood had little to offer in the way of education, Joel made the twenty-mile trek to Watonga to attend an accredited high school and paid his way by working in a pharmacy. Although the Prices lacked Native American ancestry, they lived close enough to an Indian agency in Canton for Joel to take on another part-time job as a store clerk. Gifted with an extraordinary memory, he learned enough of the Native language to hobnob with the locals and help them make their purchases. "The Native Americans loved him!" said Bill, "because they could come in and order goods in the Indian language. That's one of the ways he worked his way through school."

Graduating as valedictorian from a real high school in Watonga gave Joel the bona fides he needed to enroll at the University of Oklahoma. Accustomed to modest accommodations, he was unfazed by moving into a dirt basement. Once again, he paid his way, this time by waiting tables at a fraternity house and accepting whatever odd jobs he could find. Somewhere along the way, he set his sights on a career in medicine. As always, he balanced work and study so effectively that he completed his undergraduate degree, stayed at OU to attend medical school, and graduated as a full-fledged physician. One wonders if this adept multitasker Joel Scott Price took time to reflect on his mother's homemade incubator, which had saved his older brother's life—an early sign, perhaps, that a career in medicine was not beyond his grasp. Further motivation had come when the most beautiful surrey he had ever seen, pulled by equally beautiful horses, pulled up to his family's soddie. Joel watched in awe as an immaculately dressed gentleman stepped out of the surrey and announced that he was a doctor.

"That's when he got the call to medicine," concluded Bill about a favorite family story.

Joel's upward mobility eventually landed him as chief of surgery at Mercy Hospital in Oklahoma City. Long before the age of specialization, he performed surgeries in the morning, visited with patients and made house calls in the afternoon, and delivered babies at night. As many of his patients were too poor to pay their bills, Joel often treated them at little or no charge, and he anguished each time one of them perished from an incurable disease. Blessed with a photographic memory, ambidexterity, an incredible work ethic, an eye for business, and a capacity for thriving on almost no sleep, Dr. Price dedicated himself to raising his whole family, including his brother and sisters, from the poverty in which he had been born. But he was not averse to an occasional helping hand. When Joel broke his arm one summer and was unable to draw shots, he enlisted Bill, then a teenager, to accompany him on his house calls and help with inoculations.

"It was a moving experience," recalled Bill about treating patients at his father's side.

Not content only to practice medicine, Joel invented medical devices and collected medical equipment dating back to the Civil War. His collection found a permanent home at the Robert M. Bird Health Sciences Library at the University of Oklahoma College of Medicine, where it was exhibited as the Price Collection.

Joel's inventions unrelated to medicine ranged from a cup for toddlers, dubbed the Dandy Drinker, to irrigation machinery. Although the Dandy Drinker was as good as, if not better than, competing toddler cups and resembled sports bottles of a later age, it never made it into enough stores to gain traction in the marketplace. Joel's venture into irrigation machinery came to naught when a major equipment company caught wind of his cutting-edge contraption and stole the patent. As Bill explained about his father's modus operandi, "He was a great inventor. He wasn't a very good marketer!" Fortunately, Joel's acumen as a physician more than made up for his ill-fated projects in enabling him not only to provide for his own family, but also to pay for his older sisters to go to college and launch careers as nurses and schoolteachers.

As the son of a Cherokee Outlet homesteader, it is perhaps not surprising that Joel shared his success with his brother by investing in acreage in northwest Oklahoma for him to farm. As the oil and gas industry came roaring into Oklahoma's economy, he complemented his land ownership with leases and royalty interests. Leaving his brother to farm the land, Joel took charge of their acquisitions, obtaining leaseholds and working interests, at times, by paying cash, at other times in exchange for medical services, and occasionally through old-fashioned horse trading. Joel eventually amassed 11,000 acres of minerals in northwest Oklahoma. Without consulting his files, he could recite each well's section, township, range, and stage of production. Less successful were his attempts to become a landlord by purchasing rental homes near the Oklahoma City Stockyards, where he made house calls. "His vision was to build a whole bunch of businesses, or whatever, in the Stockyards area," explained Bill about one of his father's rare failures. "But that never reached fruition."

But most things in Joel Scott Price's life did reach fruition, and his successes made a lasting impression on Bill, who liked to describe himself as the youngest son of a youngest son. Joel was in his late forties when Bill was born—young enough to exhibit the qualities that lifted him to the pinnacle of his profession and accounted for his business acumen, yet old enough to know what it took to raise happy and successful children. Bill explained the number-one lesson he learned from his father this way: "It really did teach you that somebody with absolutely nothing could succeed in America. He had absolutely nothing! I wasn't the generation that started from nothing, but he certainly was!"[5]

Bill's other role model was his mother, Virginia, the only child of Laura and John Allison Kincheloe. She was born on March 23, 1913 at Scott Lawn near Ripley, Tennessee. Virginia was only eight years old when her parents plucked her from the family home and, after a brief stay in Conway, Arkansas, whisked her to Oklahoma City, where she graduated from Classen High School in 1930. To make sure their daughter was well-rounded and familiar with various regions of the country, Laura and John sent her to four colleges in four years. After earning her B.A. from Mills College in Oakland, California, in 1934, Virginia returned home to make her debut at the Oklahoma Club.

No sooner did Virginia marry Joel, on September 17, 1935, than she thrust herself into leadership positions that included presidency of the Pi Beta Phi Oklahoma City Alumnae Club and the Edgemere School PTA. She founded the first Mills College Alumnae Club in Oklahoma, raised money for the YMCA and YWCA, was active in the Junior League, and served on the steering committee for the inaugural Beaux Arts Ball, to benefit the Oklahoma City Arts Center. Virginia was also active in the building campaign for Westminster Presbyterian Church and raised funds for Christ the King School, where Bill attended kindergarten. But, of course, nothing compared to the joy she and Joel shared with the births of their four children, spread over thirteen years, Bob, Montine, Kelsey, and Bill.[6]

▶ ▶ ▶ ▶

Bill's birth, on October 5, 1948, put him last in the family pecking order by a long shot; Bob was already thirteen, Montine (the practical joker in the family) was ten, and Kelsey (beautiful and ladylike, even as a child) was five. As the sibling closest to him in age, Kelsey was Bill's primary playmate. But all three came to realize the benefits of having a much-younger sibling, particularly when they came up with a unique twist to hide-and-seek. "It was a form of hide-and-seek with Bill, who was about two and a half years old at the time, as the object to be hidden," explained Kelsey. Favorite hiding places for their compliant playmate included a cabinet above the washing machine and their parents' clothes hamper. "Since the house had four stories, the game could last for quite a while," continued Kelsey. "Bill seemed to cooperate by staying quiet. I think he was happy just to be part of the game. I, on the other hand, was a silent witness, happy to be too large to be hidden."

"It's almost like being an only child when your brother is thirteen years older and your sisters are five to ten years older," said Bill, who suffered from a speech impediment that made it difficult for people to understand him until he was six or seven years old. Under the guidance of a speech therapist, he was heartened to learn that some of the world's

Bill, thirteen years his brother Bob's junior, enjoys a celebratory moment. COURTESY BILL PRICE.

greatest speakers, from Demosthenes to Winston Churchill, were similarly afflicted as children.

The Prices' Spanish-style home was in Crown Heights, an older neighborhood, affluent by Oklahoma City standards and only somewhat less well-heeled than Heritage Hills, to the south, and Nichols Hills, to the north.[7] In a childhood reminiscent of *Leave It to Beaver*, Bill and his buddies enjoyed carefree days cruising the streets on their bicycles, probing for crawdads in a creek, and digging holes to fashion what passed for a golf course in the neighborhood park. Bill's proficiency in ping pong threatened to derail his relationship with Kelsey when he faced off against her high school sweetheart and, many years hence, her husband, Roland Walters. More sedentary pursuits included Risk, Monopoly, chess, and checkers. "I refused to play checkers with him because he always won," complained Kelsey. "My sister's high school dates would be thoroughly embarrassed when he beat them at chess."

On Saturdays, the boys gathered at Will Rogers Theater to binge on Westerns and cartoons. It was on one of those movie-saturated Saturdays that Bill caught wind of a Hopalong Cassidy bike, complete with fake guns and holsters—just the thing for a wannabe cowboy. All he had to do was buy enough movie tickets—or, better yet, scoop up enough discarded tickets after a show—to improve his odds of winning the lottery. "I had, literally, a thousand tickets," said Bill, the excitement in his voice undiminished with the passage of six decades. "And sure enough, I won the Hopalong Cassidy bicycle!"

Kelsey, a frequent companion at the Saturday matinees, was on hand when her brother swept those tickets off the floor and organized them in a shoebox. "Honestly, I had no idea what he was doing until later. He was organizing the stubs by number so he could find the winning ticket if he won, which he did." Although his success at the theater earned him the nickname "Lucky," Kelsey knew something far more significant was playing out. "I realize it was innovation and organization that created the luck for my seven-year-old little brother." But Kelsey did offer a caveat: "I was never envious of what I considered a boy-oriented prize."

But even wannabe cowboys had to go to school, and for Bill, that meant Edgemere, a public grade school. Even though it was a fair distance from his home, he made the trip to and from school on foot, unthinkable in a later age of parental wariness. When he wasn't at school, cruising the neighborhood on his Hopalong Cassidy bicycle, or carousing with his buddies, Bill was likely to be found in his family's library. Although Joel made sure to keep it well stocked, it was frustratingly disorganized. So what did the future U.S. Attorney and gubernatorial candidate do at the age of ten? Bill, whose love for reading had been spawned when Kelsey read comic books to him before he was old enough to read to himself, laughed as he explained how he arranged the library according to the Dewey decimal system. "I would have the stuff in the living room on one part of the Dewey decimal system, and some other part of the house on some other part of the Dewey decimal system. That way, I could find every book in the house. Maybe that's neurotic!"

Bill's reading preferences led him to Landmark Books, whose 180 volumes told the stories of men and women who had changed history. Rather than dwell on the flaws of well-known historical figures,

Landmark authors aimed to inspire young readers by emphasizing their achievements and even heroism. Whereas cynics of a later age would criticize historians who viewed their subjects through rose-tinted glasses, Bill appreciated the way those authors fostered idealism and motivated youth to aspire to principled lives.

Neurotic or just plain fastidious, Bill was equally happy organizing his coin collection, a hodgepodge of coinage, foreign and domestic, that came largely from his father's patients. As Bill explained, "Dad would bring home jars of coins from patients. They would, a lot of times, give him, for medical care, they would give him food, okra, jars of coins in the attic, and I would go through looking for rare coins. If I would find a rare coin, I would put it in the coin collection."

Bill's entrepreneurial spirit first surfaced when he went door-to-door selling pinecones with bottle caps stuck on the tops as Christmas decorations. After he joined Boy Scouts, he ramped up his game by roaming through office buildings and the OU football stadium to sell Scout-O-Rama tickets. Whenever he met resistance from potential customers who were not particularly interested in attending a Boy Scout encampment, he reminded them that their purchases were tax deductible and supported a worthy cause. That usually clinched the sale, and as a reward for his stellar salesmanship, Bill traveled aboard a private plane to Carlsbad Caverns in New Mexico.

As Bill ran through his repertoire of childhood memories, I couldn't help but wonder if this über-responsible, entrepreneurial youngster and future anticorruption crusader ever had a bad day and, more specifically, if he ever got in trouble. I was, therefore, somewhat relieved to discover that his father had occasions to send his son to fetch a stick for an old-fashioned switchin'. One time, Joel had to wait longer than usual for Bill to return, stick in hand, to face his punishment. When he went outside to see what his son was up to, he found Bill holding a double handful of rocks. Unable to locate a suitable stick, he told his father to throw rocks at him instead.

Joel melted and never spanked his son again.[8]

▶ ▶ ▶ ▶

Bill's next stop was Casady School, a college-preparatory day
school, affiliated with the Episcopal church, in northwest Oklahoma
City. Unlike Edgemere, Casady was not open to all comers. "It was
real hard, at the time, getting into Casady," recalled Bill. He knew he
was in trouble when he showed up in a testing room with a hundred
applicants—all hoping, and perhaps praying, that they would perform
well enough to get in. Their parents were, no doubt, hoping and praying
as well, knowing that a Casady diploma was a surefire ticket to the
nation's finest colleges and universities. Buoyed by a childhood spent
listening to his grandmothers' stories, absorbing lessons from his
multitalented parents, and reading countless books in his family's well-
organized library, Bill sailed through the entrance exams and enrolled
in Casady as a seventh grader in the fall of 1960.

Bill made the transition from eighth to ninth grade—and thus from
middle to upper school—to encounter two of Casady's most demanding
teachers: Margaret Tuck in English (rumor had it that her mother had
named her "Mrs. Tuck" at birth) and Richard Marble in chemistry. Bill
cringed to recall a paper that Mrs. Tuck returned with a grade of "A"
for content and "-65" for grammar and spelling. He wondered why he
had been punished so savagely for the mechanics of his writing, and
Mrs. Tuck explained in her unmistakable New England accent, surely
interrupted by a coughing fit occasioned by her incessant smoking,
that he had used "you" in the generalized sense numerous times,
warranting a ten-point deduction for each offense. Whatever lessons
Mr. Marble taught about the periodic table or after an unexpected
explosion atop a Bunsen burner were less memorable than Mrs. Tuck's
insistence on grammatical precision—a valuable lesson for a bewildered
boy who would one day rise to prominence as one of Oklahoma's top
lawyers.

As much as he learned about English composition from Margaret
Tuck and chemistry from Richard Marble, Bill felt most at home in

two other disciplines: debate, where, despite his childhood speech impediment, he discovered a knack for public speaking and formulating arguments, which would come in handy in his future career, and history—a reflection, perhaps, of his youthful immersion in biographies and a well-stocked library. Gravitating toward political history, Bill devoured books about Winston Churchill's role in defeating Germany during World War II and marveled at how close the Allies had come to subjugation by the Nazi juggernaut. Other favorites included Miguel de Cervantes' *Don Quixote de la Mancha*, Jeremy Wilson's *Lawrence of Arabia*, and Harper Lee's *To Kill a Mockingbird*, all literary works that, as Price's daughter Anne explained, "made people feel something and believe in something."

Turning to economic history, he read and reread George Orwell's *Animal Farm* and *1984*, both of which alerted him to the dangers of totalitarianism. Increasingly wary of big government and its corollary in big spending, he gravitated to the works of Friedrich Hayek, whose seminal work, *The Road to Serfdom* (1944), inspired a generation of economists to advocate minimal government interference in the marketplace. None absorbed Hayek's lessons with more enthusiasm than his disciple at the University of Chicago, Milton Friedman, whose *Capitalism and Freedom* (1962) topped the reading lists of free-market apostles throughout the world, most notably U.S. President Ronald Reagan and British Prime Minister Margaret Thatcher.

"I really felt like the free market was the way to raise the economic income of the poor, and everybody else," explained Bill about his early allegiance to conservative economics. "Free markets were generally a solution to most of our problems. In certain areas, obviously, we needed laws and regulation. But we have far too many!"

Bill's tenure at Casady was not all work and no play. He was a decent soccer player and was among the top players on the tennis team. Kelsey took some credit for her brother's flair for tennis, as the two were frequent competitors at the Oklahoma City Golf and Country Club. "Each one of us developed a lifelong love for tennis," recalled Kelsey fondly. But it was not only Bill's prowess on the court that left a lifelong impression. She continued, never suspecting as a teenager Bill's future career as a federal prosecutor: "It may sound unbelievable, but Bill has confirmed this with me," she continued, looking back on a time when she'd never suspected he would become a federal prosecutor. "Neither one of us ever remembers having an argument with each other."

Nobody was surprised when Bill ran successfully for the student council. His extracurricular experiences extended to activities off campus, and none was more valuable than what he discovered when he and other members of the student council traded classes with students from Northeast High School. Some of their teachers were exceptional. "But there were two who were poor quality—that were just muttering up there!" declared Bill. "Keeping those teachers on the faculty really shortchanged their students." Seeing poor teachers in action made Bill realize the importance of good teaching and planted a seed that would one day blossom into initiatives, some professional but mostly philanthropic, aimed at spreading quality education to all races, genders, and rungs of the socioeconomic ladder.

"That memory always stuck in my mind..." Bill's voice trailed off as he pondered an early lesson in educational disparities and his dawning awareness of a rigged system that needed correcting.[9]

Another off-campus lesson came from much farther away than northeast Oklahoma City—Tunisia and Western Europe, to be exact. Bill was fifteen years old when he learned that his French teacher, Mrs. Harrison, and her husband had hosted five air traffic controllers from Tunisia in their home for six months while they attended Federal Aviation Administration (FAA) classes in Oklahoma City. As a language teacher, Mrs. Harrison took the opportunity to learn enough Arabic to pique her interest in a trip to North Africa. She wanted her son, who was in Bill's class at Casady, and two friends of his choosing, Bill and Russ Woodward, to join her on what would surely be a life-changing adventure. Sure enough, Bill got the nod and asked his parents if he could go. For Joel and Virginia, it was a no-brainer, as nothing excited them more than providing their children with travel and educational opportunities. "I probably had the worst car in high school," said Bill about his parents' spending priorities. But when it came to education, "the sky was the limit!"

And so began Bill's first overseas trip. Thanks to the air traffic controllers' connections in their native land, Mrs. Harrison and her youthful companions experienced Tunisia as few Westerners ever had and probably ever will, from villas on the Mediterranean Sea and the Tunisian secretary of the treasury's home to grand celebrations signaling the affection people felt toward Americans. As the father of one of the air traffic controllers was a mayor, the trio arrived in his town to witness a sea of hundreds of happy Tunisians waving American flags. When the celebration was over, the mayor invited them to his villa for a fifteen-course feast. "We were treated like royalty throughout Tunisia," said Bill, still incredulous, from a distance of a half century, at his good fortune. After a month of enjoying North African hospitality, Mrs. Harrison took the boys across the Mediterranean to hook up with her husband and older brother and extend their travels to Spain, Portugal, Italy, France, and England.

"That was the experience of a lifetime," said Bill.

Joel and Virginia made sure to complement their children's education and travel with real-world experience, and that included manual labor. For Bob, that meant a summer of grueling work assembling his father's irrigation machinery. Bill's hands-on experience came in a cramped building with no air conditioning, where he and an older coworker sweated through a summer of dipping Dandy Drinker straws into scalding oil and bending them to Joel's exacting standards. Bill never forgot the lessons he learned from his straw-dipping companion—an African American of great intelligence whose life chances had been diminished when he'd fathered a child at an early age. As bent straws piled up beside them, the older man admonished Bill to heed his example and make better decisions.

Of more lasting significance than assembling Dandy Drinkers

was the training his father gave him in managing the family's oil and gas interests. By the time Bill was a teenager, Joel had acquired more than four hundred mineral deeds, mainly in his native northwestern Oklahoma. Many of those deeds were small—say, five to ten acres—and they reflected Joel's strategy of diversifying risk, which was both wise and labor intensive, as he had to respond to a flood of poolings and lease offers. Rather than hire a geologist to evaluate drilling proposals, Joel and his young executive-in-training called oil and gas companies to see if they were participating in a given well. Participants paid proportionate shares of the drilling costs and earned 100 percent of their shares of the revenue; those who opted for pooling terms risked nothing and earned less revenue. When a majority of a company's poolers decided to participate, Joel followed suit about eighty percent of the time.

Joel's tough bargaining tactics survive in a treasured family anecdote. Frustrated by Joel's refusal to budge during a negotiation, a lease broker reminded him that he couldn't take it with him when he died.

"I know that," came the reply, "so I'm going to have Virginia bring it with her when she comes." [10]

▶ ▶ ▶ ▶

"I don't know where I developed my love of politics and the law," wrote Bill in a collection of notes that he hoped would one day contribute to his biography.

I wasn't so sure. In fact, the more deeply I probed into Bill's early years, the more I was able to connect his pioneer and entrepreneurial heritage to the passions that framed his life and career: Republican politics and the law. Both of those arenas would offer opportunities for Bill to reflect on and fulfill his life's motto: *From whom much is given, much is expected.*

As I learned through dozens of oral history interviews and piles of scrapbooks and press clippings, politics was only marginally important to the Price family, and nobody (except, of course, Bill's yellow-dog Democrat grandmother, Ni-Ni) voted exclusively for either party. Like most Oklahomans, Bill's parents were registered Democrats, not so much for ideological as for historical reasons. They were open to voting for Republicans, especially in national elections, if they appeared to be the most suitable candidates. What mattered most was that voters of both parties in his parents' and grandparents' generations tended toward conservatism, and they were united in their distrust of faraway bureaucracies and the high taxes that supported them. And what was further away, and more bureaucratic, than the federal government?

About the time Joel and Reila Price were staking their claim in the Cherokee Outlet, anger toward faraway bureaucracies manifested in a visceral hatred of railroad monopolies and their ruinous prices. That anger extended to Republicans, as theirs was the party of choice for Eastern businessmen who deployed their capital in ways ruinous to farmers and laborers. Rage against monied elites crystalized in the Green Corn Rebellion of August 1917, when tenant farmers in Seminole County, crushed by debt and determined to avoid conscription into the Great War, took up arms and vowed to battle their way to Washington, subsist on unripened corn along their journey, and overthrow the government. The uprising was quickly and ruthlessly suppressed, and Oklahoma was left with the dubious distinction of having fostered the most powerful socialist movement in the nation, which nearly upended the state's two-party system. Aside from acres of uneaten corn, the most lasting legacy of the stillborn revolt was resentment toward central authority and Big Money, which outlasted the socialist movement and left its indelible imprint on the Democratic Party, which was less combative than the socialist activists.[11]

Then came the post–World War I depression and the even more consequential Great Depression of the 1930s. As New Deal legislation muscled its way into the economy, Oklahomans were naturally drawn to the Democratic Party as the nation's best hope for alleviating poverty and boosting employment. Even the thriving postwar economy and halcyon days of the fifties and sixties were not enough to sway opinion in rural and small-town Oklahoma. Convinced that the Republican Party was a bastion of privilege, whose members exerted a lopsided influence on the nation's business, rural voters could be counted on to elect Democrats to county and state offices.

At the same time, the backbone of Oklahoma's economy—farming, ranching, and oil—depended on entrepreneurs, who resented the government's meddling in their business. So even though Oklahoma was largely a one-party state tilting decisively toward Democrats, business leaders remained conservative, self-reliant, and suspicious of regulations raining down from Washington. Only in the Price family's homeland of northwestern Oklahoma was there a sizeable number of Republicans. Old-timers quipped that, in the rest of Oklahoma, they hunted for Republicans.

The most insidious consequence of Oklahoma's status as a de facto one-party state was corruption—as Bill recorded in his notes, it was *the* political issue of the 1960s. And as he explained to me with a passion undimmed by the passage of a half century, "The view was, if you've got a two-party state, you could eliminate a large part of the corruption." As rural counties lost population and urban areas swelled, rules regarding representation went unchallenged, and Democrats continued to control the state legislature. Even when the Oklahoma City and Tulsa metro areas grew to comprise half the state's population, Oklahoma and Tulsa counties retained only two seats in the state Senate and a handful of seats in the state House of Representatives. According to one startling statistic from the 1950s, a single voter in the Panhandle's sparsely populated Beaver County carried as much weight as eighty voters in Oklahoma County.[12]

The issue, then, was not so much liberal versus conservative, as both Democrats and Republicans were conservative by national standards, but the old guard versus reformers—that is, politicians and businesspeople who had grown accustomed to bending the rules to suit their pecuniary interests versus those who demanded a level playing field for everybody. Anyone who doubted the pervasiveness of corruption had only to consider the blatant malfeasance at the national level. As historians Bobby Baker and Robert Caro chronicled in their award-winning books about Lyndon Johnson and the tumultuous 1960s, special interests routinely deposited mountains of cash in legislators' laps, and nobody bothered to draw the line between campaign contributions and personal bribes.

Even though he had yet to graduate from high school, Bill perceived that Oklahoma was not okay, and he knew that he would one day stake his claim to a career in public service. His family background and education, combined with real-life experiences at home and abroad, set him on a path toward politics. His conservativism, practically embedded in his DNA, meant that the Republican Party would likely be his ideological home, and his outrage at perceived injustice kindled an awareness of the law as a vehicle to make things better. Those threads came together in an organization of young conservatives bent on turning Oklahoma into a genuine two-party state: Teen Age Republicans. It was here that Bill became acquainted with young people, many of whom remained lifelong friends, who shared his passion for reform. And it was here that he caught a glimpse of his future in Republican politics and the legal profession.

CHAPTER TWO : *Teen Age Republicans*

L ike all parents, Joel and Virginia Price knew there was something special about their children. Bill's something special was that he was ridiculously mature and serious for his age. As Bill put it, "They would always say that I was very serious and grown up, even as a child!"

Confirmation that his parents were onto something came about the time he was learning to debate at Casady School. Higher-ups in the Republican Party invited him to deliver a speech at the Oklahoma Museum of Art when it was housed in the Buttram Mansion in Nichols Hills, Oklahoma City's leafiest and toniest suburb. Bill was to be the youngest Republican at the podium; the other speaker was to be the oldest. "That was a scary place to speak," said Bill about his first experience in public speaking. Standing in front of a hundred and fifty people, Bill put on his game face and made what his listeners judged as an excellent speech. One of them went so far as to write a letter to Joel to express how impressed he had been with the young man's poise and grasp of the issues. As a registered Democrat with only a nominal interest in politics, Joel had no problem with his son's political views. In fact, he and Virginia were increasingly disturbed by Democrats' abuses of power and were beginning to vote for Republicans. All he really cared about was his son's budding skills as an orator and self-confidence in a room full of grown-ups.

"What did you speak about?" I asked, even though I was pretty sure I knew.

"It was about the Republican Party, and public policy," he said. "Back then, the Republican Party was kind of the party of reform. It was a very small minority, but it was definitely the reform party, and the party that was going after the corruption of the Democratic Party of this state. The Democratic Party was so corrupt!"[1]

What Bill needed, even more than appreciative adults at the Buttram Mansion, was a way to connect with his peers and hone his political skills on a broader stage. He found what he was looking for in Teen Age Republicans, or TARS, a nationwide organization aimed at supporting the party and its candidates and giving young conservatives an opportunity to serve their communities and country. At the same time, TARS members learned about the political process and the myriad ways that politics and current affairs affected young people's lives.

With effective club programming, TARS members often grew up to become opinion leaders with an ability to sway elections. Those people included Tulsa TARS chapter president Jack Edens, Oklahoma's own William F. Buckley, who went on to write political commentaries for Tulsa news media and, later still, helped manage Price's 1992 campaign for Congress before succumbing to a heart attack in his forties; TARS parliamentarian Bill Stemmons, who rose in the ranks to assume that role for the Republican Party; Mark Tapscott, who became a journalist with the *Washington Examiner*; Jay Bruner, who became a college executive and political campaigner; Cynthia Tapscott Canevaro, whose career in the federal government included several high-profile positions; and Marshall Snipes, the son of prominent state Republican Al Snipes, who became successful in business and supported political causes. Other TARS members who were eventually elected to public office included Jim Helm, Rick Williamson, George Dunham, and Susan Winchester, who came close to election as speaker of the Oklahoma House of Representatives. TARS was one of three Republican Party auxiliaries. The other two, both of which would soon factor into Bill's life, were College Republicans and Young Republicans; the latter was open to people between the ages of eighteen and forty.[2]

No sooner did Bill join TARS than he began scouting for members. An early recruit was Tom Daxon, an equally committed Republican who, like Bill, needed a bully pulpit from which to express his views and advance his agenda. "That was one of the smartest things I have ever done," said Daxon, whose membership in TARS was the beginning of a lifelong friendship with Bill. "There's very little, personally, that I have learned about politics that I didn't really learn through Teen Age Republicans." Although their older and wiser sponsors, Jewel Mathews and Gladys Gockel, were happy to help, the teenagers got along just fine on their own. As Daxon put it, "We didn't have a lot of adult supervision—which is probably a good thing!"[3]

Nobody was surprised when Bill was named president of the Oklahoma County TARS chapter en route to his election as president, representing the entire state. What was surprising was the way he won the statewide election and then accepted his position. Knowing that Bill was spending part of the summer at a French language immersion camp in Bar Harbor, Maine, the incumbent state president scheduled the election, confident that he would retain the presidency in Bill's absence. What the president had not counted on was his opponent's ingenuity. Having lined up his supporters in advance, Bill won the election in absentia. Upon learning of his victory, he placed a call to the TARS convention in Oklahoma City and delivered his acceptance speech through a microphone. His French teachers in Bar Harbor contributed to his triumph by making an exception to their no-English rule.[4]

Bill served as president of Oklahoma County Teen Age Republicans from 1964 to 1965 and president of Oklahoma State Teenage Republicans from 1965 to 1966.[5] During his tenures, he organized volunteers for numerous campaigns and, either alone or with Tom Daxon, established TARS clubs throughout the state. Typically, they set out early Saturday mornings for towns in which they knew not a soul, intent on starting at least three clubs before nightfall. Their first stop was at gas stations to ask whoever was working the pumps ("there were actually kids pumping gas then") to name three or four high school students who were respected for their leadership abilities. The more often they heard a particular student's name, the more confident they were that they had found a potential club leader. After whittling their list to the most likely prospects, they grabbed a handful of dimes, made a beeline for the pay phone, and asked each person who answered the same questions. Phone calls invariably led to face-to-face meetings which, in turn, led to creation of a TARS club. Mission accomplished, the duo consulted a map and made for the next town. "So that was a technique we used," explained Bill about his and Daxon's initiation to grassroots campaigning. "We had several hundred members statewide!"[6]

Of all the recruiting trips that Price and Daxon took, none left a more lasting impression than the time they took a detour off Interstate 40 in eastern Oklahoma and drove through Clearview, an all-black town that, according to Daxon's reading of a Department of Transportation report ("Daxon was even more of a nerd than I!"), boasted a population in excess of two thousand yet had not a single paved road. "It was just *awful*!" declared Price. "I can't imagine what the townspeople had to put up with in rain and snow. It struck us that the counties, the state, had just overlooked this town. And that kind of stuck in my mind, what a shame it was, the power of the county commissioners to neglect a town of that size, for not having any kind of paved roads."

During the rest of their drive back to Oklahoma City, the two teenagers talked of little else but the unfairness and misuse of power in their native state.[7]

▶ ▶ ▶ ▶

Bill did not have to travel as far as Clearview to perceive the extent of corruption in state politics. Canvassing neighborhoods in support of various candidates, he heard a familiar refrain, particularly from people who had recently moved to Oklahoma City from rural areas and had experienced firsthand the goings-on in county government: *I am not voting! They're all corrupt! They're all on the take!* Clearly, systemic corruption was having a corrosive effect not only in terms of money siphoned from the public till, but also on the very foundations of democratic governance. "You have a huge number of people totally turned off," explained Bill. "Their vote doesn't mean anything. The only thing that matters is the money."[8]

While Bill Price, Tom Daxon, and other reform-minded TARS members were knocking on doors and trying to turn the tide against generations of voter cynicism, a farm boy from North Carolina named Al Snipes was busy lifting Oklahoma Republicans out of the doldrums. Former Oklahoma congressman Mickey Edwards spoke for many in crediting Snipes with creating the modern Republican Party in Oklahoma and, in doing so, establishing a genuine two-party state. As Edwards wrote in his foreword to Snipes's 2006 biography, "He inherited an almost nonexistent political party, organized its precincts, recruited campaign workers and candidates, and almost single-handedly built the organization that made it possible for Republicans, myself included, to win." Mary Fallin, former lieutenant governor and, later, governor, put it this way: "Al Snipes is one of the true fathers of the modern Republican Party in Oklahoma."[9]

Snipes's hardscrabble youth in rural North Carolina showed little evidence of the political acumen that would one day propel him to leadership of Oklahoma's Republican Party. Following his discharge from the military after World War II, he extended a modest loan to his sister, Grace, and her husband, Herb Moore, to expand their grocery business in south Oklahoma City by installing frozen-food lockers. When their frozen-food bonanza failed to materialize, Snipes traveled to Oklahoma City to help them out. He intended to stay only long enough to get them back on their feet and get his loan repaid. But life had other plans, and Snipes, who had married Rebecca Davis Burril in 1947 and had a growing family to support, wound up staying in Oklahoma City for the rest of his life.

Committed though he was to his family's grocery store, Snipes's real passion was boxing. His successes in the ring made him instant fodder for the sports pages, where he was routinely characterized as the best 160-pound prospect anybody could remember—a handsome in-fighter with a vicious punch and a winning personality. Unfortunately, Snipes's competitive streak was not enough to overcome slim profit margins and fierce competition in the grocery business. When a fire left the store in shambles, he threw in the towel and began scouting for more lucrative opportunities. He found them in the insurance business, and by 1958, he was thriving as an independent agent and making connections with opinion leaders throughout Oklahoma.

Success in business, together with his notoriety as a boxer, opened the door for Snipes to explore his other passion: politics. Wooed at an early age into the Republican fold, he was acutely aware of the Democratic stranglehold on state politics and the corruption it had bred in the legislature and throughout the state's seventy-seven counties. As he intoned at every opportunity, Oklahoma could never move forward as long as the "good ole boys" retained their grip on the levers of power.

An early foray into politics, sandwiched between grocery deliveries and boxing bouts, came in 1951 when he joined Young Republicans— one of the Republican Party's three auxiliaries—and cast his lot with Dwight D. Eisenhower in his run for the White House. Like Eisenhower, Snipes believed that prosperity depended on smaller government and lower taxes. As the campaign gained traction, Snipes was a regular sight around Oklahoma County, handing out "I like Ike" bumper stickers and lapel buttons and proselytizing on behalf of the Republican platform. After Eisenhower defeated Illinois Governor Adlai Stevenson in the general election, he and Rebecca made straight for Washington to attend the inaugural ball and parade.

The new decade dawned, and prospects for his party remained as bleak as ever. Republicans held no statewide offices and claimed only 20 percent of the seats in the legislature. There was no grassroots organization, no serious program to recruit potential candidates, no permanent headquarters, no party newspaper, and no money. Relying on his fighting spirit and familiar face, Snipes worked tirelessly to build his party and get Republicans elected to state offices. His hard work paid off when he was elected chairman of the Oklahoma County

Republicans in January 1960; later that year, he served as assistant doorkeeper at the Republican National Convention in San Francisco, the first of five conventions that he attended.

Snipes's efforts seemed for naught when John F. Kennedy was swept into office in the election of 1960. Refusing to concede defeat, Snipes summoned Oklahoma County Republicans to regroup and prepare for battles yet to come. Prescient observers knew something big was in the wind as precinct leaders and committee members, together with Oklahoma City business leaders such as John Kirkpatrick and Frank Hightower, heeded Snipes's call for unity and attended a meeting only two days after Richard Nixon's drubbing at the polls. Pundits later described that meeting as the genesis of a modern Republican Party in Oklahoma.[10]

Headquartered in a bland office building that Snipes purchased in 1960, at 3215 South Western Avenue in Oklahoma City, Republicans spent the early 1960s launching campaigns and petition drives aimed at convincing Democrats to change parties and ending Democratic dominance in Oklahoma politics. "The opportunity was there," said Snipes. "Nixon losing in 1960 was a big motivating factor, and people were willing to work. We realized all we had to do was to work hard and take advantage of the situation. That was the reason so many people were willing to change parties."[11]

If Snipes's call to arms in November 1960 signaled a Republican awakening in Oklahoma, then Henry Bellmon's victory in the gubernatorial election of 1962 was the most tangible evidence yet that organizers' tactics were working. Bellmon's predecessor, James Howard Edmondson, had been chief prosecutor in the office of the county attorney of Tulsa County. In that role he had earned accolades for securing convictions of corrupt county and state officials. Elected as Oklahoma's sixteenth and, at the age of thirty-three, youngest governor in 1957, Edmondson made reform the centerpiece of his administration. True to his word, he pushed through the repeal of prohibition and persuaded the legislature to adopt a merit system, central purchasing, a withholding tax plan, and several measures that eased the strain on state finances. He also obtained a financing plan for two state turnpikes and supported creation of the Oklahoma Capitol Improvement Authority. But many of his proposals were rejected, including a constitutional highway commission, a legislative apportionment proposal, and the removal of gasoline tax revenues from control of county commissioners. Halfway through his administration, it was clear that he had lost his mandate.[12]

"He was kind of the John F. Kennedy of Oklahoma," explained Price, who recalled Edmondson's effort to relieve county commissioners of their authority and place all road and bridge building in the hands of the Department of Transportation as the final straw for old-guard Democrats. "After he did that, he never got anything passed in the legislature. Quite a few state legislators were former county commissioners; others recognized that county commissioners were the most powerful political leaders in their districts. He was totally destroyed after that." Such was Edmondson's fall from grace that he failed to secure his party's nomination in the election of 1962.[13] From that day forward, reform of county purchasing would become nothing less than the third rail of Oklahoma politics as commissioners clung more tightly than ever to the levers of power.

Like Bill Price, Henry Bellmon came from a large family of Cherokee Outlet pioneers. Bellmon's first experience in public service came not in politics but as a first lieutenant in charge of a tank unit that saw action in the Pacific during World War II. He survived untold encounters with Japanese defenders to earn the Legion of Merit, for his valor on Saipan, and the Silver Star for a repeat performance on Iwo Jima. Following his discharge from the Marine Corps, Bellmon returned to the family farm in Noble County and launched a campaign for the Oklahoma House of Representatives. Although he won the election in 1946, he lost his seat in 1948 and settled in for several years of farming and working behind the scenes for the Republican Party. Although he lacked notoriety outside Noble County, he made

enough friends in high places to become chairman of the Oklahoma
Republican Party in 1960. Two years later, he announced his candidacy
for governor, resigned as state party chairman, and prepared to face off
against the Democratic standard-bearer, William P. Atkinson. Thanks
to Al Snipes's vigorous campaigning and to dissention within the
Democratic Party, Bellmon trounced Atkinson by nearly seventy-seven
thousand votes to become Oklahoma's first Republican governor.[14]
As Bellmon remarked many years later about Snipes's clout in party
politics and the grassroots campaign that put him in the governor's
mansion, "Al was more powerful than any state chairman because
Oklahoma City was emerging as a Republican stronghold. There was no
doubt that Al was becoming a power in the state party."[15]

▶ ▶ ▶ ▶

Bill Price was too young to participate in either Al Snipes's party-
building activities in the 1950s or Henry Bellmon's historic victory in
1962. But his door-to-door and town-to-town campaigning on behalf
of Teen Age Republicans in the mid-1960s put him in a position to
participate in an electoral battle against his party's nemesis: Democratic
Speaker of the House J. D. McCarty.[16]

Thanks to a state constitution whose framers had been wary of
strong central authority at any level of governance, the governor was
weaker than either the Speaker of the House or the president pro
tempore of the Senate. So, even though the speaker was relatively low
in the official pecking order, he or (less likely but remotely possible) she
had ample opportunity to amass power by handing out patronage jobs
and dipping into state coffers for pet projects. Wielding influence like
feudal lords, speakers of the Oklahoma House of Representatives struck
fear into the hearts of their opponents, and none more so than J. D.
McCarty.[17]

"J. D. McCarty's control over the House of Representatives was
absolute," recalled Bellmon. "Any time he took the rostrum and pointed
his thumbs upwards, the matter under consideration passed with a

sizable majority. Any time he made the opposite gesture, thumbs down, the measure failed."[18]

Speaker McCarty came crashing into Republicans' crosshairs over "right to work," a classic labor issue that has always divided the two parties. Whereas Republicans stood firmly for a laborer's right to decline union membership, Democrats insisted that prohibiting compulsory unionism posed a mortal threat to collective bargaining and, not incidentally, weakened the unions, a traditional bastion of Democratic power. Convinced that McCarty represented good-ole-boy politics at its worst, Snipes and his fellow Republicans knew that defeating him would improve their chances of passing right-to-work legislation. Even more importantly, it would drive a wedge in the power structure and help build a two-party system. As Election Day approached, the stage was set for an historic showdown between old-guard Democrats and Republican reformers.[19]

If Oklahoma corruption had a face, it was that of J. D. McCarty, an old-fashioned party boss who had served the people of District 92, in southeast Oklahoma County, for twenty-six years. In this district a toxic brew of poverty and apathy had produced one of the most pathetic voter turnout records in the state. In the run-up to the 1966 elections, for inspiration, Snipes festooned Republican Party headquarters with posters of J. D. McCarty in full party mode at a favorite hangout in Chicago. As Price explained, if central casting had requested extras to play the roles of mobsters, a recruiter would surely have been dispatched to McCarty's favorite hangouts in Chicago, where the gentlemen sported white ties and black shirts and puffed on oversized cigars. Back at his other natural habitat, in the Oklahoma legislature, McCarty was at his best when special-interest minions showed up with sacks of cash. It was an open secret that the party-loving speaker enjoyed nothing more than sharing his bounty with House members, as long as he could count on their votes. "That was the way Oklahoma politics was run," said Price.[20] Those cash payments would later lead to McCarty's conviction in federal court for tax evasion.

J. D. McCarty's conviction was several years in the future when Snipes went scouting for an all-American, clean-cut counterpart to run against him. Snipes and a support group, the South Oklahoma City Women's Republican Club, found what they were looking for in the person of Vondel L. Smith, a World War II veteran and funeral home operator with an impeccable track record in church and civic affairs. With an attractive wife and three equally attractive children, Smith presented an ideal contrast to the cigar-chomping J. D. McCarty, whose considerable heft and bulldog jowls came as a shock to District 92 voters who might not have known what their representative looked like. The only downside to Smith's candidacy was his lack of familiarity with the issues. At an open-air meeting attended by Price and other Teen Age Republicans, somebody asked him about right-to-work legislation. Fumbling for an answer, Smith leaned in Price's direction and whispered, "Are we fer it or agin' it?"[21]

The other thing Snipes needed was enthusiastic partisans who could be counted on to get out the vote. Some of those partisans came from his and Smith's families. Working side by side in their makeshift headquarters on South Western Avenue, Snipe's and Smith's wives and children turned the campaign into a family affair, preparing mailings and working the phones. The two families, together with whomever they could enlist as volunteers, made image their major selling point, with the incumbent branded as an old-guard party boss, steeped in corruption, while his opponent stood for prayer in schools and increased spending for pensioners and teachers.[22] As for door-to-door and telephone campaigning, Snipes knew exactly where to turn: the hundred-strong posse of Teen Age Republicans. "Back then, youth were attracted to the Republican Party because it was the reform party," explained Bill. "It was the clean-government party in a very corrupt Democratic state. Basically, he used our manpower."

Snipes's directive to the young Republicans was simple and straightforward: call McCarty's constituents in District 92 and ask if they knew anything about their longtime and decidedly unphotogenic

Speaker of the House J. D. McCarty, the uncrowned king of the Oklahoma legislature, was convicted in July 1967 of two counts of income tax evasion and sentenced to three years in federal prison. COURTESY *Daily Oklahoman*; BERRY AND ALEXANDER, *Justice for Sale*.

representative. If a constituent expressed confidence in McCarty, no more questions were asked. But when comments about McCarty turned negative, Bill and his colleagues turned on the paeans for Vondel Smith, a church deacon and successful businessman who was everything that McCarty was not. Knowing that they needed only 10–15 percent of the vote in such an apolitical district for Smith to win, the youthful campaigners kept calling, day and night, right up to Election Day. It was only a few days before the election when McCarty realized he was in trouble, but by then it was too late.

In results that sent shock waves from the capitol to all corners of the state, Smith won by nearly a two-to-one margin. Waxing hyperbolic, headlines blared with words like "earthquake" and "crushing defeat." As Henry Bellmon recalled, "There will never be another election like it!" Bill Price's postmortem for the election of 1966 was equally straightforward: "That's how Al Snipes defeated the most powerful political leader in Oklahoma, in the most Democratic district in Oklahoma, with absolutely no money!"

A dispiriting postscript to Vondel Smith's upset victory over J. D. McCarty came when McCarty, notorious for underreporting his income, found himself at the center of an IRS investigation for neglecting to come clean on a $12,000 contribution from a chamber of commerce, allegedly to be used to influence legislators' votes. That transaction added credence to what was common knowledge: whenever House members got in financial trouble, they could count on McCarty to pay their bills and help them out of messy situations. This time, the wily speaker had been caught red-handed. Convicted in federal court of tax evasion, McCarty was unceremoniously shipped off to a penitentiary in Texas.

McCarty served only a few months before he was paroled. He returned to Oklahoma City and, with little of his customary fanfare, went into the insurance business. Somewhere along his convoluted career path, he paid a visit to his pals in the legislature. Price's friend and fellow TARS member Tom Daxon was launching his career in politics when he entered the capitol building one day to encounter thunderous applause erupting from the basement. He quickly learned what the hubbub was about: rapturous that their benefactor had been released from prison, legislators were welcoming McCarty home with all the panoply accorded a triumphant general.

"The legislators were cheering J. D. McCarty returning from prison!" declared Price. "I'm sure some of them were so happy that he hadn't given them up." [23]

▶ ▶ ▶ ▶

Price experienced politics on the national stage when he attended the 1964 Republican National Convention at the Cow Palace in San Francisco. The high point of the convention came when Republican presidential nominee and Arizona senator Barry Goldwater electrified the auditorium with a call to arms that resonated for many years in the hearts of conservatives: "Extremism in the defense of liberty is no vice. And moderation in the pursuit of justice is no virtue."

Electrifying indeed. But as über-conservatives, including members of the John Birch Society, rose to their feet to roar their affirmation, Price knew the jig was up. "I cringed at that," recalled Price, who had realized—as a teenager—what that meant for Goldwater's campaign. "I knew that was going to be misinterpreted." Sure enough, as he and other attendees made the long bus trip back to Oklahoma, they picked up newspapers en route to read about their candidate's embrace of extremism. "We knew that election was just totally over, in 1964."[24]

Another casualty of Goldwater's pithy declaration was a U.S. Senate hopeful for whom Price was campaigning: Bud Wilkinson. As head football coach at the University of Oklahoma from 1947 to 1963, Wilkinson had entered the ranks of Oklahoma royalty with a winning record (145–29–4), three national championships (1950, 1955, and 1956), and fourteen conference titles. Assuming that his notoriety would launch his career in politics, Wilkinson had announced, in February 1964, his plan to enter a special election to replace his friend the late Robert S. Kerr in the Senate. Skeptics doubted that a successful career on the gridiron qualified him for a career in politics, but no matter, he resigned his coaching position and cast caution to the winds, only to watch his fortunes fade when Democratic incumbent Lyndon Johnson defeated Goldwater by a 55–45 percent margin. As Price put it, "Goldwater brought down the other candidate that I was working for at the time, which was Bud Wilkinson, who was far more moderate." Neither Price nor anyone else, for that matter, could have foreseen that LBJ would go down in Oklahoma history as the last Democrat to carry the state in a presidential election through 2018.[25]

Lyndon Johnson's decisive victory over Barry Goldwater and Bud Wilkinson's failed run for the U.S. Senate revealed Oklahoma as an anomaly. Throughout the country, most cities were Democratic strongholds while Republicans held sway in rural areas. "We were exactly the opposite," explained Price, who had learned his politics under the tutelage of Al Snipes, Henry Bellmon, and other Republicans who had crafted a modern party from miniscule bases in the state's two largest cities. "The cities were becoming more and more Republican, and the rural areas were the Democratic strongholds." Oklahoma City and Tulsa, together with pockets of Republicans in the northwest and Panhandle, "were the only hope for the Republican Party."[26] Not even the most prescient politicos could have anticipated the reversal, nearly undetectable in the early 1960s but more apparent as the decades passed, that would align Oklahoma with the rest of the country, with rural areas voting for Republicans and cities trending toward Democrats.[27]

Price's other mentor was G. T. Blankenship, a lawyer from Oklahoma City who was elected in 1960 to the state House of Representatives. In 1965, his fellow Republicans chose him as the House minority leader, making him the highest-ranking Republican in the House. Aiming for higher office, he resigned his position to launch a grueling run for state attorney general.[28] Other than more Republicans to support his political ambitions, what Blankenship needed more than anything was a bus driver to ferry him around the state and take notes at his meetings. He found his dream driver (or, more accurately, thought he had) in the person of Oklahoma TARS president Bill Price.[29]

"He was a great guy," said Price about the prospective attorney general, whose marriage into a wealthy family had given him a leg up in fundraising but not, apparently, in transportation. "I was a terrible bus driver. I hated that bus. It was an RV repurposed as a campaign billboard, and hot air from the engine blew right in my face." Enduring hot air spewing in his face during a summer that was plenty hot already, Price kept one eye on the road and the other on a road map to make sure he didn't miss a turnoff. His mood darkened when he turned on the windshield wipers during a rainstorm and watched them snap off and clatter onto the highway. For many years thereafter, Price and Blankenship enjoyed getting together and regaling one another with memories of their pan-Oklahoma odyssey aboard a rattletrap campaign bus.[30]

In his run for the state Attorney General's Office in 1966, G. T. Blankenship hired Price to drive his campaign bus. COURTESY BILL PRICE.

During campaign stops, Blankenship ordered Price to pull into newspaper offices for interviews. Invariably, editors popped a question that struck at the heart of the state's endemic corruption: *Why are feds the only people that prosecute corruption, and why don't we clean up our own messes?* Just as invariably, Blankenship gave a straightforward answer: the Oklahoma Constitution included a provision for multicounty grand juries that had the potential to increase indictments, and ultimately convictions, of low-level criminals as well as their ringleaders. The problem was, there was no legislation to implement this practice. "That's up to the state legislature," explained Blankenship ad infinitum. "So until we get implementing legislation, the state cannot effectively prosecute corruption."[31] Those newspaper interviews planted a seed in Price's mind that would blossom, many years later, in his successful campaign to convince legislators to pass a multicounty grand-jury bill.

Then they were back on the road, bound for another town, another speech, another interview, and perhaps a plateful of chicken-fried steak to speed them on their way. As hot air baked his face and hoping that the bus would hold together for another few miles, Price got an earful about the defining issue in the attorney general race, which was capturing headlines across the state and nation, sending lawyers running for cover, and propelling G. T. Blankenship to victory: the Oklahoma supreme court scandal of 1964–65. Never had jurists at such high levels sunk so low; never had Oklahomans had more reason to distrust their duly elected judges. Next to the J. D. McCarty story and awareness of sleaze in the Johnson administration, it was malfeasance in the state's highest court that put the fire in Price's belly to take on the fight against corruption.

T he scandal that G. T. Blankenship described to his young and impressionable driver erupted in the spring of 1965. Day after excruciating day, Oklahomans unfolded their newspapers and flipped on the TV news to learn of bribery and extortion allegedly committed by three Oklahoma supreme court justices: former justice N. S. Corn, who was then serving an eighteen-month sentence in federal prison for tax evasion; Chief Justice Earl Welch, who resigned from the court rather than face an impeachment inquiry; and Associate Justice Napoleon Bonaparte Johnson, who vowed to fight to the bitter end. Rare, but not unprecedented, was Johnson's impeachment trial in the Senate, where he tried unsuccessfully to avoid forced removal from office. Even more consequential to reformers than the fate of Justices Corn, Welch, and Johnson was a question of paramount importance: how to jettison the election of supreme court justices in favor of an appointment system to ensure a nonpartisan judiciary. Another question, perhaps even thornier than devising an equitable system of judicial appointments and looming ever larger as the scandal reached its denouement, was figuring out what to do about dozens of court cases, some going back decades, that had been decided by tainted judges.

"The majority of the supreme court was taking bribes," explained Price about his youthful education in judicial ethics. "You can imagine the governor or the legislature, but that the supreme court of the state of Oklahoma was taking bribes was really unthinkable."[1]

Ever since Oklahoma's territorial period (1890–1907), reformers had looked for a way to establish a nonpartisan judiciary, only to see their proposals go down in flames. At the 1906 annual meeting of the Oklahoma and Indian Territory Bar Association, W. H. Korngay was more prescient than he knew when he described the nonpartisan selection of judges as "an incandescent dream." Korngay made his dreary prediction at a time when Soonerism was still clogging the court system with land disputes. At the same time, Indian lands were converting from communal to individual ownership, leaving lawmakers with two unenviable tasks: establishing boundaries between Native American, city, county, state, and federal jurisdictions and preventing swindlers from stealing Indian land and property.

Of all the injustices that have corrupted Oklahoma's judicial system, none offers a more blatant illustration of perfidy in plain sight than Indian land fraud. Like a polluted tributary feeding into a river, the theft of Indian land—aided, abetted, and often committed by people who had taken oaths to uphold the law—belied leaders' commitment to justice, and its effects lasted far beyond the territorial and early statehood periods. The most common form of theft was "grafting," which was the practice of locating non-Indians on Indian allotments. One territorial resident went so far as to claim that grafting was "the chief and most thriving industry in the whole community."[2] Although land fraud was most common among the Five Tribes in eastern Oklahoma, it cast a pall of corruption across the entire state, impoverished countless lives and communities, and contributed to endless litigation.

Chief Justice Fletcher Riley was probably not exaggerating when he described Oklahoma's courts, understaffed and starved for resources, as the most burdened in the English-speaking world. A particularly pernicious consequence of backlogs and inefficiencies in Oklahoma's court system was that ambitious lawyers perceived a judgeship as little more than a springboard to establish a lucrative practice.[3] Reformers' hopes were short-lived when, in 1961, a merit selection plan failed to get out of legislative committee. According to Earl Sneed, former dean of the University of Oklahoma Law School, the plan's opponents argued that the plan was "not grounded in the democratic process," and they equated it with the federal system—never a winning comparison among Democrats with an innate distrust of Washington politics.[4] In a page seemingly ripped from ancient scrolls, judicial reformers' task could be likened to the trials of Sisyphus, whose fate was to push a boulder uphill, only to see it tumble back down and begin another day of fruitless toil.

Pervasive in both the public and private sectors, corruption in Oklahoma seeped most famously into the governor's mansion. We therefore take a detour from Bill Price's story for a primer on corruption in Oklahoma history. Our first lessons come from five governors whose misdeeds forced the legislature to take (or at least threaten) action against them. We then turn to the supreme court scandal of 1964–65, a noxious chapter in Oklahoma history that galvanized reformers to root out the rascals and promote legislation to ensure that justice was not for sale. A glance at corruption's deep roots in Oklahoma governance and its persistence in the 1960s provides an historical context for the challenges that Bill Price, along with other attorneys of his generation, confronted while crusading to curb corruption.

Price's role as a corruption buster was far in the future during that steamy summer of campaigning for G. T. Blankenship. All he knew as he steered his bus across Oklahoma was that his candidate had increased his chances of winning the election by taking on corruption in the state judicial branch. "His claim to fame in running for attorney general was that he helped uncover the supreme court scandals," explained Price. "He had delivered a speech in the state legislature that revealed the extent of corruption on the state supreme court."[5]

The teenage Bill Price could not have suspected how significant Blankenship's example of courage under fire would become in his future career as a prosecutor.

▶ ▶ ▶ ▶

The precedent for shenanigans in high office goes back to the state's first governor, Charles N. Haskell, who served as Democratic national treasurer for William Jennings Bryan's run for the White House in

1908. Accused of appropriating six thousand dollars for legal services, Haskell was forced to resign his position in disgrace.[6] By then, everyone knew Haskell was trouble, particularly after Hearst newspapers blared his collusion with Standard Oil Company from headlines nationwide. Although his reputation certainly suffered from the usual dissonance between Republicans and Democrats, there was too much hard evidence in print to dismiss the charges against him as partisan smears.[7]

Haskell's most noteworthy brush with infamy came when he relocated the state capitol from Guthrie to Oklahoma City. The Enabling Act of 1906, which set the ground rules for Oklahoma to enter the union, in 1907, as the forty-sixth state named Guthrie as the capital until 1913, at which point Oklahomans would decide for themselves where to locate their capital city. But that was too far in the future for Governor Haskell. Declaring Guthrie to be a "Republican nest," Haskell called for a special election and, on the eve of the name-that-capital vote on June 11, 1911, dispatched his associates northward to steal the state seal and other papers and deliver them to his temporary headquarters at the Lee-Huckins Hotel in Oklahoma City. Although the U.S. Supreme Court upheld Haskell's fly-by-night thievery, the good people of Guthrie never forgave him, and he went down in history as the governor who stole the state capital.[8]

After two administrations of relative quiet, Oklahomans elected James B. A. Robertson as their fourth governor. During his tumultuous term, Robertson contended with the post–World War I depression, which forced farmers into bankruptcy and some into suicide; fended off threats from a revived Ku Klux Klan, whose dream of a white ethno-state culminated in a riot in Tulsa that marked one of the bleakest episodes in American history; and declared martial law in six southeastern counties when coal miners walked off the job. But his real problems came when a grand jury charged him and a slew of other state officials with accepting bribes to keep Okmulgee's Bank of Commerce open after they knew it was insolvent. Although Robertson managed

BARBECUE PITS, FAIRGROUNDS, OKLAHOMA CITY, OKLA.

To prepare for Governor Jack Walton's inaugural bash, trenches were carved into the prairie for a barbecue of mythic proportions. Nine months later, the governor was impeached and convicted on multiple charges of betraying the people's trust. COURTESY OKLAHOMA HISTORICAL SOCIETY.

to sidestep a trial, he did not clear himself of the allegations until after leaving office.[9]

Robertson's successor, Democratic Oklahoma City mayor John Calloway "Jack" Walton, promised throughout his 1922 gubernatorial campaign to host the mother of all parties in the event of his victory. "When I am elected governor, there will not be any inaugural ball, and there will not be a tea dansant," he promised. "I am going to give an old-fashioned barbecue. It will be a party for all the people, and I want you all to come."[10]

By the time of his open-ended invitation, Walton had secured the allegiance of tenant farmers and down-and-out urbanites, who flocked to his impromptu rallies to hear his rants about the evils of big business. Fearful that he would bring the same ineptitude he had displayed as mayor of Oklahoma City to the governorship, business leaders launched a campaign to thwart his election, but to no avail.[11] He sailed into office in November 1922 and took the oath of office twice: first, with customary dignity, at the state house; and the next day at the fairgrounds, where the party he had promised roared to life with a parade stretching ten miles across the bleak winter landscape. Floats, marching bands, high-stepping horses, pistol-toting cowboys, Native Americans in their finest regalia, and World War I battle flags wound their way to a barbecue of mythic proportions. Carcasses of multiple species smoldered in six quarter-mile-long barbecue pits, and the aroma from coffee steaming in four 8,800-gallon percolators wafted all the way to Kansas.[12] The New York Times did its best to describe the hoopla to an incredulous East: "In Oklahoma the pioneer tradition is fresh and recent. She 'steps on her gas' all the time. She is full of the joy of life, the passion for self-expression . . . Until the last notes of 'Turkey in the Straw' have died away in the state house at Oklahoma City let us rejoice in the barbecue and fiddle, the enjoy yourself-and-let-the-world-go-hang spirit of 'Jack' Walton's people's party and Oklahoma."[13]

Governor Walton's term ended less ceremoniously than it had begun. It turned out that selling pardons and paroles to the highest bidders, accepting payment for prestigious positions at local universities, handing out government jobs, and nefarious dealings with oilmen were not the best ways to ingratiate himself with the legislature. His political playbook included proclaiming martial law to prevent the legislature from meeting, attempting to suppress newspapers, and stationing hired guards with machine guns outside a federal judge's court. Somewhere along his route to ignominy, he ran afoul of the Ku Klux Klan, which was packed with state legislators who took a dim view of the governor's panache. Ten months after the party to end all parties, the House of Representatives voted to impeach Walton on twenty-three counts and sent him to the Senate, where he was convicted on eleven charges in a 41–0 vote and escorted from the governor's office.

But Walton was not done with politics. He won the 1924 Democratic primary for a state Senate seat but lost the general election. He tried to win back his job as mayor of Oklahoma City in 1931, failed, and then redeemed himself the next year with a successful campaign for corporation commissioner. Subsequent bids to become governor, county sheriff, and corporation commissioner flopped in rapid succession. Then his trail went cold. Rumors circulated that he had gone to Mexico and ended up in Texas, where he likely died.[14]

Voters had little time to catch their breath before Martin Edwin Trapp, the son of pioneers who had made the run of 1889 into central Indian Territory and had homesteaded near Guthrie—who was then serving his third term as lieutenant governor—stepped in to fill the rest of Walton's term. Toward the end of his second term as lieutenant governor, Trapp had experienced his first brush with impeachment on charges of conspiracy. In a partisan vote, the Senate declined to remove him from office. Clearly nonplussed by his enemies' aspersions, Trapp went on to earn a reputation as one of the most capable governors in Oklahoma history. He reorganized the highway commission, reformed taxes, and pushed through key legislation to create the Oklahoma State Bureau of Investigation (OSBI). As Bob Blackburn, executive director of the Oklahoma Historical Society, put it, "He was not elected by the people, but he became one of the best governors. The guy was a wonderful politician. He knew how to work the legislature. He knew how to get things done. He had personal integrity and honesty. And the people responded to him."[15]

None of that meant very much to the Ku Klux Klan. The all-powerful organization, which had struck fear into the hearts of African Americans since Reconstruction, launched a move in November 1924 to impeach Trapp on charges of neglect of duty and corruption in office, stemming from selling bonds in his second career as a businessman. Once again, Trapp found himself in the legislature's crosshairs and, once again, he managed to retain his office, this time in a highly partisan 27–16 vote in the Senate to acquit him of all charges.

In 1926, Trapp announced his intention to run for governor, only to run up against a constitutional mandate that someone who had served as governor could not succeed himself. The Oklahoma supreme court agreed, and even though the state treasury boasted a surplus at the end of his unelected term, his political options were dwindling. After a run for the governor's office in 1930 failed, Trapp returned to the private sector to busy himself in construction, oil and gas, and a bond brokerage business. Active in numerous clubs and organizations, he was a member of the Masonic order, the Independent Order of Odd Fellows, and the Benevolent and Protective Order of the Elks. Trapp died in 1951 and was buried in Fairlawn Cemetery.[16]

Trapp's disqualification and the dearth of qualified candidates in the gubernatorial election of 1926 left the field to Henry Johnston, a participant in the Cherokee Outlet opening and, long after the dust settled, a fringe politician whose ambitions exceeded his grasp. About twenty thousand people attended his inauguration, the first ever to be broadcast on radio and over loudspeakers. No sooner was Johnston settled in the governor's mansion than his secretary, Mamie Hammons, alienated the legislature with her arrogance and insistence on treating the governor like royalty. "She controlled access to the governor," said Blackburn. "And the legislature, with its recent success, did not like that attitude."

The inevitable showdown between the executive and legislative branches went down in history as the "Ewe Lamb Rebellion" because Johnston referred to Hammons as his ewe lamb and swore that he would never throw her under the bus. The House of Representatives responded, in January 1929, by voting eleven articles of impeachment against him and sending him to the Senate for trial. Over the next two months, senators waded through more than five thousand pages of testimony alleging that Johnston had illegally hired state employees and summoned the Oklahoma National Guard to prevent the legislature from meeting. Lacking his predecessor's sympathetic votes in the Senate, he was found not guilty on ten charges but guilty of a single charge of general incompetence. He left office on March 20, 1929, becoming the second Oklahoma governor to be removed from office through the impeachment process.

Following a stint in the state Senate from 1933 to 1937, Johnston returned to his original home in the old Cherokee Outlet, where he practiced law into his nineties. He died in Perry on January 7, 1965, one day after a proposal to soften his impeachment was introduced in the House of Representatives. Suggesting that Johnston was a decent man who had gotten in over his head, Blackburn offered a simple postmortem for his failure as governor: "Johnston was a good man. He was just the wrong person at the wrong time."[17]

Meanwhile, far from the governor's mansion in Oklahoma City, members of the Osage Nation were learning just how far corrupt politicians and businessmen would go to line their pockets at the expense of a vulnerable population. As New Yorker staff writer David Grann chronicles with devastating effect in his 2009 bestseller, Killers of the Flower Moon, Osages were routinely murdered for their headrights in northeastern Oklahoma's vast oil deposits. Perpetrators were duplicitous whites who did not think that Native American lives mattered, and they committed their atrocities with the complicity of law enforcement. Not since the publication of John Steinbeck's The Grapes of Wrath have Oklahomans had a more troubling testament to their state's tolerance for inequality and susceptibility to dishonorable men whose crimes were hidden in plain sight.[18]

▶ ▶ ▶ ▶

Forged in the crucible of Soonerism, Native American land theft and murders over mineral rights, and incompetence in the executive branch leading to the impeachment of three governors and the early exit of two of them, Oklahoma appeared to be in a league of its own when it came to corruption. With overburdened courts and underpaid jurists holding a porous line against lawlessness, Oklahoma was widely perceived as a risky place to do business. Cynics at midcentury had a point in claiming that nothing much had changed since territorial days, when hard-riding outlaws and nefarious businessmen had plied their trades with impunity.[19] Even though advances in technology and transportation were fostering unprecedented prosperity and giving rise to what *Time* and *Life* magazine publisher Henry Luce dubbed The American Century, public officials in Oklahoma were notorious for taking advantage of the people who had elected them to office.

Beleaguered though it was, at least the state's judicial system was beyond reproach. Surely the men in black robes could be counted on to uphold their oaths of office, and none more so than the nine elected members of the Oklahoma supreme court—the highest court in the land and the state's last line of defense against chicanery.

Then came the Oklahoma supreme court scandal of 1964–65, and all bets were off.

The story begins in 1929 when Hugh Carroll founded Selected Investments Corporation, an Oklahoma investment management company. Mired in financial and regulatory troubles, the firm declared bankruptcy in early 1958. An audit revealed that Carroll had withdrawn $200,000 from the company's trust account. Ten days after Carroll's withdrawal, the Oklahoma supreme court overturned a lower court decision that was unfavorable to Selected Investments and granted the company a judgment in the amount of $500,000. To explain his hefty withdrawal from corporate coffers, Carroll testified that he had directed the money to a French-Canadian named Pierre Laval, who was supposed to use it to buy oil properties in Canada. Instead, he absconded with the money, leaving Carroll to wonder if Laval had died and certain that he had purchased an oil-field version of the Brooklyn Bridge.

Chief Justice Earl Welch, who had served on the court since 1932, authored the majority opinion in favor of Selected Investments. Second to sign was Vice Chief Justice N. S. Corn, whose service on the court dated back to 1933, followed by Justices Denver Davidson, N. B. Johnson, Ben T. Williams, and W. A. Carlisle; Justice Floyd Jackson wrote the dissenting opinion with the concurrence of Chief Justice W. H. Blackbird. Unfortunately for Carroll, the court's decision in his favor failed to shield him and other officers from criminal charges attending the bankruptcy. On October 22, 1958, a federal grand jury in Oklahoma City indicted Carroll, his wife Julia, and three associates on thirty-one counts of mail fraud and conspiracy. They were duly convicted and appeared in Judge Ross Rizley's court for sentencing. "I don't know what you did with that money," said Rizley. "I don't think you have it. But I don't think you turned it over to Pierre Laval."[20]

Three years passed, and nothing was heard from the mysterious Pierre Laval. Meanwhile, the IRS was conducting an investigation that burst into the open, in April 1964, when a federal grand jury was asked to consider criminal charges against Justices Corn and Welch, whose taxable incomes exceeded their salaries, then $12,500 annually, by a considerable margin. It quickly became obvious that the judges' inflated incomes derived from their involvement in the Selected Investments case. Corn was the first to fall; having resigned from the supreme court and ailing, at the age of eighty, he was sentenced to eighteen months in a federal medical facility in Springfield, Missouri, and fined $11,250 for income tax evasion.[21]

Reaction in the legal community was swift. Shocked supreme court justices convened in an emergency meeting and decided to request Corn's resignation as a supernumerary judge. While Corn pondered his options, Governor Henry Bellmon called for a vigorous investigation by state agencies into what he called "a sickening and despicable corruption in the highest judicial court of our state."[22]

Welch's turn at the bar of justice came in early October 1964. Appearing before Judge Roy W. Harper in Muskogee, Welch defended himself against charges of evading $13,364.74 in taxes from 1957 to 1961. Welch also had to defend himself (unsuccessfully, as it turned out) against allegations that he had been "going with another woman" and lavishing her with money and gifts. But the real drama came when former Justice Corn arrived from Springfield to deliver his testimony.

Drama turned to frustration as he invoked his Fifth Amendment right against self-incrimination sixteen times. The second week of testimony featured Hugh Carroll, former president of Selected Investments Corporation. Speaking clearly and matter-of-factly, Carroll admitted to paying $150,000 to Judge Corn, allegedly for "campaign expenses," in return for the reversal of the lower court ruling against his company. The higher court's opinion, authored by Justice Welch, had saved Selected Investment Corporation more than $200,000. Carroll had given Corn $25,000 as a good-faith deposit and had delivered the balance after the court handed down its decision, leaving Corn to decide how to share his bounty with his coconspirators on the court.

And the duplicitous (or perhaps dead) Pierre Laval? Years of speculation ended when Carroll admitted to fabricating the whole story to cover up his scheme. It took less than two hours for the jury to find the seventy-two-year-old Welch guilty of five counts of evading federal taxes.[23]

Despite his conviction, Welch remained a full-fledged member of the supreme court, as the state constitution had no provision for removing a justice except by impeachment by the state legislature, and the legislature was not scheduled to reconvene until January 5, 1965. Governor Bellmon entered the fray with a plea for the legislature to vote on a constitutional amendment to create a "supercourt" with the authority to remove judges. Opposition to Bellmon's plan came from none other than House Speaker J. D. McCarty. For reasons best known to himself, McCarty insisted on deferring to his fellow legislators to consider such a weighty matter as impeachment.

On November 13, 1964, Justice Welch was sentenced to three years imprisonment and fined $13,500. His appeals fell flat, and he was scheduled to begin serving his sentence on February 14, 1965, just over a month after the beginning of the Oklahoma supreme court term, on Monday, January 4, 1965. "Much to my surprise and chagrin, Justice Earl Welch entered the room," wrote Associate Justice William A. Berry, who had served on the court since 1959 and had hardly expected to see

Welch on the first day of the new term. Berry was even more surprised when Welch—only a month before he was set to begin a prison sentence! —proceeded to tell his colleagues how to dispose of cases in which his vote was not needed. "His effrontery irritated me completely," continued Berry, whose book, *Justice for Sale*, survives as a firsthand account of the court's dalliance with tax evasion, bribery, and extortion. "Here was a convicted felon awaiting the start of his sentence, and he was trying to tell the court how it should conduct its business."

Judge Berry had had enough. He excused himself from the meeting and stormed out, only to confront *Oklahoma City Times* reporter Hugh Hall in the hallway. Too rattled to sit for an interview, Berry directed Hall to Chief Justice Blackbird. Hall did as the judge suggested, and the next day the paper's headline blared, "It's a Berry Boycott."[24]

▶ ▶ ▶ ▶

Judge Berry's life got a lot more complicated when, a week after his alleged boycott, he returned home and was shedding his hat and coat as the phone was ringing. His wife, Carolyn, answered it and promptly handed over the receiver.[25] After a brief exchange with the caller, Berry put his hat and coat back on and made for the door. On the way out, he explained to his startled wife that U.S. District Judge Stephen Chandler, who presided over the Western District of Oklahoma, wanted to see him on a matter of some urgency.

Berry was puzzled, as Chandler was twenty years his senior, they did not know each other particularly well, and federal judges rarely reached out to their counterparts in the state courts. Their main contact had been in Chandler's court, as Berry had served as assistant U.S. Attorney from 1947 to 1950 and had tried several cases in the western jurisdiction. As he made the twelve-block drive to Chandler's home in their posh Oklahoma City suburb, Berry tried in vain to imagine what warranted a late-night rendezvous.

Stephen Chandler, a tall and distinguished widower whose wife had been dead for many years, was known as an eccentric recluse who lived in perpetual fear for his life. Some lawyers objected to his dictatorial attitude in court and wanted nothing more than to see him off the bench. But Chandler had not summoned Berry to talk about court cases and personal peccadillos. No sooner did Berry step into his house than Chandler handed him an electrifying confession from former Oklahoma Supreme Court Justice N. S. Corn. Although he had been sentenced to eighteen months in prison for income tax evasion, Corn had wound up serving less than five months, leaving many to wonder what kind of deal he had cut to shorten his sentence.

Berry's heart sank as he read Corn's confession. "The statement Chandler handed to me told a sordid, sickening tale of bribery and collusion on the state's highest court," recalled Berry. "It made me feel sick to my stomach just to read it." In his statement, Corn went into explicit detail about the bribes he had received in connection with two supreme court cases: *Selected Investments Corp. v. Oklahoma Tax Commission* and *Marshall v. Amos*. The confession read like a classic whodunit, particularly the part in which the recently convicted Hugh Carroll had paid $150,000 to Justice Corn to reverse the lower court decision pertaining to Selected Investments. What was potentially explosive, and what nobody had heretofore suspected, was Corn's admission not only of his own sizeable take, but also that he had paid $7,500 to two other justices to secure their votes in the case: Earl Welch, who had been convicted of tax evasion three months earlier, in the U.S. District Court in Muskogee, and was still, to Judge Berry's disgust, serving on the court; and Napoleon B. Johnson, a Cherokee who complemented his service on the court with participation in tribal politics. Corn had kept the rest for himself and further admitted to having received $4,000 from an attorney for a reversal in *Marshall v. Amos*.

Transfixed, Berry reached the last page of the confession, where Corn's signature, dated December 9, 1964, proved its authenticity. Berry was further shocked to learn that Oklahoma County Attorney Jim Harrod had been sitting on Corn's confession for a month. Assuming that Harrod's successor, Curtis Harris, would sit on it as well, Chandler feared that nobody would have the courage to expose the scandal and it would simply disappear.

As the enormity of the confession sank in, Chandler asked Berry, "Now that you have read it, what are you going to do about it?"

As a federal judge, Chandler was prohibited from intervening in state courts without specific authority from Congress. His only alternative was to enlist Judge Berry in exposing the outrage and bringing the miscreants to justice. As Chandler explained to a solemn Bill Berry, "I have thought about that hard and long. It boils down to this, you're the only one I can trust. You know, there are some people out there who want to sweep this scandal under the rug because they don't want to bring shame on the court. In addition, you've got some powerful legislators out there who want to squelch any court cleanup because they like things the way they are."

Shaken to his core, Berry said goodbye and drove home in the darkness.[26]

▶ ▶ ▶ ▶

Berry returned home with a dark cloud hovering over him. Realizing that a misstep on his part could end his career, he put his legal mind to work to consider three obstacles to going public with Corn's confession: (1) Chandler had shared the document as an acquaintance and not in a court of law, thereby exposing Berry to a charge of libel (as Berry often quipped, "You don't need grounds to file a lawsuit, you only need a lawyer."); (2) Welch's and Johnson's continuing service on the court meant that his disclosure would be perceived as awkward at best and duplicitous at worst; and (3) Berry was a Democrat and Governor Bellmon was a Republican. Clearly, no support would be forthcoming from the governor's office.

After considering and rejecting several options, Berry decided to ask G. T. Blankenship, then serving as Republican minority leader in the House of Representatives, to release Corn's testimony in the legislature.

Even though Blankenship was a Republican—and the first member of the GOP to be elected in Oklahoma County since 1928—the two men had been friends since Berry had delivered lectures in his law classes at OU. With Judge Chandler's concurrence, Berry invited Blankenship to his house. As his children, Nick and Libby, played upstairs, Berry led Blankenship into his study, closed the door, handed him Corn's confession, and waited in silence while he read it.

"This is awful!" blurted Blankenship as he reached the end of Corn's revelation. "How could something like this go on right under our noses and we not know about it?"[27] Both men were aware that rumors of improprieties had been circulating for years. But now, with Corn's sworn confession, there was no doubt about it: justice was for sale on the state's highest court.

Knowing that he was about to ignite a firestorm, Blankenship agreed to put his career on the line and read the confession in the House of Representatives. If he succeeded, he would have a ticket to higher office; if he failed, he might never practice law in Oklahoma again. With one eye on the upcoming race for state attorney general and the other on his minority status in a sea of Democrats, Blankenship decided that exposing Corn's confession was a golden, albeit risky, opportunity to stimulate judicial reform. Little did he suspect that his resolve to stand on the right side of history would make a profound impression on a young bus driver who was already envisioning a future in Republican Party politics and the law.

The legislature convened in early January 1965 amidst mounting tensions over the prospect of impeaching Earl Welch. Leading the charge against him was Representative John McCune of Tulsa, chairman of the House Judiciary Committee, who insisted that Welch's conviction of federal tax evasion amounted to "moral turpitude" and "corruption" in office. Nobody was surprised when House Speaker J. D. McCarty mounted a counterattack. Determined to bury the debate in committees, the wily speaker revealed more than he knew when he suggested that, according to some lawyers, income tax evasion was not an impeachable offense and dismissed the government's case as a cock-and-bull theory.[28]

As McCarty and his cronies laid the groundwork for another whitewash, the press had a field day. A *Tulsa Tribune* editor spoke for many when he lambasted the legislature for its tolerance of corruption: "We've seen legislative committees throw tantrums because minor state employees have padded expense accounts with a few drinks or used state cars to haul their children to school. Those tribulations of our time will not diminish if the legislature repeats such investigations but permits the big ones to go untouched. Indeed, the public will either laugh the bold hunters out of office if they go after mice with shotguns but drop their weapons and run every time bigger game appears, or we'll head into a situation where everything goes, and the bigger it is, the smoother it can operate."[29]

The jockeying and grandstanding continued until January 21. On what was expected to be just another day at the state capitol, a visibly shaken G. T. Blankenship rose from his seat and asked for the floor on a matter of personal privilege. Reading from a text, he began by likening courtrooms to houses of worship—sacred spaces where citizens could count on justice and daily renewals of confidence in their legal system. And then came the bombshell: "On December 9, 1964, at Springfield, Missouri, former justice N. S. Corn made a sworn statement. This statement was sworn to before an officer authorized to administer oaths as well as in the presence of a then county attorney from Oklahoma and a U.S. Attorney from Oklahoma. This document reveals a story so sordid, sickening and discouraging, its contents must be revealed for the good of us all."[30]

Now that he had everybody's attention, Blankenship described the two cases that had been former Justice Corn's undoing: *Selected Investments Corp. v. Oklahoma Tax Commission*, for which he had received $150,000 from Hugh Carroll, and *Marshall v. Amos*, for which he had been paid $4,000. The tension was palpable as Blankenship read Corn's description of secretive meetings with his two coconspirators, Justices Welch and Johnson, and how he had handed them each a packet of hundred-dollar bills totaling $7,500, neatly bound with rubber bands. "The people's faith is shaken," declared Blankenship as he wound toward his conclusion. "It is the duty of the legislative branch to show them the difference between an unworthy individual and an unworthy court. The honest, faithful members of the court must be vindicated. An investigation by an arm of this body can, properly pursued, restore the confidence of the people and clear the innocent." Blankenship proceeded to introduce his resolution, HR 512, calling for the judiciary committee to investigate and, if warranted, invoke articles of impeachment.[31]

And then all hell broke loose. Tumult in the House chamber quickly spilled into the corridors as legislators fumbled for what to say and reporters raced for the phones. Cries of *shady politics!* filled the air, and Democrats pressed an uncompromising Blankenship to reveal his source. Even Speaker McCarty was caught off guard. "I feel as if I had just been shafted," declared the speaker off the record. Governor Bellmon called Blankenship into his office to say he wanted the Oklahoma State Bureau of Investigation to run a sweep on his home to make sure it was not bugged. His warning to his Republican friend presaged dark days ahead: "I don't know what your habits are, or who you hang out with, or what you do; but my advice is that at the close of the session every day until this matter is over, go home. Don't go anyplace where you might be compromised, either fairly or unfairly. But just look after yourself, and don't give the people involved any opportunity."[32]

▶ ▶ ▶ ▶

By late February 1965, the House Research and Investigation Committee was ready to begin public hearings into the bribery charges against Justices Welch and Johnson. Consumed by closed-door meetings and wrangling over procedures, a few legislators shook free long enough to corner Blankenship and grill him over the source of Corn's confession. But the minority leader would divulge neither Chandler's nor Berry's name, leaving both judges to share the cloak-and-dagger moniker "Mr. X." Meanwhile, back at the supreme court, Justice Welch was toiling away, clearly intent on working right up to his date with the Department of Corrections.

At the same time, a storm was brewing at the courthouse, where an Oklahoma County grand jury was investigating more bribes that Justices Corn, Welch, and Johnson had allegedly accepted. As some of those alleged bribes dated back to the 1940s, legal experts knew they would have no choice but to relitigate cases that had been decided under a veil of corruption. Included in the ever-expanding list of individuals receiving grand-jury subpoenas were former Justice Corn and Otto Arthur Cargill, a former streetcar conductor who had earned a law degree in 1916 and risen in city politics to become mayor of Oklahoma City from 1923 to 1927. Cargill's career in law and politics, which included service as Oklahoma County attorney, had coincided with the heyday of bootlegging, a business dominated, albeit briefly, by Logan Billingsley, whose Night-and-Day Drugstore reigned as the go-to place for contraband spirits masquerading as prescription medicines.[33] Known later in life as a fixer, Cargill's involvement in the government's case against Selected Investments and his relationships with Oklahoma supreme court justices set off alarm bells. Public access to the grand jury's investigation was sparse. Testimony was taken behind closed doors, and witnesses were forbidden to talk to reporters.[34]

Back at the capitol, Justice Johnson took the witness stand on March 9 and, in his first public appearance since he had come under fire, was grilled by the House Judiciary Committee. Although he insisted that neither he nor other sitting justices had taken bribes, he had plenty to say about former Justice Corn, whom he lambasted as a "self-confessed criminal." He also denied rumors that he drank on the job. A reporter on the scene thought Johnson was both vague and disingenuous, as he asked for many questions to be repeated and sidestepped others by claiming a poor memory. Johnson's testimony stood in stark contrast to that of a much feistier Justice Welch, who was called to the stand the next day and launched into a sparring contest with his questioners. Like Johnson, Welch denied any knowledge of bribery and had nothing good to say about an allegedly "confused" Corn.

To get Corn's side of the story, the committee called on the former justice, now at home in Oklahoma City following his early release from prison, and asked him to comment on the eighty-four-page statement he had authored in Springfield. He confirmed that every word was true, leaving committee chairman Lou Allard to conclude that, even though Corn was in declining health, he was in top mental condition. "I've never seen a man 80-plus who had his wits about him and better," said the chairman.[35]

Johnson's and Welch's prospects dimmed when Allard revealed "an interesting pattern" in their voting records pointing to collusion. Ultimately, the House voted for three articles of impeachment against Welch (two for accepting bribes and one for income tax evasion) and two against Johnson (both for accepting bribes). Although Welch resigned his position on the supreme court before charges were formally filed, he remained defiant to the end, insisting that he was the victim of rumors and false press reports. "The 'power of the press' under the guise of 'freedom of speech' has attained another victory," declared Welch, "and I humbly bow to what appears to me to be the inevitable, in submitting this resignation, with the hope that I, now 73 years of age, may live the remainder of my life in peace and dignity."[36]

Welch's resignation meant that Johnson, now suspended from the bench, would face his Senate trial alone, where Corn's testimony was sure to dominate the proceedings. As though Johnson did not have enough to worry about, the Oklahoma County grand jury returned indictments against him on charges of bribery.

And so began the Senate's first impeachment trial since the 1920s, when governors Walton and Johnston had come up short in their efforts to keep their jobs. Those precedents notwithstanding, senators did not have much to go on other than a constitutional mandate to impeach elected officials for willful neglect of duty, corruption in office, habitual drunkenness, incompetency, or any offense involving moral turpitude while in office. One thing was for certain: Justice Johnson's personal achievements, including his recognition as the outstanding American Indian in 1954, made him a formidable witness.[37] His questioners would not include G. T. Blankenship, as his role in bringing the scandal to public attention compelled him to decline service as a prosecutor. The trial was scheduled to begin at 9:00 A.M. Thursday, May 6, in the Senate chamber on the fourth floor of the state capitol building.

As expected, the turning point of the trial came when Hugh Carroll, former president of Selected Investments Corporation, took the stand to explain how his company had gotten into tax trouble and, barring a favorable opinion by the supreme court, faced bankruptcy. In his detailed account of their transaction, he described Corn's request that the First National Bank and Trust Company of Oklahoma City deliver $125,000 to him in hundred-dollar bills. Then, per their prior agreement, Carroll met Corn across the street from the Oklahoma County Courthouse to deliver the first installment of his bribe.[38]

Efforts to discredit Carroll under intense cross-examination fell flat. Whatever hopes Johnson had for exoneration vanished when Corn, seated no more than twenty feet from his former colleague on the court, not only corroborated Carroll's story, but went on to add a few choice details: how he had been slack-jawed at the amount of money he had been paid; how Carroll had placed his down payment of $25,000 in the glove compartment of his car, parked south of the Oklahoma County Courthouse; how he had assembled two bundles of cash, totaling $7,500 each, and delivered them, separately, to Justices Welch and Johnson; and how he had waited for Johnson to count his hundred-dollar bills before leaving his office. Toward the end of his testimony, Corn was asked if there had been a single year in his twenty-four-year career when he had not accepted money to influence his vote. The presiding officer overruled the question, but not before everyone heard Corn say, "I had arrangements . . ." Asked why he had been so stingy with his colleagues, Corn replied, "That was an arbitrary amount that I fixed...I just wanted to keep the rest of it, I guess."[39]

When he testified in his own defense, Justice Johnson dismissed Corn's testimony as false and categorically denied taking bribes and concealing information from federal authorities. But prosecutors knew enough about Johnson's finances to question him about multiple bank accounts, safety deposit boxes, dozens of cashier's checks, and shadowy deposits that exceeded his payroll checks by about $20,000 between 1961 and 1965. Asked what he did with his cash, Johnson said that he kept some of it in his bedroom over a window. He further admitted that he kept no written records of his bedroom hoard.

Finally, it was time for the roll call. Onlookers in the galleries held their breath as senators' aye and nay votes echoed through the chamber. When the roll call ended, the count stood at thirty-one ayes and fifteen nays, one short of conviction. It was up to Senator John W. Young of Sapulpa to cast the deciding vote. After a moment of silence, the clerk repeated his call for a vote. Young voted to convict.

Presiding officer Roy Grantham of Ponca City ended the roll call with a terse declaration: "Two thirds of this court having voted Aye, I declare Article One to be sustained and you are thereby under the constitution and statutes found guilty and it is the judgment of the court that you be removed from office as justice of the supreme court of Oklahoma." Grantham repeated his declaration after Article Two was sustained. The court was adjourned.

Justice Johnson met the press on the Senate floor to read and distribute his one-paragraph statement. His conclusion contained more than a hint of ambiguity: "While I am deeply disappointed with this verdict, I am glad to have had the opportunity to give the people of Oklahoma my side of the story that they may be the final judges."

And with that, former Oklahoma Supreme Court Justice N. B. Johnson exited the chamber and descended the stairway in the company of his family.

The month ended on another downbeat note when the entire supreme court, with one exception, was subpoenaed to testify at O. A. Cargill's trial. Cargill had been indicted for allegedly lying to a federal grand jury concerning his financial dealings with members of the supreme court and connections with Selected Investments Corporation. A subpoena was issued to Judge Berry, but he was absent from his office when service was attempted. The only justice who was not subpoenaed was Ralph B. Hodges, who Governor Bellmon had appointed to fill the vacancy created by Judge Welch's resignation. Former justices Welch and Johnson were asked to testify for the defense.[40]

Early on, Johnson's attorneys had asked Justice Berry if he would testify as a character witness. He replied that he would, and although he found it hard to believe that Johnson had accepted bribes, he did think he was capable of "being easily influenced."[41]

▶ ▶ ▶ ▶

Judge Berry was never called to the witness stand. Watching from the sidelines as the Senate trial ground on, he took time from his cases to think about, and eventually record, his take on judicial ethics and the damage that the scandal was inflicting on the legal system. His analysis can be summarized in three main points: (1) a judge can always rationalize his actions; (2) pressure from stakeholders—friends, business associates, civic leaders, artful lawyers, fellow judges, state legislators, and even the governor's office—can easily influence a judge's decisions (as one cynic noted, "When the pressures on both sides are equal, then you get judicial fairness"); and (3) none of those stakeholders exerted more influence than state legislators who, despite the separation of powers between the executive, legislative, and judicial branches, "wield a heavy hammer" over the judiciary. Berry pinpointed the source of that heavy-handed influence as legislators' ability to set salaries, approve budgets, decide on the number of judgeships, and establish jurisdictional boundaries.

Berry went on to describe the profound disconnect between the legislature and the judiciary as an inevitable consequence of their different playbooks. Legislators were accustomed to lobbying and trading favors with fellow legislators, opinion leaders, and constituents to get what they wanted, and they applied the same rules to their relationships with judges, who had taken an oath to remain impartial. But how were judges supposed to maintain an oath of impartiality on relatively modest salaries? When Judge Berry had been elected to the Oklahoma supreme court in 1959, his annual salary had been $12,500 (approximately $109,000 in 2019 dollars)—by no means a paltry sum, but hardly enough to mount an effective electoral campaign and less than an attorney might expect to earn in private practice. Moreover, in the absence of a state retirement plan, a judge's only option upon retirement was to become a supernumerary judge, a position that entailed minimal responsibility and very little compensation.

To illustrate the kind of pressure judges were subjected to, Berry recounted his wife's least favorite story. Whenever she received a traffic ticket, he offered "to take care of it." He would then write a personal check and mail it, never suspecting that she assumed he was getting it "fixed." At a party one evening, a guest casually mentioned that he had been cited for a traffic violation on the way to the party. And Carolyn's response? "Oh, just give it to the judge, he'll take care of it. After all, that's what friends are for."

And then there was the issue that reformers had been focused on since territorial days: the partisan election of judges. "The process was old-fashioned partisan politics, pure and simple," wrote Berry. "Each political party mounted its candidates for the supreme court in much the same manner as they elected legislators and other political officers." To finance their campaigns and curry favor with power brokers, candidates were under pressure to cut deals and make promises that did not always square with their oath of impartiality. Often, de facto payoffs to judicial candidates were made under the guise of campaign contributions, which were almost impossible to trace to

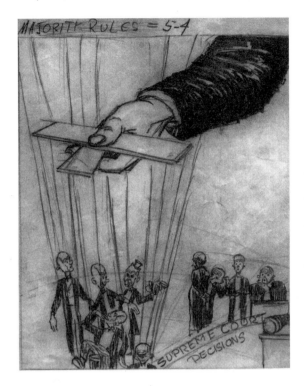

MAJORITY RULES = 5-4

SUPREME COURT DECISIONS

The publisher of the *Watonga Republican* gave this unpublished cartoon to William A. Berry during Berry's 1958 campaign for election to the Oklahoma supreme court. COURTESY BERRY AND ALEXANDER, *Justice for Sale*.

illicit transactions. And, just as rural voters exerted a lopsided influence in electing representatives to the state legislature, judicial districts were severely tilted toward rural counties. Of the nine judicial districts, two were urban and seven were rural, even though urban districts had as many practicing lawyers as the other seven districts combined. "Presumably, a wider choice would result in better candidates from which to choose," continued Berry. Finally, the qualities that made for good candidates did not always translate to qualities that made for good judges.

Toward the end of his 1958 campaign, Berry visited Art Loewen, the mayor of Watonga and his Blaine County campaign manager. Loewen introduced Berry to "Cowboy" Curtin, the publisher of the *Watonga Republican*, who promptly opened his desk drawer to show Berry a political cartoon featuring the Oklahoma supreme court in the hands of a puppeteer. Five puppets were controlled by one set of strings; the four others were standing to the side with puzzled looks on their faces. As Bill Berry was about to learn, distrust of the Oklahoma supreme court had been rampant long before Justice Corn revealed the depth of corruption in the legal system.[42]

Reforming the judiciary remained a distant dream in the summer of 1966, when Bill Price was deciding against a career as a bus driver and G. T. Blankenship was campaigning for the attorney general's office. But the possibility of reform at all levels of governance certainly gave the two campaigners, one a teenager with lofty goals and the other a seasoned politician with clear-cut ambitions, plenty to talk about on their odyssey across Oklahoma. One thing is beyond doubt: Price's interest in politics and the law, nurtured by his family and honed through his leadership in Teen Age Republicans, became more focused under Blankenship's mentoring. And the more he learned about his native state's plight, the more he wondered if he had what it took to do something about it.

CHAPTER FOUR: *Mr. Price Goes to Washington*

A year before his summer campaign trip with G. T. Blankenship, Bill Price set off for the East Coast to tour colleges. At the top of his list were two premier universities: Georgetown and Princeton. As he traveled up the East Coast by train, he alternated between reading Theodore White's award-winning *The Making of the President* (1964) and preparing for the 1966 national debate on labor issues, including arbitration, right-to-work legislation, and collective bargaining. Upon his arrival at Princeton, he was surprised to recognize his interviewer as his history teacher from Casady, who had resigned from the faculty to accept a position as a university admissions officer. Remembering Price as an ace history student, he fired off one question after another on labor issues. "I had a briefcase full of stuff that I had been researching on the way," recalled Bill about his admissions interview at Princeton. "That was the one subject area I really knew."

Smitten though he was, Price had already been granted early acceptance at Georgetown. Had he opted for Princeton, he would have had to sacrifice a guaranteed acceptance and taken his chances at the rival school. Besides, the prospect of living in the nation's capital was nothing short of exhilarating for a Teen Age Republican with a passion for politics. Having traveled through blighted cities festooned with Che Guevara posters on his way north, Price could not help but feel that his country was in deep trouble and that perhaps he, with a Georgetown diploma to his credit, might work himself into a position to make things better. On a lighter note, Price was dumbstruck at how uninformed people in the Northeast were about the West in general and Oklahoma in particular. By enrolling at Georgetown, he was about to join an exclusive club of Oklahoma expatriates who enjoyed nothing more than regaling their incredulous and gullible East Coast friends with tales of Indian raids and cowboy shoot-outs in the Wild West.[1]

Price returned to Oklahoma City from his college tour, graduated from Casady in the spring of 1966, and packed his bags for a return trip to Washington. Having enrolled in the Georgetown University School of Foreign Service, he began his classes at the same time another Oklahoman, Frank Keating, was on his way home. One of twin sons born to a prominent oil family in St. Louis, Keating had moved with his parents to Tulsa and graduated from Cascia Hall High School before making his own trek to Washington. "I knew him also in the political realm," said Price, "but he had just graduated from Georgetown as I arrived." Now it was Price's turn to field questions not only about the lawless frontier, but also about Oklahomans' apparent passion for politics. "I would get comments like, 'What is it with you guys from Oklahoma? You're all involved in politics."[2]

Contrary to the stereotype of college students as uniformly liberal, Georgetown's student body was fairly evenly divided between Republicans and Democrats. Whereas Republicans were united in their conservative beliefs, Democrats were split between liberals in the classic mode and antiwar radicals. Partisanship took a violent turn when Joseph Alito, the Democratic mayor of San Francisco, arrived on campus to deliver a speech. No sooner did he begin than a phalanx of female members of the SDS (Students for a Democratic Society) staged a protest featuring vicious groin kicks to signal their displeasure with patriarchy. Alioto knocked over his microphone as he fled through the back door. Occasional aggression notwithstanding, radicals did not represent the entire student body. Their minority status was confirmed in the presidential elections of 1968 and 1972 when Richard Nixon carried Georgetown and most other Washington, D.C.–area colleges. But wherever they stood on the political spectrum, just about everyone was skeptical of President Lyndon Johnson's approach to eradicating poverty through his Great Society programs.

Shortly after he arrived on campus, Price made contact with College Republicans. "I got involved in student politics the minute I arrived," said Price, who had been relieved to learn that conservatives were well represented on campus. "It was a very political school. Most of the people in the School of Foreign Service became lawyers and politicians and, secondarily, joined the foreign service."[3] Founded as the American Republican College League, at the University of Michigan, in 1892, College Republicans had risen to national prominence when William McKinley, then-governor of Ohio and soon to be president of the United States, gave a rousing keynote speech encouraging youth to join the Republican Party. By 1924, the organization was operating under the auspices of the Republican National Committee as the Associated University Republican Clubs. As the Great Depression cast its pall across the land, the organization merged with the newly created Young Republican National Federation to encompass both college students and young professionals. That merger lasted until the founding, in 1965, of the College Republican National Committee (CRNC). Conservative leaders who earned their spurs in the CRNC included such luminaries as Karl Rove, Lee Atwater, Rick Davis, Charlie Black, Roger Stone, Grover Norquist, Morton Blackwell, and Ralph Reed.

As the Republican Party's most effective recruiting tool, the CRNC was tailor-made for an ambitious Oklahoman who had earned his spurs in Teen Age Republicans. Such was Price's enthrallment with Georgetown University's College Republicans that he served as its president during the 1967–68 school year. Serving alongside Price in College Republicans was Andrew S. Natsios, an American of Greek origin who went on to serve in a number of high-level positions in Massachusetts and in the federal bureaucracy. Natsios served most famously as administrator of the United States Agency for International Development (USAID), where he was special humanitarian assistance coordinator for Sudan and U.S. government coordinator for international disaster assistance. Price was less enthralled by the group's treasurer, Paul Manafort, who received his bachelor's degree in Business Administration in 1971 and his juris doctor in 1974 from Georgetown. "I never warmed up to him, particularly," recalled Price. "He was sort of an operator."[4] Price was more prescient than he knew about the man who, a half century hence, would serve as Donald Trump's campaign manager in the 2016 presidential election en route to convictions and imprisonment on charges ranging from obstruction of justice and witness tampering to tax and bank fraud. Years later, as he wound down his legal career and turned his attention to public speaking, Price would spice up his lectures on corruption by displaying a photo of Georgetown's College Republicans and asking his listeners if anyone looked familiar. Only rarely did someone recognize either him or the boyish and as-yet-unremarkable Paul Manafort.[5]

Price's college career nearly came to an early and tragic end during a hazing incident that was part of his initiation (better known as Hell Weekend) into his foreign service fraternity. On what was supposed to be a routine treasure hunt, Price and other initiates ventured out in the wee hours of the morning to abscond with concrete bricks lying along the George Washington Parkway. As Price trudged through the snow with his looted treasure, a sports car driven by a drunk driver careened off the road at fifty or sixty miles per hour. In a flash, the car struck Price from behind and sent him flying into a snowbank. Had he been hit by a larger car, he might have spent the rest of his life in a wheelchair or perhaps expired on the spot. Instead, he suffered injuries, but not breaks, to both legs and was carted off to a hospital, where he was fitted with two casts that left him all but immobile, but thankful to be more or less intact after a close brush with death.

Predictably, friends and faculty demanded that the university shut down Price's fraternity. But Price, temporarily bound to a wheelchair, disagreed, as the fault lay with the drunk driver and not his fraternity. When the student council met to pass judgment, Price's friends wheeled him into the meeting and plunked him in a chair so that he could lodge his protest in person. Thanks to his insistence on placing blame where it was due, Price's fraternity was exonerated.

An amusing follow-up to Price's near-death experience came during Christmas vacation following his accident. Delivered to Oklahoma City with plaster casts on his legs, Price decided to visit his sister Montine. Recently divorced from plastic surgeon Bill Foerster and caring for their three children, Montine's challenges were compounded by a rare eye disease that was slowly robbing her of her sight. To cheer her up and make himself useful, Price plopped himself under her Christmas tree to assemble presents for her children, Scott, Steve, and Stan. "She had ordered all these toys and didn't realize they were in a million pieces," recalled Price about an unforgettable evening spent crawling on Montine's floor. "I was putting together toys until four in the morning."

Price reserved some of his vacations for his brother, Bob, who had graduated from Dartmouth College and settled in Hartford, Connecticut, where he taught classes for Hartford Insurance Company employees. On a trip to New York City, Bob met his future bride, Gudbjorg Dybing, a translator for the Norwegian consulate. Always up for an adventure, Bill often joined his brother and sister-in-law on trips to French Canada and Cape Cod. A memorable experience came when Bob's neighbor, a butcher by trade, gave him strips of filet mignon for the road. Too cheap to spring for a hotel room, they slept in their car at the Woods Hole Yacht Club parking lot en route to Martha's Vineyard. Startled awake by a security guard, they found a perfect spot to light a fire and enjoy a breakfast of filet mignon.

Bob and Gudbjorg later moved to Oklahoma City, around the corner from the Prices' home, where they raised their two children, Siri and Eirik.[6]

▶ ▶ ▶ ▶

In his third year at Georgetown, Price complemented his leadership in College Republicans with chairmanship of the District of Columbia College Republicans and service as a national committeeman for the District of Columbia Federation of Young Republicans.[7] Price attributed his position in the latter organization, which had its roots in the run-up to the Civil War, to his vaunted ability to recruit scores of College Republicans. Formally known as the Young Republican National Federation (YRNF) since 1935, and simply Young Republicans (YRs) for short, it was the nation's oldest and most influential political association for people between the ages of eighteen and forty, and it provided grassroots support for Republican candidates and conservative issues on the local, state, and national levels. Like College Republicans, Young Republicans built a solid record of producing Republican Party leaders through recruiting, training, and mobilizing its members, and they quickly learned that they could count on friendships and networking opportunities to last a lifetime. Among Price's most cherished mentors were Natalie and Peter McPherson. Peter went on to become head of the USAID (a position later held by Andrew S. Natsios) and president of Michigan State University.[8]

Price's knack for networking led him to Steve Serbe, a fellow freshman who was elected president of their class. In the same election, Price was chosen as the class treasurer. Charismatic and handsome, Serbe spent his summers at a modeling agency in New York, where he modeled for brands such as Calvin Klein. "He was great to go out with," recalled Price about his friend, who bore a striking resemblance to Robert Redford, only taller. "The girls would just flock." They roomed together and won various campus elections over the next three years, and even though Serbe was a Democrat and die-hard supporter and close friend of New York senator Robert Kennedy (he was invited to spend his honeymoon at the Kennedy family compound in Virginia), the two formed a lasting friendship based on their interest in politics and leadership ambitions. After serving as freshman class treasurer, Price was elected vice president of his class and won a seat on the student council, both in the 1967–68 academic year.[9]

When it came time to take a break from politics and listen to lecturers, there was nobody Price would rather listen to than Carroll Quigley, an American historian with a unique take on the evolution of civilizations. As a student in the School of Foreign Service, Price declared what was, in effect, a tri-major in history, foreign affairs, and government. Grateful for his Casady education, Price paid rapt attention to Quigley's lectures, particularly his spiel on the history of warfare, in which he focused on combatants' reliance on either offensive or defensive strategies. Taking an offensive position entailed the use of cannons in a drawn-out siege or tanks in a World War II blitzkrieg, whereas defensive warfare ranged from castles in medieval Europe to trenches in the killing fields of World War I. In terms of the evolution of civilizations, a combatant's approach to warfare, whether offensive or defensive, was both cause and effect of characteristics that defined its entire culture. According to Quigley's thesis, the Cold War between the United States and Russia suggested a defensive posture on both sides, as mutually assured destruction—or MAD, in one of the most appropriate acronyms of all time—compelled each nation to beef up its defenses against nuclear attack.

"Someday," intoned Quigley to the nation's future policymakers, "you will have non-state players, where you will have nuclear bombs in suitcases. Then offense will predominate, and there will be chaos in the world." Quigley died in 1977—too early to see his prediction play out in the spread of international terrorism perpetrated by non-state warriors and the chaos that ensued.[10]

Another Georgetown student who named Carroll Quigley as a favorite professor was Price's classmate and political rival Bill Clinton, whom Frank Keating likened to future Oklahoma governor, U.S. senator, and University of Oklahoma president David Boren for his extraordinary intellect and aptitude for a career in politics. "We all could agree or disagree with their politics," said Keating, who would one day make his own mark on the Republican Party, about the two Democrats, "but they are two very bright guys!"[11]

Clinton's political instincts were still a work in progress when he ran for student body president. Price and Serbe, who were completing their freshman year, served as their class's campaign managers for Clinton's opponent. Clinton won all but the freshman class by narrow margins. Such was his lopsided defeat in the freshman class that he lost the election. Although neither Price nor Serbe was fond of the future president, Serbe's dislike was palpable. "Serbe hated phonies and thought Clinton was a phony," recalled Price.

Even in his college days, Clinton's modus operandi tended toward the devious, and it was on full display when he chose a car auction to benefit the sports program as his *cause celèbre*. "The sports program was the only thing that didn't need any money," explained Price who, along with everyone else in student government, was puzzled by Clinton's priorities. "Then we finally figured it out. For his Rhodes Scholarship, he had academics, he had student leadership, but he didn't have sports. If you raised money for sports, you could qualify—it helped you qualify for the Rhodes Scholarship. That's his whole motivation. That was typical of Bill Clinton."

During his run for the White House in 1992, Clinton resurrected his student days at Georgetown and tried to pass himself off as a former antiwar activist and avid Robert Kennedy supporter. "He wasn't even remotely antiwar at Georgetown, and he wasn't known for supporting Robert Kennedy," recalled Price. Although Price campaigned for Clinton's rival for student body president, the two got along fairly well. Yet Clinton earned the everlasting enmity of Steve Serbe, whose antics at the end of an election for student body president gained notoriety during those heady days at Georgetown. They were sharing a stage with other class presidents when election results came in showing that Clinton had lost. And Serbe's response? Taking a deep drag on his cigar, he turned around and blew smoke in Clinton's face.[12] Serbe's appalling lack of respect was indefensible, and it seared itself in Price's memory as behavior he would never emulate in his own career in public service.

A postscript to Steve Serbe's enmity toward Bill Clinton came during the presidential campaign of 1992. While Clinton was barreling toward the White House, Serbe was working as an attorney on the New Jersey shore with neither wealth nor influence in the Democratic Party. Nevertheless, Clinton detoured a great distance from his campaign route to visit Serbe and try to solicit his support, but to no avail. Serbe later called Price to speculate on two possible reasons for Clinton's surprise visit: either he was obsessed with forging friendships with everyone on his radar, no matter what their past disagreements; or he wanted Serbe to keep quiet about his lack of support for Robert Kennedy. "Serbe still had the list of Kennedy supporters at Georgetown and, according to him, Clinton's name wasn't on it," explained Price. "Serbe was convinced that Clinton simply wanted to guarantee his silence." Serbe never revealed Clinton's failed attempt to win his support, and he never went public about his lack of pro-Kennedy credentials for the simple reason that he was never queried by the press. For the rest of his life, Serbe interpreted the campaign detour as evidence of the president's penchant for duplicity.

At the other end of the spectrum from Steve Serbe was Paul Prosperi, a friend of Bill (or simply FOB, an acronym later added to Democrats' vernacular) and Clinton's class campaign manager, who was already touting him for president—not only of the student council, but of the United States. After graduating from Georgetown, the two men went their separate ways, Clinton to politics in his home state of Arkansas and, eventually, presidency of the United States; and Prosperi to Palm Beach, Florida, where he practiced law and donated liberally to the Democratic Party and the arts. Not surprisingly, his philanthropy extended to his old college buddy, and in 1995, he organized the first—and, arguably, most successful—of President Clinton's fundraisers in Florida. But how quickly fortunes change. Two years after that storied event, Prosperi was convicted of fraud, filing false tax returns, and forging securities to hide his multi-million-dollar theft from a client. Even then, Prosperi remained true to his college buddy and donated his ill-gotten gains to a raft of Clinton's causes, including renovations to the White House and contributions to Hillary Clinton's brother's ill-fated campaign, in Florida, for the U.S. Senate.

"The next time I see Paul Prosperi's name is on Clinton's pardon list," said Price about the sad demise of a Georgetown acquaintance.

In one of his last official acts in the White House, President Clinton caused a furor by commuting or pardoning 175 people, including Prosperi, whose five-year prison sentence was commuted to three years of house arrest. Clinton defended his decision as the merciful thing to do for first-time offenders.[13] But few doubted that, in cases such as Prosperi's, the president's real motive was to cut his supporters a break.

Determined to take advantage of all that Georgetown had to offer to an aspiring public servant, Price leveraged his way into a small group of students invited to attend a three-hour seminar on foreign policy featuring Richard M. Nixon and about forty heads of international corporations under the age of forty-five. "It was just surprising how *bright* he was on foreign policy," recalled Price about the man who would soon rise to the presidency. "What a waste that he had all these character flaws. He was brighter than any professor of international affairs that I have ever seen at Georgetown, and more knowledgeable." Price sat spellbound as Nixon, who had barely begun his bid for the White House and had yet to draw on the wisdom of his future secretary of state, Henry Kissinger, fielded questions about obscure countries and arcane policies with confidence and supreme intelligence. "He was a deep thinker on foreign policy," concluded Price. "He outlined political and social trends and anticipated U.S. foreign policy decades into the future. He had *incredible* talent and potential. But his dark side was incredibly disturbing."[14]

Price's involvement in student government and Republican politics gave him a unique perspective on one of the most turbulent periods in American history. Gazing from the roof of his fraternity house, the young Oklahoman was an eyewitness to a revolution in the making. One antiwar rally was peaceful. Another was not. Chanting antiwar mantras and brandishing posters of Chairman Mao, Che Guevara, and Leon Trotsky, campus radicals paraded through the streets of Washington, wreaking havoc and daring the police, clad head-to-toe in riot gear, to arrest them. Then came the riots following the assassination of Dr. Martin Luther King. As Price recalled about his front-row seat at America's unraveling, "We were up on top of the fraternity house watching Washington burn. You saw areas of Washington just go up in smoke. The next morning, all along our front lawn, were soldiers with guns and bayonets facing the park where H. Rap Brown, chairman of the Student Nonviolent Coordinating Committee, had announced an upcoming rally."

True to his conservative roots, Price chose a more benign and, arguably, more effective path to change by leading a College Republicans campaign, during his senior year, to rebuild houses in poor neighborhoods. Comparing his campaign to a Habitat for Humanity project, Price was proud to strap on a tool belt and do something practical for poor people rather than wave banners and wreak havoc. "They were *talking* about doing things for the poor, and we were actually *doing* things for the poor," said Price.[15]

Price's rebuilding project attracted the attention of officials in the White House, including Egil Krogh, an attorney who had joined Nixon's team as an advisor on the District of Columbia. He later served as liaison to the Federal Bureau of Investigation and the Bureau of Narcotics and Dangerous Drugs. Krogh's association with Nixon insiders brought him into contact with the so-called plumbers—a secret team of operatives charged with "fixing leaks" on behalf of the president. One of those leaks was discovered in the office of psychiatrist Lewis Fielding, whose patients included Daniel Ellsberg, a military analyst with the RAND Corporation, who authored the so-called Pentagon Papers for the U.S. Department of Defense. Known officially as the Report of the Office of the Secretary of Defense Vietnam Task Force, the Pentagon Papers told a dreary tale of deception from 1945 to 1967, when duplicitous policymakers squandered blood and treasure in the jungles of Southeast Asia. When the Pentagon Papers went public in a *New York Times* exposé in 1971, readers learned, to their horror, about the Johnson administration's campaign of lies that led to military escalation in Vietnam and surrounding countries.

As indictments attending the Watergate scandal and related acts of treachery rained down on conspirators, the plumbers found themselves in the crosshairs of federal investigators for burglarizing Fielding's office in an effort to discredit Ellsberg and suppress the real story behind the Vietnam War. Krogh pleaded guilty to federal charges of conspiring to violate Fielding's civil rights and agreed to cooperate with prosecutors. Although he was sentenced to two to six years in prison, he was released after four and a half months.

The plumbers' perfidy was a few years in the future when Krogh, impressed with Price's can-do approach to alleviating poverty, summoned him to the White House, in the spring of 1970, and offered him a job following other Young Republicans into the Nixon Administration. Sorely tempted to accept a job in the White House, Price decided to stick with his plan to attend law school at the University of Oklahoma and declined the offer. Little did Price suspect that Krogh would one day trade his White House credentials for a prisoner number. "It was a compliment, being offered a job in the White House," recalled Price about refusing an offer that might have landed him on the wrong side of America's most celebrated scandal. "I'm glad I avoided the quagmire that put many people, including Krogh, in jail."

Price paused as he pondered, as we all do when we recall turning points in our lives, a road not taken—a road that might have led him in directions he could never imagine.[16]

Price was multitasking between his studies and politics and watching America burn from atop his fraternity house when a much-needed dose of good news trickled in from Oklahoma, where the supreme court scandal of 1964–65 had actually spurred reformers to action. As Price and his mentor, G. T. Blankenship, had discussed during their epic bus ride, Oklahoma's resistance to judicial reform had always been firm and stratified, and it was based on a toxic trifecta of historical precedent, voter apathy, and entrenched political and economic interests. The glaring weaknesses in partisan elections of judges, perpetuated by prominent politicians with a vested interest in maintaining the status quo, had led inexorably to the scandal, and in the absence of systemic changes, it was not hard to imagine more scandals to come. In the words of Abraham Lincoln, "What has once happened, will invariably happen again, when the same circumstances which combined to produce it, shall again combine in the same way." OU law school dean Earl Sneed added his own dire prediction that the "forces of lethargy, the forces of self-interest, and the built-in opposition to any change will work against" anybody who championed reform in the state's elective system of judicial selection.[17]

Happily, neither Lincoln's nor Sneed's prophesies came to pass. On July 11, 1967—less than a year after Price arrived at Georgetown— judicial reform became a reality when voters accepted two constitutional amendments under which the legislature replaced the old county courts with district courts, abolished justice of the peace courts, created the Oklahoma Court of Appeals, and established an administrative director of the courts. In what was probably the most significant change, the legislation required the governor to appoint judges from among candidates named by a judicial nominating committee which, in time, became a requirement for all state court judicial positions except special judges.[18]

As Price entered his final year at Georgetown, he could look back with pride on helping G. T. Blankenship, the whistleblower who had brought the state legislature to a standstill with his shocking revelation of corruption on Oklahoma's highest bench, to win his campaign for state attorney general, a position that he leveraged to push through reforms that had been needed for the better part of a century.

Sometimes, the good guys really do win.

▶ ▶ ▶ ▶

The other good news came when Bill went to a college mixer at Immaculata Junior College and met his future wife, Mary Lynn Slattery. Recalling that fateful day, Bill said he was immediately attracted to her smile and how animated she was talking to her friends. "She's the happiest person I ever met," said Bill. "She loves life and has a way of making everyone around her, especially me, feel appreciated. Mary is smart and pretty but also very funny!"

Mary was likewise impressed. "I was struck by how self-assured and intelligent Bill was," she said. "He came over and asked me to dance and we started talking right away. It was like we'd always known each other. I'd never met anyone from Oklahoma, but I was a big fan of Westerns and could tell that Bill was one of the good guys."

Maybe it was kismet. Bill and Mary had narrowly missed one another twice, first when they'd attended the 1964 World's Fair in New York with their parents and then when Mary had attended a party at Bill's house.

The rest, as they say, is history. Although Bill was president of Georgetown's College Republicans and Mary, a Democrat, had worked on Robert Kennedy's presidential campaign, they had a surprising amount in common. Bill's conservative, Midwestern background dovetailed with Mary's Catholic school upbringing, which had instilled the same values of faith, family, and country.

Both were avid readers with a particular interest in politics, and they loved movies. "Bill has always been a history buff," continued Mary. "Seeing Mount Vernon, the White House, and the Smithsonian through his eyes was spectacular! We took walks by the Tidal Basin during the Cherry Blossom Festival, enjoyed musicals at the National Theater (none more memorable than *Camelot* and *Man of La Mancha*!), and took in art shows at the National Gallery of Art and the Phillips Museum." Mary cherished memories of listening to incredible music at the Cellar Door on M Street, eating hamburgers at the Little Tavern, and watching movies like *Butch Cassidy and the Sundance Kid*, *Goodbye Mr. Chips*, and *The Out-of-Towners*.[19]

One of their first dates was a picnic on Roosevelt Island. They walked to what they thought would be a secluded spot, only to blunder into a ceremony where LBJ and Secretary of the Interior Stewart Udall were dedicating a statue. Long before security became a paramount issue, they had no trouble finding seats and blending into the audience.

While Secretary Udall was delivering his speech, Bill and Mary watched with mounting curiosity as President Johnson, seated on the front row and clearly distracted from what the secretary had to say, grabbed a fly. And then, lightning-quick, the president squeezed it, winced as it wriggled in his sizeable palm, threw it to the ground, and stomped on it. Fairly or not, Price never forgot that bizarre incident as a metaphor for LBJ's character—crafty, crude, and perhaps even cruel to those who had fallen out of his favor.

As their romance blossomed, Price got to know Mary's parents at family dinners. Dr. Edward J. Slattery, originally from upstate New York, was a graduate of St. Bonaventure University, where he had been a champion boxer. After graduating from Georgetown Dental School, he opened a private practice in Washington, D.C. When World War II broke out, Slattery joined the U.S. Navy and served as an oral surgeon in the Pacific theater. After returning home in 1945, he attended 6:30 mass every morning for the rest of his life. He lived his faith by ministering to the homeless and providing free dental care to the Missionary Sisters. Dr. Slattery was featured in *Time* magazine in 1951 as the first dentist to successfully implant an injured and dislocated tooth in an eight-year-old boy who had fallen and struck one of his upper front teeth on the pavement. An inventor, Slattery held many patents for medical instruments and applications. Known for his sense of humor, he teased Mary Lynn about finding the only Protestant at Georgetown.

Mary Lynn's mother, Evelyn Alber Slattery, was a third-generation Washingtonian. A flapper in the 1920s, Ev (as she was known) traded her dancing shoes for a business school diploma and worked at Massachusetts Mutual until her marriage in 1935. Ed and Ev were extroverts who enjoyed tennis, swimming, and entertaining. In addition to raising their two daughters, they took care of their invalid mothers at their home in Spring Valley, a neighborhood in Washington.

When their seventeen-year-old daughter, Jo Ann, who was Mary Lynn's older sister by seven years, was caught in a whirlpool during

Bill's parents, Virginia and Dr. Joel Scott Price, were on hand for their son's graduation from Georgetown University in Washington, D.C., in the spring of 1970. Courtesy Bill Price.

a boating excursion on the Potomac River and drowned, Ev was devastated. Her saving grace was returning to work, this time at the *Georgetown Spectator*, later renamed the *Potomac Current*. As advertising manager, Ev was well known and respected by shop owners. She loved the nation's capital not only for its vibrancy and politics, but also its beauty. As a representative of her hometown newspaper, she and Ed were regulars at diplomatic parties and theater openings. Mary Lynn's apprenticeships at the newspaper during summer vacations nurtured her love for writing and advertising.

Bill and Mary had planned to get married as soon as he graduated from Georgetown in the summer of 1970, but when her father died suddenly of a heart attack, they postponed their wedding until Christmas, when they would be on break from their respective schools.[20]

Bill remained in Washington for a few months after his graduation to be near Mary. He also seized the opportunity to secure a summer internship at the Federal Judicial Center (FJC).[21] His supervisor, Judge Alfred Paul Murrah, was born in the Chickasaw Nation in 1904, three years before the Twin Territories were united as a single state. After his mother died, he relocated with his father and brother to Alabama, where a hardscrabble upbringing inured him to life's challenges. As a teenager, Murrah took to the railways, riding freight cars throughout the South and subsisting on odds jobs along the way. In a tale seemingly ripped from a Horatio Alger novel, he returned to Oklahoma and made his way to OU, where he set his sights on a career in the legal profession. His path through the judicial system landed him in a small firm in Oklahoma City, where he specialized in workers' compensation and personal injury litigation; then as a judge at the Tenth Circuit Court of Appeals in Denver, where appeal cases in Oklahoma were heard; and finally, as director of the FJC in Washington. Such was Murrah's prominence as an Oklahoma jurist that the federal building in Oklahoma City was named in his honor. It opened as the Alfred P. Murrah Federal Building in 1978, only to be destroyed on April 19, 1995 in what was then the most destructive act of domestic terrorism in American history.[22]

For the rest of his life, Price would recall his internship under Judge Murrah as one of his most valuable experiences. Operating as the research and education agency of the U.S. judiciary, the FJC received an annual appropriation from Congress to support the efficient and effective administration of justice and judicial independence. Although it lacked policymaking and enforcement authority, the FJC provided accurate and objective information to legal professionals through analyses of policies, practices, and procedures. The agency fulfilled its educational mission by producing curricula, publications, and videos, all aimed to make sure judges and court staff had the resources they needed to do their jobs.[23]

Housed in the beautiful and historic Dolly Madison House, a block from the White House, the FJC was an ideal venue for Price and several other interns to get hands-on experience and invaluable mentoring.

One of Price's first assignments, in the summer of 1970, was to figure out how many federal judges should be apportioned to each judicial district. As attorneys general and politicians paraded by his desk on the way to meetings with Judge Murrah, Price gathered his statistics and wrote his reports, knowing that his work would have an impact on judges and lawyers across the land. Price recalled that internship as a peak experience: "There were no more than ten people who worked there. One day I was present when Judge Murrah was on the line with the attorney general recommending who to appoint to the supreme court!"

At summer's end, Price returned to Oklahoma to begin his studies at the University of Oklahoma Law School. Mary stayed behind in Washington to complete her student teaching. Although they wrote love letters and exchanged audiotapes, they never talked on the phone. As Bill explained, "Back then, no one called long distance unless it was an emergency."

With a semester of law school under his belt, Bill returned to Washington. They were married at Mary's parish church, Annunciation, on December 22, 1970. Bill's brother, Robert, was his best man; Mary's childhood friend Michelle Freeman was her maid of honor. Both of their families, along with about a hundred guests, celebrated their nuptials and attended the reception held at Kenwood Country Club in Bethesda, Maryland. Christmas decorations were everywhere, and snow was in the air although, happily, not on the ground. The newlyweds left the day after their wedding for a honeymoon in the Bahamas, thus spending their first Christmas as husband and wife in a tropical paradise.[24]

Following their honeymoon, Bill and Mary returned to Oklahoma, where Bill settled into two and a half more years of law school and Mary transferred to OU to finish her college degree. With a good record at Georgetown and enough connections to last a lifetime, Bill could have applied to any number of law schools. Yet he chose OU for a simple reason, and one that resonated with other opinion leaders who

Bill and Mary Price were married at Annunciation Catholic Church in Washington, D.C., on December 22, 1970. Courtesy Bill Price.

had attended high-powered universities: he knew he wanted to build his career in Oklahoma, and he needed local bona fides to make that happen. Once again, he looked to his mentor, G. T. Blankenship, for guidance. During his run for state attorney general, Blankenship was interviewed by countless newspaper editors who seemed ho-hum about his Yale diploma but lit up when he mentioned his juris doctor from OU. "It struck me that if you at least went part of your time to a local school, that made up for an out-of-state education," explained Price. Equally important were the connections to be made at a state college or university—indispensable for anyone aiming to build a career in Oklahoma. In keeping with Blankenship's example, he never even considered applying to another law school.

Price's Rolodex was already packed from four years at Georgetown. Now it was time to cultivate relationships closer to home. As his ambitions became ever more focused, he knew one thing for sure: he would need all the help he could get.[25]

CHAPTER FIVE: *Beginnings*

F ollowing their honeymoon in the Bahamas, the
newlyweds arrived at the University of Oklahoma College
of Law in Norman to find a far different scene than they
had experienced in Washington, where antiwar protests
had infused their academic pursuits with passion and
partisanship. Most law students were married, meaning that the Prices'
downtime would be more sedate. Moreover, many of those students had
recently returned from Southeast Asia. Whether serving in combat or
support roles, Vietnam War vets came home with a sense of purpose
that eluded students whose only experience with the horrors of warfare
was through mass media. As Bill recalled, "They were much more
conservative. It was just quite different from the feel of Washington,
D.C."[1]

The Prices were not quite done with life in the nation's capital.
After accepting a second internship with Judge Murrah, Bill returned
to Washington with Mary in the summer of 1971. Now that he had a
year of law school under his belt, Price figured he was in for expanded
responsibilities. He was not disappointed. No sooner did he arrive at
the Federal Judicial Center than he learned that the person in charge of
training federal personnel, including judges, had resigned in early June,
and his replacement was not due until the fall. Even though he knew
next to nothing about what marshals, probation officers, and judges
needed to know to do their jobs, he spent the summer designing their
training programs and soliciting speakers. Among those speakers was
Mary's cousin, Carl Imlay, general counsel to the Administrative Office
of the Courts which advised the judiciary, including the U.S. Supreme

Court, on legal issues. Thanks to experts willing to offer advice and answer his questions, Price completed his internship and returned with Mary to Norman to begin his second year of law school.[2]

Price wasted no time in joining the University of Oklahoma College Republicans and getting himself elected president for the 1971–72 school year. Among his acquaintances were Marc Nuttle, who had earned notoriety as a brilliant political strategist; and Rodd Moesel, an expert in state politics with impeccable judgement. Price was not surprised to learn that Tom Daxon, his friend from Teen Age Republicans, had been elected as president of the Oklahoma State University College Republicans in Stillwater at about the same time. Price's notoriety in Republican circles received a boost when he was recruited as a spokesperson in support of President Richard Nixon's reelection campaign. The roster of conservative campaigners read like a *Who's Who* of Oklahoma leadership: Dewey Bartlett, who had succeeded Henry Bellmon as governor in 1966 to guarantee another four years of Republican control; Attorney General G. T. Blankenship, whom Price had helped to elect in his unlikely position as a campaign bus driver; Ralph G. Thompson, who had been elected to fill Blankenship's District 83 seat in the Oklahoma House of Representatives, representing north Oklahoma City, Nichols Hills, Lakehurst, and the Village; Jim Inhofe, who had been elected to the state Senate from Tulsa's District 35 in 1968; and Mickey Edwards, a former reporter and editor for the *Oklahoma City Times*, public relations director for Beals Advertising Agency and, from 1968 to 1973, editor of *Private Practice* magazine.[3] "I was the bottom of the rung," recalled Price. If none of the higher-ups were available to deliver a speech or sit for an interview, it fell to Price to fill the breach. As a reward for his faithful service to his party, Price was chosen as an alternate delegate—and certainly one of the youngest—to the Republican National Convention in Miami Beach, Florida, in August 1972.[4]

One of Price's main responsibilities as president of OU College Republicans was to participate in college and televised debates in the run-up to the 1972 election. To balance his support for Republican incumbent Richard Nixon, former OU student council president Cleta Deatherage was tapped to represent U.S. Senator George McGovern, a Democrat from South Dakota and a longshot candidate for the Oval Office. Characterized by Price as "kind of the Hillary Clinton of Oklahoma," Deatherage practiced law in Norman before she was elected to the Oklahoma House of Representatives in 1976. Equipped with a law degree from OU and married to Dale Mitchell, Cleta Deatherage Mitchell relocated with her husband to Washington, D.C. in the mid-1990s. Rebranded as a Republican, Mitchell earned a reputation as a firebrand who expressed her new-found allegiance in IRS cases targeting conservative individuals and organizations. Another debate opponent, Eric Groves ("still a liberal, and also a friend," according to Price), was later elected to the city council of Oklahoma City.

To prepare for the debates, Price spent a week in Washington, D.C., under the tutelage of President Nixon's closest advisors: John Ehrlichman and H. R. Haldeman, both of whom were later implicated in the Watergate scandal and sent to prison. Listening to their counsel and reading their position papers, Price was struck by the contrast between Nixon's policy expertise and his character flaws, which would soon bring down his administration. Knowing more than he had a week earlier about the administration's policies, Price returned to Norman for what turned out to be a series of friendly debates with two committed liberals, often followed by nonpartisan beers at a campus hangout. "We got along great during those debates," recalled Price about his experience with Deatherage and Groves. "There was no animosity whatsoever." [5]

Price's tenure as president of OU College Republicans afforded him the opportunity to participate in the 1971 Oklahoma Intercollegiate Legislature, a mock assembly in which students throughout the state gathered at the capitol to introduce bills and vote on legislation. Having spent a summer as G. T. Blankenship's bus driver, Price knew exactly what he wanted to introduce: a bill to establish multicounty grand juries as a surefire mechanism to expand investigations and indictments beyond the borders of single counties where crimes were perpetrated. He never imagined that, nearly two decades hence, he would play a key role in pushing a multicounty grand-jury bill through the legislature.[6]

While college students were testing their mettle in the legislative chambers, Governor David Hall was orchestrating a return to Democratic policies after eight years under Republican governors Bellmon and Bartlett. "The 1970 race was rigorous," declared Hall in a retrospective a year after his upset victory and subsequent inauguration as governor. "While the infighting was tough, as it should have been, we worked to keep the dialogue clean and the campaign ethical." His inauguration came at noon on January 11, 1971—a classic Oklahoma day of crisp air and azure skies. In his inaugural address, the forty-year-old governor waxed poetic to describe the fulfillment of dreams that had fueled his ambitions: "In response to the times, A change has come. Through the power of the ballot. Our direction is new. By the will of the people, we take up the challenge." By his side were his wife, Jo, and their three children; his father, William, better known as "Red"; and U.S. Representative Carl Albert, recently arrived from Washington, D.C., for the inauguration, who was only two weeks shy of his swearing-in as speaker of the U.S. House of Representatives.[7]

David Hall, an Oklahoma City native, had showed promise at an early age. He served as president of the student body at Classen High School and paid his way through the University of Oklahoma by waiting tables and clerking at a clothing store, all the while demonstrating enough academic acumen to earn membership in the Phi Beta Kappa Society. After two years as an air force navigation instructor, he attended law school at Harvard University before enrolling at the University of Tulsa Law School to complete his education. Driving a Pepsi truck to finance his education, Hall cultivated a persona that resonated with Democrats in search of a champion. Down but far from beaten when he failed to secure his party's nomination for governor in 1966, Hall spent the next four years practicing law and preparing for the 1970 gubernatorial election.

Hall's main opponent, Dewey Bartlett, had served Tulsa County in the state Senate from 1962 until his election as governor four years later, and he seemed certain to keep his job. As the scion of a wealthy oil family who had earned his workingman's credentials as a roughneck on rigs near Dewey and Bartlesville, he could count on the endorsement of well-heeled Republicans far beyond his Tulsa stronghold. Broader support, even from open-minded Democrats, derived from his accomplishments. During his tenure as state senator and then as governor, he had provided unprecedented support for common education, promoted the virtues of the free-market system, and advocated on behalf of America's oil and gas industry at every opportunity. But Bartlett's backers were blindsided by third-party candidate Reuel Little, representing the American Party of George Wallace, who drained support from his more conservative opponent. They were also unprepared for the crafty David Hall, who politicked through backwoods counties, passed the hat at bean dinners and watermelon festivals, and borrowed heavily from banks to build grassroots support. The rumor mill had it that Hall was the first candidate to finance his campaign on a Diner's Club credit card. Prescient observers detected a whiff of duplicity when he excused himself from a restaurant one evening and raced to a friend's house to borrow enough money to cover his tab. Credited with a keen memory, Hall failed to mention the tape recorder he kept in his pocket to capture conversations with donors and constituents. Back at the office, aides were kept busy writing notes to the people whose banter was caught on tape, and who never suspected that the governor's legendary recall got a bump from technology. Running on the catchy campaign slogan, "Hall of Oklahoma for All of Oklahoma," and capitalizing on his movie-star looks, the silver-haired orator and his carefully groomed organization staged the closest race in state history to defeat Bartlett by a razor-thin margin of 2,181 votes.[8]

To his everlasting credit, Bartlett climbed back on the proverbial horse to win election to the U.S. Senate in 1972. He and Henry

Bellmon, who had served as national chairman of Nixon's presidential campaign en route to winning Mike Monroney's Senate seat in 1968, were pleased to celebrate a milestone in their state's history: for the first time in twenty-six years, and only the second time since statehood, Oklahoma had two Republican senators.

Bartlett's tenure was cut short when he was diagnosed with lung cancer. He resigned from the Senate in 1968 and returned to Tulsa, where he died on March 1, 1979, at the age of 59.[9]

▶ ▶ ▶ ▶

In Bill's final year of law school, he and Mary relocated from Norman to Oklahoma City, where she explored her new home and awaited the birth of their first child. After completing most of his law school courses in two years, Bill secured an internship with Rhodes, Hieronymous, Holloway & Wilson, a law firm specializing in product liability litigation, medical malpractice, workers' compensation, and personal injury defense cases. The firm was rebranded as Holloway & Dobson when Page Dobson, about ten years Price's senior, became managing partner. Dobson, who had offered him the internship and served as his primary mentor, waited only a year to bump him from intern to associate and began handing him more difficult cases. By the time Price graduated from OU law school with his juris doctor in 1973, he was already trying cases and writing briefs with little, if any, help from the firm's partners.

In one of his first cases, Price made the short drive to Purcell to defend General Motors against a plaintiff who had walked away from his truck and left his three-year-old child in the passenger seat. Sensing a commotion, the child's father turned around to watch in horror as the truck jumped out of gear, rolled downhill, and slammed into his barn. Although the child was uninjured, both the truck and barn were wrecked. Knowing that General Motors had issued a recall notice for the truck's motor mounts, the man filed a lawsuit to collect damages on his barn.

The case made its way to small claims court, where General Motors was willing to spend a pile of money to avoid admitting that a defective motor mount was to blame for the mishap. Certain that a small-town judge would decide in favor of a local plaintiff (known in legal vernacular as being "hometowned"), Price showed up in court with every expectation of losing. His prospects dimmed when he learned that the plaintiff was represented by his nephew, who was the judge's former law clerk, known locally as a talented attorney. The judge, Alma Wilson, went on to become a distinguished justice on the Oklahoma supreme court. Fortunately, Price was able to procure an expert witness from Detroit who swore under oath that a motor mount could not possibly cause a truck to jump out of gear. Clearly, the child had accidentally started the truck on its downhill roll. Following a five-hour trial (unusual for such a minor case) and a delay that dragged on for months, Judge Wilson finally rendered her decision in favor of General Motors.

"A defense verdict," said a surprised Price, still proud of his victory as a rookie defense attorney. "That was sort of a fun one!"

Then there was the case of the angry orangutan. Although Holloway & Dobson rarely represented plaintiffs, Price was dispatched to represent an employee of the Oklahoma City Zoo who was filing a lawsuit stemming from injuries that might have turned fatal. The trouble began at mealtime when the employee, monkey feed in hand, squeezed between steel bars and a plexiglass window to deliver an orangutan's dinner. Such was the distance between the bars and the window that the orangutan, equipped with famously long arms, reached through the bars, pulled the man toward him, and spent the next hour or so mauling him. During discovery, Ben Goff, counsel from Holloway & Dobson, learned that the unlucky employee's panicked colleagues had hastened to inform the zoo's director of mayhem at the orangutan enclosure, only to find that he was at lunch with the only key to the closet where a stun gun was stored.

"It was really a pretty good plaintiff case!" declared Bill, who has long since lost whatever affection he might have had for exotic primates.

"The orangutan..." Price paused to contemplate one of his least favorite species.

"They are *frightening* creatures!" he said finally.

Partway through the trial, Price was asked to determine whether or not zoo officials had modified the enclosure to make sure such disasters would not be repeated.

"Here's a measuring tape," said one of the firm's partners. "Go measure the distance between the enclosure and the cage."

"Is the orangutan still there?" asked Price.

"Yeah, he's still there," came the reply.

When Price arrived at the enclosure, the orangutan was nowhere to be seen. Warily, he took his measurement and beat a hasty retreat back to the office, where he reported his findings to the trial attorney. Forever after, Price could look back with pride on putting his life on the line to help secure a verdict in favor of the plaintiff. He laughed as he concluded his story about a close brush with savagery: "I could just see me getting mauled by the orangutan!"[10]

Price's law career was just beginning when he was tapped to coordinate state Senator Jim Inhofe's campaign for governor.[11] Inhofe, an eight-year veteran of the state legislature and described in the press as "youngish and rather intense," had defeated his friend, fellow senator, and minority leader Denny Garrison in the Republican primary and was waiting to see who his Democratic opponent would be in the general election. Looking at the two colorful Democratic primary candidates, Inhofe said it was impossible to predict the outcome, "but whether the winner will wear a cowboy hat or carry a broom makes no difference."[12]

As his party's best shot at a Republican victory, after four years with David Hall in the governor's mansion, Inhofe vowed to attack corruption by reforming state government and eliminating wasteful spending. At the top of his agenda was honesty in government. "There is no issue of more importance than the honesty and integrity of the candidates," declared Inhofe in an oft-repeated mantra. "Only good, honest men and women can bring good honest government." Disgusted with Governor Hall's reversal of his no-new-taxes pledge, Inhofe touted his standing as an anti-tax crusader. He was particularly proud of two bills that he had introduced in the Senate aimed at tax relief. To further his campaign promise to follow Dewey Bartlett's example and bring public education out of the doldrums, he announced a four-point agenda: raise teachers' salaries, establish lower teacher/ pupil ratios, beef up vocational and special education programs, and resist further consolidation of rural school districts.[13]

As Inhofe's state campaign coordinator, Price bought into the collective wisdom that Clem Rogers McSpadden would win the Democratic primary and, sporting his signature cowboy hat, become Inhofe's opponent in the general election. Born on a ranch near Bushyhead and related to Oklahoma's favorite son Will Rogers, McSpadden had gained notoriety on the rodeo circuit as a calf roper and bulldogger. To compensate for the waning of his youthful energy, he took to the microphone to become rodeo's premier announcer. When he was chosen as the first American to officiate at the Calgary Stampede, he made rodeo history by doing his announcing from the backside of a horse. More sedentary pursuits included service in the Oklahoma Senate from 1955 to 1973, with two terms as president pro tempore, and the U.S. House of Representatives from 1973 to 1975.[14]

McSpadden's major opponent in the Democratic primary for governor was David Lyle Boren, a baby-faced dark-horse candidate who had served in the state House of Representatives from Seminole County since 1967 and chose a broom as his campaign symbol, to represent his pledge to clean up state government. Price bought into the conventional wisdom that Boren's chances in the primary were slim to none in a contest against a genuine cowboy with a Will Rogers pedigree.[15] Energized to be running his first statewide campaign, Price was struck by the camaraderie between the political rivals. "It's hard for people to imagine now, because they are so ideologically different, but the three best friends in the legislature were Inhofe, Boren, and Ralph Thompson," explained Price about an unlikely alliance. "They were the three backbenchers that were against corruption in the legislature." Assuming that McSpadden would sail to victory and send Boren's supporters flocking to his campaign, Inhofe sang Boren's praises in every speech, a tactic he came to regret when results from the Democratic primary proved (once again!) that conventional wisdom is not the best judge of political outcomes. Based on the anticipated outcome, Price was tasked to communicate—and, in fact, coordinate—with Boren's campaign staff. But then, against all odds, the broom-wielding Boren defeated McSpadden to become his party's candidate for governor, leaving Price to recalibrate and prepare for the general election in November. He described the effect of Boren's victory on Inhofe's campaign: "Once Boren won the nomination, that just ended the campaign. Boren was going to win. He was honest and opposed to tax increases. That just took away all chances that Inhofe had, because, at that time, there was a Democratic advantage of probably 10 or 15 percent, just inherently."[16]

Inhofe's added challenge was to fend off criticism that, as an officer of an insurance company who wrote policies for the state, he had a conflict of interest. Price and Inhofe's defense was simple and straightforward: if an attorney who enforced laws written by attorney-legislators could run for office, why should an independent insurance agent be barred from submitting competitive bids?[17] On a lighter note, Price had to defend his candidate's boyish looks. During a campaign stop at a pizza parlor, a waiter asked Price to verify that his companion was old enough to order a beer. "Here I was, in my early twenties, and he was thirty-nine," said Price. "He looked incredibly young for his age!"[18]

What Price remembered most vividly about coordinating Inhofe's gubernatorial campaign were the endless road trips that threatened his health and left Mary with more than her fair share of responsibilities. During one two-week period, he visited all seventy-seven counties in the state. "What a full-time job!" declared Price. "My back went out at some point, just driving, and I was in the hospital. It was really rough!" But his marriage was never in doubt, even after Mary gave birth to their first child, Anne Katherine, in May 1973, and settled into the routine of a de facto single mother.[19]

Just as Price's recruiting trips for Teen Age Republicans had revealed inequities in state spending, so too did his campaigning for Jim Inhofe open a window into corruption in state government. Two types of corruption were particularly pernicious: the seeming inability of Democrats—including David Hall and Clem McSpadden, but definitely not David Boren—to resist offering jobs to people devoid of qualifications, usually in return for campaign contributions ("It was rampant at the time!"); and the power of special-interest groups to sway public opinion and influence policy. Crisscrossing the state for Jim Inhofe, Price discerned that workers' compensation lawyers and owners of nursing homes were unrivaled in the power they exerted over the political system. "You would see enormous amounts of money pouring into those candidates that had sold their souls to these and other special interests," said Price.

Another fount of corruption was absentee ballots. Although Price rated the state's electoral system as fairly honest in relation to other parts of the country, absentee ballots presented candidates with irresistible opportunities to rig the system. Voters in northeastern Oklahoma were especially susceptible to candidates who offered a flask of booze or a twenty-dollar bill in exchange for an absentee ballot. As Price learned during his travels, acquiring absentee ballots was preferable to simply paying for votes, as candidates could not follow voters into the voting booth to make sure they checked the right boxes. But if candidates could get their hands on absentee ballots, they could fill them out and submit them to election officials with no questions asked. During a campaign stop in Adair County, savvy voters asked Price why he had bothered to show up, as everyone knew that absentee ballots would inevitably stack up in favor of preferred candidates. Price caught a glimpse of his future as a prosecutor in the U.S. Attorney's Office when he perceived the power of an Adair County commissioner to steer elections toward his chosen candidates. "So that is the one area of election fraud in the balance that I was seeing in Oklahoma, and especially in the northeastern part of the state," recalled Price.

Price paused to reflect on the difficulty of proving what was basically hidden in plain sight. "Well, how do you prove it?" he asked rhetorically. "How do you break into that? You can't just prove it by the fact that a hundred percent of the absentee ballots go a certain direction. It is hard to prove. Knowing and proving are two different things, totally!"[20]

Far more visible than the ongoing chicanery in absentee-ballot voting was a scandal dating back to 1967 when suspicions arose that State Treasurer Leo Winters, a Panhandle native with imperial ambitions, had enlisted state-chartered banks in a campaign of bribery and extortion. As Price was carrying Jim Inhofe's doomed gubernatorial campaign to every county in the state, what had gained infamy as the Leo Winters banking scandal was reaching its crescendo in a court battle to determine the treasurer's honesty and, more fundamentally, the integrity of Oklahoma's banking system.

Indicted by a federal grand jury on nine counts of mail fraud and extortion, Winters did his best to deflect attention from prosecutors who knew that his wealth, and the clout that went with it, far exceeded the grasp of a law-abiding state treasurer.[21] "He had tens of millions of dollars in cattle loans from various banks, and tens of millions of dollars in deposits in the same banks," explained Price. "He put state deposits in the hundreds of millions of dollars in the same banks. He also would get sacks of cash from those same banks and pass them out to all the different legislators. Who knows how much he would keep for himself? Just like J. D. McCarty! He had enormous political power; he had enormous wealth. He was the wealthiest person in the Panhandle of Oklahoma!"[22]

The scandal had originated in December 1967 when M. J. Swords, vice president of the Federal Reserve Bank in Kansas City, informed

Oklahoma State Bank Commissioner Carl Sebring that Winters was mishandling the state's money by increasing deposits in the First American Bank and Trust Company of Purcell in order to obtain a personal loan in the amount of $15,000. Both Winters and Sam Ewing, president of the bank, quickly dismissed Swords's accusation as a lie, but the damage was done. After Governor Dewey Bartlett appointed a committee to investigate the charges, subpoenas came raining down on bankers across the state believed to be complicit in Winters's scheme.[23]

From day one, Winters denied that he had used his office as leverage to force bankers to make loans to him. His statement after the initial hearing was unambiguous: "The attorney general and his team proceeded all day long until he himself admitted that he had exhausted all of his evidence and failed to prove a single thing that violates my trust to the people or that I am ashamed of." Yet he did testify that he had increased state deposits in 173 banks in fifty-nine of Oklahoma's seventy-seven counties and that some of the banks from which he had received loans might have received increases in state deposits.[24]

Hearings were held, subpoenas were issued, investigations were launched, and gallons of ink were spilled to discover what Winters was doing with the people's money. In early 1972, William R. "Bill" Burkett, U.S. Attorney for the Western District of Oklahoma, got into the act to determine whether the treasurer's alleged favoritism in depositing state money in small banks was a quid pro quo for campaign contributions. Trim, intense, modest, and blessed with a quick wit, Burkett had been county attorney in Woodward County, served two terms in the state legislature, and officiated as chairman of the Oklahoma Republican Party before his appointment as U.S. Attorney in 1969. Easily recognizable for a brow that seemed permanently furrowed, Burkett was responsible for representing the United States government in all criminal and civil proceedings within his district, a sprawling expanse that stretched westward from Stillwater to the Texas and New Mexico borders.[25]

Leo Winters insisted that the "big bankers"—that is, the top brass at the First National Bank and Trust Company and Liberty National Bank, both in Oklahoma City—were out to destroy him for taking up to $300 million "in idle state funds" out of their coffers and spreading taxpayers' money around the state.[26] By the time the case made its way to trial, in April 1974, Winters and several codefendants had retained as their lead counsel one of Oklahoma's most colorful lawmaker-lawyers, Gene Stipe. Born in 1926 on a hardscrabble farm south of McAlester, Stipe had earned notoriety as a state senator and, later, as a defense lawyer whose wiliness in the courtroom was unrivaled in the history of Oklahoma jurisprudence. Stipe wasted no time in issuing subpoenas to a host of Republican heavy hitters to testify on the defendants' behalf. Among the sixty-four people summoned to Oklahoma City were former U.S. Attorneys General John Mitchell and Richard Kleindienst, U.S. senators Henry Bellmon and Dewey Bartlett, and former Oklahoma governor Raymond Gary.[27]

All eyes were riveted on the U.S. District Court in Oklahoma City when, on April 4, Judge Wesley E. Brown announced a recess so that he could consider some "legal problems." Confident that an acquittal was all but certain, a beaming Leo Winters declared, "Today is a good day for the people of Oklahoma. I have been planning for some time to announce that I will be a candidate for re-election to the office of state treasurer. The timing is appropriate for this announcement to be made today."[28] Winters went on to remind his listeners that he had collected more than $70 million in interest on taxpayers' money, an achievement that Stipe had exploited to its full potential in front of the jury. "'That figure is more than 10 times the interest collected by all the other treasurers since statehood in 1907,' said the proud treasurer."[29]

After a hung jury and before a second trial, the federal grand-jury indictment against Winters and his eleven codefendants was dropped. To explain Winters's acquittal, U.S. Attorney Bill Burkett said that elderly witnesses, all critical to the government's case, had died of natural causes after the first trial. According to their testimonies, Winters had a formula to determine how much cash to expect from bankers based on the level of state deposits in their banks. As state deposits could spell life or death for their banks, those witnesses showed extraordinary courage in testifying. Burkett lamented that he had been unable to charge Winters on tax evasion, as his so-called contributions were largely undisputed. The only allegation Winters faced was that he extorted cash from bankers in return for state deposits, a claim that he fervently denied.[30]

Others explained the government's failure to secure convictions by citing Stipe's chart showing the amount of interest income that Winters had added to state coffers during his tenure as treasurer. Simply put, the means justified the ends. Compared to his timid predecessors, Winters was a genius.[31]

As far as Oklahoma's grateful taxpayers were concerned, nothing succeeds like success.

Although Price was not involved in litigating the Leo Winters banking scandal, he knew enough about the investigation and subsequent trial to realize the extent to which bankers feared Leo Winters. Many "were scared to death of him," and for good reason: banks that drew his ire were likely to have their state deposits withdrawn. In a worst-case scenario, the withdrawal of state deposits would cause them to fail. Those fears intensified when Leo Winters was exonerated of all wrongdoing. As Winters walked out of court as a free man, he surely had a few bankers in his crosshairs for questioning his modus operandi.

"Do you think he got away with it so long because he didn't see anything wrong with it?"

The questioner was Bill's son, James, whose series of videotaped interviews constitutes a treasure trove of source material to tell his father's story and, at the same time, opens a window into lawlessness dating back to the bad old days of Soonerism and theft of Native American land.

"I'll tell you, it was the political norm in that day!" exclaimed Price. "Corruption was just uncontrolled. This same kind of corruption was occurring at the national level." As malfeasance in the Johnson administration came to light and with Watergate still fresh in collective memory, it was hard to argue with Price's assessment of high-ranking officials, at all levels of governance, with their hands in the till.

▶ ▶ ▶ ▶

From late 1973 through the first week of August 1974, all eyes were on Washington, D.C., where an embattled president and his Republican loyalists were scrambling to remain in power. Then, on August 8, the unthinkable happened: confronted with irrefutable evidence that he had orchestrated a cover-up to deny complicity in the Watergate scandal, President Nixon announced his resignation. In a scene that seared itself into collective memory, the former president and his long-suffering wife, Pat, boarded a Marine helicopter for the short trip to Andrews Air Force Base, where they would begin their cross-country trip to California and a premature retirement from the nation's highest office.

Flashing his signature victory sign and waving to his well-wishers, Nixon disappeared into the helicopter to close a noxious chapter in American history. For generations to come, Watergate would be remembered not only for the corruption emanating from the Oval Office, but also for the resilience of federal agencies in bringing the miscreants to justice. White House Counsel John Wesley Dean was more prescient than he knew in his testimony attending the Watergate hearings: "I began by telling the President that there was a cancer growing on the presidency, and if the cancer was not removed, the president himself would be killed by it."

That "cancer," and concerns over the damage it was inflicting on the Republican Party, were never far from Price's thoughts as he zoomed from the high plains to the dense forests of Oklahoma to find plenty of homegrown corruption. Office holders doling out jobs to cronies and campaign contributors, special-interest groups exerting undue influence at the capitol, wily candidates commandeering elections with phony absentee ballots, a state treasurer who owed his exoneration from charges of bribery and extortion to the state's wiliest litigator—these and other nefarious practices, long since accepted as Oklahoma's way of doing business, were a mirror image of what was happening at the national level.

In books gleaned from his parents' über-organized library and in preparation for debates, Price had learned about corruption in the Johnson administration. During a field trip to a public high school, he had learned how some students were shortchanged. Recruiting for Teen Age Republicans, he and Tom Daxon drove through all-black towns to witness firsthand the human cost of inequities in state and county funding. Under G. T. Blankenship's mentoring, he realized how deeply the supreme court scandal was eroding faith in the state's legal system and, at the same time, came to understand the limitations of single-county grand juries in investigating and prosecuting crime. And, as a student at Georgetown, he observed the corroding effects of violent antiwar protests and poverty-stricken slums on the American Dream. Now, in his dual career as an attorney and campaign coordinator, he had a portal into the underbelly of state politics. Barely out of law school and not entirely on his own, Price was formulating a future of making things better through the law and Republican Party politics.

Support for Price's endeavors came from his growing—or, more accurately, exploding—family. Despite her deteriorating eyesight, his much older sister, Montine, was a gifted artist, and she never lost her fun-loving and rebellious nature. She reminded Bill and his other two siblings, Bob and Kelsey, of a character from *Happy Days*. Her marriage, soon after her high school graduation, to Bill Foerster produced the three sons for whom Bill, on break from Georgetown and recuperating from his near-fatal accident, had assembled Christmas presents while encased in a lower-body cast. One of those sons, Steve, recalled facets of Uncle Bill that had nothing to do with Georgetown, law, or politics. "He's ten years older, so he's ten years younger than my mother, and ten years older than me," explained Foerster about his family's rather complicated genealogy. "He was kind of there for the Cub Scout meetings, birthdays—all those as a little kid. He was just kind of that guy in the background that was a big kid."

As Montine's go-to babysitter, Bill had been happy to entertain his nephews while their father went through his residency en route to a career as a plastic surgeon. As he grew to maturity, the younger Foerster watched his uncle morph from a babysitter into a high school and then college student, graduate from law school, take on cases with Holloway & Dobson, and embroil himself in political campaigns. "I am looking at him as an older guy going through those phases," concluded Foerster, who never forgot the lessons he had learned from Uncle Bill.

Following her divorce from Bill Foerster, Montine married Paul Sprehe, who entered the union with eight children from a previous marriage. Together, Paul and Montine had one child, Tia, who brought their combined tally to an even dozen. Unpretentious and gifted with a sense of humor, Montine exuded a zest for life that was nothing less than infectious. As Bill noted about his sister, she enjoyed youth and could communicate with young people "because she profoundly understood them, since she herself was young at heart."[32]

Backed by supportive parents and siblings, a cheerful wife, an admiring nephew, and a host of other family and friends, Price kept up his grueling pace of lawyering and politicking. Having learned at an early age that success in life requires a deft combination of preparation and opportunity, he knew two things: he was prepared for a life in law and politics, and there would be lots of opportunities to send his career into overdrive.

Even though the Inhofe campaign was looking like a lost cause, Price approached Election Day of 1974 with his usual buoyant optimism knowing that, in the world he had chosen to inhabit, anything could happen. Something certainly did, and it brought him face-to-face with corruption on a grand scale that would consume the next phase of his career: Governor David Hall's impeachment, trial, and conviction on charges of bribery and extortion. Past was indeed prologue as Price geared up for more lessons on how *not* to run state government.

PART II : *THE ARENA*

CHAPTER SIX : *The Rise and Fall of David Hall*

A year into his administration, Governor David Hall looked back on his track record with a mixture of pride in his accomplishments and confidence that even better things were on the horizon. "I believe we changed the tempo, altered the course and claimed new direction for Oklahoma," declared Hall in a guest editorial in January 1972. First on his agenda was reforming education, the state's most pressing obligation as well as its most rewarding opportunity. Toward that end, he led initiatives to increase per-pupil expenditures and bring teachers' salaries up to the regional average. Hall also pushed legislation to decrease the high teacher-pupil ratio, reduce class sizes, lower the mandatory school age, and mandate kindergarten attendance.

Running a close second on the governor's hierarchy of needs was the less tangible but certainly no less worthy goal of instilling renewed pride in his fellow Oklahomans. Ever since the Okie exodus to California during the Great Depression, Oklahoma had been perceived as a hardscrabble state whose fortunes were tied to the vicissitudes of nature and the boom-and-bust cycles of its energy-dependent economy. Neither a post–World War II campaign to build the OU Sooners into a football powerhouse nor the ubiquitous Okie lapel pins managed to sway perceptions of Oklahoma as a second-class state. Even more damaging in the court of public opinion was the corruption that surfaced with numbing regularity at all levels of state government. As far as Governor Hall was concerned, enough was enough. It was time for Oklahomans to leave their scandalous past behind and embrace more enlightened ways of doing business: "No slogans. No nicknames. Simply, pride in being an Oklahoman. I believe Oklahoma is first. The libel and shams of the past must be cast aside. We raise our heads to new heights. Oklahoma is best."

Returning to agenda items that required more than a PR budget, Hall described the need to beef up law enforcement in a way that guaranteed both justice and liberty. What followed was a year of initiatives, including a law enforcement task force, reforms in the correctional system, educational programs, increased court funding, and additional personnel assigned to various agencies and departments. For Hall, it all came down to leadership. "Leadership from the Governor's office, based on hard experience, seemed to be the singularly most important factor in law enforcement," declared the governor. "Oklahoma today is a more lawful, free and safe state."

Governor Hall's prison reforms were dealt a serious setback when, in July 1973, inmates rioted at the Oklahoma State Penitentiary at McAlester. Armed with knives and meat cleavers, the malcontents seized twenty hostages, including a deputy warden, and held police and national guardsmen at bay for twenty-two hours. Despite the governor's best efforts at negotiation, what became the worst riot in state history left three inmates dead and twenty million dollars in damage.

As though his top three priorities were not challenging enough, Hall had one more item on his to-do list: increase equality and opportunity for all Oklahomans. With a quarter of a million people falling below the poverty level, Hall declared that the status quo would not stand. Although tax hikes were bound to stir up trouble, Hall risked alienating tax-averse Republicans by initiating reforms to put the state on a sound financial basis and thereby mitigate the looming crisis in revenues. His tax plan was partly vindicated as the national economy boomed and increases in energy and income taxes poured billions of dollars into state coffers. Such was the success of his initiative that two of his successors, David Boren and George Nigh, were able to sponsor tax cuts and, at the same time, provide increased funding for schools, colleges, and highways, the principal beneficiaries of Hall's much-maligned tax program.

Early on, Hall was impressed by what he called "a pleasant discovery": the excellence of state employees, which stood in stark contrast to one of his biggest bugaboos: "the immobility of the federal bureaucracy." Nowhere was bureaucratic red tape more unyielding than in officials' seeming indifference to rural areas. To promote free enterprise and alleviate the problems plaguing farms and small towns, Hall reorganized and strengthened key functions of state and county government, but not to the point of consolidating school districts, a doomed strategy in counties where jobs were scarce and schools were among the few sources of steady employment.

"I can say that I have never enjoyed a job more," gushed Hall on the eve of his second year as governor. "I am proud to tackle the problems of government and, most of all, I enjoy the people." And, apparently, the people enjoyed him, so much so that Democratic Party insiders put him on their short list as a vice-presidential nominee. Hall closed his editorial with a clarion call to rekindle the spirit of 1889, especially with regard to Oklahoma's most precious resource: its youth. "Oklahoma was settled by impoverished families who rolled onto the land in wagons and on horseback. They dug into the earth and raised food. Next they built schools and churches. Those pioneers were willing to make sacrifices for religion and education. We need to rekindle that pioneer dedication to enriching the minds of youth through quality, properly financed education."[1]

▶ ▶ ▶ ▶

Governor-elect Hall was putting the finishing touches on his inaugural speech when he sent his top aide and closest confidant, Sunny Jenkins, to New York to solicit contractors for the Cimarron Turnpike, the main road between Tulsa and Enid, which was sure to raise millions of dollars through a bond issue. True to form, Jenkins returned to Oklahoma City with a pile of cash from eight New York brokerage houses that had expressed interest in underwriting the road-building project. To disguise the money as campaign contributions, one of Hall's secretaries wrote thank-you notes to the contributors, taking care to date them before the November 1970 election. Confident that he had covered his tracks, Hall proceeded to spend the money on his personal bills.[2]

Hall's hijacking of funds intended for highway construction was an early sign of his blithe attitude toward money. In the two and a half years that he served Governor Hall, Jenkins deployed his connections and entrepreneurial skills to borrow from banks or, if that didn't work, convince his boss's friends to do the borrowing. Hall's major donors got invitations to the "Governor's Club," an exclusive cadre of well-heeled supporters who received handsome plaques as evidence of their largesse. Many of those donors were contractors and architects who stood to benefit from making political contributions, known in the common vernacular as "frog hair." Jenkins insisted that he used no strong-arm tactics. "The contributors just wanted to make sure they were treated equally," he said.[3]

Governor Hall's preinaugural scheming led not only to the solicitous Sunny Jenkins, but also to the office of State Examiner and Inspector John M. Rogers. Lacking opposition in his own campaign, in 1970, Rogers slid into office with plenty of cash left in his war chest. Any doubts about what he should do with his surplus vanished when the newly elected governor suggested that he give it to him—$37,000, to be exact. As there were no laws governing either making contributions or reporting them, Hall and his campaign lieutenants cooked up a plan to launder the money by giving it to Secretary of State John Rogers, who happened to be the examiner and inspector's son. The hand-off was accompanied by a list of names that included Hall's personal secretary, Dorothy Pike, and several friends and associates who were no doubt members in good standing of the Governor's Club. The elder Rogers's campaign treasurer, surely bored after managing his candidate's uncontested run for state office, was then ordered to write checks to the people on the list. They received their checks with instructions to cash them, report the money as income on their tax returns, withhold

Governor David Hall entered office in 1971 with an ambitious reform agenda, only to see his administration unravel as the extent of his corruption became clear. He was convicted in 1975 on charges of bribery and extortion and sent to prison. COURTESY OKLAHOMA HISTORICAL SOCIETY.

enough to pay taxes, and contribute the balance to Hall's so-called campaign fund.

In another scheme that eventually fell within U.S. Attorney Bill Burkett's jurisdiction in the Western District of Oklahoma, Hall persuaded Carl Ballew, a lanky and good-natured thirty-something from south Oklahoma City who had contributed to his 1970 gubernatorial campaign, to pay his monthly expenses of $7,000 or so a month that were not covered by the governor's expense account. More to the point, Ballew was a paint contractor who regularly performed services for the state, and he was determined to remain in the governor's good graces. To compensate for Ballew's cooperation, Hall promised to put him at the top of his list of state contractors. Ballew was fortunate to be part of the construction business, a genuine growth industry that was awash in cash during Hall's administration. From 1972 to 1975, the state's construction budget for roads, state-funded hospitals and mental health facilities, and higher education rose from $325 million to more than $700 million, leaving plenty of leeway for the governor to exercise his version of gubernatorial privilege.[4]

In what became a routine transaction, Hall turned over his bills to Dorothy Pike, an attractive, forty-something blond with experience in state government. Exuding a flair for sophistication and a no-nonsense attitude when it came to ethics and public morals, she was surely vexed when her boss ordered her to deliver his bills to Carl Ballew so that he would know how much to borrow. The two rendezvoused monthly, usually at the Southwest Bank in Capitol Hill, where Pike accepted Ballew's bundles of cash and proceeded to purchase money orders from banks and other financial institutions. She was careful not to rely heavily enough on a particular money-order vendor to arouse suspicion. Finally, creditor list in hand, she used those money orders to pay the governor's personal bills. Like Secretary of State Rogers, Pike suspected that something might be amiss. But rather than conceal a recording device under her blouse, she kept a list of her transactions, complete with dates, serial numbers, amounts, and payees, in a spiral notebook under the rather prescient heading "Notes made for my protection."

Suspicions notwithstanding, Pike remained confident that the governor had her back, and she kept up her routine with Ballew through most of 1971. During her travels with the governor, she took it as a badge of honor that her room always adjoined his suite. But then came the October 1971 Governor's Conference when she found herself in a distant wing—a sign, perhaps, that Hall was taking her for granted or, worse yet, that she was falling out of his favor. Deciding she had better come clean with the authorities, she returned to Oklahoma City with every intention of visiting the nearest IRS office whose agents were empowered to investigate allegations of tax fraud with little or no involvement from either the FBI or the U.S. Attorney's Office. Clutching her spiral notebook, Pike showed up at the IRS in November 1971 with evidence that was a prosecutor's dream.

When Pike went to the IRS, Ballew decided that he had had enough of cloak-and-dagger meetings with the governor's secretary and relinquished his duties to the multitalented Sunny Jenkins. Meanwhile, Dorothy Pike did indeed fall out of the governor's favor, and she was replaced, as Hall's confidential secretary, by Nadine Ralls. Over the ensuing nineteen months, Jenkins and Ralls handled as much as $170,000 of the governor's personal expenses, all of which was disguised as political contributions. In the absence of Carl Ballew, Jenkins expanded his network to include architects, engineers, contractors, and anyone else who might benefit from state contracts. Jenkins's money-raising activities brought in an average of about $10,000 per month to meet Hall's needs. Although most of his collections went to Ralls for bill payments, Jenkins occasionally diverted a few thousand dollars directly to the governor. Records later indicated that Hall actually paid bills from his own pocket on two occasions. But even that was open to doubt.[5]

In a scheme that the IRS untangled in December 1972, Governor Hall agreed to award a construction contract for two office buildings in the capitol complex, referred to as the tax and education buildings, to Shawnee contractor E. Allen Cowan II in return for a payment of $125,000. There were two parts to this particularly convoluted arrangement: Sunny Jenkins's buddy Carl Ballew was re-enlisted to personally borrow $50,000 to help defray Hall's debts; and Jenkins arranged for the preparation of ten phony invoices in the amount of $122,000. Although that money was supposed to go to subcontractors, it somehow made its way to Hall's personal and political expense accounts.

By now, Carl Ballew was really in over his head, and even more so after he wrote a hot check that required an additional $32,000. To cover their ever-expanding bases, Jenkins agreed to deliver $80,000 in cash to his buddy Ballew. Knowing that the governor was a bit strapped, he further agreed to toss in another $10,000. To consummate the deal, Jenkins told Ballew to meet him at the Habana Inn in northwest Oklahoma City. Sure enough, Jenkins showed up at the motel with a briefcase bulging with crisp twenty-dollar bills neatly wrapped in Federal Reserve packaging.

Staring at all those Andrew Jacksons was enough to give Ballew cold feet, and he refused to carry the briefcase out of the motel. So, in an age when personal assistants did most of the heavy lifting for their bosses, he called his secretary, who dutifully arrived at the Habana Inn, with her husband in tow, to retrieve the briefcase and take it home. One can only imagine the couple's surprise when they got home and opened the briefcase. Like Dorothy Pike, they suspected nefarious goings-on, and they snapped a few photos and delivered them, along with the negatives, to the IRS. U.S. Attorney Bill Burkett put it this way: "When things began to look fishy, they gave that picture to the Internal Revenue Service."[6]

Grateful for the incriminating evidence delivered on a silver plate and certain that it foretold more cases to come, IRS special agents Jack Querry and Bill Maynard enlarged the photos to read the banknote serial numbers. A visit to the Federal Reserve Bank in Oklahoma City revealed that the money had been sent to a bank in Shawnee on December 18, 1972. Querry and Maynard's next stop was at the Shawnee bank where the banknotes had begun their journey to the Habana Inn.

"I know NOTHING about that!" blurted the bank officer under the duo's stern gaze. "You'll have to talk to the president of the bank!"

Which the agents promptly did, only to learn that, under the direction of bank president Harbour Lampl, the money had been loaned to a local contractor who needed cash for heavy-equipment purchases. As Lampl explained—and, apparently, everyone in the construction business knew—heavy-equipment dealers preferred to be paid in cash.

The plot thickened when Cowan, the Shawnee contractor, offered his own narrative. As Cowan explained to Lampl, who then passed the story to Querry and Maynard, he had intended to borrow the money for a few days and then pay off the loan with the neatly bundled banknotes in hopes that prompt payment would enhance his credit rating. To prove his innocence, Cowan insisted that the cache of twenty-dollar bills had never left his house. At least part of the contractor's story was true: he had indeed paid off his loan in record time. But he didn't do it with the crisp new bills. What he did was instruct his subcontractors to submit inflated invoices on the capitol complex building project. Cowan paid those invoices on the basis of change orders and left the larger amount for the state of Oklahoma to pay. His final instruction was for the subcontractors to return the overpayment to him (in cash, of course) so he could pay off his loan.

Carl Ballew could not have been surprised when two very skeptical IRS agents appeared on his doorstep. Confronted with clear evidence of his complicity in the scheme, he agreed to cooperate with investigators in return for immunity from both state and federal prosecution. Once again, we rely on Bill Burkett for economy of words: "David Hall's coat began to unravel."[7]

▶ ▶ ▶ ▶

As Governor Hall's criminality came to light, a federal grand jury was summoned, and *Oklahoma City Times* staff writer Jack Taylor became an indispensable source of information on its discoveries. Taylor even persuaded Sunny Jenkins to outline the operations he had spearheaded as the governor's chief aide and principal fundraiser. About the time of their interview, in late 1973, Hall began to suspect that his formerly dependable secretary, Dorothy Pike, had spilled her beans to the IRS, and he dispatched a private investigator, former state legislator Robert O. "Bob" Cunningham, to Tulsa to get to the bottom of it. Pike and Cunningham (nicknamed "Oklahoma Crude" for his vulgar language) met in a restaurant equipped with hidden recording devices. Hers was furnished by the IRS; his, presumably, came from his private-eye inventory. In a script seemingly ripped from a *Keystone Cops* episode, they took turns visiting the restrooms to flip their tapes to record on the other side.[8]

The governor upped the ante when, on January 7, 1974, he instructed his attorneys, Byrne Bowman and Frank McDivitt, to file two lawsuits, both pertaining to an increasingly elusive Dorothy Pike. Knowing that the IRS was about to commence civil and criminal tax actions against him and his wife, Hall needed Pike's testimony, and the only way to get it was to file the first of the lawsuits. The second lawsuit was filed against U.S. Attorney Bill Burkett, District Director of Internal Revenue Clyde Bickerstaff, and U.S. Marshal Gene Carrier, all of whom were allegedly using armed force to prevent Hall and his attorneys from talking to Pike. These two lawsuits, extraordinary by any standard, were referred to U.S. District Judges Luther Eubanks and Stephen Chandler, respectively.

On January 17, 1974, Judge Chandler summoned Burkett to a hearing in which he testified that he had never met Dorothy Pike and had no clue where she was. Chandler didn't buy it, and he spent the next two weeks trying to find her. In what became a numbing routine, the three defendants piled into his courtroom, for what Burkett called his "10:00 o'clock flogging," to be told, ad nauseum, that he, Bickerstaff, and Carrier were duty bound to find Dorothy Pike. Convinced that they were conspiring to keep Pike's whereabouts a secret, Judge Chandler issued her a subpoena, to be served wherever she might be.

By late January, Judge Chandler seemed to be utterly unhinged, and he commanded Dorothy Pike—in absentia, as she was still nowhere to be found—to appear in his court on January 29th at ten o'clock. After telling Bickerstaff and Carrier to ramp up their efforts to find her, Burkett hopped on a plane to Denver to ask the Tenth Circuit Court of Appeals to stop her deposition. Within a couple of hours, the appeals court gave Burkett what he had come for: a writ to quash the subpoena. But that very afternoon, a U.S. marshal found Pike in Arlington, Virginia, and served her with Judge Chandler's subpoena.

Incensed to discover how far the key witness had traveled, Chandler summoned Burkett to court. He was further incensed to discover that Burkett could not comply, as he was in Denver to get the Tenth Circuit to quash Chandler's subpoena and would have to send a substitute. Chandler's next move was to telephone Pike and order her to return to Oklahoma City for her deposition. But now that the subpoena had been

In the early 1970s, the U.S. Attorney's Office for the Western District of Oklahoma included (left to right) Assistant U.S. Attorneys Jim Peters, Drew Neville, Floy Dawson, Susie Pritchett, Bill Price, O. B. Johnston, Givens Adams, and John Green. U.S. Attorney Bill Burkett (sixth from left) held the top job from 1969 to 1975. COURTESY BILL PRICE.

quashed, she told the judge that she needed to consult her lawyer before making travel plans. But that was not the only reason for her reluctance. In an earlier affidavit, Pike had admitted that she feared for her life and had implored both the U.S. Attorney and IRS officials to keep her hiding place a secret.

Judge Chandler's rants were not enough to dissuade Burkett and his staff from presenting testimony to the federal grand jury and honing their arguments about the legality—or, rather, the lack thereof—of the subpoena. The importance of Chandler's tongue lashings became clear when, shortly after the U.S. Court Clerk's office closed for business on March 11, the judge slipped a note under the office door stating that Burkett and his four assistants—Jeff Laird, Jim Peters, O. B. Johnston, and Floy Dawson—together with IRS counsel Phil Harney, had committed perjury in not divulging Pike's location and were therefore disbarred. He then ordered the six attorneys to appear before him on March 21 to show cause why they should not be cited for civil and criminal contempt for their alleged actions in Governor Hall's lawsuits against the federal government. Burkett later quipped that Susie Pritchett, the only member of his team to avoid disbarment, owed her good fortune to Judge Chandler's preference for women.[9]

Stephen Chandler had a reputation as one of the least capable federal judges in the nation, and his antics on the bench sometimes bordered on lunacy. Bill Price tended to agree with that assessment. Price was gearing up to manage Jim Inhofe's 1974 gubernatorial campaign when word of the judge's unorthodox announcement hit the streets. Judge Chandler's alleged ineptitude gained notoriety in Joseph C. Goulden's *The Benchwarmers: The Private World of the Powerful Federal Judges*. First published in 1974 and reissued in later editions, Goulden's book illuminated the extraordinary power and arrogance exercised by all too many federal judges, whose lifetime tenure fostered malpractice in the nation's courtrooms. "Burkett didn't know where she was," explained Price, referring to Dorothy Pike. "And Chandler didn't seem to know or care that subpoenas issued in civil cases have a hundred-mile limit, whereas subpoenas in criminal cases have no such limitations. But Chandler insisted that he *had* to know where she was, and everybody in the office *had* to know, so he disbarred everybody who was working on the case except Susie Pritchett and John Green on the basis that they *had* to know where this secretary was!"[10] Judge Chandler also failed to acknowledge that a civil suit should be stayed if a criminal investigation and/or trial was underway.

Bill Burkett and the reticent Dorothy Pike were not solely to blame for Judge Chandler's pique. Even as he was pulling out all the stops to bring Pike to court, the ill-tempered judge was engaged in pretrial proceedings in the prosecution of State Treasurer Leo Winters. Accused of extorting money from state banks in return for campaign contributions, Winters was barreling headlong toward a showdown with the U.S. Attorney. The very day that Burkett learned about his disbarment in the morning paper, he was scheduled to participate in a hearing on pending motions in Winters's upcoming trial. Realizing that he "could not function very well" as a disbarred attorney, Burkett contacted Chief Tenth Circuit Judge David Lewis of Salt Lake City to explain his dilemma. As Burkett recalled, with a flair for understatement, "The Circuit was well aware of Judge Chandler's predilection for bizarre actions from the bench, and immediately ordered a stay of the order by telephone."

Unaware that Judge Lewis was ordering the stay of Chandler's order, the three other judges in Oklahoma's Western District—Fred Daugherty, Luther Eubanks, and Luther Bohanon, who happened to be in Muskogee, Oklahoma City, and McAlester, respectively—learned what Judge Chandler was up to *this* time. Long since accustomed to Chandler's oddities, all three of his colleagues on the Western District bench had shown their misgivings about the renegade jurist by stripping him of his ability to adjudicate criminal cases. In what was surely a heated three-way phone call, they agreed to let Eubanks act on their behalf to nullify Chandler's order. But by the time they hung up, their intervention was no longer needed, as Judge Lewis at the Tenth Circuit Court of Appeals had already intervened, holding that Chandler's actions "were entirely without foundation in law or fact." In the court's reversal, Tenth Circuit Court Judge William E. Doyle wrote that "the dearth of evidence in support of the adjudications is so plain that the accused attorneys are not to be subjected to meaningless procedure in connections with these contempt citations."

Even as they were preparing for Leo Winters's trial and soliciting the Tenth Circuit Court of Appeals' help in nullifying their disbarments, Burkett and his assistants kept Governor Hall in their crosshairs. In the two-pronged investigation into gubernatorial wrongdoing, the IRS was puzzling through the tax consequences of the governor's actions while the FBI looked into his alleged extortion and bribery. Thanks to the spade work of district attorneys in Tulsa and Oklahoma City, Burkett's office was able to build a case based on the testimony of five contractors, including E. Allen Cowan, the aforementioned contractor from Shawnee who had paid cash to obtain state contracts. Agreeing with IRS investigators that the kickbacks were taxable income and subjected the governor to charges of tax evasion, the Department of Justice was ready to approve the federal grand jury's indictment. Bill Burkett summarized the calamity that was steamrolling toward Judge Stephen Chandler's court: "All these disclosures, coupled with Hall's unwillingness or inability to make any reasonable explanation of them, in my opinion, effectively ended what had been a very promising political career."[11]

▶ ▶ ▶ ▶

Hastening Governor Hall toward the end of his promising political career was state Attorney General Larry Derryberry, a fellow Democrat, who was directing his investigators to focus on irregularities in building contracts. That laser-like focus led inexorably to Sunny Jenkins, Carl Ballew, and E. Allen Cowan. Lacking authority from the governor and legislature to prosecute grand-jury indictments and file criminal charges, Derryberry considered summoning a county grand jury. Derryberry needed all the help he could get, as Ballew's attorney had told him that his client would refuse to answer investigators' questions. Moreover, Ballew had already invoked the Fifth Amendment in testimony before a state Senate committee that was conducting its own probe of the governor's alleged crimes. Derryberry' s best option was to grant Ballew immunity from prosecution. When that happened, Ballew morphed from Hall's clandestine contributor and go-to contractor for painting jobs to a key witness in a case destined to implicate not only Jenkins and Cowan, but also a host of contractors, subcontractors, material suppliers, and gubernatorial associates.[12]

On Monday, April 22, 1974, Derryberry released a long-awaited report on David Hall that culminated months of prying information from reluctant witnesses. As noted in a *Daily Oklahoman* editorial, the attorney general's investigation, together with testimony presented before a federal grand jury, made it impossible "to pretend that there is nothing seriously wrong at the Capitol." The editorial went on to suggest that Hall was taking a cue from State Treasurer Leo Winters, who had contended throughout his trial that the entire brouhaha was nothing more than a Republican ploy to divert attention from the Watergate investigation. As the noose tightened around him, Hall publicly vented his fury toward U.S. Attorney Bill Burkett for crossing jurisdictional lines and sharing information with state Attorney General Larry Derryberry. Particularly disheartening to the state's largest newspaper was Hall's confusion of loyalties:

"Yet when a man occupies a high state office, his first loyalty must be to the people of Oklahoma. His loyalty does not lie with his party or to any other state officer if that means a conflict with his sworn duty

"The grave charges against the Hall administration are that public money was used to pay political debts. The method alleged was padding state contracts and kicking back the amount of the overcharge. These charges will not be laid to rest by public displays of anger."[13]

Hall's response to Derryberry's report was quick in coming. In a news conference on April 24, the governor, who had already announced his bid for reelection, denied wrongdoing and invoked the nation's most infamous traitor, branding the attorney general as a modern-day Benedict Arnold. He further claimed that he and other Democrats were being subjected to a "concerted effort to emasculate Democratic leadership in this country" to divert attention from troubles in the Republican Party. He went on to accuse Derryberry of making "false and malicious statements about him" during a trip to Washington and using the state legislature as a tool to advance his own political agenda, which included his anticipated candidacy for the governorship. Hall fervently denied previous testimonies that his campaign debt had soared to

$200,000, as his official campaign report on the 1970 election showed a deficit of about $1,000. He bristled at accusations that he had lured Dorothy Pike and other insiders into nefarious schemes. Lacking his customary good humor, he stated, "Let me make this crystal clear. I have never received any kickbacks during the time that I have been governor, I have never solicited any, I have never authorized anyone to accept one on my behalf, I have never participated in any way, form or action for any kickbacks in this administration."

In a final jab, Hall accused Derryberry of timing the release of his report to coincide with state representative Frank Keating's impeachment resolution, slated for announcement the next day in the legislature. Confident that voters would elect him to become the state's first two-term governor, Hall instructed his press secretary, Ed Hardy, to cut off reporters' questions after thirty minutes.[14]

The tit-for-tat continued when Derryberry called a press conference the next day to defend his loyalty to the Democratic Party. In a refreshing display of bipartisanship, he further defended his support for Republican representative Frank Keating's impeachment resolution. "I opened the investigation because I believed it was the only way for the public to have a statewide look at their government," said Derryberry. "At the conclusion, my choice was either to close my eyes, and my files, or to disclose what we had found. I simply could not just shrug my shoulders and walk away, just because it involved a Democrat, a big man or big interests." Knowing that he was stepping on "some big political toes," Derryberry expressed disappointment in the governor's lack of transparency and denied speculation that he had coordinated the release of his report with Keating's call for impeachment.[15]

Although Derryberry distanced himself from politics in the legislature, he had no qualms about admitting his collaboration with federal authorities representing the U.S. Attorney's Office. As Price explained, a state investigation was bound to get nowhere, as the Oklahoma State Bureau of Investigation operated under the purview of the governor. Coordination between state and federal investigators was on full display when Derryberry interrogated Carl Ballew, who had testified before the Oklahoma County grand jury in December and the federal grand jury in January, in Burkett's office.[16]

By the time he kicked off his reelection campaign in May 1974, Governor Hall's improprieties had yet to make much of a dent in his popularity, as he was still riding high in the court of public opinion. Press Secretary Hardy was pleased to report that responses to the governor's televised press conference on April 24th favored the incumbent by a ratio of five to one. Lauded for reforms in education and the criminal justice system and tax policies that had sent state revenues skyrocketing, Hall had every reason to anticipate another term in the governor's mansion. With the benefit of 20/20 hindsight, Price noted that Hall's tax-and-spend policies had done little to advance his reform agenda, and Oklahoma's national standing in education remained in the doldrums.[17]

But, clearly, events were spinning out of Hall's control, and they had all originated in his insatiable need for money. By early 1974, Attorney General Derryberry was turning his attention from the governor's office to the governor's mansion, where he found glaring mismatches between the Hall family's net worth (a modest $7,000, down about $17,000 since he became governor) and a lifestyle exemplified by an infamous hot-cider Christmas party that drew seven thousand guests. And there was not much relief to be found in his $35,000 salary and $15,000 expense allowance, particularly now that his campaign debts had ballooned to $200,000.

Having alienated people who wrote big checks with his audacious and largely successful tax program, Hall had come to rely on smaller contributions. "You need many, many small contributions," quipped Hall. "Otherwise, there is no way to do it unless you borrow and go into debt." Fearful that the time had come when only rich people could run for political office, Hall kept up a steady stream of protests against what he saw as an unfair investigation, all the while proclaiming his innocence and drawing support from sympathizers convinced that his enemies were gunning for him. To fight the court battle that was surely coming, he took time from his campaign to visit a bank, where he reportedly borrowed $30,000.

Defiant to the end, he spent his fourth year in office with one eye on his reelection campaign and the other on state and federal prosecutors, who seemed to be closing in. "I am 100% innocent of any wrongdoing," insisted Hall in a February 1974 interview in *Time* magazine. "I did not know what was going on."[18]

▶ ▶ ▶ ▶

Primaries and the general election of 1974 were fast approaching, and they came at a pivotal moment in American history. Richard Nixon's resignation, on August 8, was seared forever in collective memory, and his pardon by President Ford a month later had enraged voters who wanted to see the disgraced president punished for his chicanery in the Oval Office. Still reeling from the Arab oil embargo of 1973, Americans flipped on the evening news for daily reminders of their vulnerability to foreign potentates. Charles Lindbergh, a genuine hero, was dead; Hurricane Carmen had left a wake of destruction from Puerto Rico to Texas; and Evel Knievel's attempt to sail across the Snake River on a motorcycle had ended in a near-fatal plummet to the water's edge when his parachute failed to deploy. In faraway Oklahoma City, the daredevil's faulty parachute became a fitting metaphor for Governor Hall's far less sensational indictment by a federal grand jury, on September 6, on charges of bribery and extortion. By invoking the Fifth Amendment to protect himself against self-incrimination, Hall began his descent into dark waters of his own making—a Watergate writ small, but no less suffused with opacity and hubris. Although the U.S. Constitution guaranteed a citizen's innocence until proven guilty, Hall's refusal to answer the grand jury's questions was the beginning of the great unraveling, and public opinion began to turn against him. As Bill Burkett put it, "As time was to tell, the public was right."

At the same time, Hall needed his party's support in the primary election for a shot at a second term. His legendary handshaking and backslapping came to naught when he garnered a mere 169,290 votes compared to his two opponents: state legislator, one-term congressman, and rodeo star Clem McSpadden, with 238,534 votes; and state Senator David Boren, with 225,321 votes. Boren's upset victory over McSpadden, by almost 40,000 votes, in the Democratic runoff election put him on a collision course with Bill Price's Republican candidate, Jim Inhofe, whose youthful charm and conservative brand of politics failed to gain enough traction as Election Day approached.

Boren's victory over Inhofe put him on track to become one of Oklahoma's most effective governors before his election to the U.S. Senate in 1979. He remained in the Senate until 1994 when, at the urging of BancFirst cofounder and chairman Gene Rainbolt, he was named president of the University of Oklahoma.[19] David Hall's story was far less laudable. We turn once again to Bill Burkett for a succinct appraisal of the governor's fall from grace: "For David Hall it was the beginning of the end."[20]

But Hall, whose bid for a second term foundered in the Democratic primary, was not yet done with creative financing. As his governorship careened toward its denouement, he turned once again to Secretary of State John Rogers, his willing accomplice in laundering money intended for road building, to propose another money-making scheme. Hall had good reason to expect Rogers's cooperation, as the elder Rogers, the state's examiner and inspector, was under investigation for hiring ghost employees and was counting on his son's help to avoid prosecution. Even more helpful was the younger Rogers's chairmanship of the Oklahoma Public Employees Retirement System board of directors, which was responsible for investing money on behalf of state employees. As the state's chief executive, Hall served on the same board, and he was receptive when Dallas financier W. W. "Doc" Taylor, head of Guaranteed Investors Corporation, and his associate, Fort Worth public relations consultant R. Kevin Mooney, expressed interest in borrowing $10 million from the retirement fund, investing it in

Taylor's company, where it would earn about 8 percent interest, and then loaning it out at higher rates. Taylor and Mooney, who happened to be Hall's law school classmate, sweetened the pot with a promise to pay the governor a $50,000 kickback. To ensure the secretary of state's/ retirement-fund board chairman's complicity in convincing board members to approve the plan, Hall summoned Rogers into the Blue Room at the capitol in early December and offered to share half of the kickback with him.

Suspecting that his boss's latest scheme might not end well for either of them, Rogers, who was suffering his own money troubles stemming from his involvement in Hall's 1970 campaign, paid a visit to state Attorney General Larry Derryberry. Rogers left their get-together with an expanded job description as an undercover informant. In collaboration with the U.S. Attorney's Office and FBI agent Paul Baresel, he allowed his phones to be wiretapped, and he began to split his time between managing the state's business and, equipped with a hidden recording device, attending meetings with Hall, Taylor, and Mooney to gather evidence of their collusion. Those meetings were preceded by tutoring sessions with FBI agents who, as Burkett explained in a postmortem of what became the state's biggest corruption case of the 1970s, would "decide what John could say to evoke something incriminating from the other side."[21]

Bill Price was wrapping up his job as Jim Inhofe's campaign manager about the same time that Secretary of State John Rogers was going undercover. Price credited the U.S. Supreme Court's 5–4 decision, in *United States v. Hoffa* (1970), to allow consensual wires in federal investigations for enabling the FBI to gather enough evidence of Hall's misconduct to help Burkett build his case. "If you couldn't have consensual wires, how can you do any of this?" asked Price rhetorically. "If somebody else is tape-recording us, it is private. But if you are tape-recording me, that's *not* private." Price went on to explain that if the supreme court's decision had been reversed, prosecutors would have found it nearly impossible to win political corruption cases. "*U.S.*

v. Hoffa was a real turning point in legal history," continued Price. "Before that decision, in 1970, political corruption cases were rare. But once federal judges were authorized to accept consensual recordings, investigators were able to gather evidence on corrupt politicians and help prosecutors build their cases."[22]

Evidence that Hall was lining up favorable votes among members of the retirement fund board came in Rogers's taped conversations in mid-December. Burkett resorted to a fishing analogy to emphasize the importance of Rogers's undercover work: "Listening to these taped conversations, it was clear to the investigators that John Rogers was playing a good con game. He had the fish securely on the hook. Now it was time to start reeling him in."[23] Although there was no direct mention of a bribe or payoff, Mooney admitted that Hall was to be paid and that Rogers's share would come from him. On January 12, 1975—the day before David Boren's inauguration as governor—Mooney telephoned Rogers to warn him not to exert more pressure for payment, for two reasons: Taylor feared that he might be complicit in a felony, and Hall was afraid that Rogers was setting him up.

"David is afraid of me?" Rogers asked.

"Yes, he's scared to death," replied Mooney.

"If he don't [*sic*] understand he can trust me, he is paranoid," said Rogers. "The only guy who's done anything for him is me. I took the Fifth Amendment to keep that son-of-a-bitch out of the penitentiary. If he can't trust me, he can't trust anybody."

In an effort to set up a bribe that would enable FBI agents to make arrests, Rogers ramped up the pressure for a direct payment. In one conversation, Rogers asked Mooney, "Have you ever screwed a prostitute?"

"Yea," replied Mooney.

Rogers proceeded to explain to Mooney that politicians are basically prostitutes, as they expect payment in advance.[24]

▶ ▶ ▶ ▶

Hall was still refusing to talk openly about his pending deal with Taylor and Mooney when, an hour before David Boren's inauguration, on January 13, Hall summoned Rogers to his nearly empty office for a final chat. Suspicious that his office might have been bugged, he decided not to chat and, instead, scribbled notes on 3x5 index cards and put them in front of Rogers. Through their headsets, agents were startled to hear flushing sounds as Hall dropped shredded notes into the toilet. In his hastily composed shorthand, Hall urged Rogers to trust Taylor and Mooney and to give them a letter from the Oklahoma Public Employees Retirement System board, addressed to Taylor as president of Guaranteed Investors Corp., indicating the board's agreement to invest $10 million, at 8 ¼ percent interest and for an indefinite period of time, in Taylor's company. Guaranteed Investors Corporation had blanket authority to invest the money in unregistered securities and trade them at its discretion. Half of the money was to be delivered upon ten days' notice; the balance was due within four months. That letter was sitting on Rogers's desk. Mooney, on his way north from Fort Worth, had agreed to drop by the capitol to pick it up.

Wired with a Sony tape recorder tucked in at the small of his back and a transmitter strapped above his left hip, Rogers did his best over the ensuing twenty-four hours to pry smoking-gun evidence from the outgoing governor and his coconspirators. Even though FBI agents were confident that they had plenty of incriminating evidence, they could not keep Rogers from pushing for more.

Back in his own walnut-paneled office, the day after the inauguration, Rogers whispered into his transmitter that Mooney had just walked through the door. In the course of their conversation, Rogers upped the ante until he got Mooney to agree to pay him $31,250 plus 10 percent of business stemming from the $10-million-dollar investment. He went so far as to convince Mooney to take him off a half-million-dollar mortgage, dating back to Hall's 1970 campaign, that had been hanging over his head. Such was Rogers's success as a negotiator that he whispered into his transmitter that he might just take the deal. FBI agents, hunkered down with their headsets in a conference room on the other side of Rogers's office, were not amused.

Seated in a specially padded chair designed to improve the acoustics, Mooney studied the two-and-a-half-page letter while Rogers, under instructions from FBI agents, paced in front of the wall separating his office from the conference room. Rogers later claimed that he was not nervous in the least—apprehensive, maybe, but not nervous. "I knew that everything was handled," said Rogers. "It was figured out. Goddamn, who could be nervous? I had the FBI all over the place."

And then, on a prearranged signal, FBI agents swarmed into Rogers's office. Theodore P. Rosack, the acting agent in charge of Oklahoma's FBI office, had been waiting at the capitol since Mooney's arrival earlier that day. Flashing his identification, Rosack told Mooney that he was under arrest. Ashen-faced and clearly in shock, Mooney was frisked, handcuffed ("Are these really necessary?" he asked), and hustled out a side door and through the conference room. At about the same time, agents received word that Taylor had been arrested at the Downtowner Motel in Jackson, Mississippi, where he was attending a meeting. Booked and released on $25,000 bond, Taylor flew back to Dallas that evening. His son-in-law, James Duckels, picked him up at the airport and drove him home.[25] Whatever Taylor and his wife discussed when he walked through the door has been lost to history.

As FBI agents hustled Mooney out of the capitol and completed their protocols, Rogers shut down his office and summoned his staff to assure them that he was not in trouble.

The FBI's six-week investigation was over. Two days later, only three days after David Hall stepped down as governor, federal grand jury indictments came raining down on him and his coconspirators.[26] The indictment charged Hall with extorting $50,000 from Taylor and Mooney and then conspiring with them to bribe Rogers to influence the Oklahoma Public Employees Retirement System board to go along with their investment scheme.[27]

Now that grand-jury indictments had been handed down, it was U.S. Attorney Bill Burkett's turn to build his case. None doubted that the former governor would put up a fight. Nor did anyone doubt that Burkett and his assistants would see justice done in officialdom's most recent dalliance with its darker angels.

CHAPTER SEVEN : *Assistant U.S. Attorney – Part One*

With the Inhofe campaign behind him and eager for challenges that Holloway & Dobson could not offer, Price was receptive when, in February 1975, U.S. Attorney Bill Burkett gave him an offer he could not refuse: a position as an assistant prosecutor. "It was an amazing place when I arrived," recalled Price about the job offer that changed his life. "There were only six of us in the U.S. Attorney's Office." That tiny cadre of assistants included Jim Peters; Floy Dawson; Susie Pritchett, who had arrived the year before; O. B. Johnston, who had been in the office less than three years; and John Green, a relative long timer who ranked just under Burkett as first assistant prosecutor. Later hires Ron Pyle and David Poarch were assigned mainly to civil litigation cases.[1]

Although Price was quick to form working relationships with all his colleagues, his closest collaborator during his first few months in the U.S. Attorney's Office was Drew Neville. An Oklahoma City native, Neville had parlayed his undergraduate major in business and juris doctor from the University of Oklahoma into a job with Hanson, Peterson & Tompkins, an insurance defense firm in Oklahoma City, where he already had experience as a law clerk and legal intern. Neville spent his days preparing briefs and defending car wreck victims and estranged spouses. Relief from a mundane law practice arrived in the person of Don Cogman, his college roommate and, fortuitously, U.S. Senator Dewey Bartlett's chief administrative assistant, who asked if he might be interested in working as a legislative aide on Capitol Hill. That was a no-brainer, and Neville left the law firm in December 1973 and took up residence in Washington just in time for the Watergate hearings.

"I worked for Henry Bellmon," began Neville. "All of us had a wide variety of responsibilities—legislative responsibilities. One of my responsibilities was the Watergate investigation, to keep Henry up to speed on what was going on. That was my main job, my principal job." Other responsibilities included drafting legislation, coordinating Senate floor activities and drafting speeches, preparing position papers, and managing relations with Senator Bellmon's constituents—heady business for a recent law school graduate with a scant year of workplace experience under his belt.

When it came time to reorganize his staff, Bellmon called on his newly appointed legislative director, Charlie Waters. A native of Skiatook, Oklahoma, Waters had complemented his studies at the University of Oklahoma with working for Governor Bellmon during his first term. "I was a guard at the governor's mansion," explained Waters about his unlikely introduction to politics, "a little five-foot-six, hundred-and-forty-five-pound guy, didn't know how to shoot a gun or anything!" Following Waters's graduation from OU, Bellmon bumped him from guard to youth director in his 1968 campaign for the U.S. Senate. Bellmon won the election, and while he was making his transition from governor to U.S. senator, Waters was completing his juris doctor at the University of Tulsa and pondering a career as a law professor. But fate intervened when Senator Bellmon summoned him to Washington to join his legislative staff. "I was up there in 1973," said Waters, who had been thrilled to be thrust into the turmoil of Watergate-era Washington. "After a year or so, he put me in charge."

Given carte blanche to choose Bellmon's legislative staff, Waters zeroed in on his former fraternity brother at OU—Drew Neville. "That was my first hire," continued Waters. "I think I was his pledge trainer!"

Neville's career on Senator Bellmon's legislative staff was short-lived. Even though he was happy to work under his former pledge trainer and exhilarated to land in the red-hot center of Washington politics, Neville longed to be in the courtroom. After Nixon resigned and America collectively exhaled, Neville returned to his hometown, in late 1974, to accept Burkett's offer to join his miniscule staff of federal prosecutors. Less than a week before his arrival, Bill Price showed up. As Neville told the story, their initial meeting gave them something to laugh about for years to come: "I think Bill was hired like, one or two days after I was . . . I always, to this day, pound on Bill Price because he stole my desk and my office! I still rib him about that. I think he actually, physically, got in the office before I did, but he was hired after I was."[2]

Price and Neville went to work in the U.S. Attorney's Office just as ex-governor David Hall was careening toward trial. As Price recalled, the only reason he was thrust into such a high-profile case was that he had no other cases on his agenda. "They needed a third and fourth chair to write briefs, to do notes, to do other things in relationship to the case," he said about his abrupt immersion in one of the highest profile cases in Oklahoma history.

As Price familiarized himself with the case, he discovered why Hall's trial had been so long in coming: Burkett had been trying to build a criminal tax case against the governor, and that was notoriously hard to do. "Criminal tax, especially at the time, involved this really long process," explained Price. "They had to write up a big long report; they had to send it to D.C.; they had to go through all these committees and groups, then get approved." Eventually, criminal tax cases wound up in the IRS regional office in Dallas, where they were likely to languish for as long as five years. Frustrations mounted when IRS administrators waited until the eleventh hour—often just as the statute of limitations was set to expire—to render their judgments and allow prosecutions to proceed.

"It was a ridiculous process," said Price about an early encounter with bureaucratic red tape.

Frustrated by his inability to prosecute the governor on criminal tax charges, Burkett was relieved when Secretary of State John Rogers delivered incontrovertible evidence that Hall was conspiring with

Messrs. Taylor and Mooney to commit bribery and extortion; both charges offered an uncluttered path to prosecution. "In retrospect, if they had added a tax count on Leo Winters, it would have been enormously easier," said Price about Burkett's previous high-profile case against the state treasurer, which had ended in his acquittal. "If you have sacks of cash, it's easier to prove tax evasion than anything else! That's what finally convicted J. D. McCarty."[3]

Price and Neville were still acclimating to their new jobs when the six-week investigation into David Hall's misdeeds ended with his indictment by a federal grand jury, on charges of extortion and conspiracy to commit bribery, and Taylor's and Mooney's arrests by the FBI for their roles in the ex-governor's scheme. During those tense weeks of wiretapping and clandestine recordings, secrecy had reached the point where investigators and their collaborators avoided meeting in the FBI's offices, preferring to hold briefings and debriefings— sometimes three times a day! —in an underground garage.[4]

David Hall, "Doc" Taylor, and Kevin Mooney (represented by state senator and attorney Frank Keating) faced their accusers in Chief U.S. District Judge Fred Daugherty's courtroom in early March 1975. Not for the first time, and certainly not the last, pundits drew comparisons between Hall's trial and that of State Treasurer Leo Winters a year earlier. Both men were Democrats whose charges of conspiracy by federal grand juries had been orchestrated by Republican U.S. Attorney Bill Burkett, and both had been accused of peddling influence. There was also precedent in previous occupants of the state's highest office: Charles Haskell, who avoided impeachment but not the opprobrium that came with his various dalliances with corruption; James B. A. Robertson, who was indicted by a federal grand jury while still in office, only to have his charges dismissed without trial; and Jack Walton, Martin Trapp, and Henry Johnston, all of whom ran afoul of the state legislature and, in various iterations, faced impeachment.

In contrast to Messrs. Haskell, Robertson, Walton, Trapp, and Johnston, David Hall was indicted three days after he left office. His predecessors' experiences, significant though they were in the chronicle of gubernatorial misdeeds, provided scant cover as he braced for what was sure to be a bruising trial.

▶ ▶ ▶ ▶

Although Price neither called nor questioned witnesses, he viewed his participation in Hall's trial as a great experience. For the most part, he prepared briefs and sat with Burkett and Assistant U.S. Attorneys O. B. Johnston, Susie Pritchett, and Jim Peters at counsel table.[5] Price, Susie Pritchett, and Drew Neville wrote many of the government's briefs, both at the trial level and, later, for the Tenth Circuit Court of Appeals. "It was so exciting to be in on all of the interviews, and at the back of the room, or whatever, and then being there at the trial," Price said. "I was writing most of the briefs, and occasionally writing notes for Burkett of a question I may have thought of." During cross-examination, Price suggested that Burkett read the official oath of office required of all public officials that they would never accept money in connection with their positions and ask Hall if he had violated it. Nobody was surprised when Hall answered in the negative, but that was not the point. Price wanted the jury to reflect on the gravity of the charges against the former governor. As his career developed, Price had ample opportunity to think about the oath of office and the consequences of ignoring it in pursuit of personal gain.[6]

"I always considered him as part of the Hall prosecution team," said Neville, who Burkett tasked with much of the pretrial research and writing. "As the trial progressed, Bill became a lot more involved than I did. Bill kind of took the load on what research and writing needed to be done during the trial." The primary litigator, of course, was Bill Burkett, who used Secretary of State John Rogers's recordings as the lynchpin of the government's case. Price surmised an added incentive for Rogers to cooperate: his wife, from all appearances an upright Christian woman, was speaking to him in Burkett's office, her voice just audible enough for Price to overhear. "John," she whispered in a tone that surely got his attention, "if you don't tell them the whole truth, I'm leaving you!"

That was all Price needed to hear. Whereas Burkett believed that Rogers's deep-seated honesty drove him to confess, Price was convinced that Rogers had been corrupt all along and was merely trying to keep his new marriage intact. Price further theorized that Hall was smart enough not to approach Rogers with a bribe unless he was confident that he would accept it.[7]

For three weeks, what Burkett later described as "a knock-down, drag-out free-for-all" met Hall's expectation of a vigorous prosecution and gave Oklahomans yet another lesson in high-stakes corruption.[8] Closing arguments came on Tuesday, March 11. "Outside this courtroom there are millions of people who are entitled to know if there are honest officials," declared Burkett, his voice cracking from the strain. "They want to know whether the kind of distorted, appalling, sordid, disgraceful and outrageous conduct that you've seen from these two men is going to be condoned or condemned." Under David Hall's withering glare, Burkett took an hour and thirteen minutes to deliver his summation, in which he urged jurors to remember Hall's and Taylor's tape-recorded conversations. Hall's attorney, D. C. Thomas, adopted entirely different tactics, comparing the government's probe to Christ's crucifixion. Although he never mentioned the Savior by name, he went so far as to compare Hall's prosecution to another man's appearance before a magistrate, who commanded soldiers to nail him to a cross. "They thought they were through with him," concluded Thomas, "but for 1,975 years they've found out they were wrong." He then fast forwarded to the government's high-handed attacks attending the Watergate break-in. Thomas saved some of his firepower for Rogers for confessing during his testimony that he was trying "to nail Hall."[9]

Doc Taylor was fortunate to have James P. Linn in his corner. Known in legal circles as one of the feistiest, most accomplished, and (to borrow from the sports lexicon) winningest trial lawyers of his generation, Linn was a Texas Panhandle native and World War II combat veteran, and he had expressed his bellicose nature throughout his fifty-year career as a lawyer while representing such illustrious clients as rock star David Bowie and the Philippines's First Lady, Imelda Marcos, who seemed to thrive on the ragged edge of the law.[10] In Taylor's defense, Linn accused the federal government of "constructing a crime" through its investigation. In contrast to Burkett's assertion that John Rogers was a hero for going undercover, Linn referred to his tape recordings to reveal the secretary of state as a foul-mouthed bully— hardly the all-American boy that Burkett claimed he was. Both Thomas and Linn were outspoken in their determination "to rake Rogers over the coals" and bring out "every skeleton in his closet" to discredit his testimony.

Linn was tough, but he was also ethical. In Mooney's pretrial interview, Burkett discovered that Doc Taylor had written a check that seemed to be evidence of a bribe and recorded it on the check stub. When Burkett subpoenaed the check stub, Linn could have risked obstruction of justice charges by denying its existence. Even though obstruction of justice would have been difficult to prove, Linn did the right thing by complying with the subpoena. Linn's courtroom behavior was matched by the way Judge Daugherty, a former general in the U.S. Army who had earned famously high marks at the Army War College (higher, it was said, than Douglas MacArthur's grades!), conducted the trial. Daugherty took notes in shorthand and referred to them constantly to determine the propriety of rebuttal testimony. In dealing with objections, he asked counsel to approach the bench and subjected them to Socratic questioning based on Tenth Circuit Court of Appeals cases. When attorneys came up short, he asked them if they wanted to withdraw their objections. Almost invariably they did, leaving Daugherty's record for allowing no grounds for appeal intact.

On Wednesday, March 12, the defendants' case fell into the hands of the seven men and five women on the jury. Hall and Taylor, both of whom refused to talk to reporters, went immediately to their wives, Jo and B. G., respectively, to await their fate. They were relieved to learn that the state House of Representatives was considering impeachment charges against Secretary of State John Rogers. "It should have happened about two months earlier," said Jo Hall.

Huddled with his wife, his attorney, and a few close friends, Hall displayed his customary good humor. But his insides were in knots, as he knew that a guilty verdict could send him to prison for thirty-five years and deprive him of $40,000 in fines. When he and the other defendants were summoned back to Judge Daugherty's court, the verdict was swift in coming. Former governor Hall was convicted and sentenced to a three-year term in federal prison, at Swift Trail Camp, near Safford, in southeastern Arizona. He was scheduled to begin his sentence on November 22, 1976.[11]

As a postscript to the governor's conviction, the legislature's charges of incompetence, corruption, and moral turpitude against John Rogers were too much for the secretary-turned-informant, and he resigned as secretary of state in the summer of 1975. Rumors swirled that Rogers's real crime had been angering legislators by collaborating all too freely with the FBI's investigation. Although there was surely a hint of politics in Rogers's resignation, it certainly deepened suspicions among those looking for evidence of a corrupt political culture.[12]

▶ ▶ ▶ ▶

Price's involvement in the state's other high-profile case came when Leo Winters filed a civil lawsuit against Bill Burkett. "He had the audacity to then sue Bill Burkett in civil court for prosecuting him!" said Price. He was further astounded when his boss, Larry Patton, dropped the case in his lap. He soon discovered that the presiding judge would be none other than U.S. District Judge Stephen Chandler—the same famously idiosyncratic judge who had summoned Bill Berry to his home to discuss Supreme Court Justice N. S. Corn's confession.

"Somehow or other, I got by, winning the case in the circuit without getting disbarred by Chandler," explained Price. "But the fascinating thing about this case was the deposition of Leo Winters. I deposed him for about twelve hours, and the hubris of this fellow—he didn't deny that all these bankers came by with sacks and sacks of money, huge amounts of money, that he never kept track of. He never kept track of how much he kept, and how much he gave out to other people. His only contention was that there wasn't a formula! But he wasn't denying the huge amounts of cash from these same banks that he is putting money in!"

Price marveled at Winters's alacrity in writing checks. "He had to have spent five hours a day writing checks and making deposits. He had the biggest check kite I had ever seen in my life, on cattle!" Not for the first time since the banking scandal started making headlines, Price was struck by Winters's hubris not only in orchestrating a statewide scam in plain sight, but also in filing suit against the man who had prosecuted him. "Of course, the prosecutor has immunity, so we won at the circuit," said Price about what was a relatively simple, albeit unnerving, case. "Can you imagine the thought process by which you're willing to sue, and you're willing to admit to these hundreds of thousands—or untold amounts of cash coming in sacks from bankers?"[13]

Although Drew Neville was less involved than Price in David Hall's trial and not involved in Leo Winters's lawsuit, he quickly discovered that he had stepped into his dream job, and he had no doubt that Price felt the same way. "It was wonderful!" gushed Neville at a remove of four-plus decades. "It was the best job I have ever had!" What made the job so enjoyable was the camaraderie that Bill Burkett fostered among his tight-knit group of assistants. Then there was the variety that kept everybody on their toes. "We had to handle civil cases as well as criminal cases. We didn't have a criminal division; we didn't have a civil division; we didn't have an appellate division. You had to do it all!" For Price, this variety was reflected in the steady stream of criminal cases he handled. Fraud in institutions ranging from banks to nursing homes, government scams, embezzlement, and robberies were all in a day's work, and their common denominator was corruption. When a union official was caught stealing from the coffers, hundreds of union members showed up in court to cheer for a stiff sentence. The checkerboard of Indian allotments in western Oklahoma compelled the U.S. Attorney's Office to act as the local prosecutor when someone of Native American ancestry was involved in a crime or when a crime took place on tribal land.

When they were not in the office or roaming the Western District, assistants were liable to be in Denver, arguing cases in the Tenth Circuit Court of Appeals. For the sake of efficiency, assistant U.S. Attorneys went to Denver to argue not only their own cases, but also others that their colleagues had entrusted to them. Price holed up for days on end at the Brown Palace Hotel to read transcripts and briefs, some fifty pages in length, in preparation for his appearance before the appellate judges. Whereas many attorneys skirted over the facts of the case and concentrated on rebutting allegations of error by opposing counsel, Price presented the facts in exacting detail. His approach was based on a simple calculation: as no trial is devoid of minor mistakes, judges should be encouraged to weigh technical errors against the evidence. Convinced that most errors at trial were basically harmless, Price directed judges' attention to the facts of the case without skirting over minor mistakes. As a result, he never lost a case on appeal.

Closer to home, Neville and Price spent more time than they might have anticipated at the Federal Correctional Institute in El Reno, where drug trafficking, stabbings, and even murders were common, and whose lawsuits landed in the U.S. Attorney's Office because the alleged crimes were federal offenses. Because it housed young prisoners with a bent toward violence, the El Reno facility was known as the gladiator school of federal prisons. A typical government case involved a victim, a small group of witnesses, a guard who had discovered the crime, and a physician to explain the victim's injuries. With numbing regularity, witnesses told defense attorneys that they had seen the crime—most often, a stabbing—but could not identify the perpetrator. All they knew was, it was not the defendant! But there was an upside for up-and-coming prosecutors. As Price explained, "The prison cases were a great school to hone your cross-examination skills."

Although Neville could not recall trying cases with Price, they and their colleagues enjoyed the same energizing routine of large caseloads of three or four cases per month, plenty of diversity, and friendships destined to last a lifetime. Included in their network of crime fighters were the FBI agents who investigated crimes and brought them to the U.S. Attorney's Office for prosecution.

"It was a very high-energy office," concluded Neville. "We had an awesome time!"

In August 1976, Neville accepted Bill Burkett's invitation to follow him into private practice, in a firm whose star defense attorney, Jimmy Linn, had tried unsuccessfully to keep Doc Taylor out of jail. That firm, Linn, Curtage & Burkett, eventually became Linn & Neville and rose to prominence for defending some of the nation's highest profile businesses, lawyers, and accountants who had been implicated in securities violations. But switching from prosecution to defense did not mean he had to sacrifice friendships, with either his former colleagues or FBI agents. "All of us were very close to the FBI," continued Neville, who went on to earn bragging rights as the only defense lawyer to receive invitations to the FBI's Christmas parties.[14]

Bill Burkett's successor, David Russell, had served on Senator Dewey Bartlett's staff since his election in 1972. When Russell got the nod to replace Burkett as U.S. Attorney for the Western District of Oklahoma, he asked his counterpart on Senator Bellmon's legislative staff, Charlie Waters, to consider a change of career.

"I wanted to be a trial lawyer," recalled Waters about the opportunity that came knocking. "So even though I was in a pretty good position in Washington and could have branched out and made a career up there, I thought the best place to learn to do trial work was in the U.S. Attorney's Office." With a tinge of regret at resigning from a job he loved, Waters packed his bags and followed Russell back to Oklahoma City.

"It was there I first became acquainted with Bill Price," continued Waters. "When I got there, there were about ten assistants. It was a small office. Everybody there had civil work or criminal work." As the low man on the totem pole, Waters was not surprised to inherit cases that nobody particularly wanted, including crimes at the Federal Correctional Institute at El Reno and run-of-the-mill DUI violations at military bases. Ignoring Waters's protests that he had never tried a case and knew nothing about courtroom protocols, Price dragged him to Fort Sill to prosecute soldiers for driving under the influence. As Waters put it, "They stuck me in the library with a desk, and that's how I started my career. It was a great training ground. I tried a whole bunch of those cases."[15]

Far more consequential than prosecuting unruly inmates and drunken soldiers was shattering a drug distribution ring headed by Ramon D. Martinez, aka the Milkman ("He had been a milkman, way back there," explained Price about the drug kingpin's unlikely moniker), from Dona, Texas, and Charles Robert "Churn" Mathes of Jones, Oklahoma. At the end of an exhausting and often dangerous investigation by state and federal authorities, Martinez, Mathes, and nearly two dozen confederates, including two underlings identified only as the Rat and the Beast, were named in a fifteen-count indictment charging them with distributing high-grade Mexican marijuana and cocaine through a network spanning Oklahoma, Texas, West Virginia, Tennessee, Arkansas, and Ohio.[16] "The Milkman would have truckloads of marijuana and cocaine driven from Texas to a farm in the Edmond area owned by Churn Mathes," explained Price about his and Charlie Waters's introduction to international drug trafficking. Upon its arrival in Edmond, the contraband was loaded into dozens of vans and distributed nationwide—until the long arm of the law caught up with them. While investigators were probing for incriminating evidence, Price was fielding calls from attorneys throughout the country who thought they could trace drugs shipped into their jurisdictions to Churn Mathes's farm.

Although Martinez was willing to testify against his American accomplices, he balked at implicating Mexicans. "He told one story that was interesting," explained Price, with a flair for understatement:

"'I was crossing the Rio Grande with this huge truck full of drugs, [Martinez said] and all of a sudden, from every direction, lights appear. It's the *federales*. I just know that I am dead. And they arrest me and seize the load, and then they tell me to run. And I am sure that I am going to be shot in the back.'

"They didn't shoot him!" concluded Price about the Milkman's hair-raising tale. "They kept the load!"

But that was not all. The Milkman's home, near the porous border between Texas and Mexico, put him in the crosshairs of drug smugglers who took a dim view of anyone who testified against them. To punish people for testifying or threatening to testify, their henchmen employed a diabolical tactic: they crept up to their homes in the dead of night, turned off their gas at an outside meter, turned it back on, and then called them on the phone.

"The little spark of the phone call..."

Price paused to ponder the various forms that death took for those with the temerity to rat on drug smugglers.

"The gas would tend to asphyxiate you," said Price finally, "but the little spark of the phone call would tend to blow you up. Their whole family would be blown up! I always thought that was a good reason not to testify against drug gangs in Mexico!"

The sordid saga continued with Price and Waters's star witness, Diana Beckerdite, who revealed more intelligence through her advanced degrees in chemistry than in her choice of a marriage partner. Diana's husband, Ernest, held a full-time job as one of the governor's top aides; on the side, he dealt drugs. After one of Ernest's customers was implicated in his murder, rumors swirled that Diana was having a fling with the killer, who was later convicted, which raised the question: was Diana involved with the man who shot Ernest? If so, defense attorneys would have a field day. The plot thickened when investigators came across Ernest Beckerdite's customer book—a treasure trove that included many prominent Oklahomans and implicated Ernest in the Milkman's distribution network. The thickening continued, a few weeks before the trial, when Price asked the police department for Beckerdite's customer book. The book was known to contain the names of many prominent Oklahomans, and it had turned up missing from the police property room. Price took the problem to Police Chief Tom Heggy, but a long night of polygraphing department employees failed to turn up the missing book.

Disappointed that nobody would plead guilty, Price huddled with Oklahoma State Bureau of Narcotics agents on Saturday to prepare for trial on Monday. During their pretrial huddle, an agent told Price about a person who had attended a previous drug conspiracy meeting. On the off chance of finding him, Price picked up the phone book and started calling everyone with that name. On his fourth call, Price hit pay dirt. The woman who answered admitted that her son had suffered from drug addiction and was part of the drug conspiracy on trial. She then explained that he had been high on cocaine when, about three years earlier, he had dived headfirst into a pool, broken his neck, and emerged as a quadriplegic. "He spends his life speaking about the dangers of drugs," said the boy's distraught mother. I will bring him into your office right now, and he will testify against everybody!"

Thrilled with the prospect of enlisting "the best witness on earth" in their prosecution of the Milkman and his gang, Price and Waters welcomed mother and son when they arrived for the trial. "She wheeled him into the U.S. Attorney's Office that afternoon, and he turned out to be an unimpeachable witness!" explained Price about the beginning of the end of the Milkman's drug business. Although defense attorneys felt confident that they could challenge Diana Beckerdite's and other coconspirators' testimonies, there was not much they could do to discredit a young man in a wheelchair who was on a mission to put drug dealers behind bars.

Thus began the great unraveling as the Milkman and his accomplices, eager for plea agreements to reduce their sentences, admitted their guilt and implicated others. The pleading and implicating continued through the weekend. At midnight Sunday, Price called U.S. District Judge Ralph Thompson and asked him to delay the trial. Already vexed by the circus that would soon play out in his courtroom, Thompson had brought in extra chairs and moved tables to accommodate dozens of defendants and their attorneys. Thompson granted the delay and told Price to keep him informed of the fast-changing developments.

By the time the sun rose on Monday morning, all the defendants had pled guilty, concluding one of the biggest drug busts in Oklahoma history.[17]

▸ ▸ ▸ ▸

Ralph Thompson, who had served in the Oklahoma House of Representatives from 1966 to 1970, had become acquainted with Price during the run-up to the presidential election of 1972, when they had teamed up with Dewey Bartlett, G. T. Blankenship, Jim Inhofe, and Mickey Edwards to campaign on Nixon's behalf. Fourteen years Price's senior, Thompson was an Oklahoma City native whose father, Lee, was a prominent lawyer and whose maternal grandfather was Dr. William Bennett Bizzell, president of the University of Oklahoma from 1926 until 1941. Bizzell's grace as a gentleman and scholar exerted a profound influence on his grandson. Like Price, Thompson attended Edgemere School; unlike Price, he went to Harding Junior High School and Classen High School before enrolling at the University of Oklahoma, first as an undergraduate and later as a law student.

After two years of law school, Thompson was commissioned in the U.S. Air Force's pilot training program. Since the air force had more pilots than it needed, he was reassigned as a special agent in the Office of Special Investigations (OSI), a division that Thompson likened to the FBI, where he put his two years of law school to work in criminal investigations and counterintelligence activities. Assigned to southern Taiwan (formerly Formosa), Thompson found himself on the front line of defense against Communist China, whose Red Army, flush from its triumphs in mainland China, was expected to invade any day.[18]

Fortunately, that never happened. Upon release from active duty, Thompson returned to OU to complete law school. Realizing how much he had enjoyed his stint with the OSI, he considered applying to the foreign service and actually sat for the CIA examination. Then he met his future bride, Barbara, and the allure of an overseas career faded. As Thompson explained about his decision to remain stateside, "I knew that life as a covert CIA officer was not a good career for a family man, and I opted out of that." He and Barbara were married in 1964, and Thompson settled in for what he assumed would be a less exhilarating, but more stable, career at his father's side in a private law practice.

But that was not Thompson's only reason to opt out of government service abroad. His career aspirations were still a work in progress when G. T. Blankenship dropped his bombshell in the state legislature and pulled back the curtain on a corrupt legal system. Thompson spoke for his generation of young and idealistic attorneys who built their careers in the wake of the Oklahoma supreme court scandal: "I had been raised in a great lawyer's family and held the profession of law in the highest regard. For all of us who shared those feelings, and all of us did, it was just a dagger to the heart of us young lawyers. We committed ourselves to working for judicial reform, to establish, by constitutional amendment, a system that would help prevent that ever happening again, taking politics out of judicial selection, to the extent possible."[19]

Thompson entered the fray when he ran successfully for the seat in the Oklahoma House of Representatives that his friend and fellow attorney G. T. Blankenship had vacated, in 1966, to make his own successful run for state attorney general. "I was elected and served for the primary purpose of working on judicial reform," continued Thompson. "I was able to be a principal author of the constitutional amendment proposals, which were enacted, and to this day, it is one of the most satisfying things I have ever been able to be involved in, in public life."[20]

Thompson upped the ante when he accepted Governor Dewey Bartlett's invitation to run on his ticket as a candidate for lieutenant governor in the gubernatorial election of 1970. Although Thompson claimed to have no interest in holding state office, he was honored by Bartlett's invitation to join his team. Their hard-fought campaign ended when they lost, by the narrowest electoral margin in Oklahoma history, to David Hall and his running mate, George Nigh. He then resigned his seat in the legislature and returned full time to his and his father's law practice. After four years in politics, he could look back with satisfaction on the judicial reforms he had crafted and pushed through the legislature. He also took solace in knowing that his good friend the newly elected lieutenant governor, George Nigh, would wield some clout in the coming Democratic administration.

Thompson's only flirtation with national politics came when he asked Bill Price to test the waters for a congressional campaign. "Ralph decided I would be the perfect person to send out a letter, 'Draft Ralph Thompson for Congress!'," recalled Price. "He just wanted to see the response." But he never got his chance, as the Watergate scandal was grabbing headlines and making Republicans reconsider their political ambitions. "This wasn't the year for Republicans," continued Price with a flair for understatement. "Anyway, we never did it."[21]

Thompson did not have to wait long for his next life-changing opportunity. At the recommendations of U.S. senators Henry Bellmon and Dewey Bartlett, the Senate Judiciary Committee considered nominating him to replace retiring judge Stephen Chandler as U.S. district judge for the Western District of Oklahoma. Not surprisingly, Thompson's former gubernatorial running mate praised him as "an exceptionally well-qualified candidate for the federal judiciary" whose "experience, intelligence, age, training, temperament, and character uniquely qualify him for the federal bench." After a unanimous committee vote, the full Senate confirmed his nomination without debate or dissent. On October 14, 1975, President Gerald Ford put his stamp of approval on the appointment. Six days later, the forty-year-old Ralph Thompson took his oath of office to begin yet another career, this time succeeding Judge Chandler and, alongside Western District judges Fred Daugherty, Luther Bohanon, and Luther Eubanks, serving as a member of Oklahoma's federal judiciary. Thompson recalled Judge Daugherty with special fondness: "Judge Daugherty was not only a close family friend and one of my dad's best friends, but he was a mentor, and a wonderful example to me of what a federal judge should be and do. I always appreciated that very much. He was a *very* distinguished federal judge."

"I had enjoyed being a lawyer," continued Thompson, long since retired and clearly wistful, recalling a career dedicated to honesty and fairness in the judiciary. "I enjoyed the advocacy of it. But the prospect of being a federal judge was beyond anything I would realistically have expected of my opportunities!"

"Were you the junior member—the youngest member of the foursome?" I asked, even though I was pretty sure I knew the answer.

"Very much junior! I was one of the youngest federal judges in the country, at the age of forty, which in those years was extraordinarily young. I think there were only two others in the country who were my age at the time."[22]

A few years before Price, Neville, and Waters settled into their jobs in the U.S. Attorney's Office and Thompson launched his unexpected career as a federal judge, Frank Keating made his first foray into a career in law enforcement. He complemented his degree from Georgetown, where he had graduated in 1966, with a juris doctor from the University of Oklahoma. Following his graduation from law school in 1969, he packed his bags for the West Coast, where he spent a couple of years as an FBI agent in Seattle and San Francisco. As an investigator, he presented his cases to U.S. Attorneys on a regular basis. Before long, he decided that what he really wanted to do was prosecute crimes rather than investigate them. To make that happen, he returned to Tulsa to accept a position as an assistant district attorney.

Like Price, Neville, and Waters, Keating hankered to test his mettle as a trial attorney. "I wanted to get into the courtroom, and that was a way to get into the courtroom," explained Keating about his career change. In 1972, Keating married Catherine Heller and launched yet another career, this time as a representative from District 70 in the Oklahoma House of Representatives, a position that he held until his election to the state Senate in 1974.[23] No sooner did Keating settle into his Senate seat than he agreed to defend Kevin Mooney in the David Hall trial—a case that did not go well for any of the defendants.

Included in the 1960s generation of reform-minded Oklahomans was Tom Daxon, Price's comrade-in-arms from Teen Age Republicans who, like his friend, had joined College Republicans, soon after arriving at OU's archrival, Oklahoma State University in Stillwater. En route to a bachelor's degree in economics, Daxon took a two-year sabbatical to join Campus Crusade for Christ, an organization through which he met his future bride, Linda, and that dispatched him to California and the University of Maryland in suburban Washington, D.C., to spread the Gospel.

Daxon was excited to absorb all that the nation's capital had to offer. "I was really interested in politics," explained Daxon. "It was a natural place for me to go." Discovering that his Christian values did not obligate him to serve as a Campus Crusade staff member, Daxon returned to OSU, where he spent his senior year as president of College Republicans before graduating in 1974. His next step was at Hurdman & Cranstoun, a boutique firm in Tulsa where he put his expertise in accounting to work in examining clients' books. He remained there for four years—plenty of time to grow weary of the mergers and acquisitions that were steamrolling through small and midsize firms such as his, leaving him to wonder if there was not a better way to make a living for a young, energetic, and idealistic Republican with a yen for balancing books and a distaste for immoral politicians.[24]

Young, energetic, and idealistic—a perfect trifecta of attributes that Bill Price, Drew Neville, Charlie Waters, Ralph Thompson, Frank Keating, and Tom Daxon shared in their journeys to leadership positions in politics and the law. Although they came from different directions and exhibited a variety of skill sets, all six men were on the same page when it came to confronting Oklahoma's sordid history of corruption. Experience had taught each of them that their state was definitely not okay. Sharing Ralph Thompson's anguish over the Oklahoma supreme court scandal ("a dagger to the heart of us young lawyers," as Thompson so eloquently put it), they and other idealists of their generation knew that Oklahoma could do better. They also knew that they would have to fight, each in his own way, for meaningful change in a state named for ne'er-do-wells, where disrespect for authority seemed embedded in its DNA.

▶ ▶ ▶ ▶

Coincidentally, one of Price's first victories as a federal prosecutor came in Purcell, thirty-six miles south of Oklahoma City, the same town where, as a rookie attorney with Holloway & Dobson, he had successfully defended General Motors against a local and heavily favored plaintiff whose truck had mysteriously slipped its gears. Price's second courtroom victory in Purcell also involved a truck. Only this time, the truck was parked in a motel parking lot, its motor mounts were beyond suspicion, and it was chock-full of stolen liver. Working with fellow assistant U.S. Attorney Susie Pritchett, who sat as second chair, Price pieced together a nefarious tale that had begun when the truck driver reported the theft but neglected to provide the actual scene of the crime. Price and Pritchett quickly discovered the truth behind his duplicity: he had violated his company's policy by picking up two hitchhikers, a brother and sister, and then committed further violations by taking the woman to a motel, perhaps to relieve the stress of driving a truck piled high with organ meat. While she and the driver were otherwise occupied, her brother absconded with the cargo. When news of the hijacked liver hit the streets, he panicked and scattered his stolen property in lakes and ponds throughout the area.

Witnesses, including one Mutt Mooney, were duly summoned to U.S. District Judge Ralph Thompson's courtroom. Although the truck driver's wife wanted to be in the courtroom during her husband's testimony, Price knew better, as he had no interest in seeing their inevitable separation escalate in the courtroom. After some deft maneuvering, which included issuing a subpoena to the defendant's wife (who, to the detriment of courtroom drama, was a no-show), Price and Pritchett prevailed. Price credited this and other successes to their complementary skills: Pritchett excelled at gathering sufficient detail to extract testimonies that bolstered their cases, and Price was adept at cross-examinations and closing arguments.[25]

During his prosecution of the liver heist, Price came to realize that I-35 between Oklahoma City and Ardmore was a popular corridor for theft of interstate shipments. "There were all kinds of gangs that would steal cargo of semi-trucks," recalled Price about his robbery prosecutions in the U.S. Attorney's Office. Price had barely settled into his job when a two-year FBI investigation culminated in the arrests of gang members charged with stealing a semi-trailer truck loaded with 50,000 pounds of steel plates, valued at $12,000, from a truck stop in Pauls Valley, between December 6 and 9, 1974. Two of the alleged thieves, Ted Almon Pigg and Freeman Morris "Corky" Wadley, were arrested in Pauls Valley and Paoli, respectively. Also charged in the crime were Lawrence Wigley, whose home had been used to offload the steel plates, and Bugs Buthurum, who had helped to offload the steel. As Buthurum was the only one who did not profit from the theft, he was acquitted. The gang's activities expanded to Lake Charles, Louisiana, where three more confederates—Wadley, Rufus Byrd, and the aforementioned witness in the liver heist, Mutt Mooney—were arrested. Under the stern gaze of the arresting officer, FBI agent Chick Dickie, Messrs. Wigley, Wadley, Pigg, and their coconspirators were handcuffed and jailed. In due course, they landed in Judge Thompson's courtroom for trial. Thompson could scarcely contain himself when Price announced the defendants' names in his opening statement. FBI agents in Oklahoma who sent requests to other districts, to prove that the shipment had crossed state lines, were convinced that someone was pulling their leg.

"Half of the law enforcement in southern Oklahoma was there to see me put away Byrd and Harold Moss Morris, who were the biggest fences in southern Oklahoma, and they were excited," recalled Price. Mutt Mooney got a severance from the other defendants, and Price got him convicted in a separate case. Mooney had been a witness on another interstate shipment case, saying something for the defense. "It was a whole gang of thieves," concluded Price. Following his closing argument in the case against most of the defendants, a clerk ushered him into another courtroom to deliver his opening statement in the Mooney trial. The Garvin County sheriff later told Price that, after the gang had been put out of business, crime in his county dropped 80 percent.[26]

Price chalked up a first when Bob Fitzpatrick, a veteran FBI agent who had earned accolades for participating in a takedown of the Detroit Mafia, moved to Oklahoma and dropped a grisly case of police brutality in his lap. "I had the first civil rights case tried in Oklahoma," said Price. The case went public on November 6, 1975, after a federal grand jury indicted Detective O. Ray Summers of the Oklahoma City Police Department on a charge of assaulting seventeen-year-old Dana W. Wiley for stealing a set of automobile tires. Filed in U.S. District Court in Oklahoma City, the indictment accused Summers of violating Wiley's constitutional right not to be deprived of liberty without due process of law.

Price winced as he explained what happened when Summers, a hefty 230 pounds and towering above the eighty-pound Wiley, arrested him after midnight and cuffed his hands behind his back.

"Where are the lug nuts for these tires, and where are the car keys?" Summers demanded.

Wiley, immobilized by handcuffs, struggled to pull the keys out of his pocket. His hands shaking, he dropped them to the ground, and Summers decided he had had enough. The prosecution later alleged that Summers shoved his hapless prisoner to the ground and, sporting a sturdy pair of cowboy boots, stomped on him until his spleen ruptured and pancreas split. "His pancreas was cut in half along his backbone," declared Price in disgust. "The blow was *so hard*." Summers's partner admitted, under questioning, that Wiley had never resisted arrest and had tried to cooperate, but to no avail. He further admitted that he had looked in the other direction as Summers meted out his punishment. Summers later claimed that he had slipped and fallen on the suspect.

As soon as Fitzpatrick handed him the case, Price knew two things: he could charge Summers with a federal civil rights violation, and the best he could hope for was a misdemeanor charge, as all such cases were tried as misdemeanors and carried a maximum penalty of a year in prison and a thousand-dollar fine, regardless of the extent of injuries, unless the victim died. Price knew he was in for a tough fight, as prosecutors found it all but impossible to secure convictions in civil rights cases. He had been presented dozens of civil rights cases in which FBI investigations had been based on allegations of excessive force against resisting felons. Price and FBI agents agreed that excessive force cases in which a suspect had attacked a police officer were highly questionable and should be declined. But Wiley's case was different. Summers had cuffed his hands behind his back, and he had posed no threat to the arresting officers. Although Price could have left Wiley's case to be handled by the Civil Rights Division in the U.S. Department of Justice, he was determined to send a message that police brutality would not be tolerated in his native state. Moreover, he knew it was the right thing to do, whatever the odds of conviction, and he knew that putting a local prosecutor in front of an Oklahoma jury would increase the chances of a successful outcome. Nevertheless, defense attorneys played the hometown card by referring to Price's cocounsel from the Civil Rights Division as a Washington lawyer who tried to tell Oklahomans how to treat criminals.

"It's one of the few cases I lost," said Price, still angered by Summers' acquittal when the evidence against him had been so compelling and his victim's injuries had been so severe. "What it was, the jury members said afterward, 'That kid got what he deserved for trying to steal tires.'" But that was not all. Throughout the investigation and trial, the police department and the Oklahoma County D.A.'s office closed ranks around Summers and effectively ostracized the FBI. "It was like they didn't want to cooperate with the FBI," continued Price. Before Summers's trial, Fitzpatrick actually caught grief from a few fellow FBI agents who had decided that defending Wiley was not worth the cost of losing the police department's collaboration in its crime-fighting mission. As Price concluded, "Contrast that to today, where police officers are almost *presumed* to be guilty of police brutality. Back then, it was really, the people that accused were ostracized." Until the day Bob Fitzpatrick died, Price seized every opportunity to extol the agent's bravery for trying to do the right thing.[27]

The variety of cases that assistants found so exhilarating continued with the case of Marvin Acree, a wealthy banker in Chickasha, whom Price described as "probably one of the worst people I have ever prosecuted."[28] A native of Jefferson County, Acree had begun his banking career at the age of fourteen in Ringling, the only town in southern Oklahoma named for a circus. His rather unfocused resume included chairmanship of the First National Bank of Blanchard, Oklahoma; employment as a national bank examiner throughout the Midwest; and owning and operating variety and auto parts stores, automobile and insurance agencies, a funeral home, a ranch, and an oil and gas business. Acree eventually founded his own company, Marvin Acree Investments, in Chickasha. He complemented his business career with leadership positions in civic and business organizations, and he was a member of the eponymous Marvin Acree Memorial United Methodist Church in Ringling, whose name bore witness to his extraordinary largesse. Yet Acree's generosity was not all that it seemed. Word on the street was that the church had acquired its name after a depositor in Acree's bank died and bequeathed part of her estate to build it. As Acree was in charge of her estate, he decided to name the church after (who else?) himself. Parishioners recalled Acree's warning to the pastor that keeping the collection plate in the church overnight put him at risk of theft. To ensure the safety of the church's collections, Acree deposited the cache in his bank and wrote a personal check to the church in the amount of the collections. Ever mindful of his tax liabilities, he deducted those checks on his taxes as charitable contributions. Meanwhile, Acree's wide-ranging career and substantial wealth afforded him ample opportunities to pack his Rolodex with names of politicians at the state and national levels.[29]

Acree was no stranger to the legal system. He had once been convicted of bank fraud in the Western District. To avoid prison, he had convinced Judge Daugherty that he was dying of cancer, a claim that proved to be false. His run-in with the U.S. Attorney's Office originated when he was incriminated in a heroin ring's scheme to bring stolen Cadillacs from Detroit to Chickasha, where Acree bought them at a steep discount. Aiding and abetting Acree's business activities was his African American mistress, Ida Brown, represented by Red Ivy, whose husband owned a funeral home and was only too happy to buy discounted Cadillacs, presumably at the cost of his wife's indiscretions. According to his Detroit-based driver, who turned state's evidence with the assistance of a hidden wire, Acree asked him to burn down his house, or perhaps find an arsonist in Detroit to do it, to collect the insurance. The driver later told investigators about Acree's incendiary plans.

Seeking to avoid implication in a murder plot, Acree's driver asked him when his wife would be home.

"I don't care if she goes!" shouted Acree. "If she burns up, it doesn't matter!"

The driver further claimed that his boss wanted him to find a hit man in Detroit to kill a former partner, with a yen for expensive jewelry, who was on a key man insurance policy listing Acree as the beneficiary. Upon hearing this, Price summoned the man to his office to warn him that his life was in danger. His fingers studded with flashy rings, the former partner was surprised to learn that Acree had been paying his insurance premiums long after they had dissolved their partnership. The plot fell through when Acree refused to pony up for a targeted killing that was more expensive than he had bargained for.

"He would feast on the black community," continued Price, about a man whose treachery extended to attending funerals for no other reason than to drum up business and breaking his promises not to foreclose on his customers' properties.[30]

In June 1976, the long arm of the law caught up with Acree and the Browns. Indicted on twelve counts of receiving and disposing of stolen automobiles through interstate commerce, the trio were tried and convicted in federal court. Documents indicating the origin and destination of their stolen cars, duly obtained with search warrants, revealed addresses in Michigan and Oklahoma.[31] Even their notorious attorney, Gene Stipe, was unable to convince a jury of their innocence. Unwilling to be fooled a second time by the wily Marvin Acree, Judge Daugherty sentenced the defendants to prison.

Price paused to reflect on his prosecution of Marvin Acree, someone who left his legacy in wrecked lives and damaged businesses and whose unsavory business practices resurfaced when he and Ida Brown were prosecuted for peddling drugs.

"He was just such an *evil* man,"[32] concluded Price.

The Marvin Acree story has long since faded from collective memory, except, perhaps, in Chickasha, where memories of his crime spree might still linger as a noxious episode in Grady County history, and in the U.S. Attorney's Office in Oklahoma City, where Price and his successors had access to file cabinets and digital records of noteworthy cases that have retained their instructional value. The same is true of other cases that wreaked havoc, grabbed headlines, and allowed lawyers and judges to gain valuable experience before fading into history.

But for the generation of jurists who came of age in the sixties and seventies, something new was in the wind. Run-of-the-mill crimes such as bank robberies, embezzlement, check kiting, and even Mafia-related activities had always ranked at the top of criminal investigations, and nobody expected them to go away anytime soon. But times were changing, and nowhere were these changes more apparent than in what was coming into focus as white-collar crime.

Old-fashioned mayhem and thievery, long since recognized as a cost of doing business in Oklahoma, were sharing the limelight with more sophisticated types of criminality that were broader in scope and harder to investigate and prosecute. At all levels of law enforcement, new strategies were called for and new technologies were needed to bring miscreants to justice. But better strategies and more effective crime-fighting tools would be largely ineffective without the fundamental reforms to state and county governance that activists in Oklahoma had been promoting for the better part of a century.

Coupled with the need to reform state laws, dating back to statehood, was the need to enhance prosecutors' ability to try cases.

"The structure of the prosecution laws makes more of a difference..."

Price took a moment to reflect on the Achilles heel of Oklahoma's legal system, which he confronted as a rookie assistant in the U.S. Attorney's Office and that would consume his energies as U.S. Attorney: prosecutorial laws aimed at protecting citizens from an overreaching government but whose effect was to stymie investigators and prosecutors trying to enforce the law.

"What I'm saying is, laws on the books don't matter near as much as the *structure* of prosecution," concluded Price.[33]

Price's crusade against corruption had barely begun, and already he was imagining ways to make things better for all Oklahomans. Although he had lots to learn, he was certain of one thing: in the absence of structural changes in both government and the courtroom, elected officials would forever be susceptible to corruption, and law enforcement would forever be stymied in its efforts not only to root out the rascals but also to reduce the temptations for would-be rascals to game the system.

CHAPTER EIGHT : *Assistant U.S. Attorney –*
Part Two

t was a considerably leaner and tanner David Hall, clad in the
inmate's khaki uniform, who greeted reporters on the eve
of his release from prison in Safford, Arizona. Flashing his
trademark smile, which had helped send him to the governor's
mansion in 1970, Hall declined to issue a formal statement.
But as the sun cast its late afternoon shadows across the desert on that
Sunday evening of May 21, 1978, the former governor was nothing
short of jubilant, clearly happy to be pushing a cart loaded with his
possessions from the prison that had been his home for a day short
of eighteen months. With his wife, Jo, by his side, Hall responded to
reporters by name and carried on his usual good-natured banter, all the
while counting down the minutes before he would walk through the
gates as a free man, at six o'clock the following morning.

One of the reporters asked Jo if she was excited about his impending
release.

"Oh, no," she replied with a smile.

Queried Monday morning about his post-prison plans, Hall
explained that he and Jo were headed for San Diego, where his family
had a home. Although his plans had yet to firm up, he had spent a
year and a half thinking about his next moves. After being convicted
on charges of bribery and extortion, losing his appeals in federal
court, suffering disbarment by the Oklahoma supreme court, and
being sentenced to three years in prison, David Hall had some serious
rebuilding ahead of him.[1]

As it turned out, trading the plains of Oklahoma for the sunny
climes of southern California was easier than changing his ways. Like
his supporters back home, Californians found Hall to be an energetic

and funny guy, always effusive in his praise for others and flattering to everyone who drifted into his orbit. "He's also deep in debt," declared an exposé in the *San Diego Union-Tribune* in May 1995, exactly seventeen years after he walked out of prison to begin rebuilding his life. "And so is his organization." That organization, the nonprofit San Diego Senior Olympics, was known nationwide for giving older athletes a chance to compete, and it was tailor-made for the genial promoter from Oklahoma. As the self-designated poster boy for senior athletics, Hall let it be known that he had shaved sixty pounds from his once-hefty frame.

Few of Hall's associates knew much about his shady reputation as governor. Better known in his new circles were his varied business interests, including oil deals in Oklahoma that went dry, a four-vehicle rental car company that collapsed, and a venture aimed at mitigating the effects of acid rain that, like puddles in the California desert, evaporated. Once-buoyant investors were left with nothing but worthless stock certificates and broken promises. Asked about his collection of failures, Hall gushed, "Oh, gosh, I can't tell you about them. There have been so many." En route to his most recent ignominy, Hall racked up about $300,000 in court judgments, and his checks kept "bouncing like a basketball."

"I never, ever intentionally tried to harm anybody," said Hall about his debts. "Every bit of the money that I took went into legitimate business and the fact is that those businesses weren't successful." Hoping to prevent the San Diego Senior Olympics from suffering the same fate as his other ventures, Hall led with his game face. "My forte is inspiring people to do more than they might otherwise do," he said. And then, perhaps with unwarranted enthusiasm, he continued: "When I got involved in this in 1992, it had a zero deficit. Now it's at $100,000."

To broaden its exposé, the *San Diego Union-Tribune* reached out to a few of Hall's fellow Oklahomans. "He's a nice fellow but he lives off his personality," said Tulsa attorney Don Dees, who once loaned Hall $14,000 to invest in a struggling furniture manufacturer in Tijuana.

The best Hall could do was repay $3,000; Dees knew better than to expect more. "He was a consummate politician," continued Dees, "a real likeable fellow, a real glad-hander, except he was completely and thoroughly dishonest." Tom Brett, a federal court judge who counted himself among Hall's lifelong acquaintances, thought he knew what was behind the ex-governor's string of bad debts: "Politicians are always going around with their hand out hitting up their friends and supporters. They do it with the mentality that their supporters will be paid with some kind of favor or another from their political favors bag."

Hall, unrepentant to the end, remained convinced that the San Diego Senior Olympics' signature event, the Senior Sports Festival, could turn its dismal financial picture around through the sizeable donations that he was sure were coming. Sam Cohen, who had founded the organization in 1988, was not so sure. "We kept asking for a budget and there never was a budget," declared Cohen with more than a trace of bitterness in his voice. "He put up pie-in-the-sky claims. You can't run a program like that."[2]

▶ ▶ ▶ ▶

In a retrospective published in January 1980, the *Oklahoma City Journal Record* characterized the rise and fall of David Hall as "one of Oklahoma's most traumatic political events of all time." A decade later, as the former governor was finding new opportunities to lose money and defraud his associates in southern California, former U.S. Attorney Bill Burkett chimed in with his own retrospective at a meeting of the International Credit Association of Oklahoma City. Of all the crimes that he had been called on to prosecute as the government's representative in western Oklahoma, none matched David Hall's trial, and it made 1974 a year never to be repeated.

"It was a most exciting and eventful year," said Burkett. Now that the Hall trial had long since faded from the headlines as well as collective memory, Burkett regaled his listeners with tales of a convoluted trail that began with tips supplied by the governor's secretaries and confessions from contractors who had accepted state money under the table and led to the secretary of state's undercover work for FBI agents.[3] What Burkett failed to mention in his lecture on the bad ole days was the other sensational trial of 1974—that of Treasury Secretary Leo Winters, who had played a shell game with the people's money and shown favoritism toward bankers willing to line his pockets with supposed campaign contributions. Winters's exoneration and subsequent reelection as treasury secretary set a new standard for fiduciary chicanery and gave subsequent prosecutors much to think about in their campaigns to root out corruption in public office.

Bill Price's retrospective began with a fishing story, and it came not from Hall's trial but from a related trial that was part of the IRS Hall investigation—that of Charles M. Montgomery, one of several businessmen implicated in the governor's money-making ventures, who remained subject to prosecution long after Hall's conviction. The Friday afternoon before Montgomery's trial was set to begin, in July 1977, Price learned that U.S. marshals had not served Sunny Jenkins, David Hall's fixer and a key witness for the prosecution, who was set to testify first thing Monday morning. Jenkins was thought to be at the Moose Head Lodge in Ontario, Canada, a fishing camp accessible only by hydroplane. By five o'clock Friday, a desperate Bill Price had located a U.S. State Department official with the authority to issue an international subpoena. But then Price had to figure out a way to serve it. And who do you ask to serve a subpoena in the wilds of eastern Canada? The Canadian Mounted Police, of course! Price managed to find a Mountie to serve the subpoena, and he in turn found the lodge, but not the witness—turned out he was fishing from his hydroplane in a remote section of the lake and was nowhere to be seen. So the Mountie nailed the subpoena to his cabin door and left the rest to fate.

"When he comes back from fishing, he gets the subpoena, and he flies back in time," said Price about a close call in the U.S. Attorney's Office. "That's moving heaven and earth! And he didn't know the trial was coming up."

Now that his witness was back from the wilderness, Price was ready to prosecute Charles Montgomery, owner of Montgomery & Associates Insurance Company in Oklahoma City. Montgomery stood accused, in U.S. District Judge Fred Daugherty's court, of dipping into his company's till to cover $30,000 of Hall's campaign expenses, claiming that amount as a business expense and deducting it on his federal tax returns. Montgomery's star character witness was none other than University of Oklahoma football coach Barry Switzer, who testified that he would go to the mat for his buddy Charles.

"Charlie is an honest person," declared Switzer under oath. "I'd stake my reputation on it." Although Switzer's football acumen was beyond reproach, Price had reason to doubt his character judgment. By claiming such a huge deduction back in 1971, Montgomery & Associates Insurance Company had paid a trifling $350 in federal taxes, thereby saving about $8,600. Montgomery insisted that the contributions had been legitimate business expenses and, moreover, that helping get Hall elected was his ticket to the governor's inner circle and a prerequisite to attracting business in Oklahoma and from other states.

But that was not the end of Montgomery's association with the governor. He testified that he continued to curry Hall's favor by joining several other investors in financing construction of an office building near the capitol. Governor Hall inflated the building's value by filling it with state employees before Montgomery and the favored owners sold it to an out-of-state investor at the inflated price. After Montgomery et al. pocketed their profits, those same employees could be relocated to another building owned by (no surprise here!) another of the governor's cronies.

Montgomery "tried a quasi-bribe defense, which is amazing," said Price about the defendant's unusual and, ultimately, unsuccessful strategy. In his closing arguments, Price accused Montgomery of having the audacity to buy influence from the new governor and the temerity to claim ignorance of what $30,000 had paid for. "The jury did not buy this defense," concluded Price. Convicted of tax fraud, Charles Montgomery joined David Hall's legion of supporters who had learned too late what their allegiance would cost them.

Reflecting on his experience in Hall's trial and the prosecution of Montgomery in a subsequent trial, Price described the extent of the ex-governor's corruption and what it taught him about the dark side of human nature. "Before he became governor, he was a D.A. in Tulsa, and he was honest," began Price about the ex-governor he had helped to put in prison. "And when he ran for governor the first time, his aide said he was honest. But there was something about..."

Price paused, as was his habit when he was searching for just the right words.

"He saw that money made a huge difference, and he could see the temptation of getting huge amounts of money, and what a difference it would make on his ability to win," said Price finally.

> And he changed completely, and he was willing to sell that office to the highest bidder. That does not speak well for a political system that can change a normally honest person, or previously honest person, into somebody totally corrupt and willing to sell the office to the highest bidder; to sell positions in office to contractors; to do anything to get the money to try to win political office. That's the tragedy that I saw in this thing. It not only destroys the public's faith in our Republic, but if unprosecuted, it can persuade otherwise honest candidates and businesspeople to decide that corruption is the only way they can compete and be successful.

Price's other takeaway from Hall's trial was the importance of consensual tapes in bringing miscreants to justice. "I think, without the ability to have consensual tapes, corruption in America would have never been caught," he said. Not for the first time, Price referred to *United States v. Hoffa*, the seminal U.S. Supreme Court decision, in 1970, against teamster boss Jimmy Hoffa, whose links to organized crime sent him to prison, in 1967, on the strength of evidence gleaned from consensual tapes. In its 5–4 decision, the court denied any expectation of privacy when someone records a conversation on audiotape. "People don't realize how *significant* that was," explained Price about a decision that revolutionized the way undercover investigations were conducted. "Obviously, you are displaying to that person what you're saying. It's not like you're wiretapping the conversation. One person is tape-recording the conversation, and you don't have an expectation of privacy with that individual."

As Price learned from his participation in the trial, Hall and his codefendants, Doc Taylor and Kevin Mooney, would never have been convicted without Secretary of State John Rogers's consensual tapes. "Sure, you can prosecute low-level crime without it," continued Price. "You can't prosecute high-level crime, or people that are important, and in important positions, without consensual tapes. If you can't do consensual wires, you can't *prosecute* political corruption!" What is more, when consensual tapes provide incriminating evidence in an investigation, they can help make the case for filing an affidavit to install wiretaps on phones, an expensive and time-consuming procedure that law enforcement agencies undertake only as a last resort and only when there is sufficient evidence to warrant it.[4]

What Price's fellow rookie in the U.S. Attorney's Office, Drew Neville, recalled most vividly was Governor Hall's need for coconspirators to carry out his fraudulent schemes. "Hall could not have gotten his plan done without Rogers," said Neville. "He couldn't have done it himself. So what you learn from it was that, if corruption is to survive, you have to have people in place to make it happen. Hall could not have operated without John Rogers." Nor could Neville or any of Bill Burkett's assistants, for that matter, have led or assisted in successful prosecutions without help from one another. Describing Bill Price, Susie Pritchett, and himself as "a band of brothers" whose youth and lack of experience put them at the lower end of the totem pole in the U.S. Attorney's Office, Neville spoke once again about the camaraderie that he had found so fulfilling throughout his year and a half as Bill Burkett's assistant.[5]

As David Hall was tried in U.S. District Judge Fred Daugherty's court, Ralph Thompson was not directly involved in the case. But, like everybody else in Oklahoma, he paid rapt attention. Like the Oklahoma supreme court scandal, which had been so formative in charting Thompson's career, David Hall's trial and the trail of deceptions that led to it revealed corruption in a coequal branch of government, which he found utterly abhorrent.

"Sadly, public corruption trials became very much a part of what the federal courts were called upon to handle," said Thompson with an unmistakable tone of sorrow in his voice.

"And why, exactly, were public corruption cases such as David Hall's tried in federal rather than state court?" I asked.

"Almost none of them [were tried] in the state system," explained Thompson, now sounding more like a jurist than a saddened citizen. "The federal government—the federal courts—are sufficiently independent of local politics, were completely independent of state politics."

"So who makes decisions with respect to jurisdiction?"

No doubt about it now. This was the jurist talking: "It depends on the facts of the case, whether the facts give federal government jurisdiction in each instance. That depends on the facts of the jurisdictional statutes, as applied to those facts. It could be mail fraud; it could be any number of things that implicate federal jurisdiction. It might not appear to at first blush. The public corruption cases didn't end with David Hall, but certainly occupied very much of Bill's career, and mine. They were in the federal realm."[6]

For a glimpse into the defense, we turn to Frank Keating, who was serving in the state legislature when he got word that one of David Hall's codefendants, Kevin Mooney, needed a lawyer.

"So I went down, and there was this guy, and he had on an orange jumpsuit," recalled Keating, then in his late twenties and only beginning to learn about the underbelly of Oklahoma politics. "As I recall, he had a diamond Rolex watch. In those days, you could keep stuff like that. He looked like a very prosperous guy!"

Introductions were duly made, and Keating settled in to get his prospective client's story.

"Why am I here?" asked Mooney. "Look, David Hall is my friend. David Hall told me he could have my company represent the teacher retirement fund. I pay finder's fees and bonuses for people who bring me business. And he brought me business. So what am I doing here?"

Summoning rhetorical skills that would one day propel him to the governor's office, Keating replied, "In the private sector, it's called a finder's fee or a bonus. In the public sector, it's called a bribe."

"Then I'm going to plead guilty, because that's what happened!" declared Mooney.

Kevin Mooney did indeed plead guilty, and his testimony helped put both of his friends, David Hall and the third member of the trio, Doc Taylor, in prison.

"That was my introduction to public corruption involving the governor, who went to prison," concluded Keating. "The rest is history."[7]

▸ ▸ ▸ ▸

David Hall's lesson in how not to run state government was still very much on people's minds when Tom Daxon, Bill Price's friend from Teen Age Republicans, started looking for an exit ramp from his accounting firm as mergers and acquisitions upended his industry. At the urging of Price and an older and wiser mentor, Herb Johnston, Daxon toyed with the idea of running for state office. Inspiration for a political career also came from Al Snipes, one-time chairman of the Oklahoma County Republicans who, along with Henry Bellmon and with tactical support from Teen Age Republicans, had breathed life into the state party in the 1960s. "I was kind of a protégé of Al Snipes," recalled Daxon with a trace of nostalgia.

Considering and then rejecting a campaign for state treasurer in the wake of the Leo Winters banking scandal (as Daxon put it, "I wanted to take out Leo—I really was kind of a big-game hunter . . ."), Daxon settled on the office of auditor and inspector as the most likely venue for someone with his background in accounting to instigate reforms. Knowing that former secretary of state John M. Rogers's father and longtime examiner and inspector John Rogers, Sr., had violated the people's trust during his tenure, Daxon overcame his worries that the position was too "nerdy," resigned from his accounting firm in Sand Springs, and tossed his hat into the political ring. Technically, a victory would make Daxon the state's first auditor and inspector, as the state legislature created the title in 1977 and set 1979 as the deadline for merging the office of auditor with that of examiner and inspector.

"I had a real simple campaign," recalled Daxon. "I would get up and say, 'My name is Tom Daxon. I am running for auditor-inspector. I am a CPA and would appreciate your support.'" Promising to run the auditor and inspector's office like a CPA firm, the thirty-year-old Daxon brought Rogers's twenty-year tenure to an end in the elections of 1978. What Daxon remembered most vividly about the campaign was his close shave in getting on the ballot. "I was the subject of a lawsuit," said Daxon. "They tried to kick me off the ballot because you have to be thirty-one years of age when you're elected. I turned thirty-one on December 19. The election was in November."

Fortunately for Daxon, both the Election Board and the Oklahoma supreme court looked favorably on his situation, and he sailed to victory, with a margin of 372,308 to 314,355 votes, to begin a four-year tenure as one of the state's youngest elected officials. He was also the first Republican elected to a secondary statewide office in Oklahoma who had not ridden in on somebody's coattails.

No doubt with the best of intentions, the outgoing examiner and inspector offered to ease Daxon's transition in any way he could. "If you want anyone on my staff, you're welcome to interview them," said the magnanimous Rogers. "I'd recommend them all." Daxon's appreciation turned to disappointment when he discovered how incompetent Rogers's staff was. "They didn't know what they were doing!" declared Daxon, still amazed, at a remove of four decades, at the fiasco he had inherited. "And I had promised I was going to run the office like a CPA

firm. I spent a lot of time trying to make a silk purse out of a sow's ear."
As he set about recruiting a staff he could actually work with, he came
to an epiphany: "You don't really have to be that good, as long as you
find really good people, and don't get in their way!"[8]

Halfway through his first year in office, Daxon began to receive
reports confirming his worst fears about shoddy recordkeeping in at
least a third of the state's seventy-seven counties and irregularities
that made his jaw drop. A common line in the audit reports read
simply, "The county does not now use a receiving report to document
receipt of materials and services." Auditors who fanned out across the
state, together with FBI agents who had begun their own probe into
county governance, searched in vain for records indicating that county
commissioners had purchased supplies through a competitive bidding
process. Open meeting laws were routinely violated, and evidence
began to surface that county commissioners were relying on sloppy
accounting methods to hide kickbacks and purchases of fictitious road
and bridge supplies.

"For all practical purposes, we had not audited county government
for 25 years," said Daxon. "What we did, was for the first time in the
history of the state, go out and audit counties in Oklahoma in the
same manner that a certified public accountant goes out and audits
a business." No sooner did audit reports land in Daxon's office than
he fired them off to district attorneys for review, all the while trusting
that his position as auditor and inspector would give him the leverage
he needed to get to the bottom of what was building into a scandal of
historic proportions.[9]

Daxon's discoveries and the FBI's suspicions came at the end of a
decade of protests that presented law enforcement with unprecedented
challenges, from the American Indian Movement's armed stand-off
with federal agents at Wounded Knee, South Dakota, to the left-wing
Symbionese Liberation Army's campaign of terror, dramatized by
the sensational kidnapping and subsequent enlistment of newspaper
heiress Patty Hearst into its antiracist and anticapitalist crusade.

Closer to home, rumors circulated that Oklahoma Senator Dewey Bartlett had been targeted for assassination for reasons long since lost to history. Less violent, but no less troublesome to law enforcement, were protesters who aimed to topple the U.S. government's financial underpinnings.

"The main ones were tax protesters," explained Price. "They were a little crazy!"[10]

Crazy or not, tax protesters in the 1970s were determined to reduce Benjamin Franklin's short list of inevitabilities, death and taxes, from two to one. Among those disgruntled taxpayers was Richard Davis, a twenty-seven-year-old grocer from Edmond, Oklahoma, who led seminars on the federal government's "oppressive, tyrannical, and unconstitutional" taxes. His organization, Tax Facts, was in the vanguard of a national movement to abolish them. "You can't fight the Internal Revenue Service on moral grounds and win," explained Davis to his eager listeners. "But you can do it on constitutional grounds and win 99 percent of the time." Although Davis's day job was in his family's grocery business, his passion was the U.S. Constitution, and he cited passages as glibly as he told his customers the price of his produce.

As Davis's listeners learned in his seminars, the IRS routinely violated citizens' Fourth Amendment right to be secure in their persons, houses, and papers and their Fifth Amendment right to due process and protection against self-incrimination. Like-minded confederates around the country called themselves by a variety of names ("patriots" and "constitutionalists" tended to crop up most often), and their numbers were growing exponentially as young and old, liberals and conservatives, and city folks and farmers railed not only against the way taxes were collected, but also how they were spent on everything from foreign aid and abortion to social programs, subsidies, and excessive regulations.

Pundits and politicos watched with deepening concern as the tax revolt spread, and many of them voiced concern that the nation's finances were entering uncharted territory. Columnist Jack Anderson estimated that fed-up taxpayers were joining the movement at the rate of two thousand per day. One-time U.S. secretary of the treasury William Simon went on record to report a drop in compliance with tax laws. "We are faced with an incipient taxpayers' revolt," warned the former secretary. Mike Kelly, Oklahoma's acting IRS director, preferred not to talk about it at all, perhaps for fear of fueling the resistance.

"In two or three years there will be a constitutional crisis," declared Richard Davis at one of his seminars. "This thing is mushrooming. When enough people realize their rights and stand up for them, the IRS system will collapse." Asked about his alternative to income taxes, Davis suggested that the government rely on a national sales tax combined with import duties.[II]

Bill Price came face-to-face with the tax revolt in the person of Thomas Erickson, a tax preparer in Anadarko, Oklahoma, whose acumen in unburdening clients from their taxes had gained him nationwide notoriety. "Erickson was really unique," said Price. "If you went there at three in the morning, there would be a line of hundreds of people. He was preparing taxes, and everybody that went into Erickson's ended up with a tax return that showed no taxes owed!" Unions and other organizations chartered buses that jostled for space with private citizens in the once-sleepy streets of Anadarko. On display were license plates from coast to coast and even Alaska.

"He had dozens of tax preparers," continued Price. "If you walked in, he would ask questions like, 'Do you fish or hunt?', 'Do you ever show anybody how to fish or hunt?', and 'Do you keep your gun or your fishing pole in your house?'" When clients answered in the affirmative, they were thrilled to learn that if they kept hunting or fishing equipment in their homes—*presto!* —tax bills went *poof,* as they could claim the value of their real estate as a deduction. And if they transported sporting equipment in their cars? Well, of course auto expenses were likewise exempt from taxes. On one occasion, Erickson told a client that simply carrying a shoe catalog in his car was enough to put him in the shoe business.

Aided by his wife, Aneta, Erickson must have known that, sooner or later, the IRS would come calling. Sure enough, the IRS ended its five-year investigation when agents swooped into Anadarko and shut down Erickson's office. Price, who was personally acquainted with IRS agents who had spent years on the case and had reached their wits' end, described a press interview that was captured on videotape and broadcast on the evening news: "Right after he's charged, he's trying to talk to the press, and his wife charges out. You see her charging from behind a glass door, pulling him in, and hollering at the top of her lungs, 'You idiot! Why are you talking to the press?' He's holding onto the door, trying to talk to the press as his wife drags him inside."[12]

In what was considered the largest tax-fraud scandal in Oklahoma and surely set national records, Assistant U.S. Attorney Price secured the Ericksons' conviction on forty-two criminal counts, alleging they had failed to pay their own taxes and had falsified tax returns for scores more. Even though their income had grown from $20,000 to $89,000 from 1976 to 1978, they had never bothered to file tax returns. Between 1976 and 1979, Erickson Tax Service completed tax returns for as many as five thousand clients whose savings in unpaid taxes ranged from $20,000 to $30,000 each. During the May 1980 trial, a psychiatrist took the stand on behalf of the defense to confirm that Erickson suffered from the delusion that federal tax laws were unconstitutional and that he and his staff were innocent of wrongdoing.

The Tenth Circuit Court of Appeals in Denver upheld the lower court's conviction, and the Ericksons, no doubt clinging to their constitutional delusions in a pique of righteous anger, appeared before U.S. District Judge Fred Daugherty for sentencing. Deeming Thomas Erickson to be a "danger to the community," Daugherty sentenced him to eleven years in prison and ordered him to pay a $27,000 fine. Aneta Erickson was sentenced to nine years in prison and was slapped with a slightly lower fine of $25,000. Thus began what were reputed to be the longest prison sentences ever handed down on tax charges.

"He had duped and hurt literally thousands of people," said Price in his postmortem of one of his most bizarre cases. "There were some civil IRS agents during those years who did nothing but audit tax returns prepared by Erickson."

Another tax scheme originated with disgruntled Oklahoma County taxpayers, who resented a recent countywide property reassessment that had caused a spike in property taxes. When they complained to the assessor's office, they were directed to L. O. Peak, a notorious bagman, or another shady "consultant" of his ilk who charged a fee to get their taxes lowered. Part of those payments were funneled to an official in the assessor's office, one of whom went so far as to set up a consulting firm to charge taxpayers for advice on how to lower their taxes. As there were no policies against moonlighting, Price gathered sufficient evidence to open what became a successful prosecution for violation of criminal tax codes.[13]

▶ ▶ ▶ ▶

Price's satisfaction in sending rascals to prison was tempered by tragedy in the summer of 1979 when his older brother, Bob, perished in a Scandinavian blizzard.

Bob's untimely end seems ripped from the pages of a Jack London novel. After his marriage to Gudbjorg and the birth of their children—a daughter, Siri, and a son, Eirik—the family spent as much time as they could in her native Norway, and there was nothing they enjoyed more than hiking through that majestic landscape. During what was supposed to be a routine hike, a freak storm blew in. Knowing he had to act fast to save his family, Bob scooped his children into his arms and carried them through frigid water to safety.

Gudbjorg and the children survived the ordeal. Bob did not.

"I would have been in my sophomore year in college," explained Bob's nephew and Montine's son, Steve Foerster. "I remember getting a call from Bill. He was calling my mother, and I happened to be at home, and I was leaving that day for Arizona State University in Tempe, Arizona. I could tell by his voice, something was wrong. He asked for my mother. She broke down crying. Her older brother had died on a hike of hypothermia."

Not surprisingly, it fell to Bill to deliver Bob's eulogy. In attendance at his funeral were Bill's family, Gudbjorg, Siri, and Eirik; their mother, Virginia; and their sisters, Montine and Kelsey. Depicting his late brother as supportive and kind, Bill told the story of a man who was always willing to fix a computer program at work, no matter what the hour, help his mother puzzle through problems in their family's oil and gas business, read his children to sleep, and lend a sympathetic ear to whoever needed it.

"Bob was always there," said his grieving brother. He went on to describe Bob as a person who personified and lived Christian ideals, whose highest priorities had always been with his family and his church, and who was surely at peace with God. "Never was there a man better prepared to meet his maker," said Bill. "The big brother who protected us as children continued to spiritually lead and protect us all as adults." At some point during their mourning, Gudbjorg told Virginia that she was fortunate to have had Bob for forty-two years, and she was fortunate to have had him for twelve.

Sympathy notes that arrived in the days and weeks after the accident told much the same story: "I've never heard Bob say an unkind word"; "I've never heard him say a jealous word"; "I've never heard him complain or even to be truly angry toward anyone." Virginia spoke for family and friends to declare that her son "was truly pure in heart."[14]

Bob's death weighed heavily on Bill's mind as he returned to work in the U.S. Attorney's Office. By the time of his brother's death, his skills as a prosecutor were earning him not only an increasing workload, but also accolades from his higher-ups as well as other law enforcement agencies. In 1976, he received a commendation from the director of the Federal Bureau of Investigation; in 1978, he received another one from the district director of the Internal Revenue Service; and for three consecutive years, 1977–1979, he was named as the Outstanding Assistant U.S. Attorney.[15]

Price's prosecutorial skills were tested as never before as Auditor and Inspector Tom Daxon's inquiries and simultaneous IRS and FBI probes began to raise serious concerns about business as usual in Oklahoma's seventy-seven counties. Only three years into his job as assistant U.S. Attorney for the Western District of Oklahoma, Price could not possibly have anticipated the scandal that would define his career, give his fellow Oklahomans one more reason to wonder about their susceptibility to corruption, and cause the rest of the nation to look askance at a state named for cheaters. Nor did the state's legion of county commissioners suspect that their once-tranquil offices would soon be upended and that their peculiar methods of paying for county improvements were about to reap the whirlwind.

CHAPTER NINE : *Okscam – The Investigation*

Tom Daxon was new to his job as auditor and inspector when, in early 1979, he was invited to deliver a speech to the Association of County Commissioners of Oklahoma. Before he took to the podium, the Pittsburg County commissioner—a beefy gentleman who would have passed for a bar bouncer ("a rough-as-the-Devil kind of guy," as Daxon put it)—gave him a terse introduction.

"Our next speaker is our state auditor and inspector, Tom Daxon. I want it understood that there will be no loud talking, or rude remarks, during his speech. If anybody feels otherwise, you can deal with me after the meeting!"

And with that, Daxon rose to deliver a speech whose contents have been lost to history but whose context provides a fitting prologue to a scandal that rocked county governance to its core.

"That, literally, was my introduction!" said Daxon about an incident that retained its shock value some four decades later. Deciding that humor might be the better part of valor, Daxon did his best to win over a room full of scowling county commissioners.

"Well, I guess, according to the introduction, somebody out there must have some rope!"

I was startled when Daxon banged on the table for emphasis and nearly sent my digital recorder tumbling to the floor.[1]

Moments passed. Then, calmer and clearly lost in memories, Daxon proceeded to tell me about his and his friend Bill Price's participation in the FBI's broadest investigation to date into political corruption: the Oklahoma county commissioner scandal. Known rather inelegantly as

Okscam (i.e., Oklahoma scam) and, alternately and equally inelegantly, as corcom (i.e., corrupt commissioners), the scandal consumed Daxon's single term as auditor and inspector, launched Bill Price to prominence as the state's star prosecutor, and etched itself into collective memory as one of Oklahoma's—and really, the nation's—deepest dives into systemic corruption on a grand scale.

▶ ▶ ▶ ▶

State Auditor and Inspector Tom Daxon was by no means the first to question the way counties governed themselves. In 1950, a statewide constitutional study committee had issued the dispiriting message that incompetent and even dishonest men remained in office.[2] Shortly after leaving office in 1955, Governor Johnston Murray seized an initiative that he would never have risked as the state's top executive in calling for a thorough review of county governance. During his career in public service, he had gathered plenty of reasons to be critical of the way county commissioners did their jobs. In allegations published in an April 1955 interview in the *Saturday Evening Post*, Murray told a sordid tale of elected officials whose spendthrift habits had practically forced them to shift their burdens to the state. Murray made special reference to the "county lobby"—a complex web of ideas and institutions that supported rural values and did not always align with the checks and balances that are supposed to underlie all levels of American government. Rooted in agriculture and barely a half century removed from the frontier, Oklahoma was a land divided between metropolitan centers of business and commerce (Oklahoma City and Tulsa, with Lawton coming in a distant third) and rural areas that resisted the seductive lure of modernity.[3]

Three years after the former governor's interview in the *Saturday Evening Post*, the Oklahoma state legislature released the Sandlin Report. Pieced together by a joint select committee, the Sandlin Report relied on public hearings and interviews with public officials and businesspeople to illuminate purchasing practices in the state's seventy-seven counties, each of which was staffed by three elected commissioners, who ruled like lords of independent fiefdoms over their allotted thirds. Its twenty-seven separate findings portrayed a system gone bad, and it was significant for two reasons: (1) it provided, in shocking detail, purchasing practices that had defied reform for decades and would continue to do so until the eruption of Okscam two decades hence; and (2) it revealed yet another instance of the legislature's failure to enact reforms, even though serious flaws in county governance were now exposed for all to see.

Stripped to its essentials, the Sandlin Report made the following allegations: county commissioners did not meet as boards, as they were supposed to; supplies often cost 20–25 percent more than their market price; competitive bidding laws were routinely flouted; some supplies were purchased but never delivered; county law enforcement was weak, ineffective, and seemingly impervious to the state auditor and examiner's recommendations; and money meant to build and maintain roads and bridges was often diverted to private property and charitable organizations. As the authors of the report concluded in no uncertain terms, "We believe that the system in its present form invites the unscrupulous to take advantage of it, and that too many times it has been a spawning ground for corruption and misuse of funds."

Right on cue, reform-minded Oklahomans chose the election of 1958—the same year that the Sandlin Report was released—to elect J. Howard Edmondson to succeed Raymond Gary as their sixteenth governor. Dubbed by Bill Price as "the John F. Kennedy of Oklahoma," Edmondson kicked off his term with his "Prairie Fire" campaign, a crusade aimed at bringing decades of reform initiatives to fruition. Included in his action-packed agenda were updating liquor laws to permit the sale of intoxicating spirits, creating a system of centralized purchasing, and installing a merit system in state hiring. Edmondson went so far as to tackle the thorny issue of reapportionment, thus unleashing a long-simmering battle between urban and rural interests that was probably doomed from day one. Incensed that Edmondson aimed to strip them of their power and vest more authority in the state, county commissioners swarmed the capitol and guaranteed that his stay in the governor's mansion would be limited to a single term. George Nigh, who was then serving as Edmondson's lieutenant governor, had a front-row seat at the unraveling of a promising career. As Nigh put it twenty years later, during his own term as Oklahoma's governor, "It caused his total administration to go down the tubes."[4] In the end, neither the Sandlin Report nor Governor Edmonson's reform agenda succeeded in bringing county governance in line with the needs of a robust and efficient economy and the protocols of accurate bookkeeping.

Edmondson's defeat, in 1962, served as a warning to would-be reformers to keep their hands off the counties. They pretty much complied, even though the Oklahoma Public Expenditures Council reported in 1964 that seventy-one of the state's seventy-seven counties routinely violated the state's purchasing laws. In 1972, that same group reported that most county commissioners paid 20 percent more for culvert pipe than highway contractors. Although these and other allegations never made it to the floor of the state legislature, lawmakers and administrators whispered about commissioners' unchecked power. Typically, a close-knit cadre of county officials that commissioners knew they could count on, known collectively as a courthouse clique, included the county sheriff, tax assessor, treasurer, and clerk—a formidable power bloc that legislators confronted at their peril.[5]

Business as usual prevailed more or less unbridled until the fateful year of 1978. That's when Mrs. Billy McCartey, a homemaker in Stephens County, became fed up with the dilapidated roads and bridges that endangered her children on their way to school. A bit of sleuthing revealed that county commissioners were purchasing lots of lumber but bridges remained in a dreadful state of disrepair. Much the same was true for roads that never seemed to benefit from the purchase of road-building materials. So Mrs. McCartey did what any concerned mother ought to do to keep her children safe: she spearheaded a petition drive to look into county purchasing.[6]

Mrs. McCartey's activism bore fruit when, on April 10, 1978, a Stephens County grand jury launched what became a two-month probe into county commissioners' purchasing practices. More than fifty witnesses were summoned to the county courthouse in Duncan, and members of the grand jury roamed the countryside to unravel the disconnect between mountains of expensive supplies and construction projects that never seemed to get done. Charles Muse, an auditor from the state auditor and examiner's office (soon to be the auditor and inspector's office), discovered that Stephens County was unable to account for about $1.9 million that was supposed to have been spent on infrastructure during the period of his audit. Muse reported the missing money and other deficiencies to the Oklahoma State Bureau of Investigation (OSBI), only to learn that his findings were being shuffled off to the same county commissioners who he was investigating! It did not take a great deal of imagination to suspect tolerance of Stephens County commissioners and maybe even collusion between them and officialdom in Oklahoma City.

The Stephens County grand jury ended its probe by charging two county commissioners with "gross neglect of duty," for failing to account for a million dollars, and four suppliers with fourteen counts of fraud. One of those suppliers, Don Skipworth, would soon gain notoriety in the federal probe that had yet to coalesce. As Stephens County officials launched ouster proceedings against its wayward commissioners and speculated on how to find honest suppliers, law-abiding citizens had reasons to celebrate: both the local grand jury and the auditor and examiner's office had done their jobs, and parents could stop worrying about their children's perilous trips to school.

And that's when things got squirrely. Much as the Sandlin Report and Governor Edmondson's attempts at reform had failed to gain traction, Stephens County law enforcement sputtered its way to irrelevance. First, the district attorney disqualified himself in the case against the four suppliers. Next, the district judge who was supposed to adjudicate the charges against them disqualified himself. But the real problem was the Stephens County grand jury's lack of jurisdiction over witnesses. As one county's grand jury was barred from requiring witnesses from other counties to testify, some wondered if it was not time to call in a state prosecutor.[7]

As accusations and recriminations reached fever pitch, the county's leading newspaper, the *Duncan Banner*, reported what most people had already figured out: nobody wanted to move the case forward. Little wonder that Charles Muse from the auditor and examiner's office decided to call in the big guns. In a replay of Oklahoma Attorney General Larry Derryberry's decision to share his investigation into Governor Hall's malfeasance with the U.S. Attorney's Office, Muse gave up on state investigators and turned to federal officials for help.

Sharing Muse's frustration was the newly elected head of the rebranded office of auditor and inspector, Tom Daxon, who hit the ground running in early 1979 with his own probe into county purchasing. His chilly reception from the Association of County Commissioners of Oklahoma, together with CPA-worthy audits that failed to exonerate a single commissioner, told him that troubles in Stephens County were only the tip of the iceberg. Thwarted by state laws prohibiting him from doing more than passing information to prosecutors and making recommendations, he, too, opted for the federal route.[8]

Daxon quickly discovered that his old buddy Bill Price was one step ahead of him.

► ► ► ►

Suspicions that Oklahoma's county commissioners were cooking the books arose at a time when the FBI was shifting attention from traditional street crimes to what had entered the lexicon as white-collar crimes—that is, nonviolent misconduct, ranging from embezzlement to tax fraud, that otherwise "respectable" people committed to improve their bottom lines. Watergate, culminating in President Nixon's resignation on August 9, 1974, stands out as the most obvious marker in a paradigm shift that sent FBI agents in pursuit of criminals in business suits. At the end of the decade came Abscam, an FBI sting operation that capped a two-year investigation and led to the convictions of six members of the U.S. House of Representatives, one senator, and dozens of prominent politicians and businessmen. The codename, Abscam, was a contraction of "Arab scam," as the initial complaints originated with the American-Arab Relations Committee. Initially aiming to track stolen property and unmask shady business dealings, the investigators set up an undercover company and broadened their operation into a probe of public corruption. Although the scandal paled in significance to Watergate in eroding Americans' confidence in their elected officials, it certainly gave the public one more reason to be skeptical of their elected leaders, and it justified law enforcement's increasing focus on white-collar crime.[9]

As political corruption fits rather neatly into the broad range of white-collar crime, the FBI responded to reports of stonewalling in county commissioners' offices across Oklahoma by launching its own investigation. The FBI found common cause with its counterpart in criminal tax complaints, the IRS, whose agents had their own reasons to look into county commissioners' alleged misappropriation of taxpayers' money.

Bill Price was working primarily in the economic crime and public corruption unit when his boss and Bill Burkett's successor, Larry Patton, told him to look into Stephens County's purchasing system. With a few years' experience in public corruption and criminal tax fraud under his belt, he knew something was amiss in Stephens County. But proving it was sure to be difficult. "Some crimes are easy to recognize, bank robberies for example," explained Price. "But the public rarely knows about business crimes." Often hidden in plain sight, crimes such as price-fixing and bribery wreaked more havoc in the public sphere than bank robberies and embezzlement put together. Most offensive to Price were the perpetrators—often wealthy and always well-connected criminals in business suits who invariably hurt the people who could least afford it. As a burgeoning expert in economic crime, Price knew that bringing them to justice was the only way to end systemic corruption. As Price put it, "We try to prosecute the high-level people so that we can bring down the whole organization."[10]

As Price suspected, something was not quite right in Stephens County. "There was enough lumber bought in one year in Stephens County to rebuild every bridge three times!" declared Price, whose conversations, in 1978, with then-auditor and -examiner John Rogers (whose son, former Secretary of State John Rogers, Jr., had resigned in disgrace following David Hall's trial and conviction), together with intelligence trickling in from the FBI and IRS, were about to put him at the red-hot center of Okscam.

Price had reason to be skeptical of Tom Daxon's predecessor, John Rogers, Sr. As Price explained, "the FBI didn't hold him in very high esteem." That was not the case with a much-younger Charles Muse, whose work on behalf of the auditor and examiner's office was beyond reproach. Price was, therefore, receptive when Muse suggested a meeting at FBI headquarters in 50 Penn Place, a high-rise in northwest Oklahoma City, for a briefing on the goings-on in Stephens County. Others summoned to the meeting included two representatives from the FBI: Jim Elroy, an extraordinarily innovative and dedicated agent; and Hank Gibbons, a highly respected general counsel and case agent whose judgment Price could count on. Price's inner circle would later include IRS agent Dale McDaniel, a sleuth with special skills in uncovering tax evasion.[11]

▶ ▶ ▶ ▶

"I am a Chicago boy," began Hank Gibbons in our 2019 interview, clearly proud of his roots in the Windy City. His Midwestern twang had somehow resisted four-plus decades in Oklahoma. En route to a juris doctor from the Kent College of Law, he had fallen under the influence of a professor who had worked as an FBI agent before opting for a career in academics. Wondering if that might be a career worth pursuing, Gibbons came across an article in the *Saturday Evening Post* about Hogan's Alley, an FBI training camp that specialized in marksmanship.[12] His mind swimming with visions of a career in law enforcement, Gibbons was more susceptible than most to the spate of 1950s television programs featuring swashbuckling FBI agents. So, when it came down to deciding between enlistment in the Navy and applying to the FBI, his decision was pretty much made.

"I chose the FBI," said Gibbons.

Following his graduation from the FBI Academy, in December 1969, Gibbons was assigned to the Kansas City office before landing in New Orleans. As he settled into his position as legal counsel in one of America's notoriously crime-ridden cities, the FBI was undergoing its historic shift from run-of-the-mill street crimes to white-collar crime. "Starting with the 1970s, white-collar corruption increased," said Gibbons. "We got into a lot of white-collar corruption. It just showed the shift at the FBI, going into bigger con schemes than check passing!"

At the same time, the agency was negotiating its way through U.S. Supreme Court decisions aiming to redirect law enforcement from adherence to complex and often conflicting state laws and criminal procedures to being guided by the U.S. Constitution. Gibbons cited two court cases in the 1960s whose effect on FBI policies and procedures had been profound. The first, *Mapp v. Ohio*, declared that evidence obtained in violation of the Fourth Amendment, which protects against "unreasonable searches and seizures," could not be used in criminal prosecutions in either state or federal courts.[13] The second and far better known decision, *Miranda v. Arizona*, held that both inculpatory and exculpatory statements made by a defendant in an interrogation could be admissible at trial only if (1) the defendant had been informed of his or her right to consult with an attorney, and (2) the defendant not only understood his or her rights, but had waived them voluntarily.[14]

"It was law enforcement by the federal Constitution, the Bill of Rights, versus the state constitution," explained Gibbons about the sea change in law enforcement. "It was a sweeping, sweeping change!"

As he delivered lectures and organized workshops to keep his fellow agents apprised of the shifting legal landscape, Gibbons came face-to-face with Louisiana's corruption, which rivaled machine politics in his native Chicago. Gibbons cited his adopted state's mantra—"Louisiana doesn't tolerate corruption; it demands it!"—to describe the hornet's nest that had become his jurisdiction. It was therefore an experienced and somewhat jaded Hank Gibbons who arrived at his next post in Oklahoma City in 1977—two years after State Treasurer Leo Winters had escaped conviction and Governor David Hall had not, and just before Okscam mushroomed from its spawning bed in Stephens County into a statewide imbroglio.

"The FBI was into trying to figure out corruption," continued Gibbons. "As an agency, corruption had come to the forefront." When he wasn't choking down food that was several notches below New Orleans standards, Gibbons was traversing Oklahoma, teaching workshops and delivering lectures, and trying to figure out his responsibilities as a case agent. Answers came in the person of Buck Revell, a native Oklahoman who had worked his way through the FBI hierarchy to become special agent in charge in Oklahoma City. One of Revell's first meetings at his new post was with Larry Patton, newly ensconced as U.S. Attorney, in March 1978, whose upbringing in Pottawatomie County had enlightened him to the ways of county government, and who was delighted to have an FBI agent in town who shared his commitment to tackle corruption head-on.[15] As Gibbons explained, Revell knew about prosecutions of county commissioners in Arkansas. "He wanted our office to attack it," said Gibbons. "He assigned an agent named Jim Elroy and me to develop the investigation here."[16]

And what better place to begin developing an investigation than in a meeting with Assistant U.S. Attorney Bill Price and Charles Muse from the auditor and examiner's office?

Anything could happen.

Something certainly did.

▶ ▶ ▶ ▶

While Abscam was rocking the nation's capital, the group assembled at 50 Penn Place was hatching a plan to uncover corruption closer to home. As far as an increasingly frustrated Jim Elroy was concerned, county commissioners' alleged pilfering was hidden in plain sight. During his investigation in Pottawatomie and Lincoln counties, complaints surfaced that a county commissioner had ordered steel that was never delivered. Gibbons explained what happened when Elroy joined other law enforcement officials in a visit to a county supply yard: "All of a sudden, the steel turns up, and the D.A.'s investigator goes out there and rolls the steel over, and the grass is still green under it!"[17]

Taking a cue from Abscam, Price and his collaborators decided to set up an undercover company to pose as a supplier of road- and bridge-building materials. As they soon discovered, setting up a sham company was no easy feat. Price put it this way, to explain his group's foray into clandestine work: "To get an undercover company done, you have to appear in Washington in front of twenty of the greatest experts on undercover companies, and spend a day being grilled on how you're going to run this undercover company."[18]

After a day of the requisite grilling in Washington, Price, Elroy, and Gibbons returned to Oklahoma City with authorization to proceed with their sting operation. Dubbed S&J Materials, their fake company was staffed by FBI agents whose purpose was to muscle their way into the supply business, earn a reputation as compliant partners in county construction projects, and solicit bribes from county commissioners. To convince prospective buyers that S&J Materials was a legitimate company, agents procured plastic cups and other promotional items, slapped a logo on them, and went on the prowl for commissioners on the take.

No sooner did S&J Materials open for business than Gibbons's task force started running into trouble. As Gibbons explained, "All the county commissioners figured out pretty soon that it wasn't a legit company."[19] Price described their fake company as "the fly in the ointment" insofar as it fueled suspicions that the FBI was closing in. Gibbons and Price further realized how difficult it was to insert a new company into a supply chain that had been in operation for decades. "Having a brand-new bunch of people coming into Oklahoma is not a good recipe for an undercover company," said Price about their initial attempt to bring county commissioners to justice. Moreover, the company's low bids on construction supplies had the unintended effect of infuriating county commissioners and suppliers who had no interest in paying low prices, as that would diminish whatever they could skim off the top. As Price explained, bids established a base price, and neither commissioners nor suppliers wanted anything to do with low prices, which diminished their profits.

On the bright side, S&J Materials was serving two important purposes, which eventually helped to crack the case: it created opportunities to gather intelligence on what was going on in the counties, and it served as a warning to miscreants that the FBI was onto them. "Taped confessions supplied by undercover participants in which they referred to S&J Materials as an FBI operation left no doubt about their criminality," concluded Price. No matter how clumsy its methods, S&J Materials sent an unmistakable message to county commissioners and their suppliers: "Hey, watch out for this undercover company! They've got to be FBI!"[20] Even though they knew they were under investigation, Okscam participants continued to arrange ten-percent deals, confident that nobody would catch them. Their only concession to caution was to curtail their far more flagrant thievery in purchasing nonexistent materials.

Price thus had much to think about as he worked through his to-do list. Among his responsibilities in the U.S. Attorney's Office was prosecuting abuses of the tax system that were often key to political corruption cases. Criminal tax cases would have been easier to prosecute with cooperation from the IRS, but they were rendered maddeningly difficult by the firewall (as Price described it, "a Chinese wall") that stood between the federal government's premier crime-fighting agencies: the Federal Bureau of Investigation and the Criminal Investigative Division (CID) of the Internal Revenue Service. The disconnect dated back to Watergate and President Nixon's effort to compel the IRS to launch criminal investigations of his enemies. As Price explained, "There became a brick wall between the IRS and the prosecutor. They became so afraid that, like, Nixon was trying to get the IRS to investigate people for tax, the IRS might be able to communicate to the U.S. Attorney's Office." Not for the first time, Price complained about the time required to push criminal tax cases through the system: "They go through local, regional, and federal reviews. Then, finally, they land at the U.S. Attorney's Office." The cases sometimes arrived in the U.S. Attorney's Office after a five- or six-year review process and six months before the statute of limitations was set to expire.

Stymied by S&J Materials' failure to crack the county commissioner case and frustrated by his inability to coordinate investigations between his office, the FBI, and the IRS, Price was somewhat relieved when Larry Patton asked him to fill in for Susie Pritchett and look into a case of old-fashioned arson near Britton Road in northwest Oklahoma City, where a restaurant owner was suspecting of torching his building to collect insurance. "That's usually the suspicion," explained Price, whose range of responsibilities extended to arson only when Patton needed him to substitute for Pritchett. He arrived at the site to encounter a swarm of policemen, firemen, and agents from the IRS, the FBI, and the Bureau of Alcohol, Tobacco, Firearms, and Explosives (ATF). Hobnobbing with his friends in the various agencies and departments and looking for signs of arson, Price was only half listening when an agent he had never met from the IRS's Criminal Investigative Unit (CID), Paul Elledge, bent his ear about an all-too-familiar case: Erickson Tax Service of Anadarko, a case that had just been approved for prosecution.

Price perked up when Elledge dropped a recognizable and somewhat unusual name, Opal, as he recalled a woman by that name who had worked in the Ericksons' tax-fraud factory. Price's radar went on high alert when Elledge blurted out her last name: Hester.

"Paul, are you talking about Opal Hester, one of the materials suppliers in Stephens County?" asked an incredulous Bill Price.

"No, no, Bill. I meant Gibson—Opal Gibson. I don't know why I said Hester."

But Price knew. Elledge had simply misspoken, and his gaffe took Price's breath away.

"The woman he was referring to in the tax case was Opal Gibson, not Opal Hester," explained Price about a casual remark that had the potential to break the county commissioner case wide open. Opal Hester was an unusual name, and it happened to be the name of a corrupt supplier in Oklahoma City with direct ties to Stephens County.

Assigned to substitute for Susie Pritchett in a run-of-the-mill case of suspected arson, Price had blundered into proof that the IRS was investigating wrongdoing in Stephens County. Elledge later told Price that the IRS had been preparing to close its county commissioner investigation when Providence intervened in the unlikely form of a burned-out restaurant. Elledge's face lit up when Price promised "to move heaven and earth" to convince the U.S. Attorney General to designate a joint grand-jury investigation.

Price was on cloud nine when he strode into the office the next morning. Pulling Pritchett aside, he told her all about his conversation with Paul Elledge and his unintended tip-off that the IRS knew more about county commissioners that it had heretofore divulged.

Price knew something else: as one of thirteen suppliers who had been implicated in the Stephens County probe, Opal Hester surely knew another woman whose name came up time and again in discussions about county purchasing practices.

Her name was Dorothy Griffin.[21]

▶ ▶ ▶ ▶

Standing a fraction above five feet and weighing in at two hundred pounds, Dorothy Griffin seemed an unlikely conduit to white-collar crime. But if appearances can be deceiving, then she was surely a master (mistress?) of deception. As Price was soon to learn, this unassuming woman, with a fondness for billowing Hawaiian muumuus, was his entrée into a goldmine of incriminating evidence.

Dorothy Griffin, who had started selling lumber and supplies from the back of her hay wagon in 1963, was the sole proprietor of Griffin Lumber Company near Farris in Atoka County, some 130 miles east of Stephens County, where much of her business originated. Her location in the forested hills of southeastern Oklahoma made her an ideal supplier of lumber for county commissioners, who were always on the prowl for building materials. Upon closer inspection, those commissioners might have been surprised by the modesty of her operation. As FBI agent Jim Elroy once quipped, "On a good day, they couldn't make a set of toothpicks."[22]

Like so many people in her part of the state, Griffin was poor, and her precarious grip on solvency had taken a turn for the worse when her husband's health went into decline. As her medical bills piled up and 'round-the-clock caretaking threatened to put her out of business, she was receptive when a supplier to county commissioners throughout the state, including Stephens County, suggested a scheme that might be far more lucrative than routine lumber sales and, in the process, dovetail with their own interests. "All these bills were stacking up," explained Griffin about her slide to the dark side. "We're just poor country folks. We didn't know what we were getting into. But ignorance is no excuse."[23]

Thanks to the intelligence they were gathering through S&J Materials, Price and his corroborators were learning, in sobering detail, exactly how Stephens County commissioners—and, presumably, their peers across the state—conducted their affairs and why they needed people like Griffin to help. The most common form of corruption involved 10-percent kickbacks, known in commissioners' rather uninspired lexicon as "ten percents." Generally, commissioners ordered supplies such as timber, gravel, and sand from suppliers who agreed to return—that is, kick back—part of the cost. If the supplies were indeed delivered (which was not always the case—see below), the kickback was 10 percent. To cover the cost of kickbacks, suppliers simply jacked up their prices. Those jacked-up prices were listed on price-and-bid lists that suppliers provided to their customers. According to age-old custom, suppliers' bids never determined who got the sale; they merely set prices. And, of course, there was no incentive to bid low. All that did was make everybody mad and reduce profits.

Ten percents were low risk, and oversight was minimal. Moreover, at this lower level of sleaze, someone with Dorothy Griffin's business acumen did not have to be part of the picture, although the money she gave suppliers from her cashed checks enabled them to hand over 10 percent to commissioners and pay for nonexistent materials. In fact, if it were not for systemic corruption, suppliers would not have to be involved at all, as commissioners could just as easily order supplies directly from wholesalers and bypass middlemen altogether. Most suppliers did not even go to the trouble of maintaining yards and transporting materials. They simply traveled around the state to deliver kickbacks and conducted their business with wholesalers by phone. But bypassing middlemen would have jeopardized a lucrative source of income that many commissioners came to recognize as part of their compensation for conducting the county's business. What is more, it did not take much entrepreneurial savvy for commissioners to boost their income even more by purchasing materials of inferior quality, as shoddy construction opened up more opportunities to purchase supplies and rake in kickbacks.

Far higher on the sleaze meter was the second most common form of corruption—50-50s, known more lyrically to insiders as blue-sky deals. Here is where Dorothy Griffin and her ilk rendered their services. Whereas ten percents depended on supplies that were actually delivered, blue-sky deals depended on supplies *not* being delivered. In these transactions, suppliers split the purchase price of nonexistent materials with commissioners on a fifty-fifty basis. Visibly embarrassed, Price borrowed a line from suppliers' vernacular to quote a taped conversation in which a commissioner asked a supplier to define blue-sky deals. Without a trace of subtlety, the supplier responded, "You get fifty percent, I get fifty percent, and the county gets F-U-C-K-E-D!"

Blue-sky deals tested commissioners' ingenuity on two levels. First, commissioners needed proof that whatever they had purchased actually existed. To solve this problem, they and their suppliers hit on the ingenious idea of arranging a minor sale—say, a box of nails—and finding someone in the supply yard to sign the delivery ticket. Before sending it to the county clerk for payment, the commissioner would tack on a few thousand dollars' worth of nonexistent materials, knowing that whoever had signed the ticket would never recall the details of such a trivial delivery. And *presto*—instant documentation! But then how to account for materials that had never existed? That problem, too, called for ingenuity. Commissioners solved it by confining their orders to gravel, lumber, tinhorn, sand, and other expendables that were difficult to trace. Upon questioning, they could plausibly claim that the materials had been put to good use, perhaps to pave a stretch of highway or shore up a bridge.

Blue-sky deals presented suppliers with a different set of problems. If a supplier was paying a commissioner 50 percent in cash and receiving a check from the county for the full amount of the invoice, on which taxes were owed, there was no profit, particularly when tax rates were close to 50 percent. And what was the supplier supposed to do when an officer of the law, or perhaps a grand jury, came snooping around and asked where his materials came from?

The solution to both problems arrived in the person of Dorothy Griffin. Typically, a supplier met with her, maybe once a month, to tally up invoices for nonexistent materials that commissioners had purchased. Griffin's part of the deal was to prepare matching invoices to make it look as though the materials existed. The supplier then wrote a check to her for 90 percent of the quoted price, leaving her to cash the check and return 90 percent in cash. As the reward for preparing the phony invoices, Griffin kept 10 percent. The supplier could then claim a tax deduction for the cost of goods sold and pay taxes only on the supposed profit. Invoices and cashed checks were all they needed to prove their innocence to pesky investigators.

Unlike ten percents, blue-sky deals could not be dismissed as benign forms of extra income generation that injured nobody. Adept in the art of denial, many commissioners who routinely accepted 10-percent kickbacks insisted that their counties had not been cheated in the least, as materials had been bought and paid for at the established (albeit inflated) prices. Suppliers made sure to tell the tiny minority of commissioners who would not accept kickbacks that they would not reduce their prices for the tiny minority who refused to accept kickbacks. Such was not the case with blue-sky deals, an insidious form of corruption and the hardest to rationalize. The miscreants knew exactly what they were doing, and even the glibbest among them could not excuse their behavior as a time-honored way of doing business. As one lawyer remarked, commissioners and suppliers who engaged in this level of corruption were nothing short of "scumbags."

The third form of corruption involved leasing and purchasing heavy road equipment, such as road graders, rock crushers, and bulldozers. Understandably, these transactions were less frequent than ten percents and blue-sky deals. Really, how many road graders, rock crushers, and bulldozers did a commissioner need for his or, less likely but certainly possible, her third of the county? But when it came time to beef up the county's inventory of heavy equipment, commissioners took the initiative to negotiate prices with their suppliers that included—you guessed it!—negotiated kickbacks. As with ten percents, suppliers raised their prices to cover the requisite payments. Although commissioners deluded themselves about counties' losses resulting from ten percents, they knew perfectly well that heavy-equipment kickbacks inflated prices paid by the counties. Whenever suppliers sold used equipment, they added kickbacks. No kickbacks were paid on new equipment unless commissioners demanded it. In those cases, prices were inflated to cover kickbacks.

Price never thought that all types of corruption were equal. In his sliding scale, the worst offenders were commissioners and suppliers who split their commissions on nonexistent materials on a fifty-fifty basis. The second worst were commissioners who extorted money from suppliers in the form of kickbacks on heavy equipment. But no matter where it landed on Price's sliding scale of culpability, each form of fraud cost the state untold millions in lost revenue and, in some instances, put public safety at risk. In Price's estimation, ten percents and blue-sky deals caused counties to lose 40 and a 100 percent, respectively, on every transaction; extortions on heavy-equipment deals deprived counties of the amount of the kickbacks and, in some cases, caused the purchase of unneeded equipment. As Okscam hit its stride in 1980 and 1981, estimating Oklahoma's lost revenue became something of a cottage industry. But there was no way to estimate the havoc wreaked by potholes and unsafe bridges and, perhaps most troubling of all, the erosion of values in a system steeped in corruption.

So when and how did county purchasing go so far off the rails? The fact is, nobody knows for sure, although some suggested the transitional period between territorial status and statehood (that is, around 1907) as the crucible of county-level corruption. After all, Oklahomans were still grappling with the effects of Soonerism, theft of Indian land was rampant, and the up-and-coming "ole bidness" was offering unlimited opportunities for creative financing. So why not creativity in county purchasing? Fast forward to the Stephens County investigation in the late 1970s, and you have second-, third-, and maybe even fourth-generation Oklahomans who stepped into their positions to discover purchasing practices that their predecessors had long since accepted as normal. Those who wanted to keep their jobs—that is, pretty much all of them—simply learned how things were done and proceeded to keep the game going, never suspecting that the end was in sight.[24]

▶ ▶ ▶ ▶

Price knew that Dorothy Griffin was not a hardened criminal. Nefarious as her activities had been, she was really just a poor country woman struggling to keep her husband alive. And now that her lumber business was on the skids, she might be persuaded to switch teams and help the U.S. Attorney's Office gather evidence against county commissioners and their suppliers. In investigative shorthand, Griffin had the potential to be "turned."

As he contemplated what to do with his potential undercover agent, Price counted himself fortunate, as he did not have to put up with Oklahoma's jurisdictional restrictions. Even if the Stephens County district attorney had been a dedicated anticorruption crusader, he would have gotten nowhere as long as grand-jury investigations stopped at the county line. Besides, the ubiquitous Gene Stipe had already quashed Griffin's grand-jury subpoena in Stephens County. If the subpoena had been enforced, she could have invoked her Fifth Amendment right to protection against self-incrimination. In the absence of a statewide grand jury, the district attorney would have been unable to prosecute her for tax evasion. By contrast, federal investigators and prosecutors had free rein to leverage testimonies in Stephens County, Atoka County, where Griffin lived, or anywhere else in the state's three federal districts.[25] As G. T. Blankenship had explained ad infinitum during his 1966 campaign for attorney general, the absence of multicounty grand juries had always been state prosecutors' biggest roadblock in bringing high-level criminals to justice. Little did Blankenship's youthful bus driver suspect that he would one day grapple with the shortcomings of Oklahoma's single-county grand-jury system. Nor did he suspect that he would ever be in a position to do something about it.

The first order of business was to acquire tangible evidence of Griffin's subterfuge in supplying Stephens County's thirteen suppliers with phony invoices. IRS Criminal Investigation Division Agents Paul Elledge, Howard Turner, and Dale McDaniel went to Atoka County, on February 7, 1980, to confront Griffin with the evidence they were gathering against her, including her tax returns and a fistful of her canceled checks.[26] Price's plan was to supply IRS agents with copies of Griffin's canceled checks that the FBI had discovered all over Oklahoma. If Griffin's tax returns did not match the canceled checks, Price was sure he could convince the U.S. Attorney General to launch a joint grand-jury investigation.

One imagines Griffin's jaw dropping when she opened the door to her trailer home to confront three frustrated IRS agents who had been trailing her for months.

Then came the tears—lots of them.

The agents waited for Griffin to regain her composure before trudging behind her through the snow to her lumber barn, where she proceeded to dig up a cache of phony invoices, stuffed in garbage bags, worth about $1.6 million. As Price explained, "The reason why she buried them is she was afraid of being burned out by the suppliers, and to hide the evidence. It was kind of an insurance policy."

With her garbage bags in tow, Griffin was taken to a Holiday Inn in Midwest City, where Elledge, Turner, and McDaniel, now joined by Special Agent Thomas C. Kemp, subjected her to a series of interviews on February 8th and 9th.[27] Satisfied that they had uncovered a goldmine of incriminating evidence against suppliers, the agents hastened to a meeting in U.S. Attorney Larry Patton's office. Others in attendance at that meeting, held on a Saturday morning to signal its importance, included Bill Price and FBI agents Hank Gibbons and Jim Elroy. No sooner did Patton close his door than everyone in attendance (except, perhaps, a sullen Dorothy Griffin) realized they had a problem. "It was so strange," recalled Price. "The IRS couldn't give the documents to the FBI or the U.S. Attorney's Office because of the law." To breach the firewall between the agencies, the IRS agents returned the invoices to Griffin, and she in turn handed them to Price and the FBI agents. After photocopying the invoices, they handed the originals back to the IRS agents, who were also present. "That way, we complied with the law," said Price triumphantly. "The IRS didn't turn it over to us."

Standing before her accusers in Patton's office, there was nothing Griffin could do but admit her crimes, agree to plead guilty to charges of conspiracy to commit mail fraud and tax evasion (charges that most cooperating witnesses agreed to plead to), and turn state's evidence against Stephens County's suppliers. If anyone doubted the veracity of her story, all they had to do was consult her diary. As Price put it, about this particular stroke of good luck, "She had written a diary saying how guilty she was, and how remorseful she was. That was incredibly good evidence that her testimony wasn't just made up!" On April 2, 1980, FBI Special Agent Hank Gibbons and Griffin affixed their signatures to an agreement to signal the beginning of her new career as an informant.[28]

The next step was to designate a joint grand-jury investigation that would enable the FBI and the IRS to cooperate in an investigation outside the confines of a single county. At the time, only two people in the federal hierarchy had the authority to make this happen: the U.S. Attorney General and his deputy. Under the auspices of a joint grand jury, the IRS and FBI would be able to circumvent firewalls and a tangle of red tape and, potentially, shave years off their investigation.

Already designated to spearhead the investigation as soon as a joint grand-jury probe was approved, Price got busy comparing Griffin's invoices, her tax returns, and the checks that she had cashed. The FBI had long since discovered that she had visited banks throughout southeastern Oklahoma, cashing multiple checks under the reporting limit of $10,000 each, and likely kept 10 percent for herself with nary a thought to withholding enough to pay taxes. "She has to have cheated on her taxes," said Price. "These checks from various suppliers are always turned into cash!" On a larger stage, he was about to summon the tools he needed to enable his office, the FBI, and the IRS to collaborate in a joint grand-jury investigation to gather the evidence they needed to launch the most comprehensive series of prosecutions ever conducted in Oklahoma. None suspected the magnitude of the public corruption scandal they were about to unravel. As Price put it, "It is certainly the largest investigation of political corruption, in terms of sheer numbers, in the nation's history."

Before sending Griffin into the field with a tape recorder to gather evidence of criminal activity, investigators needed to give her a plausible reason to talk with her former coconspirators, as everyone knew by then that she was out of the phony-backup-invoice-supply business. "If she just pops out of the blue, and wants to talk to these people, that's going to be ridiculously suspicious," explained Price. "How in the world do we utilize this woman? Because they have dropped her like a hot potato for two years!" Their challenge was compounded when they learned that Stephens County suppliers had gotten wind of the Griffin investigation and ponied up a thousand dollars each to hire Gene Stipe to represent her in the Stephens County case that would surely lead to their doorsteps.

The story Price and his confederates devised was that the IRS had opened a civil case—as opposed to a criminal case, which would have scared suppliers off—and discovered the checks she had been cashing. As those checks did not quite match the income reported on her tax returns, the IRS sent her a tax bill for slightly less than $13,000— exactly the sum that suppliers had raised to hire Gene Stipe as her counsel. IRS agents went so far as to create a phony civil tax bill and prepare a formal letter for suppliers to inspect. The story made sense, as Griffin clearly needed help, and where better to turn than to the suppliers on whose behalf she had prepared a million and a half dollars' worth of phony invoices?

"That was a perfect excuse for her to go back to the suppliers with," explained Price. "It made a good story. It gave her a reason to go back and talk to these people."

Equipped with a plausible reason to contact her former customers, Griffin went to work. A female FBI agent, Melanie Beum, was assigned to travel with her to make sure she was properly wired. Meanwhile, Victor Hamilton was back in the office trying to tie Griffin's invoices to the ones investigators had discovered in the counties. Among her successes as an informant was convincing all thirteen Stephens County suppliers to pay their portions of her taxes. "It made for great conversations on tape," said Price about an early victory in Okscam. She told them that, since they got nearly half, the commissioners got half, and she got only 10 percent, it was not fair to stick her with the entire tax bill. The suppliers either agreed or remained silent, and silence constitutes legal consent. So we got them all tied in. They all paid her tax bill. That's a pretty good indication of guilt![29]

▶ ▶ ▶ ▶

With Dorothy Griffin in their camp as an informant, Price and his collaborators geared up for the avalanche of prosecutions that was surely coming. As he pondered the ten percents, blue-sky deals, and kickbacks from purchasing and leasing heavy equipment, he obsessed over the sixty-four-dollar question that everyone was asking: Why?

With the benefit of hindsight and untold hours in the company of corrupt officials—and, much later, with their tape-recorded confessions—Price offered and then refuted five rationalizations, all shaded in gray and mostly overlapping, that county commissioners used to explain their pilfering of the public till.

First, commissioners thought that they were underpaid—that is, their salaries failed to reflect the difficulty of the job they had been elected to perform. But if that were true, why were the highest paid commissioners, particularly those in Oklahoma County, some of the most corrupt?

Second, kickbacks were an open secret. They had been flowing for generations and would no doubt continue to flow to generations of commissioners yet unborn. But if kickbacks were such an open secret, why were commissioners so guarded about it? There were never any witnesses, and commissioners were loath to testify against one another, even if they worked in the same county.

Third, kickbacks were part of their salaries. In fact, a glance at its etymological roots showed that their profession was so designated because they were entitled to *commissions* when they purchased supplies and construction materials on behalf of their grateful constituents. This might have been the easiest rationale to refute, as commissioners had sworn under oath to refuse payments for anything of value and to rely solely on their salaries. Kickbacks were not part of the oath they had sworn to uphold.

Fourth, many commissioners routinely dug into their own pockets to help constituents in need. In light of their generosity, it was only fitting for them to get it back, plus a little. But for the most part, their small subsidies were meant to keep them in office by making voters happy. Besides, the money they gave away paled in comparison to the kickbacks they received.

Finally, refusing to accept kickbacks served nobody's interests and made nary a dent in county budgets. True, blue-sky deals defied rationalization. No amount of linguistic parsing could explain them away, and the money commissioners received on heavy-equipment deals clearly inflated costs to counties. But as suppliers explained, prices on ten percents were already factored into the cost of kickbacks, so why should commissioners refuse their rightful cut of the action?[30]

Maybe, because they were stealing. As Price explained, with a nod to the state's history of corruption, "A majority of the purchases made in the state of Oklahoma, probably since statehood, did not exist! That means that untold billions of dollars did not go into the roads and bridges of Oklahoma, but rather went into the pockets of suppliers and commissioners. The ten percents that actually *did* exist cost the counties in aggregate and the state about forty percent in higher prices."[31]

In short, no matter how deftly they rationalized their methods of income augmentation, county commissioners were not engaged in victimless crimes. Price actually thought of some of them as victims, as many had come into office as honest public servants and allowed others, by example and through persuasion, to corrupt their souls. Like all white-collar criminals, if county commissioners were left to conduct business as usual, otherwise honest people might decide to seek similar opportunities to game the system without suffering the consequences. As Price insisted time and again, failing to prosecute white-collar crime creates an environment in which only the strong in character can resist temptation.

The main victim in Okscam, of course, was the broader public, not only in terms of squandered money and deteriorating infrastructure, but also in the erosion of faith in government. The very constituents whom county commissioners championed paid for their malfeasance whenever they navigated between potholes and rumbled across unsafe bridges. Sometimes they made it to their destinations without incident. And sometimes they never arrived at all, never realizing, or perhaps not caring, that the taxes they paid to support county infrastructure were disappearing into a neighbor's pocket. Taxpayers might not have known the sordid backstory to county corruption, and law enforcement might have been stymied in its efforts to investigate and prosecute. But everyone knew, or at least suspected, that county governments were rotten at their core. Erosion of faith in institutions has brought down civilizations throughout history. Absent vigorous law enforcement, there was no reason to assume that America would escape their fate.

Such were the late-night musings that put the fire in Bill Price's belly to gather enough evidence to make the transition from investigation to the next phase of the inquiry: prosecuting the offenders.

CHAPTER TEN : *Okscam – Pleas and Convictions*

C aught red-handed with canceled checks that led straight to her bags of phony invoices, there was little a teary-eyed Dorothy Griffin could do but agree to turn state's evidence against other suppliers and the county commissioners who had bought their materials. Next on Price's agenda was to give her a reason to approach suppliers she had not seen in a couple of years and try to make them say something incriminating. The story that Price and his confederates cooked up—that Griffin's check-cashing sprees had failed to register on her tax returns, and she needed help to make good on her back taxes— seemed like an ideal narrative. As Price recalled, "That was the whole key to it!"

The more Price got to know Dorothy Griffin, the more he realized that her outward appearance and dearth of education were camouflage for two traits with the potential to break the case wide open: an incisive intellect and a flair for the thespian arts. "She was a pretty good actress," continued Price. "We would coach her, especially in the office where she was phone calling. We had all kinds of contingencies." Among those contingencies were instructions to let it slip that she kept a diary and had entrusted it to her sister. If things turned ugly, Griffin's sister had been told to turn it over to the FBI.

In the absence of clear links between Griffin's cashed checks from suppliers and the phony invoices she had prepared for them, the most egregious crime that Price could bring against her accomplices was tax evasion. What he really wanted was proof of public corruption, and that could be obtained only if he could complement tax evasion with mail fraud, a crime that was committed every time someone dropped a bogus check or invoice in the mail.

What Price was referring to was the Mail Fraud Act of 1872, in which Congress put state and federal officials on notice: from now on, using the U.S. mail to advance "any scheme or artifice to defraud" is a criminal offense. In 1927, the Mail Fraud Act was broadened to criminalize the theft of honest services from a guileless public. In the ensuing years, mail fraud became the statute of choice for prosecuting self-dealing officials who used their positions for personal gain and to advance their interests. Although defense attorneys objected to the extreme latitude afforded by the mail-fraud statute (if the public was not adversely affected, how could there be a crime?), most courts held that defendants acted illegally by withholding the loyal and faithful services that their positions required. As the Ninth Circuit Court explained in 1975, "When a public official is bribed, he is paid for making a decision while purporting to be exercising his independent discretion."[1]

"That incorporates everything they did," said Price about his requirement that everyone plead to a charge of conspiracy to commit tax evasion and mail fraud. "We liked that because it gave credit to the IRS, it gave credit to the FBI, and it encapsulated every bit of their conduct."

Meanwhile, Dorothy Griffin was getting a crash course in espionage. With an FBI wire tucked beneath her prized Hawaiian muumuus, Griffin spent the early months of 1980 amassing an astonishing collection of taped confessions. Collecting those confessions called on skills that did not quite align with her rustic mien.

"She slept with several of these people," said Price about his multitasking informant. "One date was to McDonald's. She was a pretty cheap date!" Griffin continued her unorthodox methods of gathering evidence when Price's task force sent her south of the Red River to make deals with county commissioners in northeastern Texas. Although she had branded herself as a phony invoice supplier in Oklahoma to earn her 10-percent commissions, she offered real materials, as well as the occasional tryst, to Texans. Griffin found it easy to record 50-50s on tape, as commissioners in Texas were not aware of the publicity about the Stephens County case. As she admitted from the witness stand, when her case wound its way to court in the summer of 1981, "At the time, I was working for the government, and I said and did anything to get them to open up and get information for the government."

Griffin's amorous exploits were a cause for concern when FBI agents strapped on her wire.

"We were later worried, because she had the wire right here..."

Price paused, pointed to his chest, and left the rest to my imagination.

"We listened to Dorothy Griffin's tapes for three weeks—180 tapes!" continued Price about his own immersion in the dark arts. Huddled with his task force in front of a chalkboard, Price listened intently for incriminating evidence that might help him build psychological profiles of his next targets. Did a supplier go fishing with his kids? If so, maybe he was a devoted family man with a sense of right and wrong and could be induced to cooperate with authorities. Fishing with a county commissioner, on the other hand, signaled a good-buddy relationship that would be hard to crack. And how about signs of intelligence? The smart ones were likely not only to seek leniency by turning state's evidence; they would also be effective witnesses in front of a judge and jury. And the dumb ones? Presumably, they would maintain their innocence all the way to the penitentiary.

Although many of Griffin's undercover adventures were stressful and even dangerous, some were the stuff of comedy. Such was the case with Bill Klutts, a supplier in Shawnee who suspected that FBI agent Jim Elroy was onto him. Confirmation came at a chance run-in with Elroy at a filling station. Feeling playful, Elroy struck up a conversation with the increasingly fidgety target of his investigation.

"I just love my job!" declared Elroy. "You know, you get new toys every day—new things that they provide the FBI. One of the latest things is a gun-type thing that you can point at a window, and you can hear all the conversations through the window. It's just amazing, all the different, fun toys you can have!"

Shortly after his wake-up call at the gas station, Klutts arrived at a motel rendezvous with Griffin in a state of agitation.

"Be quiet!" he barked to a startled Dorothy Griffin. "Don't get near the window! Elroy has a thing that he can listen through the window! Let's go in the bathroom!"

His voice reduced to a whisper, Klutts escorted Griffin into a shower stall. He proceeded to hand over a thousand dollars to help cover her tax liability, never suspecting that the real microphone was just inches away, nestled discreetly beneath Dorothy Griffin's ample breasts.[2]

▶ ▶ ▶ ▶

At this point in the investigation, Price had tax cases against the thirteen suppliers. Yet the only solid cases he had against county commissioners were the ones against Texans who had dealt directly with Griffin. The only case in Oklahoma that showed promise was the one they were building against Guy Roy Moore, a former high school teacher from Midwest City who had been selling road- and bridge-building materials to county commissioners for the better part of three decades. Except for the phony invoices that Griffin had prepared for him, there was no way to match invoices to specific nonexistent material deals. Absent incriminating evidence, Price would never be able to prove which invoices were fraudulent, and commissioners' crimes would go unpunished.

To identify fraudulent invoices, FBI agents descended on county courthouses to subpoena clerks to produce their invoices. To avoid tipping off clerks and commissioners to the invoices they were targeting, agents did not request photocopies. Instead, they relied on old-fashioned handwriting to record dates, descriptions of purchases, and amounts that appeared to match Griffin's phonies. But matching dates, descriptions, and amounts were insufficient to prove beyond a reasonable doubt that particular purchases were for nonexistent materials.

For iron-clad proof of suppliers' subterfuge, Price hit on a clever ruse: he provided FBI agents with what he called "act dumb subpoenas." Under instructions to "act dumber than hell," FBI agents descended on Stephens County to deliver subpoenas to the thirteen suppliers who had paid cash for Griffin's phony invoices. Unaware that agents with an aw-shucks attitude were trying to link their cash payments to invoices for nonexistent materials, suppliers unwittingly gave them the evidence Price needed to implicate them in what would soon mushroom into Okscam. They and their attorneys then spent weeks attempting to match their sales with purchases from Griffin. Ironically, their efforts to prove their innocence wound up proving their guilt.

What might have been the riskiest phase of the investigation came when Price's team dispatched Griffin to visit commissioners she had never met, but whose invoices matched the phonies that she had prepared for Guy Moore. The script they handed her went something like this: "You don't know me, but I supply phony invoices for Guy Moore. According to those invoices, Griffin Lumber Company is the supplier. When the FBI questions you, you won't be able to describe my truck or my son, who supposedly made the deliveries. In short, you won't know how to lie."

About half the commissioners were skeptical and told Griffin to get lost, thereby avoiding self-incrimination. The other half took the bait and asked for the color of her truck (for the record, it was yellow) and a description of her son. Some thanked her for the heads-up.

▶ ▶ ▶ ▶

Day after day, Price and agents from the FBI and IRS sifted through Dorothy Griffin's tapes to find a supplier who might be induced to turn state's evidence. They knew they had to choose carefully. "If we approached the wrong supplier, he would tell other suppliers and commissioners, and it would be all over," explained Price about his task force's winnowing process. "That would have been the end of the case.

If we brought back the same people to a federal grand jury, they would just lie to us, just like they had lied to the Stephens County grand jury.

"We found out, later on in our investigation, that this was not an unusual occurrence. They had all lied to numerous county grand juries in the past, without any problem whatsoever. They weren't worried about it at all! In fact, on tape, they would laugh about it, that they had lied in multiple counties many years ago. All the suppliers had lied; the commissioners had lied; and they were never able to prove it."

Largely at Jim Elroy's insistence, they settled on Guy Moore. U.S. Attorney Larry Patton and Price cosigned a letter to Moore on September 19, 1980, in which they left no doubt that his sales career was over and his new one as an informant was about to begin: "From the evidence accumulated thus far in the investigation, we have found that there are many suppliers like you and a large number of County Commissioners involved in a state-wide ongoing pattern of bribery and fraud costing state and federal taxpayers massive amounts of money . . . It is therefore essential to the investigation and prosecution of all those involved in these crimes that a supplier like you agrees to co-operate in the investigation and truthfully testify concerning these matters."

Although Moore was one of the thirteen suppliers implicated in the Stephens County probe in 1978, his most lucrative territory stretched northwest from Oklahoma County through the Panhandle. Listening to his taped conversations with Griffin, Price agreed with Elroy that Moore ranked a notch above his competitors in terms of intelligence. Moore also fit the psychological profile of a devoted family man—puzzling, given his life of crime, which was about to be revealed—who avoided fraternizing with his customers, meaning that he was more likely to cooperate with authorities than protect his buddies. Best of all, the phony invoices that Moore had obtained from Griffin were linked to transactions in specific counties, a convergence that was not always obvious in suppliers' convoluted paper trails. As Price put it, "That was by far the best kind of invoice to have."

Another source of incriminating evidence came from the Fifteenth Street crowd, a supplier's clique that operated from a nondescript office in southwest Oklahoma City. Their secretary and fellow supplier, Opal Hester, ran an Oklahoma City–based supply business, and she was well known to investigators. She had surfaced when IRS agent Paul Elledge blurted out her name to an incredulous Bill Price at the arson investigation. "Opal Hester was kind of the secretary and ran that office and did deals on her own," said Price. "We also subpoenaed all the Fifteenth Street records. They were literally out in the alley and ready to be thrown away. They were ready to go in the garbage, and we got them just in time. So many of these things just barely happened!"

As it turned out, Elroy's instincts were spot-on. Confronted with Patton and Price's no-nonsense letter, requiring that he cooperate in the investigation, and Dorothy Griffin's tapes, Moore knew the jig was up, and he joined his former phony invoice supplier in turning state's evidence against other suppliers and, eventually, county commissioners. Once again, fate looked kindly on Price's task force. Subsequent efforts to convince other suppliers to turn state's evidence came to naught, meaning that their first choice turned out to be their only choice. "We were *so fortunate!*" declared Price.

Price and his task force were shocked to learn that, over the course of his twenty-eight-year career as a materials supplier, Moore had doled out almost eight thousand bribes and kickbacks, worth more than $1 million. A quick calculation quantified Moore's duplicity at 5.5 bribes per week for a total of 286 per year. An old story dating back to the 1930s, perhaps apocryphal but revealing nonetheless, began to make the rounds about county commissioners' demand for a raise from their forty-five-dollar weekly salary. The raise never came through, prompting somebody to comment that, if they weren't smart enough to figure out how to make more money, they didn't deserve to be county commissioners.

As Price pointed out on more than one occasion, the system itself was "an ideal breeding ground for corruption."

Moore's instructions were to return to his customers and conduct business as usual, making sure to record their conversations. At one point in the investigation, Moore actually warned commissioners to beware of Dorothy Griffin—a warning that was unnecessary among commissioners who were plenty suspicious already.

Like Griffin, Moore needed a plausible reason to meet with other suppliers, many of whom were beginning to suspect that they were under investigation. Mulling over their options, Price's task force decided that Moore should attend a county commissioner convention and initiate conversations about the state attorney general's new regulations pertaining to competitive bidding. For as long as anyone could remember, low bids on materials had determined only prices with no effect on who earned the contracts. Not surprisingly, suppliers tended to bid high to increase the kickbacks they could dispense. But now, the attorney general was forcing commissioners to purchase their materials from the low bidders. To keep their high kickbacks, suppliers had no choice but to collude with one another—something they had never had to do and an ideal icebreaker for Guy Moore to use in meetings with other suppliers.

In a best-case scenario, shop talk about the new regulations might morph into reminiscing about corrupt practices that had been their stock-in-trade for longer than anyone could remember. Confident in their ability to obtain confessions without running the risk of entrapment, FBI agents fitted Moore with a recording device and dispatched him to a county commissioners' convention in Oklahoma City. To ensure robust attendance, commissioners held their annual convention to coincide with the National Finals Rodeo, Oklahoma City's marquee event before Big Money wooed the event to Las Vegas. Moore's recording device, paired with a hidden camera installed in his room, captured Bourbon-saturated boasting about county grand juries they had outfoxed over the years and county commissioners with an insatiable appetite for kickbacks. When salesman "Cotton" Irwin's attorney, Bill Berry (no relation to Oklahoma supreme court

Justice Bill Berry), heard his client confess on tape to kickbacks and lying to grand juries, he asked Price (facetiously, one assumes) where he had found an actor who sounded just like his client. But not even the most incriminating evidence was enough to convince Irwin and other suppliers to turn state's evidence until it was too late to improve their chances of a lighter sentence. Clearly, Price's team made the right decision in approaching Guy Moore as the supplier most likely to cut a deal.

Even with alcohol-saturated confessions, investigators had a hard time matching Griffin's phony invoices with specific deals for nonexistent materials. To figure out which invoices were fraudulent, FBI agents dropped into county courthouses with subpoenas for records of materials purchases. To avoid tipping off clerks to which invoices they were targeting, they did not ask for photocopies. Instead, they parked themselves at a desk and recorded by hand the dates and amounts of invoices that appeared to match the phony ones that Griffin had produced. The next step was to subpoena suppliers for invoices to prove how and where they had obtained their materials. Suppliers and their attorneys then spent weeks comparing their records with Griffin's invoices, no doubt assuming that they could thereby prove their innocence. But with paperwork from all parties, investigators were actually enlisting suppliers to prove their own guilt.

Price, still incredulous, at a distance of four decades, at suppliers' brazen dishonesty, described the gold mine of self-incrimination that poured from Moore's recordings and the FBI's videotapes, all corroborated by mounting stacks of paperwork: "They would sit there and talk about all the grand juries that they had appeared at for the last forty years, and how they had all lied! The old-timers would say that fifty percent of the materials didn't exist—since statehood! That's the kind of conversation that you would get!" Moore's grand-jury testimony came on May 6, 1981; Griffin took the stand the next day.[3]

As their collection of audiotapes from Dorothy Griffin and Guy Moore piled up, Price began to wonder if *anyone* in the county commissioners' supply chain was actually honest and, more to the point, if he could find an honest supplier to cooperate with investigators. In an effort to answer those vexing questions, Price's task force launched Operation Diogenes, so named for the Greek philosopher (nicknamed the Cynic) who, lantern in hand, scoured the countryside in search of an honest man. The results were not encouraging. Moore, arguably one of the busiest and most successful suppliers, knew of only five of his sixty or so customers who refused to partake in kickback and extortion schemes. When other suppliers in the ever-widening probe implicated themselves on tape and agreed to turn state's evidence, they identified the same county commissioners as frustratingly honest. Confirmation of those depressing results came from Auditor and Inspector Tom Daxon, whose separate investigation revealed that only three counties—Tulsa, Washington, and Comanche—maintained tight enough bookkeeping practices to preclude wrongdoing. Daxon's other insight was that Oklahoma's tiny cadre of female commissioners was uniformly honest. Without waxing sociological about women's penchant for honesty and suspected lack of expertise in repairing roads and building bridges, Daxon said simply, "We had four who were elected and, as far as I could tell, did fine!"

In the end, Operation Diogenes failed to gain much traction. "It wasn't very successful," explained Price, "because a lot of these people were just honest to the core, and they just couldn't change. They couldn't act dishonest. They couldn't disappoint people in their community to do it." Some members of that select club served as church deacons; others were opinion leaders in their communities who refused to compromise their principles by informing on their neighbors. One was a retired pro football player. Even when Price enlisted agents with strong religious leanings and who could recite Bible passages to rally honest suppliers to his cause, nobody budged.[4]

But then, in March 1980, an unexpected visitor showed up in the FBI's Tulsa office: Wagoner County Commissioner Rufus Young. As he explained to an astonished agent, he was fairly new to his job when a materials supplier approached him about doing a ten-percent deal.

That sounded not quite kosher to Young, and he hightailed it to the nearest FBI office, which happened to be in Tulsa, to etch his name into Okscam as the only honest county commissioner to turn state's evidence. After his visit to the FBI office, Young overcame whatever scruples he might have had about clandestine work and, duly wired, spent the rest of 1980 gathering evidence for an ever-expanding pool of investigators. He was careful to target only the suppliers who had previously suggested kickbacks, as secretly recording conversations with suppliers he did not know would open him to charges of entrapment.

One imagines Diogenes the Cynic breathing a sigh of relief as he snuffed out his lantern.

Not long after he went undercover, Young was approached by a supplier interested in doing a blue-sky deal.

"What's that?" asked Young.

"You don't know?" asked the supplier, perhaps amused to find a young man so unschooled in the basics of his job.

"No, I guess not," he said, or something to that effect.

The supplier answered with a refrain that alerted Young to more nuances of his job: "That's when I get fifty percent, you get fifty percent, and the county gets fucked!"

As it turned out, Young's service to Okscam was limited. Griffin and Moore's collection of audiotapes was nearing saturation, to render additional taped confessions superfluous. For the most part, Moore's reach extended through northwestern counties, far from the bucolic hills of eastern Oklahoma. "Operation Diogenes was not successful," said Price. "Rufus was only able to do about four tape recordings."

But that did not stop the U.S. Attorneys from all three of Oklahoma's judicial districts from joining the FBI and IRS in a celebratory dinner, held long after the investigation ended and the trials started, to honor Rufus Young for his courage in bucking the county commissioner system. In a cookies-and-punch party that began with the Pledge of Allegiance and a rousing chorus of "God Bless America," Rufus was feted as a man "willing to do something" about what he saw going on around him. "I really don't know what to make of all this," said Young on the eve of the party. Among those called on to deliver laudatory speeches were Oklahoma's three U.S. Attorneys and Edwin Enright, who had been appointed as special agent in charge of the FBI office in Oklahoma City in April 1981 and had been coordinating much of the probe ever since.

"He did what I describe as taking the extra step," said Enright.[5]

▸ ▸ ▸ ▸

Rufus Young's celebratory dinner was more than a year in the future when, in the spring of 1981, the U.S. Attorney's Office in Oklahoma City, in conjunction with the FBI and IRS, launched its version of the D-Day invasion. "After using Guy Moore to the nth degree and being turned down by twelve other suppliers, we had to hurry to convince those twelve to turn state's evidence before word hit the streets," explained Price. "Choosing Moore as our first supplier, after Dorothy Griffin, turned out to be a good decision!" In the pre-dawn stillness, as many as a hundred agents mustered in FBI headquarters at 50 Penn Place to receive their final instructions before setting off in all directions to corral county commissioners in a simultaneous statewide round-up. If all went according to plan, agents would confront them before word leaked out that their freewheeling days were over.

And so began the great unraveling. Agents' first order of business, upon arriving at their destinations, was to preclude defenses of any kind and make sure that commissioners had no business dealings or legitimate debt owed by their suppliers. Next, agents forced their interviewees to acknowledge their oaths of office prohibiting them from receiving compensation beyond their salaries. Then, all too predictably, came their denials that they had accepted kickbacks. Those denials proved unconvincing when agents flipped on their tape recorders and waited as commissioners listened to incriminating evidence against them. Satisfied that they had adhered to their protocols, agents produced preprinted plea agreements, which Price had signed, charging conspiracy to commit tax evasion and mail fraud. That single count was all-encompassing, and it carried a maximum sentence of five years. Commissioners who cooperated on the spot were asked to consent to taped phone calls with their suppliers to warn them that the FBI was closing in and, in the process, obtain incriminating admissions. Agents encouraged commissioners to hire attorneys. Although some saw the wisdom of cooperating right away, others chose to resist their day of reckoning until the bitter end.

Most commissioners came quickly to two realizations: (1) their guilt was seared into audiotaped confessions, most collected by Dorothy Griffin and Guy Moore, that dashed all hope of exoneration; and (2) copping a plea and implicating others in their crimes would lighten their punishment. As word spread of the U.S. Attorney's willingness to seek leniency for those who agreed to plead guilty, offenders practically tripped over one another in their haste to cooperate with authorities.

"It's a snowballing situation," said one person. "One commissioner will be implicated and he will cop a plea and start singing on suppliers and other commissioners, and then some of them will decide to cooperate, and it just keeps getting bigger."[6]

The D-Day invasion and its sequel, a short time later (conducted not with tape recordings, but with suppliers' or commissioners' written testimonies), were milestones in Okscam insofar as invoices for county purchases could now be linked to specific suppliers whose forms of corruption—ten percents, blue-sky deals, and extortion—had been revealed for all to see. The second D-Day invasion differed from the first insofar as agents confronted commissioners with multiple suppliers' statements; similarly, they confronted suppliers with multiple commissioners' statements. If blue-sky deals were involved, they relied on testimonies of backup phony invoice suppliers such as Dorothy Griffin to show that purchases never happened. Although most agents confronted subjects with multiple witness statements, one agent was assigned to confront a commissioner with a single supplier's witness statement. Wondering how to lower the boom on the commissioner, the agent hit on a creative solution: he made six copies of the same statement and fanned them across the commissioner's desk face down like deck of cards. He then told the commissioner to pick one.

The commissioner promptly complied. Caught red-handed, he managed to cough up a confession, but not without posing a question that amused Price and his collaborators forever after:

"I only took kickbacks from five suppliers. How come you had six statements?"

The agent's response has been lost to history.[7]

▸ ▸ ▸ ▸

Now that the investigation was winding down, Price's task force geared up for the next phase of Okscam: prosecuting the offenders.

Much as the Okscam task force had agonized over which supplier to try to turn before choosing Guy Moore, they now had to prioritize trials for those who had refused to plead guilty. "We drew up, and debated back and forth, the first ten that we wanted to go to trial," said Price. "Those ten kept changing as defendants agreed to plead and new defendants were added." Determined to send a message that corruption in county purchasing would no longer be tolerated, they sorted through mountains of three-by-five index cards to zero in on Blaine County commissioner Orville Pratt and Caddo County supplier Donald Skipworth. As the owner of Caddo Material and Equipment Company, with offices in Anadarko and Oklahoma City, Skipworth's massive fraud in Stephens and Okfuskee Counties branded him as one of the most nefarious deal-doers of them all.[8]

On June 24, Price and his second chair, Susie Pritchett, secured Skipworth's conviction on twenty-six counts, including tax evasion and mail fraud. As Skipworth was not a public official but, rather, a private businessperson, they could not charge him with a violation of the Hobbs Act, a congressional statute, enacted in 1946, that criminalized extortion by a public official acting under the color of official right—that is, obtaining payments to which the official was not entitled, knowing that it was made as a quid pro quo. The Hobbs Act defined extortion as "the obtaining of property from another, with his consent, induced by wrongful use of actual or threatened force, violence, or fear, or under color of official right." Along with the Mail Fraud Act, the Hobbs Act became a tool of choice for prosecuting public officials on extortion charges, and its effect in honest service cases was to empower juries to determine what constituted corruption.[9]

Among the witnesses called to testify in Skipworth's trial was Emil Montgomery, a county commissioner in his eighties who might have come straight from central casting. "Oh my God, I want forgiveness for all the things that I have done wrong!" wailed Montgomery from the witness stand. "This is the biggest thing I have ever done wrong!" Montgomery's mea culpa found its match in another tearful confession, from a defendant whose name neither Bill Price nor Hank Gibbons could recall, but whose message surely resonated with others who were led blinking into the light: "Boy, I sure hate to admit it, but I am about to meet my maker, and I don't want to meet my maker having lied here in court!"

After Skipworth's trial, U.S. District Judge Luther Eubanks called Price aside to recommend that he allow Montgomery to plead guilty right away. "I knew what was going on," continued Price. "He wanted Emil Montgomery so he could give him a light sentence, so that it would encourage more pleas." But if other defendants expected Montgomery to set a precedent for leniency, Judge Eubanks's rulings over the ensuing weeks came as a severe disappointment. "They all got six months, or a year," said Price. "Most of them got eighteen months and got out in six months." Those sentences were not lost on the hundreds of attorneys, representing other Okscam defendants, who attended the trials in hopes of picking up pointers for their own defense strategies.

And Donald Skipworth? In a ruling that sent shock waves through the materials supply business, Eubanks sentenced Skipworth, on

July 2, 1981, to twenty years in prison. "Skipworth's was a great case!" exclaimed Price. "Skipworth was a good case to lead off with. We had as good a case as you could ever have on Skipworth, and the amount of money was phenomenal."[10]

As the government's lead prosecutor in the Okscam cases, Price had his hands full when his boss and acting U.S. Attorney John Green's successor, Larry Patton, resigned from office in June 1981. As was customary in America's de facto spoils system, Patton and thousands of other presidential appointees lost their jobs when Jimmy Carter lost the election of 1980 to Ronald Reagan. Upon the recommendation of U.S. Senator Don Nickles, David Russell resumed his former job as the government's top attorney in the Western District.

Asked to comment on the three-year Okscam investigation, Russell began by giving credit to Larry Patton, Bill Price, the FBI, and the IRS. And then he waxed pessimistic. "In a way, it has been disillusioning— to see the scope of wrongdoing," said Russell. "It's an indictment of human nature as well as of citizens. It is sad that people can't resist such temptation." At the same time, Russell was heartened by the public's support for the investigation and indictments. He also praised Judge Eubanks for handing down sentences with an unambiguous message: If you get caught in a serious crime, you will pay the price.

Like all investigators and prosecutors in what had exploded into the largest public corruption scandal in U.S. history, Russell felt strongly that county government needed to be reformed. "We can win all of these cases," continued Russell, "but, if the system is not changed, our apparent success may prove illusory." The good news was that the investigation and vigorous prosecutions were already yielding results. By the time of Russell's appointment, some counties were already seeing 20–30 percent reductions in the costs of building and repairing roads and bridges. Although nobody was ready to issue a clean bill of health, there was no doubt that the probe and prosecutions were making a difference.

Russell was sworn in on Friday, as he was set to prosecute Blaine

County Commissioner Orville Pratt on Monday. In what he described as "a crash course in Orville Pratt," Russell huddled, over the weekend, with Price and FBI agents to prepare for what he later considered to be the government's weakest Okscam case to date. Although Pratt was forced to resign, convicted on two counts on June 18, and sentenced to seven years in prison (a sentence that encouraged a tsunami of plea agreements from other defendants), neither Russell nor Price, who sat as first chair, were satisfied with their prosecution, and they resolved to learn from their errors. Such was the trajectory of their learning curve that, by late July 1981, they had racked up an undefeated record—twenty-three to zero! —in court and plea-bargain conferences.

Price described Pratt's defense as one of the strangest ones in the entire slew of prosecutions. Revealing a flair for undercover work that might have surprised his colleagues, Pratt testified that he had suspected his fellow county commissioners of corruption and opened his own investigation. The county commissioner turned private eye claimed to have had every intention of turning his evidence over to the Blaine County district attorney, but he hadn't quite gotten around to it.[11]

What was arguably the highest profile (and, perhaps, the tawdriest) trial was that of Oklahoma County Commissioner Jewel Parke Richardson. In September 1981, he pleaded no contest to a fifteen-count indictment for extortion, mail fraud, and charging padded contracts totaling $96,481.02 in three years. Active in Republican circles, Richardson relayed through his attorney that he had saved the county money. Russell, whose prosecutorial skills had apparently improved since Orville Pratt's trial, disputed Richardson's boast as "absolutely ludicrous." Russell went on to cite figures indicating that the cost of goods in Oklahoma County had dropped 25–30 percent after Richardson left office. But Richardson, ailing and confined to a wheelchair, refused to go down without a fight.

"I'm innocent," he insisted to Judge Eubanks. "My family knows I'm innocent. Jesus Christ knows I'm innocent."

And Eubanks's response? "You're just as guilty as sin."

At the eleventh hour, Richardson's fate was sealed when the judge listened to a tape recording of Richardson's conversation with his supplier, the infamous Guy Moore, who was, as usual in such circumstances, wearing an FBI wire.

"What are you going to do with this money?" asked Moore.

"With this kickback money, I'm going to go buy me some pussy."

That was all Eubanks needed to hear. Just before his tape was to be broadcast for the entire courtroom to hear, Richardson pleaded no contest to fourteen mail-fraud charges and one extortion charge. Eubanks then handed him the second longest prison term to date for a county commissioner—seven years and six months in prison—and levied a fine of $24,000.[12]

▶ ▶ ▶ ▶

Federal investigators, prosecutors, and judges were not the only ones struggling to keep pace with Okscam. Over at the capitol complex, State Auditor and Inspector Tom Daxon was sending a chilling message to his colleagues in state government: he had lost all confidence in the counties' financial statements, and he could no longer vouch for the accuracy of his audit reports. In some counties, commissioners' board minutes showed nary a trace of competitive bidding in purchasing, and laws pertaining to open meetings were routinely violated. Daxon offered a description of the money lost to kickbacks that only a CPA could appreciate. "You wouldn't call it kickbacks receivable, but that's what it is," explained Daxon. "It's an asset of the county." In conversations with suppliers, he became convinced that nobody could do business with counties without paying kickbacks.

As Oklahoma's only statewide Republican office holder, Daxon was making enemies throughout the state by challenging a system dominated by Democrats. Many accused him of using civic organizations and clubs as bully pulpits to launch a 1982 gubernatorial bid. Yet it was hard to argue with two of his key recommendations: (1) write guidelines for multicounty grand juries, a provision of a constitutional amendment that had been approved by voters in 1971 but never implemented; and (2) compel counties to police themselves to deter dishonest suppliers and report illegal activity to the Association of County Commissioners of Oklahoma. But that might have been a stretch, as the association was just beginning to wake up to the problem. Association president Fred Jordan of Pawhuska gave credit to the Okscam probe for illuminating misconduct within its ranks. "We just didn't think the problems existed to the extent that they do," he said. Jordan's suggestion that somebody rein in county commissioners' "unbridled independence" seemed disingenuous at best and, at worst, hinted at a cover-up. In a lament that rings through the ages, Daxon said, "Unfortunately, due to the lack of profit motive in government entities, there seems to be more incentive to acquire power through bigger government and more programs than to cut costs and increase efficiency." [13]

For historical perspective from a capitol insider, we turn to state Senator Herschal Crowe of Altus. "This has been a poisonous subject in the Legislature for years," said Crowe, who ranked corruption among county commissioners as "the worst kept secret in the state of Oklahoma." Crowe went on to explain that reform efforts had been doomed from the start because legislators, many of whom were former county commissioners, relied on the same grassroots support that kept commissioners in office. Happy to have their driveways paved and potholes filled, most folks turned a blind eye to commissioners who came into office with modest means and left as landed tycoons. "The only way to stop this (corruption) is take the road-building fund from this bunch of thieves," concluded Crowe. "Hell, it's happened all over the state of Oklahoma. The old system we have was meant for horse-and-buggy days." Crowe's alternative, hardly original and seemingly impossible to implement, was to appoint professional, bonded administrators to oversee county purchases. [14]

Elsewhere in the capitol, Governor George Nigh was assembling a thirty-five-member task force, under the leadership of Phillips

Petroleum Company president William C. Douce, to recommend ways to eradicate "kickbacks, payola, and corruption in office." Nigh's initiative came as U.S. Attorney David Russell issued a dire prediction that more than 250 people would be implicated in Okscam. "Our worst fears have come true, and every day it gets worse than the day before," said Russell. "It is so widespread, you'll have to assume it will spill into other areas of government. If it leads us there, we will go there." Price went on record urging legislators to eliminate commissioners' sole discretion over county purchasing and to approve state funding for district attorneys. "If you don't eliminate the sole discretion from one person's hands and spread it out among several officials, you'll have the same problem again in three to five years," Price said.[15]

Conjuring up a literary analogy for task force members to think about, Democratic Senator Finis Smith from Tulsa cited *The Legend of Sleepy Hollow* to suggest that county government was operating like the headless horseman who pursued Washington Irving's tormented schoolmaster, Ichabod Crane. "County government today is in need of a head," declared Smith, who advocated home rule and the appointment of professional managers as the most sensible reforms that would allow county residents to change the form of their governments. Enraged as never before, reform-minded Oklahomans were finally in a position to compel legislators to do the right thing. "It's going to be like voting for motherhood next year," said Smith.

Nigh's task force's proposed overhaul of county governments' revenue-raising capabilities included the appointment of county administrators to oversee all purchasing, creation of a county road department, and enforcement of competitive bidding requirements. In terms of probes and prosecutions, the task force recommended multicounty grand juries, under the supervision of the state attorney general, and state-funded district attorneys, who would be less inclined to sweep local corruption under the rug. In a familiar refrain, task force members criticized a system that "invites waste, fraud, no accountability and hampered service delivery." Although Nigh encouraged legislators to participate in the task force, both houses set up their own committees to study county corruption.

In late August 1981, Nigh called a special session to consider the vexing question of how to fund special elections occasioned by the early exits of so many county commissioners. Legislators were given the choice between appropriating $1 million to pay for those elections or letting him fill vacancies through appointments.[16] Nigh preferred option two, prompting Republicans to accuse him of playing politics, as he would surely appoint Democrats to increase his popularity. The governor insisted that he would replace each commissioner with someone from the same party, thereby dismissing their concerns about his political motivation.

Among the governor's most vocal critics was Tom Daxon. Speaking to Nigh's task force on county reform, Daxon, described by his friends as "squeaky clean," blasted the governor for ignoring a crisis that had been brewing for generations and for exercising patronage at the expense of fair and honest government. "Should a man who has been in state government for twenty-five years and yet has admitted that he was unaware of the existence of corruption in county government now be given the right to appoint two hundred new county commissioners?" asked Daxon. "I am prepared to fight this proposal in every town and city in this state." Daxon urged Nigh's task force and, indeed, all Oklahomans to join the battle for democracy.[17]

As summer faded into the fall of 1981, several bills spawned by Okscam received the legislature's stamp of approval and reflected the public's growing intolerance for corruption: (1) to Daxon's delight, counties were authorized to receive state reimbursement for special elections; (2) officials implicated in the scandal were to be either ousted or suspended; and (3) officials suspected of bribery were no longer immune from prosecution.[18] More good news came when David Russell and Bill Price reported to Governor Nigh's task force that prices of road- and bridge-building materials had fallen by 20–25 percent since Okscam went public. In a familiar mantra, the two attorneys reminded their listeners that reform of county government required two key ingredients: (1) a statewide law enforcement system; and (2) statewide, multicounty grand juries to broaden the scope of investigations and prosecutions. Price concluded his remarks with a message born of experience: "Unless these reforms are made there can be no true prosecution of political corruption."[19]

▶ ▶ ▶ ▶

The great unraveling continued apace through the fall and winter of 1981–82. As county commissioners from the Western District wise enough to enter into plea agreements followed one another into the legal system, resignation letters piled up on Governor Nigh's desk bearing the same message: "This is to advise you that I have recently entered into a plea agreement with the U.S. Attorney's office for the Western District of Oklahoma in connection with the FBI investigation of the county commissioners in Oklahoma and specifically in [name that county]." By early December, seventy-four sitting commissioners had tendered their resignations. Thirteen counties had lost all three of their commissioners.[20]

Although most of the action to date was in the Western District, Frank Keating, whose tenure as U.S. Attorney for the Northern District of Oklahoma had begun on June 12, 1981, said he was "ready to go" as soon as the probe shifted to the northeast. The eleven counties in his jurisdiction included Craig, Creek, Delaware, Mayes, Nowata, Osage, Ottawa, Pawnee, Rogers, Tulsa, and Washington. "I've had a lot of people call, a lot of inquiries about county commissioner cases and about future prosecution of them in this district," said Keating at his office in Tulsa. "Some of the callers didn't understand that we don't investigate. We prosecute." Keating did not have long to wait; by late summer, investigators were looking into misconduct in Mayes and Delaware counties. Cases were also cropping up in Oklahoma's third judicial district, based in Muskogee.[21]

Frank Keating served as U.S. Attorney for the Northern District of Oklahoma during the county commissioner scandal. COURTESY OKLAHOMA HISTORICAL SOCIETY.

A sampling of press reports provides a glimpse into dramas playing out across Oklahoma as the county commissioner system crumbled. Okscam came full circle in its crucible, Stephens County, where a grand jury impaneled in 1978 had recommended the ouster of all three of its commissioners—Eston Ruel Fisher, Jack Davis, and O. L. Damron—for neglect of duty. Nobody was surprised when they claimed innocence. In the absence of jurisdictional authority to hear evidence from other counties, the grand jury had no choice but to end its investigation. But when the FBI and IRS were authorized to launch their joint probe, the jurisdictional boundaries melted, and all bets were off. Although all three commissioners pleaded guilty, Fisher's case set a standard for thievery: he was tried on sixty-seven charges of accepting bribes on more than $100,000 worth of material purchases from 1976 to 1980. Faced with the same charges that he had denied back in 1978, Fisher told U.S. District Judge Lee West, "I'm sorry for this your honor." Davis was equally concise. "I'm just sorry it happened," said the former commissioner, "and I wish it was over."

Of Stephens County's four main materials suppliers, three pleaded guilty: Opal Hester, who supplemented her secretarial work for the Fifteenth Street crowd with her own supply business, and whose name had surfaced when Bill Price was looking into the arson investigation in northwest Oklahoma City; Ed Wilson; and Don Smith. The fourth, the aforementioned Don Skipworth, made the unwise decision to have his day in court.[22]

By mid–January 1982, 150 people had been convicted or pleaded guilty. "It has really been disillusioning," said David Russell. "You see the broad sweep of people involved, and you ask yourself whether the system is bad or whether humans are just corrupt." Not surprisingly for an accountant, Tom Daxon's focus was on the millions of dollars that had been squandered through fraudulent purchasing by county commissioners who seemed to believe that they were stealing not from friends and neighbors, but from a faceless bureaucracy that collected taxes for the state. For Bill Price, it was all about a founding principle of the U.S. Constitution. "The commissioners were czars in charge of their own districts," he said. "There were no checks and balances."[23]

Our sampling of press reports continues with six former commissioners from six different counties who appeared before U.S. District Judges West, Daugherty, and Thompson in late January to answer corruption charges. A few weeks later, former Jefferson County Commissioner Ike Roberts pleaded guilty to accepting 10-percent kickbacks, but not before admitting that he had known about county commissioner graft since he was a boy. The legislature "knew what was going on for years," declared Roberts. "That's why they kept the salaries so low."

An early case to go to trial, with multiple witnesses and no tapes, was that of Major County Commissioner William T. Boston. With U.S. District Judge Luther Eubanks presiding and Susie Pritchett sitting as second chair, Price faced off against a familiar foe: defense attorney and state senator Gene Stipe. Price was grateful that he had admonished agents never to suggest to witnesses who they should implicate, as each supplier who took the witness stand identified the same commissioners as either honest or guilty. Stipe's standard argument that witnesses were implicating others to please the prosecution fell flat, leaving Price and Pritchett to argue effectively that witnesses were telling the truth, as all of them, independently and without suggestion, had implicated and exonerated the same people.

Suppliers described Boston as "a tough bargainer" who was notorious for demanding kickbacks. Boston denied the charges but, rather disingenuously, admitted under Price's cross-examination that he had told an FBI agent, in September 1981, that a lone supplier had offered him a kickback and nothing had come of it. Boston became visibly agitated by suppliers' testimonies, prompting one of them to announce, "If you want me to say he's a liar, I will. He's a liar." The jury found these witnesses more credible, and Boston was found guilty of fifty-four counts of accepting kickbacks. Boston's conviction, without tape recordings as evidence, prompted yet another round of plea agreements.

As Frank Keating had predicted, grand-jury indictments were starting to flow in his district. Included in the northern round-up were Henry Campbell, the chairman of the Mayes County Commission, who was named in thirty-two counts of mail fraud; and Coy Smith, a former Delaware County commissioner, who was named in six counts. Both men refused to accept Keating's offer, which had become commonplace in all three judicial districts: plead guilty to mail fraud, resign from office, make restitution, and cooperate in the federal investigation.[24]

In the scramble to compel plea bargains and try cases, some folks took a step back to reflect on Okscam's causes and long-term significance. Enid lawyer E. B. Mitchell, a member of Governor Nigh's task force, voiced what everyone pretty much knew about county commissioners: "Out in the boondocks, the rural areas, they're the ones who get the roads and bridges fixed, the ones who order all the

equipment and do all the hiring and firing. In the cities, of course, you've got the city to take care of some of these things. But in the boondocks, the commissioners run the government." A capitol aide chimed in with a homespun expression that seemed to sum up the public's attitude: "It's the ole saying, 'He may be a son of a bitch, but he's our son of a bitch'."

Maybe so. But not everybody was ready to let their elected officials and materials suppliers off the hook. According to Bob Renbarger, an aide to Governor Nigh, who spent his days fielding phone calls, "These are people they sat in the coffee shop with. There's a lot of frustration and anger and hurt out there."[25]

A through-line in commentaries and reflections that dominated the headlines throughout Okscam was that the county purchasing system was tailor-made to turn honest people into crooks. For decades—maybe since territorial days—the ingredients for graft had been percolating in a toxic brew of low salaries, sloppy safeguards, limited accountability (either to state officials or fellow commissioners), and materials suppliers without a moral compass. What more was needed to create an incentive for "good ole boys," as they were rather derisively and perhaps unfairly known, to pocket taxpayers' money? Perhaps the amazing thing

Syndicated cartoonist Garry Trudeau brought Okscam to the nation's attention in his comic strip, Doonesbury. DOONESBURY © G. B. TRUDEAU. REPRINTED WITH PERMISSION OF ANDREWS MCMEEL SYNDICATION. ALL RIGHTS RESERVED.

was not that so many had been corrupted, but that a few remained untainted. "There are honest commissioners," mused David Russell. "But there needs to be a real long look at our present system and what changes can be made in it. There obviously have been widespread abuses. Anytime you have the kind of money available to county commissioners that is available, you have to have some oversight." Washington County Commissioner Lee Chew agreed: "I think there is a line where we probably all are susceptible to temptation. It's just that our lines are at different levels. The salaries of the county officials have not been sufficient to support a full-time position. I don't care who you are, you have to make a living." [26]

For a thirty-thousand-foot perspective, we turn to Buck Revell, the number three man in the FBI's Washington headquarters, on assignment in Oklahoma City, who addressed the downtown Kiwanis Club, in March 1982, about street crime. His words applied equally to white-collar crime. "The streets belong to the hoodlums," said a decidedly pessimistic agent as heads surely bobbed around the room. "If we don't do a better job we are on the verge of losing certain areas of our country to the criminal element." Although he had nothing but praise for law enforcement in Oklahoma City, he knew that more was needed to mitigate the breakdown in morality and decline of family values that lay at the heart of the nation's troubles. "The institutions we use to punish criminals are not equal to the job," said Revell. "We do not have room to lock everybody up. We have to come up with alternative methods of punishment. Frankly, all of us have to do a better job."[27]

On a lighter note, not all the talk about Okscam was doom and gloom. In the fall of 1981, it fell to cartoonist Garry Trudeau to point his rapier-sharp wit toward Oklahoma. His nationally syndicated comic strip featured Mike Doonesbury, a Tulsa native who returned home from college back east to find that his uncle Henry, a longtime county commissioner, had been accepting bribes. In a visit expected to last a couple of weeks, Doonesbury did his best to render aid and comfort to his uncle. To join in the parody, Price wrote a spoof letter to the fictitious Henry Doonesbury in which he encouraged the disgraced commissioner to cooperate with investigators "and truthfully testify." Price went so far as to enlist his boss, David Russell, to send Trudeau their standard plea agreement to pass along to Henry. The plea agreement appeared on Russell's official stationery. He and Price duly affixed their signatures, careful to leave space at the bottom for Henry and his attorney to sign.[28]

▶ ▶ ▶ ▶

In December 1981, President Ronald Reagan appointed David Russell as a federal judge to fill the vacancy until a permanent appointment could be made, John Green, an African American with a strong track record in civil rights lawsuits, stepped in, for the second time, as acting U.S. Attorney and appointed Price as his first assistant. During Green's brief tenure in office, one person stood out as Russell's most qualified permanent successor: Bill Price. Having served as assistant U.S. Attorney since February 1975, and acting under U.S. Attorney John Green as his first assistant, the thirty-three-year-old Price was poised to become the first assistant ever elevated to the top job in the Western District. He scored another first in being the youngest.

Price's appointment came as Okscam in the Western District was winding down, and the focus was shifting to eastern counties. By then, the probe and ensuing prosecutions had ensnared 175 sitting commissioners, former commissioners, and materials suppliers who had either been indicted, pleaded guilty, or signed plea-bargaining agreements. Insiders estimated that two hundred people, and probably more, would be charged with corruption before it was all over.[29]

Among Price's early supporters were U.S. Senator Don Nickles, a Republican from Ponca City; and Mickey Edwards, another Republican, who represented Oklahoma's Fifth District in the U.S House of Representatives.[30] "I've been following your work on the county commissioner investigation and have been tremendously impressed," wrote Edwards to Price in November 1981. "What a great job you've done! You're a great asset to Oklahoma and I'm very, very proud of you."[31]

Predictably, Price's nomination passed quickly up the chain of command. In April 1982, President Reagan announced his intention to nominate Price to be U.S. Attorney for the Western District of Oklahoma for a four-year term. His nomination sailed through the Senate, and his swearing-in was scheduled for Friday, May 7. A White House press release commended Price for spearheading Okscam, earning the Outstanding Assistant U.S. Attorney Award for three years in a row (1977, 1978, and 1979), and receiving the U.S. Department of Justice Special Achievement Award for prosecuting public corruption, criminal tax, and major fraud cases. A congratulatory note from the White House read, "We know Bill will continue to do a splendid job!"[32]

Interviewed a few weeks before his swearing-in, Price belied the image of a hard-nosed, hard-driven, and relentless prosecutor. That refreshing image gained traction in profiles published in *Time, U.S. News and World Report*, the *Wall Street Journal*, and other national publications that took an interest in scandal-ridden Oklahoma. Those traits became "hardworking," "conscientious," "dedicated," and "energetic," tempered by a jovial personality—hardly the makings of a vindictive crusader. What is more, Price was positively excited to take on a job "where in everything you do you feel like you're helping people, you're doing something good, having a positive impact, you're not just making money or representing a client." To give credit where it was due, he cited cooperation between his office, the FBI, and the IRS as the reason that all but about ten of almost two hundred people charged in Okscam (so far!) had agreed to enter pleas rather than face trial. Convinced that his office enjoyed broad public support, Price cited innumerable occasions when jurors had thanked him for bringing wrongdoers to justice. "That's reward right there to a prosecutor," said Price, whose track record of losing only two cases in seven years testified not only to his success as a prosecutor, but also to his dedication to ensuring honesty in public service.

Price went on to explain why he was so committed to his work. As a federal prosecutor, he had the latitude to ignore community pressure, sidestep state officials who did not share his broad authority and district attorneys who were reluctant to prosecute their neighbors, and take action against people regardless of their wealth, social standing, or political clout. From the David Hall trial to Okscam and in plenty of cases in between, he had tackled corruption with a laser-like focus on seeing justice done.

Reflecting on his earliest encounters with the judicial system, Price had come to believe that transparency in office was a cornerstone of fair and effective governance. Elected officials who put their own interests above those of the people they were sworn to serve were guilty of nothing less than undermining the nation's core values. "If you don't prosecute on cases like those, it can have a demoralizing effect on an entire nation," said Price. "People begin not to believe in their country. To have corruption not being prosecuted is far more demoralizing than having corruption revealed."[33]

Price was sworn in as U.S. Attorney for the Western District of Oklahoma at 11:00 A.M., Friday, May 7, 1982, in Chief U.S. District Judge Luther Eubanks's third-floor courtroom in the federal courthouse.

With thirteen prosecutors and a staff of thirty, Price's office was larger than the Eastern and Northern districts combined. "I'll have to do more administrative chores," said Price in an interview on the eve of his swearing-in. "But I see it as the challenge of being able to work in many areas.

"A lot of times, we're the prosecutors of last resort," continued Price, who credited the federal judiciary for empowering him and his colleagues in the U.S. Attorney's Office to venture where state officials either could not, or would not, tread. "I had the opportunity to watch the federal prosecution of (former Oklahoma governor) David Hall. I saw the ability of this office to take on extremely powerful people and be able to successfully prosecute them." As always, Price lavished praise on the investigators who had enabled him to prosecute offenders. "We've been especially skilled in prosecuting major fraud cases and white-collar crime," he continued with a flair for understatement. But that did not mean that his office would relax its prosecution of violent criminals and drug traffickers. He concluded his interview on the effusive note that had become his trademark: "It's a fun job. We're able to deter crimes— do some good for the public." Price later commented that he liked criminal cases because he was always on the right side. On the rare occasions when he was not, he dismissed the case.[34]

Price's swearing-in went off without a hitch, and he stepped to the podium to deliver his acceptance speech. It came as no surprise when he acknowledged his debt to family and friends who were gathered in the room. Family members on hand for the occasion included his wife, Mary, his "best friend and the sharer of all my triumphs and defeats," and his children James (better known as Jimmy) and Anne. Although both were happy to have a day off from school, Jimmy's excitement seemed less than robust when he yawned in the middle of the ceremony. An alert photographer made sure to telegraph his apparent ennui on the front page of the next day's newspaper, giving the Price family something to rib James about for years to come. Only two-year-old Eileen was absent. By way of explanation, Price said that he and Mary had decided that not even the seven judges in the room could order her to sit still. Price's only regret was that his deceased father and brother were not there. Special thanks went to U.S. Senator Don Nickles, in absentia, for making his appointment possible.

After due deference to his predecessors—former U.S. Attorneys Bill Burkett, Larry Patton, and David Russell and acting U.S. Attorney John Green—Price launched into a paean to the U.S. judicial system: "All the components of this judicial system, from the court clerks to the Marshals, the Probation Office, the attorneys and support staff of the United States Attorney's office, the investigative agencies and judges, determine not only how pleasant it is to do our job, but the quality of justice in the Western District of Oklahoma." He then quoted Bill Burkett, who often said he was amazed that he actually got paid for doing something he loved.

As a die-hard Republican, Price was particularly mindful that the job was nonpartisan. "In the political corruption area, we have never hesitated to prosecute corrupt politicians regardless of party, and we will continue to do so in the future." He was also grateful that the bad old days of patronage were long gone: "The business of fighting crime and representing the government is too important a task to be based on any criteria other than excellence." He vowed to continue the battle against crime, especially political corruption and white-collar crime. With his usual nod to the federal system of justice, he reminded listeners that the "effective prosecution of these crimes is essential to the preserving of the free institutions we hold so dear."

Price reserved special opprobrium for drug peddlers, who wrecked young lives and escalated the nation's soaring crime rate. Only a return to fundamental values could mitigate the wreckage caused by the narcotics trade: "Unless moral and religious values and public awareness of the problem increases, law enforcement will never stop the drug traffic, but we can certainly try to slow it down.

"The office of United States Attorney is both a great honor and a great challenge and responsibility," declared Price as he wound toward his conclusion. "I pledge to you today that I will always seek to use the authority of that office to the best of my skill and ability, to seek to do justice, to prosecute the guilty, to protect the innocent, and to uphold the system of justice that I love so much."[35]

PART III : *FROM WHOM MUCH IS GIVEN*

CHAPTER ELEVEN : *Top Job – Part One*

n the months leading up to Bill Price's appointment as U.S.
Attorney for the Western District of Oklahoma and for many
months thereafter, Okscam blared from headlines nationwide.
Other than cartoonist Garry Trudeau's lighthearted take on the
scandal through the persona of Mike Doonesbury, the national
press was not amused. In September 1981, *Newsweek*'s Ronald Henkoff
preferred its alternate moniker (corcom, for corrupt commissioners)
to describe Abscam-style audio and video recordings that had revealed
$25 million in kickbacks, bribes, and phony purchases in the span of
a decade. Asked to weigh in on the scandal, Governor Nigh expressed
dismay that the perpetrators continued to feign innocence. "The shock
is that a lot of these people didn't think they were being dishonest,"
said the governor. "They were told that this is the way you do business."
Asked about investigators' modus operandi, Price singled out Guy
Moore, who had apparently needed a little coaching in his transition
from materials supplier to FBI informant, as a key to breaking the case:
"We simply had Moore do business like he had for 28 years."[1]

Time came knocking in October. By then, the contagion had spread
to Texas, where Dorothy Griffin's undercover trysts led to six guilty pleas
and one conviction after trial. "It certainly is the largest investigation of
public corruption in terms of sheer numbers in the nation's history,"
explained Price to his incredulous interviewer. For a glimpse into
Oklahoma-style corruption that played out in county maintenance
barns and pickup trucks across the state, *Time* restricted its sample to
a twenty-eight-year-old rock-crushing machine worth $5,000 that was
purchased for $42,000 and a used road grader worth $14,000 whose
year-long lease came to a whopping $27,500.

Canadian County Clerk Betty Eisenhour, an unwitting intermediary in the graft, always wondered how county commissioners earning $991.00 a month (later raised to about $1,500) managed to come into office with nothing and leave with everything from Lincolns and Cadillacs to farms, businesses, and racehorses. She also wondered why she was paying a middleman for county purchases. "Now I know," said the enlightened clerk. "The commissioners were good old boys, but just between you and me, they were thieves."[2]

When Okscam made headlines on the West Coast, Californians caught a whiff of former Oklahoma Governor David Hall's troubled relationship with the truth. Of particular interest to the *Los Angeles Times* and the *San Francisco Chronicle* was the character of so many of Oklahoma's swindlers. Most were highly respected members of their communities—churchgoers all, with a heavy sprinkling of farmers and ranchers—who looked after their neighbors' welfare and made sure the roads were paved and the bridges were up to snuff. How could they have looted $25 million over the previous decade from the public coffers, and what did that have to say about their professed values? Cimarron County Commissioner Bill Murdock alerted his interviewer to a disturbing pattern: "You're going to find that good Christian men who go to church every Sunday did it. It had been going on so long, it didn't really seem there was anything wrong with it."

Price chimed in, with a familiar refrain, to disparage the county purchasing system as "an ideal breeding ground for corruption." Asked to elaborate, he explained that Oklahoma was divided not so much into seventy-seven counties (what University of Oklahoma history professor Arrell Gibson called, in a *Washington Post* interview, "77 satrapies") as into 231 districts in which commissioners deployed their power like big-city bosses, complete with separate employees, budgets, maintenance barns, and equipment. Although local district attorneys were theoretically responsible for keeping county commissioners in line, their offices were often across the hall from the commissioners' in the courthouse, and they depended on them for their budgets. Price's friend and, since 1982, Oklahoma Auditor and Inspector Tom Daxon, who had dedicated part of his youth to Campus Crusade for Christ, might have been onto something when he invoked the need for divine guidance: "What we may be looking at is not a problem that can be solved through legislation. It may be more a spiritual problem than anything else."[3]

But not everyone clung to delusions of innocence. When Barry Siegel of the *Los Angeles Times* caught up with former Blaine County commissioner Cecil Parker, he found a self-described "good ole boy" who had been farming wheat, cotton, and corn since 1928 and, more to the point, had taken kickbacks "from every vendor who sold me lumber and tinhorn." At the time of his interview, Parker had long since pleaded guilty and testified before a federal grand jury, and he was awaiting sentencing. Talking about Okscam "helps get it out of my system," explained Parker. "I heard about these things all my life, even before I was elected. I've talked to some real old fellows and they say it's been happening ever since statehood, ever since God made county commissionering (*sic*). I just didn't know how it worked until I got into office."

Parker went on to explain business as usual in his former line of work. Materials salesmen never obfuscated when they listed their prices, and when they dropped by to collect payment, they left behind, say, $150 or $170 on a $1,700 purchase. As far as Parker knew, the cash came from their profits and had no effect on the county's bottom line. In his defense, Parker denied being "hoggish." Had he been more aggressive, he could have had "the biggest damn farm in Blaine County."

"But it was the taxpayers' money, I guess," continued Parker. "It was wrong. I guess the kickbacks were figured into the prices. I've done a lot of things I'm more proud of (*sic*) than this. I regret taking the damn money. Hell, I wasn't raised that way." Then again, farming has never been easy, and even though he worried about the impropriety of it all, he gladly accepted kickbacks when times got tough.

The long arm of the law caught up with Parker in early 1981 when federal agents showed up at his house with tapes, likely recorded by Guy Moore, implicating him in Oklahoma's shame. They were "really nice young fellows," he said about the agents who launched him on his journey through the legal system. And the man who would become his prosecutor? Bill Price was "as nice a guy as you can meet. When I saw what I was into, I figured I couldn't lie." Such was Parker's despondency that he considered suicide. But talking to his neighbors made him reconsider his options. "It's turned out that people here treat me just the same. When I'm setting [sic] down in the coffee shop talking on it, people say, 'If I'd been you, I'd have done the same.' No one jumps up and eats me alive."[4]

Far to the southeast, a thoroughly repentant Carl White submitted his resignation to Pittsburg County District Attorney Don Roberts and County Clerk Champ Hodgins. Like Cecil Parker, White revealed a descent into a dark night of the soul. "I am very sorry for the wrong I have done," said White. "I am a Christian man, but my life got in a backsliding condition which weakened me to the point of doing wrong. I have rededicated my life before my church and want the future for myself and my family to be brighter."[5]

County commissioners implicated in Okscam might have learned a belated lesson from Keith Hoar, a vocational agriculture teacher from Pond Creek who ran successfully for the Grant County Commission, where he earned a reputation for honesty. Hoar's resistance to salesmen's blandishments was lost on his fellow commissioners, Leonard Johanning and Clifton Honeyman, who resigned after signing agreements to plead guilty to accepting kickbacks. Although Hoar was highly critical of county commissioners' salaries, which all but guaranteed a dearth of honest and qualified candidates, he saw no reason to compromise his principles. "I'm pretty hard-nosed and I think they know I would just tell them to go to hell," he explained about his relationship with suppliers. "I don't even drink a cup of coffee with them unless I pay for it." At the same time, Hoar admitted to feeling

In one of many editorial cartoons aimed at spoofing the county commissioner scandal, the *Sunday Oklahoman* compared county commissioners' resignations and exits from office— "The Run of '81"—to the run of April 22, 1889, which opened central Indian Territory to non-Indian settlement. COURTESY SUNDAY OKLAHOMAN; BILL PRICE.

isolated ("out on a limb being an honest commissioner," was how he put it) and alienated from friends who had been targets of federal probes. Without excusing their behavior, Hoar pointed to an antiquated county purchasing system that spawned corruption. "Hell, it was an accepted business practice," he said.

But not for Commissioner Hoar, who was clearly embarrassed to be singled out for his honesty. He concluded an interview in the *Tulsa World* with an insight worth pondering: "I don't think honesty should have to be congratulated."[6]

Although Monday-morning quarterbacking from the supply side was a bit harder to come by, the *Wall Street Journal* did manage to catch up with the little woman who had started this great scandal: Dorothy Griffin.

"I'm just a dumb old country woman standing out here in my bare feet," she said when queried at her trailer home in Atoka County, "but I do know that you don't do wrong and get by." In her case, doing wrong meant writing more than $1 million in phony invoices for nonexistent transactions between suppliers and fifty-seven county commissioners representing twenty-nine counties, stashing them in garbage bags, and burying them in her lumber barn. One imagines Dorothy Griffin casting furtive glances toward the dirt road that ran by her house, wary of unannounced visits from her erstwhile business partners. Even her dogs were on high alert.

"Some of my friends haven't stopped by in a long time," she said with more than a hint of sadness, "because they're afraid some FBI people might be around."[7]

As county commissioners and one phony invoice supplier were expressing their postmortems of the scandal that was upending their lives, their fellow Oklahomans were busy electing replacements in a statewide spate of special elections, many of which resulted in good-ole-boy Democrats being replaced by Republicans. Perhaps surprisingly, in a state dominated by Democrats, Price had prosecuted a disproportionate number of Republicans. That did not mean that Republicans excelled in corruption. Rather, it reflected Guy Moore's extraordinary success in peddling kickbacks throughout Price's heavily conservative Western District, where lots of Republicans served as county commissioners.

Where some saw disaster unfolding in Democratic strongholds, Republican National Committee (RNC) chairman Richard Richards saw a "golden opportunity" to elect more Republicans to local offices. Toward that end, the RNC put $100,000 in a campaign war chest in hopes of striking more of a balance between the state's two hundred Democratic and thirty-one Republican county commissioners.

Closer to home, legislators and opinion leaders were mulling over three changes in state government. One aimed to create a statewide criminal investigation force and finance district attorney operations from state, rather than county, funds. The second would require counties to hire professional managers and convert commissioners from de facto czars into non-salaried boards of directors. The third would resurrect Governor Howard Edmondson's proposal, long since relegated to the dustbin of Oklahoma politics, to grant control of road and bridge building and repairs to the state. If enacted, such proposals held the promise of ending Democratic control of county politics in a state where voters tended to favor Republicans in national elections, even as they picked their local officials in the Democratic primaries.

A snapshot of how that reform program might play out came from Cleveland County, where Commissioner Billie R. Pool was relieved of his position, required to pay more than $17,000 in restitution for the kickbacks he had taken, and replaced in a special election by Republican Evelyn Orth.

Her first day on the job, Commissioner Orth paid a visit to the county maintenance barn, where workmen asked if they could continue to fuel their pickups at the county gas pump.

"I just figured it wasn't right," said Orth, "and I decided not to let them do it."[8]

▶ ▶ ▶ ▶

As though there was not enough business in his own district, Price was called on to send assistant prosecutors to Muskogee, in the Eastern Judicial District, where the U.S. Attorney's position was temporarily vacant. To face off against defense attorney Gene Stipe in the trial of Murray County Commissioners Bird Lance, Jr., and Jimmie Primrose, he dispatched Charlie Waters to U.S. District Judge Frank Seay's courtroom. "This was not the environment and the culture of Ralph Thompson's courtroom, and this was not Fred Dougherty's courtroom," recalled Waters about his trial by fire in Muskogee. Voir dire began when Judge Seay asked prospective jurors if any of them might have a conflict of interest with either the defendants or the prosecutor. When none responded in the affirmative, Judge Seay popped his next question:

"Does anyone here know Senator Stipe, and have any reason to believe that it might impact their thinking in the case?"

And with that, the floodgates opened. For the next half hour, prospective jurors rhapsodized about the latter-day populist who had tailored his career, both political and legal, to the wants and dreams of the common man. "I started out with a credibility problem," recalled Waters, whose big-city credentials were not what he needed to sway a Muskogee County jury. Stipe, on the other hand, was in his element. He had long since earned his workingman's credentials by successfully litigating workers' compensation cases. When he was not burnishing his image in the courtroom, he kept himself busy buying up tag agencies and media outlets throughout southeastern Oklahoma. Revered as a kind of godfather in his native Little Dixie, Stipe spent his Sundays dishing out favors to constituents who lined up outside his office in McAlester.[9] Keenly aware of what he was up against, all Waters could do was record the names of prospective jurors in thrall to Gene Stipe in hopes of keeping them off the jury.

By noon, Waters was convinced that the government's case was veering off the rails, and he took advantage of a recess to visit the Lunch Box, a local eatery next to the courthouse. Like small-town restaurants anywhere, the Lunch Box was arranged with a cash register near the entrance, booths lining the walls, and two or three tables in the middle. Waters recalled a surreal scene as he walked through the door: "I walk in there, and sitting there, right in the middle, at the table facing the door, is Senator Stipe, and he looks at me, grinning from ear to ear. 'Come on in, counselor!' The one thing that I noticed, right off the bat, is who else was in there. Do you know who else was in there? All the jurors! This was in the middle of the trial, and the jurors were lined up and down eating there, and the only people in there were Gene Stipe and the jury!"

"This is improper as hell!" thought Waters. Reluctantly, he answered Stipe's beckoning and took a seat. Under the withering gaze of jurors, he endured good-natured banter from Stipe and winced as the defense attorney slurped his soup in true down-home fashion. "He would let everybody know he was one of them," continued Waters. "He was slurping that soup pretty loud."

And then came a moment never to be forgotten: "He spilled some soup on his pants. I swear to God—this was all right next to us, this was all real close—there was a juror in a booth, no further away than we are. He literally grabbed his napkin, went to his knees, and started wiping the soup off Stipe's pants!"

Stipe's unseemly relationship with jurors continued when Stipe announced to his fellow diners that he was looking for a landman. It turned out that one of the jurors was seeking just such employment.

And then it was back to Judge Seay's courtroom, where Waters had a front-row seat at more of Senator Stipe's antics. Those included pulling his shirttail out, inch by inch, until, by the end of the day's proceedings, it hung below his suit coat. "He was letting those people know that he had to wear this coat and tie, but he really wasn't a coat-and-tie sort of guy," said Waters. "He was just one of them." A trick that Waters found particularly annoying was Stipe's habit of patting him on the back whenever Judge Seay asked them to approach the bench. Whereas Waters found it condescending, the jury seemed to lap it up as yet another sign that Stipe was their kind of good ole boy. As Waters put it, with more than a hint of distaste, "I had to be careful when I went up there, because I didn't want him to do that."

Then there was Stipe's mastery of manipulating jurors' emotions. "He always tried a case with a young associate," explained Waters. When it was time for closing arguments, he allowed that associate to argue the facts of the case and the finer points of the law. But when his associate sat down, it was Stipe's turn to morph from attorney to storyteller. "Gene Stipe had all his stories that had nothing to do with the facts, nothing to do with the law, but had great appeal," continued

Waters. Whether his topic was baseball or a miscarriage of justice, Stipe's monologues seemed more suited to a Rotary Club luncheon than a courtroom, and they all aimed at stirring jurors' emotions to the point where they were likely to acquit his defendant. Prosecutors who argued against Stipe on more than one occasion quickly realized that, although his themes were consistent, he altered the details to support his cases. "That's how he makes his money," concluded Waters with a laugh. "He probably gives that same stuff in any case he tried!"

And the defendants? Waters turned pensive when he reflected on Lance, Primrose, and other county commissioners he helped put in jail: "These weren't just terrible people. These were nice people— people you would associate with in your community. Most of them were well thought of, or they wouldn't have had the job. This was just a horrible thing to have happen to them!"

Waters's anxiety in Judge Seay's courtroom was all for nothing. "Stipe was notorious for his lack of pretrial preparation" explained Price. "He once called in a character witness to vouch for a county commissioner's sterling reputation. Much to his chagrin, the witness testified that the commissioner had shoved his wife down a flight of stairs!" Jurors were left to decide the fate of a defendant whose identity Price could not recall, but whose anger issues were hardly the makings of a virtuous citizen.

Neither Stipe's antics nor his oratory were enough to save the defendants from conviction on sixty-six counts. Even the juror who wiped soup off of Stipe's pants was unswayed by his courtroom flourishes. Waters all but guaranteed those convictions in his closing argument when he challenged the master storyteller to actually answer questions about the case.

"He couldn't do his thing!" crowed Waters with undisguised glee. "It pissed him off royally! He had to answer, and he couldn't answer those questions!"

"Gene lost all his cases on county commissioners," said Price. "We had no problem in any part of the state with convictions and no problem with even Gene Stipe being on the other side. I never lost a case to Gene Stipe."[10]

In addition to Price's oversight of his assistants' trials, he served as the go-to consultant for Frank Keating, whose appointment as U.S. Attorney for the Northern District of Oklahoma, in June 1981, coincided with a spate of county commissioner indictments in his eleven-county jurisdiction. "I had been a witness in a number of federal criminal trials, but I had never been a prosecutor," said Keating about his learning curve in his district's top job. "I had been a prosecutor on the state side, but not the federal side. So I tried a lot of cases." Keating credited an extraordinary cadre of assistants, one of whom was old enough to be his father, for tutoring him in the protocols of federal criminal trials. "I am sure Bill Price was in the same boat," continued Keating. "You learn from your assistants."

Keating resigned as U.S. Attorney to accept a position as associate attorney general of the United States, a job that placed him directly under U.S. Attorney General Ed Meese and gave him authority over federal district attorneys nationwide. "They reported to me," said Keating during our wide-ranging interview in his Oklahoma City office. "So I knew Bill, and we talked periodically about his cases. The conviction rate was really impressive! They were just airtight bribery cases."

Although I had known Keating for many years, there were lots of gaps in my knowledge of the former Oklahoma governor's resume. His multifaceted career in law enforcement and politics was much in evidence in an office festooned with memorabilia and photographs.

"So you were working under Ed Meese. Were there opportunities to share this information with him?"

Keating replied in the affirmative and proceeded to tell a poignant tale that he had shared with his boss in Washington, D.C. and was now sharing with me. It was a tale that revealed yet another nuance in the Okscam narrative.

One individual that came to see me was a Native American, probably a Cherokee, with a withered arm. I just felt sorry for him. He was told this was all part of the compensation—a package, and that he would get ten percent of the cut. He probably did not know that that was not the case! And I am not depreciating the crime that needed to be punished. But I think a lot of those guys had *no clue* what it was they were doing wrong. More enlightened commissioners from other areas of the state—it probably never dawned on them that this was anything *but* corruption. These other guys, in the very small counties, and certainly in eastern Oklahoma—I don't think they really appreciated the seriousness of what they were doing."[11]

A similar story came from Drew Neville, Price's former teammate in the U.S. Attorney's Office, who had resigned to enter private practice and whose involvement in Okscam had been limited to his defense of Pottawatomie County Commissioner Edward Leroy Strickland. At the time of our interview, Neville was only a few days into his new position at McAfee & Taft in downtown Oklahoma City. Wedged between storage boxes and a random scattering of furniture, I listened intently to a story that revealed what was surely the number-one challenge in mounting an Okscam defense.

Neville's story began with an irate Commissioner Strickland storming into his office, shocked that he had been targeted by federal investigators for doing what he had been elected to do. No doubt about it: Strickland was innocent, and he needed Neville to prove it.

Then came this from the indignant commissioner:

"All I did was take my salary, *plus 10 percent!*"

Boom! With no warning, Neville roared and pounded his desk, nearly spilling my coffee but, happily, leaving my digital recorder intact.

Neville's powers of persuasion prevailed, and Strickland pleaded guilty to charges of accepting kickbacks, becoming the first commissioner to plead guilty to both state and federal charges, including mail fraud and conspiracy to commit tax evasion. Each charge carried a maximum penalty of five years in prison and a thousand-dollar fine. Strickland's troubles continued in September 1982, when a federal grand jury indicted him on thirty-seven counts, alleging that he had accepted kickbacks on purchases from materials suppliers. He pled guilty to a single count and agreed to cooperate with the probe, and prosecutors dismissed the other thirty-six counts, leaving the former commissioner to reconsider his declaration of innocence.[12]

For a judge's take on Okscam, I asked Ralph Thompson to talk about some of the cases that wound up in his court. What I got was not so much the minutiae of particular cases as a broad perspective of a scandal that had swamped his and his fellow Western District judges' calendars in a steady stream of litigation.

"What was your first real involvement in corruption?" I asked, knowing that Thompson had been appointed as a federal judge in the Western District of Oklahoma in October 1975, just three years before Stephens County became ground zero for corruption in county purchasing.

We were kept very busy for the four or so years of the investigation. We all had a lot of those cases! Many pled guilty because of the evidence being overwhelming. There was just no way out, really. But we tried some, and we sentenced all of them, except, I think, the one who was not convicted out of all of them! I think there was just one who went to trial. So we were involved in all the pleading stages of the cases. Of course, there were many pleas of guilty. The sentencing process, with the numbers involved, occupied a great deal of our time and attention. It was one of, or perhaps, at the time, the largest political corruption, public corruption, case in the country.[13]

As summer yielded to the fall of 1982, public attention yielded to the governor's race between incumbent George Nigh and Auditor and Inspector Tom Daxon, whose vigorous investigation into Okscam had given him the leverage he needed to challenge a popular Democratic governor. After waging what U.S. Senator Don Nickles called "an outstanding campaign" against Neal McCaleb in the Republican primary, Daxon enlisted President Ronald Reagan's support in what promised to be a bruising fight. Crediting Daxon for exposing corruption in county purchasing, the *Sunday Oklahoman* urged Oklahomans to vote for the former accountant, whose conservative campaign was based on his commitment to honest government, lower taxes, and spending cuts. The state's largest newspaper waxed biblical to portray Daxon as the David in his uphill battle against George Nigh, a Goliath in Oklahoma politics. According to an editorial in the *Sunday Oklahoman*, "Tom Daxon shows no hesitation to face tough, controversial issues. George Nigh ducks, dodges and dances around anything that might make someone mad . . . Oklahoma needs new leadership now. Serious Oklahomans should elect Tom Daxon on Nov. 2."[14]

Buoyed by Reagan's landslide victory in 1980 and ongoing support in Oklahoma, Daxon and his wife, Linda, crisscrossed the state in their bright red motor home, driven by former University of Arkansas quarterback Tom Rystrom, to convince voters that George Nigh was just another liberal politician, cast in the mold of Jimmy Carter and the Kennedy clan. But Nigh's freewheeling, casual, witty persona was too sharp a contrast to Daxon's deadpan deliveries. Even Linda's efforts to loosen him up failed to keep him from droning on about political patronage, waste in government, and investment of idle public funds— heady topics, to be sure, but unlikely to spawn a Republican revolution in a sea of Democrats. "The people are with us on the issue of lower taxes," declared Daxon a month before the election. "Every place we go we find that people are beginning to wake up and are learning there is an election. And we're finding we're right on the issues. We're finding we are catching up, if we haven't already caught up."[15]

But, of course, Daxon did not catch up, and George Nigh sailed to victory for a second term as governor. But Daxon's defeat could not diminish the role he had played, and continued to play, in the ongoing crusade to ferret out corruption in county purchasing and bring the rascals to justice.

▶ ▶ ▶ ▶

Two months after Bill Price was sworn in as U.S. Attorney for the Western District of Oklahoma and four months before Tom Daxon's loss to George Nigh in the governor's race of 1982, bank customers swarmed to the northwest corner of Penn Square Shopping Center in northwest Oklahoma City to witness one of the most consequential disasters in the history of American finance: the FDIC takeover of Penn Square National Bank. Rested from a weekend of splashing in tepid pools and feasting on barbecue over the Fourth of July holiday, the people who milled anxiously in the bank parking lot on that Tuesday morning, on July 6th, had good reason to doubt the safety of their deposits and the soundness of their loans. Few suspected that the entire oil-patch economy was about to go from boom to bust.

Penn Square Bank's collapse had its roots in the oil shocks of the early 1970s, when members of the Organization of Petroleum Exporting Countries (OPEC) turned down their spigots and gloated as oil prices quadrupled, spawning what was likely the greatest nonviolent transfer of wealth in history.[16] The Arab oil embargo of 1973 was on and, for once, the arcane lingo of economics was crystal clear: oil producers were running surpluses on their balance sheets, and other countries were not.[17] A familiar chant rang from the halls of Congress to the oilfields of Oklahoma and Texas: *Drill, baby, drill!*

But drilling for more oil was only part of the answer. As geologists became more familiar with the Anadarko Basin, which covers much of western Oklahoma, they realized that vast deposits of natural gas, primarily methane, were trapped in formations more than 15,000 feet below the surface.[18] Although they were convinced that even deeper sedimentary layers were ripe for development, they were stymied by a simple equation: the deeper you drilled, the more money you needed. Until the price of natural gas below 15,000 feet could be deregulated— that is, until its price could be separated from the price of shallower gas and brought in line with the high cost of extracting it—then the riches of the Anadarko Basin would remain beyond reach, and Americans would need to look elsewhere to solve their energy dilemma.

Predictably, geologists and their lobbyists went to work. "Everybody in Oklahoma was trying to get decontrol of natural gas," recalled Price. "It was real close in Congress between Democrats and Republicans. Republicans wanted to decontrol all natural gas. Democrats wanted to not decontrol natural gas."[19] In the end, free marketers won a compromise victory with passage of the Natural Gas Policy Act (NGPA) of November 9, 1978, a seminal piece of legislation whose goals were threefold: (1) to create a single natural gas market; (2) to equalize supply and demand; and (3) to allow market forces to establish the wellhead price of natural gas.[20] Drillers, bankers, and investors let out a collective cheer when they learned that price controls on natural gas below 15,000 feet were about to be lifted. Henceforth, the price of gas above 15,000 feet would be controlled, while gas below 15,000 feet would be sold at prices commensurate with the high costs of drilling. Price drew an analogy between establishing layers of price deregulation and outlawing ladders to harvest apples but allowing helicopters.[21]

Joining in that collective cheer was Robert A. Hefner III, whose company, GHK, had pioneered deep-gas exploration and drilling in the Anadarko Basin. Such was Hefner's conviction that deregulated deep gas had the potential to sever America's dependence on foreign energy resources that he rented an apartment at the Watergate Hotel in Washington, D.C., to facilitate his incessant lobbying and testifying before Congress. Hefner eventually teamed up with U.S. Secretary of Energy Jim Schlesinger and his right-hand man, Les Goldman, to craft the legislation that was now upending the natural gas industry and clearing the way for energy independence. Even though the NGPA was not slated to go into effect for a year, pipeline companies were already building incentives into their contracts for drillers to ramp up production.[22]

What became known as the "deep gas play" in the Anadarko Basin took on new urgency, in January 1979, when Iranian revolutionaries toppled the Shah Mohammed Riza Pahlavi and installed a theocratic regime bent on destroying America, excoriated by the Ayatollah

Khomeini as "the great Satan." Day after hellish day, Americans turned on the evening news to witness Old Glory engulfed in flame, black-clad imams cradling their Korans and imploring the faithful to resist Western seductions, and hordes of bearded zealots chanting *"death to America!"* But nothing etched itself more indelibly into America's collective consciousness than footage of fifty-two blindfolded hostages force-marched from the American embassy in Tehran and paraded before a seething mob. CBS anchor Walter Cronkite became the unofficial scorekeeper for a game that nobody wanted to play by ending each newscast with a tally of how many days the hostages had languished in captivity.

In a decade that began with an Arab oil embargo and ended with daily reminders of their unpopularity in the Middle East, Americans were fed up with foreign oil suppliers. And who was more equipped to come to their rescue than homegrown oil and natural gas developers, who could deploy their resources in the cause of energy independence? But, of course, financing a surge in production was not that easy. Barring piles of their own capital, where were those developers supposed to find the money to drill to mind-boggling depths?

The answer arrived in the form of Penn Square Bank.[23] Its chairman, William P. "Beep" Jennings, was raised in southern Oklahoma, and as the only child of a small-town banker, he was weaned on community banking. Undeterred by his own lack of experience in energy lending, Jennings decided to do his part for energy independence by creating an oil and gas division. Jennings's business plan was based on a modus operandi that had yet to be tested in a really big way: a bank did not have to lend its own assets if it could tap into another bank's assets.[24] He further suggested that his bank partner with money-center banks on the hunt for loan participation. In the evolving oil-patch lexicon, banks with lots of capital were "upstream," and banks with less capital were "downstream." If correspondent relationships with upstream banks could be properly cultivated, then Penn Square Bank, perched downstream like a fly fisherman in a mountain brook, would rake in millions in loan origination and servicing fees, all at minimal risk to shareholders and maximum benefit to the bank's asset base, which in 1977 was just shy of $70 million.[25]

Jennings was dreaming big when he hired William George "Bill" Patterson, a former assistant cashier at the First National Bank and Trust Company of Oklahoma City, whose legendary fraternity pranks at the University of Oklahoma (where he earned the nickname Monkey Brains) complemented his reputation as a man who "could sell snowmobiles to Okies."[26] Affable and always up for a good time, Patterson leveraged his insider status with Beep Jennings to become one of the bank's most influential movers and shakers.

The fun-loving Patterson had been on board for about a year when Jennings put him in charge of oil and gas lending. "Jennings was largely an absentee boss," explained Price. "He wasn't there a large part of the time. He gave carte blanche to Patterson."[27]

By the time of Patterson's rise in the ranks, Americans had had enough of Muslim fanatics and were more anxious than ever to wrest themselves from Middle Eastern oil. Determined to capitalize on the superheating oil-patch economy, money-center bankers sent their loan officers to Oklahoma and Texas to find local lenders in need of upstream capital. As Price recalled about the lending frenzy of the early 1980s, "The banks were desperate to find borrowers out there! They had also loaned to a lot of countries, and those had all gone bad. They were really desperate for loans!"[28]

Like latter-day gunslingers with a license to deal, those lenders found their way to Penn Square Bank, whose bland three-story edifice, poking out between fashionable shops and eateries, gave little evidence of the powerhouse it would soon become.

Nor did Bill Patterson signal that he would be the one to set it all in motion.

▶ ▶ ▶ ▶

Oklahomans in the early 1980s were witnessing a convergence of two powerful narratives destined to shape the course of their state's development for generations to come: Okscam, a scandal of such scope that it left a permanent scar in the body politic and spawned reforms that had been stymied since statehood, and a deep gas play that contained all the ingredients of an economic boom. As the public's attention shifted from corruption in county courthouses to the goings-on in the Anadarko Basin, bankers and their intrepid borrowers had little reason to doubt that they stood to make a pile of money. Staid bankers who stayed on the sidelines were chided for their conservatism. Among them was Citizens Security Bank of Bixby President and CEO Carlisle Mabrey III, a conservative banker who resisted the siren song of easy money, but not without plenty of soul searching. As he commented many years after the frenzy was spent, "We were the ones sitting around wondering, 'Are we the only dumb guys around?' We're not doing this, and there was pressure to do it!"[29] In Duncan, bank consultant Bob McCormack watched a boom that had all the hallmarks of a bust in the making. "Everybody that I knew and talked to—we all knew it wouldn't work," he said. "It couldn't last! It was just going too fast!"[30] With his consulting business headquartered a few blocks from Okscam's spawning grounds in the Stephens County courthouse, McCormack knew better than most that bonanzas don't last forever.

And why was it going too fast? Cue Bill Patterson, Beep Jennings's star loan officer, with a distaste for stodgy protocols and a nose for upstream money. "These banks were just chomping at the bit to take every one of Patterson's loans!" explained Price about the man who could sell snowmobiles to Okies. "So you've got this little bank in Oklahoma, and supposedly the most sophisticated banks in the world are buying Penn Square loans. It's hard to show that they were defrauded in many ways. What Patterson was doing was—and Jennings was allowing him to do—was making wild and crazy loans based on the theory that the price of gas would continue to rise. But that's not a criminal act."[31]

Not criminal, but certainly unorthodox, and definitely risky enough to make Penn Square Bank's rapid-fire growth a matter of concern to regulators. A quick calculation showed that the bank's growth rate was putting it on track to become the third largest bank in the country by the end of the century. Stunned, a senior official in the Comptroller of the Currency's office in Washington, D.C., remarked to a colleague, "There's something in Oklahoma City that's growing. It's weird. It's just weird."

Upstream lenders from such behemoths as Continental Illinois, Chase Manhattan, and Seattle First who made their way to Patterson's office in search of loan participations encountered a high-energy loan officer who never let paperwork bog down a deal and a master of delegation who promoted secretaries to managers of multimillion-dollar portfolios. As a former bank officer who preferred to remain anonymous put it, "You could walk in the door without a financial statement or any formal written proposal, and if what you outlined verbally sounded feasible you could sit down and sign your name to a note and maybe some oil and gas mortgages all prepared in blank." Overdrafts and sloppiness were all in a day's work. When the workday ended at Cowboys, Junior's, or another of Patterson's favorite hangouts, where food fights were a favorite mode of entertainment and quail was Patterson's preferred projectile, deals were scratched on cocktail napkins.[32]

Even as Penn Square Bank's oil and gas division was celebrating its successes, an implacable logic was casting a pall across western Oklahoma, and it confirmed economics' designation as the dismal science. Frenzied natural gas production, OPEC's diminishing clout in manipulating fuel prices, and slackening demand attending the new conservation ethos (epitomized when President Carter turned down the White House thermostats and donned his cardigan sweater) were conspiring to produce an oversupply of natural gas and push prices in the wrong direction. Ominously, pipeline companies were becoming overextended on their take-or-pay contracts and buying more natural gas than they could possibly sell. Oil-field service companies were having a tough time collecting their money from contractors, and bankers were beginning to reminisce about other booms that had ended badly. Like the proverbial canary in the coal mine, the stock market foretold dark days to come. By late 1981, prices of most oil and gas common stocks were down 30 percent from the previous year. According to lease broker Steve Knox, "The whole Ponzi scheme stopped in January."[33]

Back at the financial epicenter of the deep gas play, National Bank Examiner Steve Plunk was conducting Penn Square Bank's final and most damning review. Among Plunk's discoveries, duly reported to his supervisor, Clifton Poole, regional administrator for the Office of the Comptroller of the Currency in Dallas, were overlending, an absence of controls in the energy department, poor supervision by the bank's directors, and inadequate documentation. Last-minute attempts to find a buyer with deep pockets came to naught. Efforts became ever more frantic as the Fourth of July weekend approached.

Any doubts that the wheels were coming off the bus vanished when Plunk dropped into Patterson's office one day with a stack of loan documents that he wanted to review with him.

"I could not keep him focused," said Plunk in his lilting Tennessee accent. "He would jump up on the couch, point at a map of Oklahoma, and tell me how many oil and gas reserves there were!"[34]

Penn Square Bank's moment of truth came Monday evening, July 5, 1982, when Comptroller of the Currency Todd Conover called Plunk and recited a scripted run-up to declaring the bank insolvent. After dispensing with the formalities, Conover told Plunk, "I have become satisfied that the bank is insolvent. I have appointed the FDIC as receiver. Please advise the bank that we are closing it and appointing the FDIC as receiver effective at 7:05 P.M, Central Daylight Savings Time."[35]

▶ ▶ ▶ ▶

"I still remember so well when Penn Square Bank collapsed in 1982," recalled Price. "There were many parts to this case that were a

Penn Square Bank's closure by the FDIC on July 5, 1982, was both cause and effect of the worst economic downturn in the oil-and-gas patch since the Great Depression. COURTESY OKLAHOMA HISTORICAL SOCIETY.

prosecutor's nightmare. Number one, everybody in the state thought that, if there was criminal activity, it had to be Jennings at the heart of it." To prosecute the avalanche of lawsuits that was surely coming, Price assigned Assistant U.S. Attorneys Susie Pritchett and Terresa Black; when needed, he participated in their prosecutions. Based on piles of documents that FBI agents had uncovered in a year of careful sifting and a raft of interviews with potential witnesses, Pritchett and Black concluded that, although Jennings was civilly responsible for the bank's collapse, he could not be held criminally liable. But they were building a criminal case against Patterson, and if he could be compelled to testify that Jennings knew what was really going on, they would be able to charge the beleaguered bank chairman with criminal violations.

That was bound to be difficult. As Price explained about Jennings' plausible deniability, "You would have Patterson doing something and saying, 'Don't tell Jennings.' You would have not only Jennings not knowing; you would have positive evidence to the contrary that *he was kept in the dark!*"

Jennings may have dodged a bullet, but others in the bank's hierarchy were not so fortunate. After a year of scrutinizing the remains of Penn Square Bank, federal regulators had discovered evidence of more than 340 possible criminal violations, mostly involving the bank's freewheeling lending practices. Thomas R. Procopio, the FDIC's liquidator in charge of the bank's receivership, described several possible criminal violations, including overline lending (loans for amounts above the bank's legal lending limit), insider loan transactions, and misrepresentation of the purposes of loans, all of which he reported to the U.S. Attorney's Office and the FBI. Enough evidence was gathered to prompt indictments during the next month's grand jury session, set to begin on July 18, 1983.[36]

The nightmare was compounded as interested parties, including insurance companies representing some of the nation's largest banks, lined up to file lawsuits. Price continued: "Everybody and their brothers were suing each other, and you had civil suits where everybody was being deposed. It was, literally, every time you put on a witness, there might be a room full of depositions to go through. You've got witnesses getting deposed by twenty different attorneys!" To further complicate a prosecutor's case, Patterson had played a shell game with loans, deftly moving them from bad to good borrowers with nary a word to whomever he chose to saddle with bad debt. "You've got all the motive in the world for the good borrowers to say that it wasn't their loan!" said Price.

Among the most nefarious bank officers to join Patterson in Price's crosshairs was Thomas Sidney Orr. "We did, successfully, prosecute some other folks," continued Price. "There was a guy named Tom Orr. Actually, he was higher up than Patterson. It was an old-fashioned kickback scheme in which he was lending money on horses, and he was getting part of the proceeds."[37]

As an executive vice president, Tom Orr thought he had the cover he needed to run a horse brokerage business from his office. A bank customer who did business with him noted that working with Orr was "like trying to do business at the OK Corral." From the fall of 1979 to the spring of 1981, when Orr resigned his position, millions of dollars in horse deals were consummated in his office. Many buyers were disappointed to discover that their acquisitions were not quite the champions that Orr claimed they were.

When Orr's case was about to go to trial, witnesses from as far away as New Mexico and Florida were ready to testify that they had bought horses through Penn Square Bank. Orr had also used the bank to finance sales of his own horses, and he had violated customers' trust by concealing commissions on deals that he had encouraged them to make. Such was Orr's audacity that he disguised some of those deals as oil and gas investments. Nor was he above making outright threats. New Mexico horseman Billy Underwood, Jr., alleged that, on one occasion, Orr threatened to call a previous note unless he bought another horse from him.[38]

In January 1984, Orr waived a grand-jury indictment and pleaded guilty to tax evasion and fraud. Price called Orr's admission "the first breakthrough and the first major step in the investigation of criminality at Penn Square Bank."[39]

For all the attention accorded Beep Jennings, Tom Orr, and other top brass at Penn Square Bank, public outrage was directed mostly toward Bill Patterson. In July 1984, he was named in a thirty-four-count federal indictment (later reduced to twenty-five counts) charging him with wire fraud, misapplying bank funds, and making false entries.[40] No sooner were jurors seated for the trial than they were asked to identify the real Bill Patterson: either "an egotistic master of deceit who built a house of cards with bad loans" or the fall guy in "a treacherous, insidious plot" designed to offer him up as a scapegoat for Penn Square Bank's collapse.[41]

Whether he was an evil genius or stooge, the U.S. Attorney's Office faced two challenges in securing his conviction on criminal violations. First, the prosecution had to prove that Patterson, who was a major shareholder as well as an officer of the bank, was guilty of deliberately defrauding his bank. "Patterson had no motive to defraud Penn Square Bank," explained Price. "His motive was to keep this whole thing going by keeping examiners at bay until he could unload bad loans on upstream banks." The prosecution's second challenge was to show that Patterson was deliberately defrauding upstream banks and deceiving bank examiners by shifting loans from bad to good borrowers, hyping the profit potential in oil and gas investments, and paying interest on nonperforming loans to conceal their deteriorating status. As FBI agent Hank Gibbons put it, "With bank fraud, you've got to have the intent to defraud. That became the crux of the issue. It's kind of hard to say you have an intent to hurt the bank when you're trying to save the bank."[42]

A key aspect of defense attorneys' strategy was to challenge the credibility of good borrowers who had discovered, to their dismay, that Patterson had saddled them with other borrowers' bad debts without their knowledge. Allegations that honest borrowers were lying to protect their assets lost traction when prosecutors described the way Patterson had manipulated those loans. Most damning of all, borrowers who had been duped were uniformly absent at Patterson's loan closings. A turning point came when one of Patterson's devoted assistants told Price and Pritchett about an off-the-cuff comment that Patterson had made in her presence. Testifying under oath, the assistant recalled Patterson saying that one of the bank's upstanding borrowers, Joe Dan Trigg, had a new partner and did not even know it.

All eyes were on the federal courthouse when U.S. District Judge Lee Roy West gave the jury its instructions, and they confirmed Price's, Pritchett's, Black's, and Gibbons's worst fears. "Our indictment had alleged a scheme to defraud upstream banks and to deceive bank examiners, not to defraud Penn Square," recalled Price about the moment he realized the prosecution's case was lost. "Contrary to our indictment, the instruction said that we had to prove that he had the intent to harm Penn Square. Frankly, once we had that instruction, I couldn't hardly even argue it. That killed us!"

As Price further explained, a legally wrong instruction is a death sentence to any prosecutor's case. Although defense attorneys can appeal an instruction and get a new trial, the prosecution cannot appeal an instruction, secure its reversal, and try the defendant again. Double jeopardy is attached at the beginning of a trial and precludes retrial.

Patterson's acquittal, on September 27, did indeed hinge on the issue of intent. As one juror, who requested anonymity, explained after the trial, evidence of Patterson's alleged intent to defraud Penn Square Bank or any other bank "just wasn't there." Price heard much the same story from a college professor who had served as jury foreman. "When I heard the facts, I was sure we were going to have to convict," said the juror. "When I heard the jury instructions, I knew we were going to have to acquit."

As his attorneys helped him stand up and exit the courtroom as a free man, while weeping and choking, all Bill Patterson could say was, "Nobody knows what I've been through the past two years. I'm just so tired I can hardly stand up." He went home, went to sleep, and awoke to the unwelcome news that a Chicago grand jury had issued a sixteen-count indictment against him for the damage he had inflicted on Continental Illinois National Bank.[43]

Clearly, litigation attending the rise and fall of Penn Square Bank was far from over. Nor was Okscam ready to fade into history. These and plenty of other narratives steeped in crime and corruption stayed in the headlines to remind Oklahomans that their state had not yet outgrown its outlaw past. If there was a silver lining, it was that officials in other states were calling federal prosecutors in Oklahoma to learn how to conduct their own probes. Price and Gibbons responded by delivering lectures at national conferences, where FBI agents and prosecutors learned firsthand how to investigate and prosecute county commissioner corruption. "I've gotten calls from U.S. prosecutors across the country as to how to conduct similar investigations in other states," said Price as Okscam was winding down and a few months before Penn Square Bank muscled its way onto his calendar. Probes modeled on Okscam were launched in Texas, Mississippi, Alabama, Tennessee, Kentucky, Colorado, and Georgia.

As in Oklahoma, federal prosecutors in those states were basing their cases on three charges that were bound to snare miscreants, no matter where they stood in the criminal hierarchy: mail fraud, conspiracy to commit tax evasion, and extortion per the Hobbs Act under the color of official right. Those states were also looking to Price's reliance on plea agreements to hasten their investigations and prosecutions. "We required cooperation so the probe wouldn't just get a few people and stop," said Price, whose notoriety was beginning to spread beyond the borders of his native Oklahoma.

From investigators and prosecutors nationwide, Price found that corruption followed a common pattern and relied on schemes that had become all too familiar: ten percents, negotiated kickbacks on heavy equipment, blue-sky deals for nonexistent materials, and back-up systems for phony invoices.

"I guess the same idea occurred to people in different states," he said finally. "It's fascinating that it's exactly the same scheme."[44]

CHAPTER TWELVE : *Top Job – Part Two*

The same day that Bill Price was sworn in as U.S.
Attorney for the Western District of Oklahoma, state
Senator Gideon Tinsley was accused of accepting
kickbacks on material purchases while he was a
Canadian County commissioner. Darwin L. "Bill" Allred,
owner-operator of Allred Supply Company, testified under oath that he
had paid kickbacks to Tinsley and fifty-six other commissioners and
former commissioners between January 1970 and July 6, 1981. Like
so many materials suppliers who had been caught red-handed, Allred
pleaded guilty to mail and tax fraud.

Price's red-letter week turned out to be a busy one for his friend
U.S. District Judge Ralph Thompson. In addition to Allred, two
others entered guilty pleas before Judge Thompson on that stressful
Friday of May 7. Former Washita county commissioner Kenneth
Elwood Jones admitted to accepting kickbacks from seven materials
suppliers and Lewis Allen Miller, a salesman for Thurman Bridge
and Block Company, admitted to paying kickbacks to more than thirty
commissioners. The three defendants were released on unsecured
$5,000 bonds.[1]

A month later, it was Meeker equipment salesman Ernest
"Cotton" Irwin's turn in the spotlight. His testimony came not in
Judge Thompson's courtroom in Oklahoma City, but in Judge Seay's
courtroom in Muskogee as part of Charlie Waters's prosecution of
Murray County Commissioner Bird Lance, Jr. Irwin, the founder
of Independent Industries and Machinery Parts & Service, had
been in prosecutors' crosshairs for months. According to his own
estimates, he had made ten thousand payoffs to at least twenty-seven

county commissioners over the past seventeen years. "It's part of the system," explained Irwin, who figured that he had paid an average of one kickback a day. "It's been going on for years." Weighing in from Oklahoma City, Bill Price identified Irwin as the state's number-one purveyor of kickbacks. Unrepentant to the bitter end, Irwin described Bird Lance as his friend and, in the process, corroborated Price's assessment.

"I done business with him for 17 years," asserted Irwin. "I gave him money in the morning, afternoon and night for 17 years. If he needed $200, I'd give him $200. If he needed $300, I'd give him $300."[2]

Although the public's attention was turning to Penn Square Bank's collapse and mounting troubles in the Anadarko Basin, Okscam continued to provide fodder for front-page news. In mid-July 1982, former Cotton County commissioner Theodore Jones and four materials suppliers were arraigned before U.S. District Court Judge Fred Daugherty. Jones and his fellow Cotton County commissioners, Hoss Williams and Kenneth Kirkpatrick, had resigned their posts en masse after signing plea agreements and agreeing to cooperate with the ongoing probe. Their resignations gave Cotton County the dubious distinction as the thirteenth county to lose all three of its commissioners simultaneously.[3]

Bill Price was three and a half months into the government's top job when he admitted that his six-month estimate of Okscam's longevity had been overly optimistic. "It could take up to another year and it could very well result in three hundred people or so being charged," said Price. Prosecutors in the Eastern District hit a snag—and, much to their chagrin, suffered a rare loss against Senator Gene Stipe, who wound up defending more than forty Okscam targets before it was all over—when a federal jury in Muskogee returned a not-guilty verdict against former Pontotoc County commissioner Johnnie Boring. That verdict went down in prosecutorial history as one of only three instances in which an Okscam defendant was hauled into court and left with neither a jail sentence nor a fine. There was only one not-guilty verdict rendered in the Western District. The other not-guilty verdicts were handed down in the other districts.

Undaunted by a temporary setback, federal prosecutors in Muskogee soldiered on to convict Seminole County Commissioner James Whitt, represented by the indefatigable Gene Stipe, on twenty-seven counts of mail fraud and six counts of extortion. Gary Richardson, newly appointed as U.S. Attorney in the Eastern District, said that Whitt's conviction was significant because, for the first time in his district, a jury did not throw out extortion charges, which carried a penalty twice as stiff as mail-fraud charges. Whitt's conviction concluded a bad week for Senator Stipe. A few days earlier, in the Western District, he had failed to win acquittal for Ponca City supplier Herb Neal on thirty-three kickback-related charges. Neal's conviction helped to extend the Western District's winning streak against 170 commissioners, former commissioners, and materials suppliers, all but one of whom were either convicted or had agreed to plead guilty.[4] The Western District racked up more victories, on September 2, when six former county commissioners were sentenced to prison: Ira McHendry and Ray Fields from Garfield County; Leonard Johanning and Clifton Honeyman from Grant County, neither of whom had learned much from their squeaky-clean colleague, Keith Hoar; Dwight Hughey from Alfalfa County; and J. C. Bradford from Woods County. All six men resigned their posts after pleading guilty to the standard charges of conspiracy to commit mail fraud and income tax evasion.[5]

If Price and his assistants had any doubts about the efficacy of their prosecutions, the Tenth Circuit Court of Appeals in Denver put them to rest, in January 1983, when it upheld Donald Skipworth's conviction on twenty-three counts of mail fraud and three counts of income tax evasion. In spite of attempts by Skipworth's attorney, Garland Bloodworth, to brand Dorothy Griffin's and Guy Moore's undercover work as "outrageous conduct by government agents," the appeals court sanctioned the use of secret recordings. "It's a very important hurdle to have the first one affirmed, and this strongly, too," commented Price about the appeals court's decision. "It certainly helps in affirming the cases of the 205 commissioners and suppliers who have either been convicted or have agreed to plead guilty. It shows there was nothing wrong with this conviction, and the other cases involved very similar issues and indictments."[6]

The appeals court's decision was significant for other reasons: it highlighted the need for state prosecution of crimes that spanned multiple jurisdictions, and it accentuated Oklahoma's need for statutes to expand the scope of statewide investigations and allow for multicounty grand juries. As Price declared at every opportunity, the state was hindered from uncovering most Okscam cases because they involved kickbacks from multiple counties.[7]

Skipworth's case was only one of many Okscam appeals that made it to the Tenth Circuit Court's docket. Such was the volume of appeals that the court diverged from its protocol of handling cases as they trickled in and, instead, assigned entire days to Okscam appeals. To argue the United States cases from the Western District, Price chose Susie Pritchett as his go-to litigator. Interviewed in October 1991, Pritchett shared what Price had taught her about courtroom demeanor, which she could not quite emulate but found inspirational. "The juries loved him," said Pritchett about her mentor. "They liked us, but they *loved* him!" Appearing slightly rumpled and sporting an infectious grin, Price exuded a little-boy persona that jurors found irresistible. More often than not, all they had to do was look at his smooth, honest face, listen to his melodious voice, and absorb the wisdom gleaned from a lifetime of reading serious literature to return a guilty verdict. Anne who, as of this writing in 2021, is a lawyer and director of Student Affairs Contracts and Business Partnerships at the University of Nevada Las Vegas, explained why her father's courtroom presence would inspire her own career as an attorney, "I would not have wanted to be a defense attorney on the other side of it!"[8]

If there was a silver lining to Okscam's steady stream of arrests and indictments and pleas and convictions and appeals, it was in the state legislature's passage of House Bills 1518 and 1578. In one fell swoop, that spelled the beginning of the end of decades of business as usual in county governance. Commissioners now faced a maze of paperwork (eleven forms, to be exact—eight for the commissioner's staff and three for a county purchasing agent) and a bureaucratic chain of command whenever they purchased supplies. "I don't know who thought all this up, but they didn't have much on their mind," complained Dewey County Commissioner W. C. Baker. "Every time the boys come in and get a quart of oil, it has to go through the consumable items report." Uncertain how to purchase supplies, Blaine County Commissioner Lewis Hood halted road repair work in his district. Tom Terry with the state Department of Transportation said bluntly, "That's what all the bitching is about—the paperwork."

Price, too, had his doubts about the efficacy of paperwork. "You can get around paperwork," said Price. "Besides, all it really does is cost money and expand bureaucracy. Nor do I think it's proper to move road- and bridge-building to the state, as that would eliminate local control. What you really need is structural reform of county governance."

Confusion extended from county courthouses to the capitol. State Auditor and Inspector Clifton Scott barely had time to settle into his new job when county commissioners sent his phone ringing off the hook. Scott answered their queries as best he could and then spent sleepless nights wondering if he was inadvertently breaking the law by giving out bad advice. He went so far as to close his office, in January 1983, to obtain a legal opinion. Among other stringent regulations, any purchase in excess of $750 required county commissioners to request competitive bids. That meant long waits to obtain equipment and materials. As Pushmataha County Commissioner Finnis Whiteside put it, "If they don't modify this a little bit, we're going to have a hard time carrying on in county government."[9]

▶ ▶ ▶ ▶

Thanks largely to Dorothy Griffin's and Guy Moore's taped conversations (110 and 160, respectively), U.S. Attorneys Bill Price in Oklahoma City, Frank Keating in Tulsa, and Gary Richardson in Muskogee got to the bottom of the most widespread case of public corruption in U.S. history. Price spoke for federal prosecutors statewide when, in a March 1983 interview with the *Sooner Catholic*, he described the insidious nature of economic crime: "When wrongdoing continues, people grow skeptical about law and justice. We prosecuted. We had to send people to prison. That's the only way you can stop a practice. Some got from six months to three years. Those who lied got from seven to twenty years."

The most tangible evidence of successful prosecutions was the plummeting cost of materials. The state's central equipment purchasing agency reported that the cost of machinery had dropped 40 percent since pre-Okscam days. "That's the part you really enjoy," explained a justifiably proud Bill Price. "It's gratifying to see the state save money and to put an end to temptation."[10] Thanks to reductions in prices and reforms enacted by the state legislature, Price estimated annual savings in the post-Okscam era at $100 million to $200 million annually.[11] Delmas Ford, acting director of the state's Central Purchasing Division of the Board of Public Affairs, credited Price with saving the counties millions of dollars, and he expected that trend to continue for many years. "Certainly, the people of Oklahoma are getting more for their dollar today than they were a year or two years ago," he said.[12]

In terms of prosecutions, the final tally was 230 guilty pleas or convictions, including 165 county commissioners (110 of whom were in office when they were accused of federal crimes) and, of course, their suppliers. Okscam's tentacles touched sixty of the state's seventy-seven counties. Although a few more pleas and convictions were in the offing, Price was ready to call the case closed in early February 1984.[13]

Now that I knew more than most about Okscam, I couldn't help but wonder if Price had ever felt threatened in his war against corruption. Although he insisted that he never gave much thought to his personal safety, his family certainly did. His and Mary's oldest child, Anne, recalled late-night phone calls and suspicious clicking noises that made her suspect that their lines were bugged. "I remember thinking there were suspicious people working on the telephone lines," said Anne. "I tried to see if they actually had a marked telephone company car versus an unmarked car." Frank and Cathy Keating's daughter and Anne's childhood friend Carrie had much the same experience during her father's stint as U.S. Attorney for the Northern District of Oklahoma. During sleepovers, the girls shared their anxieties about the trouble their fathers were courting in their respective prosecutions.

"It was always a very brave thing for him to do," concluded Anne about her father's line of work. "But these things aren't without some consequences."[14]

Those consequences nearly turned fatal after a harrowing case that Price and Charlie Waters prosecuted against Kingfisher County Commissioner Billy L. Lightle, represented by Gene Stipe. "We tried him and convicted him," said Price. "All of his people were there, angry. There were probably thirty, forty, or fifty people that were friends."

Satisfied with another success in the courtroom, Price shrugged off the steely glares coming his way from Lightle's supporters, walked to the parking lot, and climbed into his car. As usual in the days of light security, his car was parked in the spot labeled "Reserved U.S. Attorney."

When Price hit the road, his car began to accelerate uncontrollably until it reached sixty miles per hour. Slamming on the brakes failed to slow it down. In desperation, he turned off the ignition and was relieved when his car rolled to a stop. A check-up the next day with a mechanic confirmed his worst suspicions.

"Somebody put ball bearings in my carburetor," he said matter-of-factly. "It stuck."

From then on, Price's parking spot was less obtrusively labeled, "Reserved."

Price went on to characterize Colombian cartels, drug peddlers, and white-collar criminals as smart enough to leave U.S. Attorneys alone, knowing that, if harm came to them, they would simply be replaced. But supporters of errant county commissioners were another story.

"That guy was totally uncontrite," said Price about Commissioner Lightle, "and his supporters were just full of animosity!"[15]

Even though Price was ready to put Okscam behind him, the curtain was not quite ready to drop—that is, not until suppliers-turned-informants Dorothy Griffin and Guy Moore received their sentences. Their day in Ralph Thompson's courtroom came on November 8, 1984, when conspiracy charges were filed against them and a third supplier, Hugh Wein of Enid, whose cooperation with authorities came as Okscam was winding down. All three pleaded guilty and settled into an anxious wait for sentences that might have included five years in prison, $10,000 in fines, and restitution to the counties. A very different fate awaited Bill Price, who learned that same week that he would receive Oklahoma Common Cause's 1984 Award for Outstanding Service in the Public Interest. Price also stood to receive the U.S. Department of Justice Special Achievement Award.[16]

Even as he basked in the glow of public approval, neither Price nor anybody else, for that matter, expected corruption to vanish without a trace. As Okscam faded from the headlines, the *Daily Oklahoman* posed the sixty-four-dollar question: "What will it take to cleanse the corruption from our political environment in Oklahoma?" Already fading from collective memory were three scandals of enormous import: Oklahoma Supreme Court justices' complicity in bribery and extortion, State Treasurer Leo Winters's alleged favoritism in depositing taxpayers' money in banks that contributed to his political campaigns, and former Governor David Hall's conviction and imprisonment on charges of extortion. And never mind the ancient history of Indian land theft, the Osage murders, two gubernatorial impeachments, the often-cozy relationship between legislators and the Ku Klux Klan, the Tulsa race riot that laid waste to the city's thriving African American community, and the relegation of African Americans to segregated neighborhoods and squalid communities.

Given the scope and variety of wrongdoing, Oklahomans had reason to doubt that Okscam would be the end of it. A glance at the goings-on in the state legislature in December 1983 seemed to confirm their skepticism. Speaker of the House of Representatives Dan Draper of Stillwater and Majority Leader Joe Fitzgibbon of Miami had been convicted of absentee-ballot fraud, Senate Finance Committee Chairman Mike Combs of Bethany had been convicted of extorting a payoff from a drug dealer, and House Judiciary Committee Chairman Don Denman of Oklahoma City was awaiting trial on charges of using the power of his legislative office for personal gain. For the most part, federal authorities had accomplished what state officials could not, and even though Democrats were the main culprits, Republicans likely would have succumbed to the same temptations if they had constituted the state's dominant party. On the upside, opportunities were knocking on both parties' doors: Republicans could brand themselves as the anticorruption party, and Democrats could challenge the reigning establishment that had brought such disgrace to the state.

Although the *Daily Oklahoman* had no surefire remedies, it did suggest reversing the trend toward a full-time legislature as a step in the right direction. "Through voter neglect and apathy, too many legislators are allowed to serve too long," declared the state's largest newspaper. "They became captives of the system, with no interest in changing it." Like Cincinnatus of Roman lore, who traded his sword for a plowshare at war's end, Oklahomans might have been persuaded to revive the concept of the citizen legislator, who would serve for one or two terms and then go home. "The bleak alternative is more of the same, but with a steadily increasing price tag," warned the *Daily Oklahoman*. "Better start thinking about it. Is that what you want?"[17]

That certainly was not what Bill Price wanted, but it was what he feared. Even though middlemen's exodus from county purchasing was driving prices down by as much as 40 percent, there were troubling signs that kickback schemes might have been making a comeback as suppliers changed the names of their companies and muscled their way back into business. What Price really wanted was for Oklahoma to emulate its northern neighbor, where part-time commissioners and full-time county managers, who were often honest-to-goodness road engineers, performed their jobs with integrity and professionalism. As Price explained, "We need more of a system like Kansas. You get a higher quality commissioner when they're willing to work part-time. And when you have full-time county managers, you tend to have professionals who are less likely to be corrupt." Moreover, under Kansas's county management structure, a county maintained a single supply yard, duplication in spending and overlapping in responsibilities were minimized, commissioners shared supplies and equipment regardless of how well they got along, and systems of checks and balances ensured that officials worked in harmony, just as the founding fathers intended.

Although repeated calls for county consolidation never gained much traction, reformers and honest commissioners would have settled for consolidation within counties under the purview of a county manager. "I'm sure, today, that most county commissioners are honest and hard-working," said Price about the values that have taken root in the four decades since Okscam. "Nevertheless, the county manager system not only promotes these values; it also reduces costs, as there's only one manager on the payroll." For Price, extending home rule (also known as county option) to the counties by legislative fiat would have preserved local control and, at the same time, replicated the efficiencies and honest governance that Kansans took for granted. The legislature allowed cities and towns to choose their governmental structures. Why not counties?

As evidence that Kansans were onto something, suppliers who dealt in northern Oklahoma and southern Kansas told Price that 95 percent of their business in Kansas was honest. By contrast, the same percentage of their business in Oklahoma was corrupt.

In the criminal area, to prevent corruption from seeping back into county governance and to address multicounty crimes, Price advocated for a state system that could prosecute crimes on a statewide basis. The state's primary investigative agency, the OSBI, could investigate only at the request of local authorities, the governor, or the attorney general, and even if its agents had tried to parallel the federal investigation, they likely would have run into interference from the courthouse cliques that held sway in most counties. Concerns notwithstanding, Price remained cautiously optimistic that the "fear factor," together with the obvious benefits of a system that promoted honesty, would keep sitting commissioners on the straight and narrow for the foreseeable future. "I don't think it will ever go back to the way it was," said Price.[18]

Neither the OSBI's constraints nor courthouse cliques stopped Oklahoma Attorney General Mike Turpen from filing criminal charges and civil lawsuits against firms and individuals who paid the kickbacks. "The federal prosecution, while effective, didn't go after the corporations but only the individuals," explained Turpen. "We are filing criminal charges against the corporations to bar them from doing any more business with the state or its counties. We also are preparing civil cases to recover the ill-gotten gains and restore money to the counties." According to Assistant A.G. James B. Frank, gathering evidence independently from the federal probe was "just the beginning" of efforts to recover damages from firms and individuals. Price encouraged district attorneys to follow the attorney general's lead and offered to cooperate with state prosecutors. In federal criminal cases, judges almost always imposed restitution orders along with prison sentences and fines.[19]

Even as Price envisioned structural reforms and cooperation between state and federal authorities as antidotes to corruption, he was losing sleep over his two Okscam informants, Dorothy Griffin and Guy Moore, whose guilty pleas had exposed them to harsh punishments. "What scared the devil out of me was that I was worried that Dorothy Griffin and Guy Moore might go to jail!" exclaimed Price. "I really made an impassioned plea on both of them for probation. I just thought both of them did so much, that of all the people in the world, they shouldn't

Unfortunately, She Was Also Wired for Sound

Law enforcement's use of hidden wires to implicate county commissioners in corrupt practices became fodder for Garry Trudeau's Doonesbury. DOONESBURY © 1981 G. B. TRUDEAU. REPRINTED WITH PERMISSION OF ANDREWS MCMEEL SYNDICATION. ALL RIGHTS RESERVED.

go to jail. When somebody spends a year or two going wired, and all the things that go with that, they deserve probation."

At a remove of three-plus decades, Price still cringed to imagine Griffin and Moore languishing in prison.

"Did they get it?" I asked.

"They got it, probation!" came the reply. "You can't imagine how scared I was."

In his soul searching about sentencing, Price thought a lot about repentance. "Maybe it was the Catholic in me," began Price as he struggled to express the confluence of law and faith. "Being repentant makes a difference," he said finally, "the fact that people feel sorry for what they did." Repentance, together with their enormous contributions to Okscam, certainly counted in Griffin's and Moore's favor. In Griffin's case, being a woman did not hurt. "I was more confident that Dorothy wasn't going to go to jail, because she was female," said Price.[20]

Two years' probation and a two-thousand-dollar fine did not mean the end of Dorothy Griffin's troubles. Back in Atoka County, a burned section of her house served as a reminder that her turning state's evidence was far from forgotten. She remained wary of passing cars and continued to receive threatening phone calls. "I guess they're beginning to come out of prison," said Griffin, then fifty-three years old, about her former customers. Threats became reality when someone set fire to her home while she and her husband were gone. If not for a light-sleeping granddaughter at home, it would have burned to the ground.

With her lumber company long gone and an ailing husband to take care of, Griffin got by on housesitting. She had little to show for her work as an informant, a temporary gig for which she had been paid minimum wage and expenses.

One thing Griffin did have was pride in never seeking immunity from prosecution. "I knew what I was doing was wrong, and I felt I had to pay for what I did," she said. Griffin estimated that she had received about $100,000 for her crimes. Nearly all of it had gone toward medical bills. Having sold her dryer to cut down on utilities, she shared her story with reporter Manny Gamallo, from nearby McAlester, as her and her husband's laundry flapped forlornly in the breeze.

Griffin toyed with the idea of accepting the government's offer of a fresh start under the Federal Witness Protection Program. Her husband, clearly well enough to express some homespun wisdom, talked her out of it.

"You don't go so far but what you can be found," he said.[21]

▶ ▶ ▶ ▶

Price's concern for Dorothy Griffin and Guy Moore's sentences carried over to all the cases that his office prosecuted. "I would literally advocate for lower sentences on people that were less involved," explained Price about his determination to see that punishments were commensurate with crimes. "If they were penitent, and came in and pleaded, I didn't care about sending them away for ten years. A year or year and a half, even six months, is enough to deter the crime. So it's whatever deters the crime."

As a corollary to his concern for sentencing, Price targeted the higher-ups in white-collar crimes, including CEOs and members of the country-club elite. "We didn't just prosecute little guys," declared Price, now sporting his infectious grin. He reserved special empathy for heavy-equipment salesmen, whose miniscule commissions and commissioners' demands made them susceptible to their employers' instructions to bend the rules. "I felt like those people ought to get probation. And generally, they did. Those were the only ones that I really felt sorry for."[22]

It was a short step from thinking about fairness in sentencing to pondering the lessons from Okscam. As the scandal receded from public attention, there was lots of speculation about Oklahomans' apparent tolerance for corruption. Price was skeptical about that. As he put it, "I really don't believe that very much!" To illustrate his rejection of the culture of corruption theory, Price cited an article about a commissioner who was reelected when he was under indictment. After he read the article, Price contacted the FBI agent who lived in the commissioner's jurisdiction and had participated in his indictment. Price was shocked to learn that the agent had voted for him! Upon further questioning, the agent explained that the commissioner's opponent, who had been out of office for more than five years, was even more corrupt. Unfortunately, the statute of limitations meant that he could no longer be charged. The commissioner then under indictment, however, would surely be convicted and leave then-governor George Nigh to appoint an honest commissioner to replace him.

"Governor Nigh really enjoyed that story when I told it to him," said Price. "It showed that voters were by no means tolerant of corruption. The fact was, they often didn't have a choice in who they voted for."[23]

Further evidence that Oklahomans were not uniquely tolerant of economic crime comes from political science professors Harry Holloway and Frank Meyers, whose 1993 book, *Bad Times for Good Ol'*

Boys, cited liberally in these pages, stands as the definitive academic study of the county commissioner scandal.[24] The authors relied on historical research, questionnaires, oral history interviews, and statistical measurements to support their hypothesis: Oklahomans were uniquely *intolerant* of corruption. The authors cited the shady goings-on in Louisiana and big-city political machines in New York and Chicago as far better evidence of the public's tolerance for sleaze in politics.

The real problem lay not in Oklahomans' collective DNA, but in the structure of government that, as Holloway and Meyers insisted, would have corrupted most saints. Nowhere was the absence of saints in government and the need for structure more eloquently expressed than in *The Federalist Papers*, in which the founding fathers hammered out the principles embodied in the U.S. Constitution. As noted in *Federalist No. 51*, with an unmistakable Madisonian flair, "If men were angels, no government would be necessary. If angels were to govern men, neither external nor internal controls on government would be necessary." Although the U.S. Constitution was built on a system of checks and balances, counties were largely left to their own devices.

Of course, nobody expected corruption to vanish with the stroke of a pen. The best those champions of Enlightened thinking could do was find the right combination of a vibrant civic culture and political rules.[25] For *On Corruption in America* author Sarah Chayes, those Enlightened thinkers might have been disappointed in the heirs to their creation: "In the United States, serious and damaging public corruption is not getting punished. That means, by default, that we deem it to be just fine."[26] Perhaps they would have caught a glimpse of a brighter future in the Okscam prosecutions. As far as federal prosecutors in the late 1970s and 1980s were concerned, corruption was not just fine in Oklahoma.

At Okscam's core, cited time and again by reformers since territorial days, was a toxic combination: (1) all-powerful yet underpaid county commissioners with too much taxpayers' money on their hands and not enough oversight; and (2) a political culture steeped in agrarian populism that severed local governments from officialdom at the state capitol. One observer with a knack for shorthand dubbed it "road districtitis"—a disease that spanned generations, was resistant to reform, and was infectious nationwide.[27]

Debates about how to cure that disease continued throughout the 1980s. A case in point comes from state representative Emil Grieser, a Democrat from Hobart who wanted the House Committee on County and Municipal Government to look at ways to beef up county coffers. He quickly ran into a conundrum: although counties relied on property taxes for most of their operational money, county assessors had to keep a lid on taxes to stay in office. And, of course, those assessors had close ties with the courthouse cliques that had enabled ten percents, blue-sky deals, and kickbacks on heavy-equipment leases and purchases to flourish for generations. As Ken Neal observed, in a June 1991 editorial in the *Tulsa World*, "County government is indeed starved for funds in Oklahoma. But much of it is the doing of county officials intent on perpetuating their own office. As long as Oklahomans insist on inflicting a horse-and-buggy government on themselves, there is no reason to get too worried about providing more money for the counties. If, however, there is a serious effort to move county government into the modern era, more money will be needed."[28]

We leave the final word on Okscam to convicted commissioners who drew the harshest sentences. Former Murray County commissioner Bird Lance, Jr., one of six men sent to a federal prison in Fort Worth, had the misfortune to draw the stiffest sentence (sixteen years and nine months) for accepting kickbacks. Since his prosecution by Assistant U.S. Attorney Charlie Waters, his conviction in Judge Frank Seay's courtroom in Muskogee, and the denial of his appeal at the Tenth Circuit Court of Appeals in Denver, Lance had maintained his innocence and even bragged about his seventeen-year record as a Murray County commissioner. "I don't think the people of Murray County thought I was doing a bad job," said Lance, who described his lengthy sentence as retaliation for taking his case to trial. "Otherwise I wouldn't have been elected all those times." He recalled fondly the way his constituents had rallied to his defense after his indictment and continued to fight for his early release from prison.

"It's not as if he got caught selling drugs or something," said his brother and Sulphur, Oklahoma, mayor Jim Lance. "This is the first time he's ever done something wrong and we think he's spent enough time in prison." Classified as a hardened criminal, the best Lance could hope for was parole in October 1989.

Former McIntosh County commissioner Marvin James had much the same experience. Accused of dozens of kickback-related charges, he was sentenced to thirteen years in prison, but not before his constituents showed their support by holding bake sales and rallies to pay for his lawyer. Bill Price recalled similar displays of affection for convicted commissioners all over Oklahoma. He suspected that those die-hard supporters would have changed their minds if they had listened to the undercover tape recordings. "The transcripts of the tapes make fantastic reading!" said Price. "They show how much they (the commissioners) knew just how dishonest it was. The pitch wasn't subtle at all. They'd be doing it even knowing they were under investigation. What they didn't know was that anyone would ever catch them."

Bird Lance's fellow commissioner from Murray County, Jimmie Primrose, was likewise classified as a hardened criminal, and he was similarly frustrated by his inability to secure an early release from his thirteen-year sentence at the federal correctional facility in El Reno. Primrose's son-in-law, Sulphur City Councilman David Pittman, noted that his father-in-law's punishment hardly fit his crime of taking $766.28 in kickbacks. "There are Penn Square bankers and oilmen in prison with him, and I'll bet you they'll be getting out before him," said Pittman. Like Lance, Primrose maintained his innocence. Amplifying his son-in-law's observation, Lance complained about drug dealers in nearby cells who had drawn lighter sentences. Clearly the commissioners' most steadfast fan, David Pittman was confident that, given the chance, Lance and Primrose would be reelected in a landslide.[29]

► ► ► ►

While Okscam was ending, litigation attending the FDIC takeover of Penn Square Bank was grinding on. The final act in a drama that upended Oklahoma banking for decades to come played out not in Oklahoma City but in Chicago, where Penn Square's favorite upstream bank, Continental Illinois National Bank of Chicago, was making history for spawning the first federal bank bailout in U.S. history. With nearly $40 billion in assets, it ranked as the sixth largest bank in the country; and with $1.2 billion in Penn Square loan participations, there was nothing it could do to stem the loan defaults when drilling in the Anadarko Basin came to a virtual standstill.[30]

The banking cognoscenti saw the handwriting on the wall when the bank became the butt of jokes. "If I had known how easy it was to get a loan from Continental Illinois," quipped Chrysler head Lee Iacocca, the beneficiary of federal largesse at his own ailing company, to the Economic Club of Chicago, "I would never have gone to the government."[31] The audience howled. Washington's $4.5 billion rescue package confirmed Continental Illinois' place in history for igniting the "too big to fail" argument.

At the center of the whirlwind was Penn Square Bank's über-lender, Bill Patterson, whose acquittal on twenty-five charges of fraud and misapplication of bank funds in Oklahoma City was the prelude to his prosecution in Chicago. His trial in Continental Illinois' backyard on eleven similar counts ended in a hung jury on May 3, 1988. Patterson spared himself the anguish of a second trial when he entered a guilty plea. Bill Price, whose office had turned over mountains of evidence to the Northern District of Illinois, had expected this result. "All I should be saying is that justice was done and I'm glad to see the case resolved," said Price when he heard about Patterson's guilty plea. Sentencing was set for August 30, 1988. Patterson's plea left no cases pending in Penn Square Bank litigation—a sordid spectacle that cast yet another spotlight on Oklahoma corruption. Patterson's two-year sentence was likely the penalty he would have received with a guilty plea in Oklahoma, a choice that would have spared him the agony and expense of two trials.[32]

Patterson received a two-year sentence and was ordered to report to a federal prison on October 11, 1988. Joining him on the appointed day was John R. Lytle, a former vice president in charge of oil and gas loans at Continental Illinois Bank, whose three-and-a-half-year sentence stemmed from his enthrallment to Patterson's hype. More specifically, Lytle had accepted $585,000 in kickbacks on unsecured personal loans between 1980 and 1982.

Testifying before his sentencing, Patterson had held his head and cried. "I'm sorry for the people in Chicago and Oklahoma," he wailed between sobs. "I think of that a lot."[33] In Patterson's defense, Price acknowledged that, unlike a career criminal, he had never set out to defraud banks or steal money. On the contrary, Patterson had scrambled to keep Penn Square Bank afloat in the midst of an economic meltdown. "He wanted to save Penn Square, and in effect, he guaranteed the failure of Penn Square," said Price. "You have more sympathy toward that person than just a plain-out crook that was out to steal as much as possible."[34]

As usual, Price looked for lessons in the Penn Square Bank imbroglio, and he found them in two errors of judgment that were repeated decades later in the financial crisis of 2008.

First, there was no connection between energy loan originators and the upstream banks that bought them. As Price explained, "That was the lesson in the 2008 crisis, where we separated mortgage originations from the people that ultimately bought the mortgages. The people that originated the loans at Penn Square were separated from the companies that ultimately bought them. When you separate them, you don't have the intimate knowledge of what they are. That caused the mortgage crisis."

Price drew his second lesson from old-fashioned ethics. Lenders in the energy boom of the 1980s and subprime mortgage crisis of the late 2000s used income from old loans to service new ones, and they rationalized what had become a shell game by insisting that they would put things right as soon as the immediate crisis passed. In both instances, short-term solutions morphed into long-term problems. "You think you're going to pay it back, and it gets worse, and worse, and worse, and worse," said Price. Like gamblers who don't know when to fold, bankers threw good money after bad in an effort to stave off disaster. As a result, their debts piled up and salvation receded like a mirage on a desert highway.[35]

Chicanery at Penn Square Bank fits rather neatly into yet another category of corruption: commercial bribery. Broadly speaking, commercial bribery makes its appearance whenever potential buyers of goods and services seek unfair advantage over their competitors by cultivating corrupt relationships. Unlike political corruption, commercial bribery does not necessarily involve government personnel or facilities. But it does involve kickbacks, better known in commercial circles as "payola."

A typical example of commercial bribery comes when a seller of goods or services from one company offers an agent or buyer from another company a payment, often directed to a personal account, to ensure an ongoing business relationship. The most common venues for commercial bribery include the entertainment industry, sports gambling, labor unions, and nongovernmental contracts where bid rigging creates an unlevel playing field.[36]

Recognizing my puzzled expression, Price offered a simple explanation of commercial bribery as a violation of an agent's or employee's obligation to provide "good and faithful services" to an employer. As Price put it, "You're taking money for something that is contrary to the interests of your employer."

Among Price's most surprising revelations as U.S. Attorney was that the Oklahoma legislature had never enacted statutes pertaining to commercial bribery. His account of how that oversight was corrected began, as so many of his stories did, with State Senator Gene Stipe.

As the story goes, a well-known and respectable attorney from southeastern Oklahoma dropped by Price's office to report that Stipe had offered him $100,000 to get his client to settle a commercial lawsuit.

"Stipe came in with that offer?" I asked.

"Yeah!" exclaimed Price. "That's the epitome of commercial bribery."

That got Price to wondering about commercial bribery statutes. "I looked it up, and we didn't have one. Without a commercial bribery statute, I would have been hamstrung, and the state was hamstrung. That's just *wrong*."

A few days after the attorney's visit, Price went to lunch with state Representative Don McCorkle from Tulsa. Knowing what Price had accomplished in Okscam, McCorkle wanted to brainstorm about reforms in county government, including legislation to establish multicounty grand juries. When their conversation turned to commercial bribery, Price told him about statutes from Texas. Although they made no specific references to attorneys, Price knew that, with a bit of tweaking, Texas statutes pertaining to commercial bribery would work just fine in Oklahoma.

After his lunch with McCorkle, Price returned to his office, spread the Texas statutes on his desk, and did the requisite tweaking. A few days later, he handed the revised Texas statutes to McCorkle.

"I couldn't believe it," said Price. "Three weeks later, Don McCorkle and I were standing by Governor George Nigh as he signed into law the commercial bribery statute that I had scribbled out. I couldn't believe how quickly he got it accomplished. McCorkle got it passed in both houses, and onto the governor's desk, in about three weeks!"

"Why do you think they rushed it through?" I asked.

"I think because it was private, not political. Who knows? Political corruption was harder to get through the legislature, I suppose. That's how we have a commercial bribery statute in the state of Oklahoma."

Getting that done was one of Price's proudest accomplishments as U.S. Attorney, and for good reason: commercial bribery was almost surely costing American business more than shoplifting, and it often resulted in companies purchasing inferior products for inflated prices. Although commercial bribery permeated American business, it was rarely prosecuted.[37] Just as public corruption destroys faith in government, so, too, does commercial bribery destroy faith in the free enterprise system. If left unprosecuted, otherwise honest people can easily slide down the slippery slope of corruption.

Nowhere was commercial bribery more rampant than in the oil and gas fields of Oklahoma, where operators took a page from Okscam and purchased drilling mud, steel pipe, and other necessities for inflated prices and shared the surplus with their suppliers. "Instead of wells costing a half-million dollars, the new, deep wells below 15,000 feet were costing ten million dollars," explained Price. "And the main office of the oil company wouldn't have any concept of, really, what this well *should* cost, and how much mud was really needed, or how much pipe, or whatever it was. It was the perfect environment for corruption, with few checks and balances. As in Okscam, there were ten percents and blue-sky deals." Oil-field suppliers complemented their under-the-table cash kickbacks with multimillion-dollar budgets that included cocaine and prostitutes—popular fringe benefits that oil and gas companies shared with their lenders at Penn Square Bank and their upstream partners across the nation.

Then there was the blatant theft of oil and gas, often accomplished with kickbacks and the connivance of the person who read, recorded, and reported readings from volume and temperature gauges on oil holding tanks. In the pre–computer age, it was a simple matter to siphon oil from their holding tanks and falsify the reports. "The oil company never knows that you're stealing," said Price. "This is a perfect theft! You don't have any idea you have been stolen from!"[38] In the absence of checks and balances (and, of course, integrity), commercial bribery pervaded energy-rich counties and, in lockstep with Okscam, contributed to Oklahoma's reputation for outlawry.

Corruption in Oklahoma's iconic energy industry included not only outright thieves, but also oil reclaimers who were contracted to clean storage tanks and process the residual oil for sale. Price had reason to suspect that much of the reclaimed oil was stolen rather than collected legitimately. Chief among the culprits were pumpers who read the gauges and oil company higher-ups who accepted payoffs and kickbacks as high as $40,000 to $50,000 to falsify logbooks and permit thievery.[39]

The U.S. Attorney's office set a precedent in combatting commercial bribery in the oil and gas patch in October 1983 in the case of Gordon G. Atwell of Enid, a former executive with Houston-based Major Oil Company. In what became the first commercial kickback case in the Western District of Oklahoma to rely on federal mail-fraud statutes, Atwell was accused of defrauding his employer in various schemes that involved a drilling firm, a workover rig service firm, and a supplier of drilling fluids. Testifying in Ralph Thompson's courtroom, Atwell claimed that his employer, John "Jack" Holden, knew all about the $350,000 in commissions he had earned over two years as the energy boom was turning to bust. He further swore that Holden had hired him, in 1979, with assurance that he could make his own deals in Oklahoma. As Atwell's lawyer, Merle Gile of Oklahoma City, explained to jurors, "That's not fraud."

Serving as the lead prosecutor, Assistant U.S. Attorney Wesley Fredenburg begged to differ, and he presented a compelling case of an employee bilking his company. Jurors had reason to doubt both men's testimonies when Judge Thompson gave Fredenburg leeway to mention Holden's eleven-and-a-half-year sentence in an Ohio prison for embezzlement in the mid-1960s. Holden, who had suspected Atwell of demanding kickbacks from subcontractors and fired him in August 1982, insisted that Atwell's compensation had been limited to an annual salary of $75,000 and 1 percent working interest in the company's wells, mainly in Major County. Jurors agreed with Fredenburg that Atwell had been defrauding his company, and they found him guilty of sixteen counts of mail fraud in extorting kickbacks from subcontractors.[40]

TG&Y, represented here by a store at 23rd and May Avenue in Oklahoma City, was a home-grown retail chain that became a breeding ground for commercial bribery and extortion. COURTESY OKLAHOMA HISTORICAL SOCIETY.

For evidence that no business sector was immune from commercial bribery, we turn to one of Oklahoma's most beloved retailers: TG&Y. Aiming to give people what they wanted at prices they could afford, Rawdon E. Tomlinson of Frederick, Enoch L. "Les" Gosselin of Cordell, and Raymond A. Young of Kingfisher pooled their resources, in 1935, to form Central Merchandise Corporation. Operating from a nondescript warehouse in Oklahoma City, the trio purchased merchandise in bulk directly from manufacturers rather than wholesalers. In 1936, they opened their first variety store in Norman and branded it with the initials of their last names, from oldest to youngest. Incorporated in 1946, TG&Y became the go-to retailer for thrifty shoppers, first in rural communities and later in urban centers and shopping malls, which were ubiquitous in the 1960s. By the early 1980s, the company had expanded to 930 outlets.[41]

And then came the unthinkable: in a slew of lawsuits, TG&Y accused its wholesalers of lavishing buyers with gift certificates, expense-paid vacations, electronics, clothing, jewelry, and fine dining experiences. Some buyers with a yen for international intrigue maintained bank accounts in Hong Kong to make it safe and convenient for wholesalers to deposit their kickbacks. Accusations against more than a dozen of its domestic and overseas wholesalers ran the gamut of commercial corruption from bribery, racketeering, and fraud to antitrust violations. In its lawsuits, TG&Y claimed that the cost of bribes had been factored into wholesalers' prices and made products more expensive than they should have been.

The damage inflicted on TG&Y from loss of income and a tarnished reputation was certainly extraordinary, but it was nothing new. In one form or another, commercial bribery is probably as old as business itself. Yet it was subject to government and corporate regulation, and it flouted IRS requirements that recipients of so-called gifts report them as income. In the absence of industry codes of ethics, most retailers simply warned their buyers against accepting kickbacks and gifts and fired them if they did it anyway. Nobody wanted to subject their companies to the humiliation of a public scandal.

But there was another reason commercial bribery remained hidden from public scrutiny: it was notoriously hard to prove in court. "These types of actions have gone on forever," said Assistant U.S. Attorney Karla McAlister. "People have just thought this is business and not crime. It's really a new area."[42]

Based on Okscam's precedent, federal prosecutors relied on mail-fraud statutes. Success depended on proving three basic elements: (1) there was a scheme between buyers and wholesalers to defraud the retailer; (2) either the U.S. Postal Service or electronic communications were used to perpetrate the scheme; and (3) harm was done. Proving actual harm was particularly difficult, as defendants might argue that a wholesaler charged high prices because it provided exceptional service. Also standing in harm's way were consumers, who were stuck with inferior merchandise and artificially high prices—a disastrous combination for any retailer, and potentially fatal for a chain that prided itself on its founders' promise to give people what they wanted at prices they could afford.[43] As Price said, about a scandal that snaked its way from Oklahoma to Taiwan, "That tends to run you out of business eventually, when you're up against a Walmart."[44]

Fierce competition from discount retailers and a series of corporate buyouts forced TG&Y to downsize. When its final upstream buyer, McCrory Corporation of York, Pennsylvania, went out of business in 2002, TG&Y closed the last of its stores. That same year, TG&Y cofounder Raymond Young, the youngest of the original trio, was laid to rest.

About the same time that TG&Y's troubles were grabbing the headlines, the FBI and the Justice Department's antitrust division were called on to investigate Washita Construction Company of Ardmore and its president, Billy Ray Anthony, on allegations that the company had participated in bid rigging on highway construction projects. In the indictment that followed, Anthony was accused of conspiring with others to decide who among them would be the low bidder; the rest would either withhold their bids or submit high, noncompetitive bids that they knew would never be accepted. According to Price, bid rigging impacted highway construction costs for two reasons: it inflated construction costs of a particular project and, if done on a continuing basis, it tended to raise engineers' estimates and pushed future contracts to artificially high levels.

During Price's tenure as U.S. Attorney, indictments rained down on companies for participating in bid-rigging schemes. Specific charges included violating the Sherman Antitrust Act, making false statements, and committing mail fraud. Firms violating the Sherman Antitrust Act faced a possible fine of $1 million; individuals found guilty of the same charge could be fined $100,000 and sent to prison for three years.[45]

▶ ▶ ▶ ▶

Price was fortunate to join other U.S. Attorneys from around the country on advisory committees aimed at helping the Department of Justice devise national policies. Two of those committees stood out as both memorable and effective: the U.S. Attorney's Advisory Committee on Drug Education and the National Environment Council, where he typically sat between Richard Daley, Jr., then district attorney of Cook County and later mayor of Chicago, and Skip Humphrey, the son of former vice president Hubert Humphrey, who served as Minnesota's attorney general from 1983 to 1999.

Price's influence was felt most strongly on the U.S. Advisory Committee on Public Corruption, a group of six U.S. Attorneys headed by Bill Weld, who served as U.S. Attorney in Massachusetts before his election as governor. Price's invitation to join the committee came at a critical juncture in federal prosecution of corruption. For many years, federal prosecutors had been relying on mail- and wire-fraud statutes to attack state and local bribery, commercial bribery, and other species of fraud. The Hobbs Act—referenced earlier as legislation designed to curb extortion by obtaining money under the color of official right— was of limited use, as it applied to public officials rather than private citizens who were doing the bribing. In mutual bribery schemes, it was sometimes difficult to prove that a bribe was extorted. To make mail-fraud charges stick in nongovernmental cases, prosecutors had to show that there was a conspiracy to deprive an employer of his or her good and faithful services—intangible rights, to be sure, but ones that private employers and public officials violated at their peril. In cases of public corruption, the employer was whatever governmental agency the official worked for.

In June 1987, the U.S. Supreme Court rendered a landmark decision, in *McNally v. United States*, that invalidated the use of the intangible rights theory, heretofore embedded in the mail-fraud statute, to prosecute public corruption. Government lawyers had employed the mail-fraud statute for nearly fifty years in prosecuting corrupt public officials. But in the McNally ruling, the supreme court held that the mail-fraud statute could not be used for prosecuting officials who defrauded citizens of their intangible rights, including the good and faithful services that their constituents expected. In short, the U.S. Supreme Court effectively rejected arguments that citizens had a proprietary right to honest government. According to the court's ruling, criminal charges of corruption applied only when there was proof of monetary loss.

Yet corruption does not always depend on such a narrow interpretation. If someone bribes a judge, the governmental entity that employs him or her does not lose money. When Illinois governor Rod Blagojevich was convicted of auctioning his Senate seat to the highest bidder, the state did not sustain a monetary loss. Closer to home, prosecutors in the David Hall case faced the impossible task of proving that Doc Taylor's scheme would have cost the state more than any other investment. Although ten-percent deals in Okscam cost counties 40 percent higher prices, it would have been difficult, if not impossible, to prove that a commissioner's refusal to accept a bribe lowered costs to the county.

Clearly, insisting that bribery and extortion charges applied only to transactions resulting in monetary losses could have put an end to Okscam prosecutions and the others that were surely coming. To U.S. Attorneys nationwide, that was a recipe for disaster. As Weld put it, soon after the ruling, "I have consulted with a good number of district attorneys and state attorneys on an appropriate response and whether they feel it is an appropriate response to do nothing and stay out of the state and local corruption thicket. The nearly unanimous response is 'no'."

What solved the problem came to be known as the "McNally fix," and that required a federal statute. To make that happen, Price and the other five members of the U.S. Advisory Committee on Public Corruption had to gain the support of U.S. Attorney General Edwin Meese. Unfortunately, three of Meese's top assistant attorneys general, including future National Security Advisor John Bolton, were opposed to a McNally fix. As über-conservative Republicans (more conservative, even, than Bill Price!), they believed that the federal government had no business in prosecutions of state and local officials. The stage was set for a showdown between two irreconcilable factions: U.S. Attorneys, dubbed by the *Boston Sunday Globe* as "cowboys" who were itching for federal laws to help them round up miscreants; and conservative ideologues, branded as "federalists" in the same newspaper, who preferred to leave prosecution of corruption to state and local officials.

Meeting in Boston prior to a U.S. Attorneys' conference, Weld's committee came up with a strategy to win Attorney General Meese's support. Knowing that an upcoming conference would be full of new U.S. Attorneys who were unfamiliar with the issue, the six committee members split conferees into the same number of groups and, in small-group sessions, set about convincing them to support a McNally fix to ensure federal help in prosecuting corruption. "If your political system is corrupt, there is no real democracy," explained Price, a lead wrangler for the cowboys, in an interview for the *Boston Sunday Globe*. He spoke from experience when he said that fighting official corruption on the federal level "has had the greatest impact in this country of anything we have done."

At the end of the conference, all six groups voiced their support for the McNally fix. In a dramatic conference finale, Meese sided with the U.S. Attorneys and cowboys and, against his assistants' objections, announced his support for the McNally fix. The cowboys let out a collective cheer when both houses of Congress voted in their favor and sent the McNally fix to President Reagan for his signature. Henceforth, state and local prosecutors could count on help from the U.S. Department of Justice.

Price spoke for the rest of the nation's cowboys in extolling the federal government's role in the ongoing war against corruption:

One of the basic ways to keep conservative government close to the people is to have checks and balances, and have a viable and honest approach to local and state corruption. If there were some hue and cry from local and state government, that would be one thing, but the hue and cry from state and locals is for help. If the federal government came in and told them how to run county roads, that would be one thing, but assuring honesty is another.[46]

▶ ▶ ▶ ▶

In one of our interviews, Price departed from his usual deep dive into history to reflect on the threat that corruption posed to the broader culture.

"How prevalent was commercial bribery during your career in the U.S. Attorney's office?" I asked. While Price was gathering his thoughts, I glanced at the red light on my digital recorder. I knew this was something I wanted to get right.

"I think it was *so* prevalent!" came the reply.

And then came this:

If you don't do at least a modicum of prosecution in those areas, and they become endemic over time, it encourages even normal, average people to become corrupt, because they see everybody else getting away with things, over time. It really corrupts the whole culture. That's what I was trying to get at, so much, was the corruption of culture.

In his videotaped interviews, James Price asked his father many of the same questions. And he responded with the same answers.

"Commercial kickbacks cost this country, cost businesses, far more than any other form of business loss," Price explained. "People talk about higher prices due to shoplifting. It is nothing like the cost of commercial kickbacks! Commercial kickbacks are a very similar type of process to kickbacks in the county commissioner scandal or in other forms of political corruption."

James then returned to the FDIC takeover of Penn Square Bank and its corollary in corruption in the oil and gas fields.

"How does thievery in the oil and gas fields fit into the broader narrative of corruption in this state?" asked James. "Do you see any sort of overall pattern there?"

"It fits into the whole thing that I have talked about before," replied Price. "It was ripe for corruption! You had no checks and balances from the main office, of knowing what a well would cost. So, therefore, when you had a million-dollar well, the main office would have a pretty good idea of what a well would cost and have a pretty good idea of the amount of oil-field mud that would be needed, and what the pipe would cost. When the cost of deep wells soared to ten million dollars, the main office lost track of expenses. The situation was ripe for corruption."

The pattern that Price was describing reflected two observations— metaphorically speaking, two sides of the same coin—that fueled his prosecutorial zeal: (1) in both the public and private spheres, structures based on checks and balances were key to mitigating corruption; and (2) in the absence of investigations and prosecutions, corruption was bound to flourish, erode the public's faith in institutions, and degrade cultural norms.

As vexed as Price was about political and commercial corruption and its dire consequences for the broader culture, he reserved special contempt for drug dealers who plied their trade with no regard for its effects on vulnerable populations, especially young people. To protect the nation's youth from the scourge of drugs, Price launched a crusade that guaranteed his legacy not only as a U.S. Attorney, but also as a political campaigner and, later still, a philanthropist who never lost sight of his father's biblical admonition: *From whom much is given, much is expected.* [47]

CHAPTER THIRTEEN : *From Whom Much Is Given, Much Is Expected*

n 1973, Richard Anthony Riley was working as a salesman under sales manager Mike Combs at Craig Ayers Chevrolet in Edmond. Looking for greener pastures, the two men parted ways and embarked on very different careers. Combs went into the insurance business and, in 1978, parlayed his affability into election as a Democratic state senator from Bethany. His former salesman took a turn to the dark side and opted for a life of crime. When the law caught up with him, he was implicated in a massive sting operation that resulted in fifty arrests and the recovery of thousands of dollars in stolen property. Facing a stiff prison sentence, Riley pleaded guilty to six felony charges and went undercover for the Oklahoma City Police Department. That proved to be a wise move. What might have been a lengthy stay in prison was reduced to a month in jail.

Upon his release, Riley found his career options severely compromised by a criminal record and a lack of money. Opportunity came knocking in the form of counterfeit narcotics, known in the trade as "turkey dope." The business model was simple: purchase a thousand pills for $3.00 each, sell them for up to $80.00, and *presto*—instant riches! To facilitate his rise to the top of the turkey dope underworld, he renewed his friendship with his former boss, Mike Combs, who later coauthored legislation to legalize turkey dope. Assured of piles of perfectly legal profits, Riley, a bearded and fast-talking former jailbird and police informant, thrust himself into a world of fast cars, jet planes, and beautiful (usually blonde) women.

To incorporate his business as Mid-States Distribution Products, Riley retained the services of William C. Page, an attorney in private practice who would later become an assistant district attorney and, later still, a judge. Headquartered on South Western Avenue in Oklahoma City with branches in Atlanta and Albuquerque, Riley shared his office suite with attorneys and oilmen who looked askance at their neighbor's ostentatious displays of wealth, including flashy cars and frequent trips aboard Mid-State's corporate jet. "And that office . . ." remarked a former tenant who preferred to remain anonymous. "That S.O.B. was furnished. Full wet bar. And I do mean full."

With controlling interest in Cowgirls, a popular strip club, Riley had ample opportunities to burnish his taste for jewelry and furs. In a phone conversation preserved in an FBI wiretap, Riley boasted that one of his girls was heading to Chicago to pose for *Playboy*. As an acquaintance commented: "When a guy doesn't work and wears fine clothes and drives nice cars, you know he's either an oilman or a druggie. And Richard wasn't in oil."

But all good things must end. When the state started cracking down on turkey dope, Riley revised his business model and began selling the real thing: marijuana, quaaludes, cocaine, and methamphetamines. Among his associates was Patrick Henry Earley, Oklahoma's most renowned racketeer. Now that he was a genuine drug dealer, in cahoots with known criminals, Riley should not have been surprised to find himself in law enforcement's crosshairs. The beginning of the end came in November 1981 when, in the course of closing a meth deal, he told his buyers about his association with William Page. Then working in the Oklahoma County district attorney's office, Page had the poor judgment to accept Riley's periodic payments. Riley and Page tried to convince authorities that they were car payments. When that raised eyebrows, they decided that they were actually overdue legal fees.

On April 19, 1982, FBI agents arrived at Riley's opulent home, on Nichols Road in the tony Oklahoma City suburb of Nichols Hills, and outlined their case against him and Page, both of whom had been snared by wiretaps. For the second time in his criminal career, Riley agreed to become an informant. This time, he was obliged to wear a wire in his meetings with Messrs. Page and Combs. In revealing glimpses into Riley's dark side, a recording captured his threat against his wife Sharon's family: "I'm gonna have to kill her brother and half her [expletive deleted] family if they get smart with me." When Riley found out that Cowgirls was being mismanaged, he threatened to use a stick of dynamite "and blow it clean off the foundations."

The U.S. Attorney's Office amassed more than enough evidence to bring charges against William Page and Mike Combs. As a star witness in both trials, Riley exposed the depths of Oklahoma's narcotics industry and at least two officials' complicity in keeping it awash in cash. To argue the United States cases, Bill Price assigned Wes Fredenburg, whom he counted among his most competent assistants. Fredenburg rose to his reputation: Page was convicted of racketeering and extortion, and Combs was convicted of attempted extortion. The lawyer and the legislator trudged off to jail to signal the end of the line for Oklahoma's turkey dope kingpin.[1]

An entirely different business model arrived in the person of Graham Lee Kendall, president of Oklahoma Aircraft Corporation. As a major supplier of aircraft for the general aviation market, Kendall was in an ideal position to augment his income by retrofitting airplanes to import dope from Colombia to the U.S. "Remember, the FAA (Federal Aviation Administration) in Oklahoma City does all the licensing of planes throughout the country," explained Price. "Airplane brokers, title cases, and everything else originates in Oklahoma City. Graham Kendall was putting bladders and secret compartments in planes for drug organizations throughout the country." Price routinely heard from U.S. Attorneys across the country whose prosecutions of international drug smugglers led them directly to nefarious goings-on in Oklahoma City.

Kendall's sideline as a drug smuggler came to a crashing halt in August 1982 when his Piper Chieftain, piloted by Benjamin Patrick Callihan and loaded with 1,680 pounds of high-grade marijuana worth $1.1 million, made an emergency landing in Louisiana en route from Cancun, Mexico to Miami, Oklahoma. Kendall and four residents of Aspen, Colorado, were charged on three counts of a seven-count federal grand-jury indictment. In what counted as the third indictment against Kendall's operation, investigators found that the plane's seats had been removed and a waterbed installed as an auxiliary fuel tank to accommodate extra cargo and enable long-distance flights.

It fell to Assistant U.S. Attorney Jim Robinson to argue the United States case in Judge Ralph Thompson's courtroom. Among those implicated in the conspiracy was David Robert Zamansky, a part-time plumber and one-time professional skier from Aspen who had clocked downhill runs at 123 miles per hour. Testimony included tales of multimillion-dollar air and sea operations, gigantic cash bribes to Mexican officials and American lawyers, and a hair-raising takeoff as the plane struggled to gain altitude. Evidence notwithstanding, Kendall denied all charges.[2]

Robinson's challenge was not so much to prove Kendall's guilt as it was to prove that his planes had been used to smuggle drugs. "We *couldn't necessarily* prove this plane over here, in Florida, beyond a reasonable doubt, was being used for drug trafficking," explained Price. "We *could sure* prove that it's more probable than not that this plane was going to be used, or had been used, for drug trafficking, by the fact that it's got a secret compartment and it's got a bladder, and it's really dangerous to cross the Caribbean without refueling!" Taking advantage of drug seizure laws, authorities seized airplanes and thereby secured enough evidence to implicate brokers and drug dealers nationwide.

"That's what created the *preponderance of evidence*," continued Price. "They wouldn't be able to prove it came from Colombia. But it came from Graham Kendall, and he had put a bladder and secret compartments in it. That was enough proof to seize the plane and start a criminal investigation."[3]

The U.S. Attorney's office relied on drug seizure laws in its prosecution of the Bowie Boys, a Mafia-style organization led by Benito Bowie whose members were primarily African American and Hispanic. With well-funded cells in Las Vegas and Oklahoma City, the gang operated sixteen crack houses in Oklahoma City and, as Price put it, "killed witnesses right and left. They were the worst drug dealers I had ever seen." To build their business, the Bowie Boys turned to a Colombian cartel in Florida to obtain enough cocaine and marijuana to flood their distribution network each month with contraband carrying a street value of $1.2 million. According to Oklahoma City Police Chief Robert V. Wilder, the Bowie Boys' drug ring was "the single most significant criminal organization" operating in the metro area." Price was particularly galled by the Bowie Boys' specialty: peddling rock cocaine to teenagers. Better known as crack and smoked rather than snorted, the drug was a hit among teenagers, who inevitably became addicted to the intense high it offered—much more satisfying than that offered by run-of-the-mill cocaine.

Following a massive investigation—which included wiretaps—the FBI, the Drug Enforcement Agency (DEA), and the Oklahoma City Police Department prepared to make their move. In a replay of the D-Day invasions that marked the beginning of the end of Okscam, dozens of agents gathered before dawn and, in a coordinated series of arrests, swooped down on the unsuspecting gangsters.

Even as they were handcuffing gang members and hustling them off to jail, agents seized assets to support the prosecutions that the U.S. Attorney's Office was already preparing. In what Price reckoned as his district's largest asset seizure from a criminal organization, agents appropriated cars, furs, jewelry, and other items, valued at $1.7 million.

"The thing is, how do you prove an asset?" asked Price rhetorically.

Noticing the quizzical look on my face, Price clarified his earlier explanation of asset seizure laws.

"I mean, their only business was drugs. But how do you prove an asset—say, a house that they owned—was derived from drugs, when it was paid for four or five years before?" As with Richard Riley's sports cars and Graham Kendall's retrofitted airplanes, seizure of the Bowie Boys' assets supported preponderance of evidence (alternatively, more probable than not), a standard of proof that relieved prosecutors of the need to link a particular drug deal to an asset.

"You will never, on most cases, prove that the asset ties to a particular drug deal," continued Price. "But what other businesses were the Bowies in? They owned real estate; they owned all this *stuff* while they were dealing drugs. By the preponderance of the evidence, you can take everything. The Bowies only did drugs. They owned this house. Is it more probable than not that the proceeds to buy this house came from drug sales? Yes! Can we prove it beyond a reasonable doubt? Probably not."

The law has always treated asset seizure differently from criminal prosecution. Under a preponderance of evidence standard, anyone can file a civil suit in hopes of seizing a defendant's assets. Yet only the government can put someone in prison under the beyond a reasonable doubt standard. To prevent law enforcement from abusing drug seizure laws, Price recommended two reforms. First, law enforcement agencies should not be incentivized to keep seized assets. Instead, the proceeds should be deposited into the general fund of whatever branch of government was involved in the seizure. Second, if a court determines that assets were improperly seized and the aggrieved party is compelled to hire an attorney, that party should be able to file suit and recover attorney's fees.

At the federal level, funds derived from seized assets never went to a law enforcement agency; rather, they were deposited into the government's general fund. On the rare occasions when parties whose assets had been seized provided a reasonable explanation for holding large amounts of cash, Price's office never hesitated to return their assets. Price recalled a case in which cash totaling hundreds of thousands of dollars was seized from people of a South Asian ethnic group whose culture predisposed them to deal in cash. When they proved that their hoard had been earned through a legal business transaction, Price had no qualms about returning it. But that was far from the norm. "I can't remember a single case in which asset seizures were contested in court, much less determined to have been wrongfully seized," said Price.[4]

Relief at the Bowie Boys' arrests and seizure of their assets was palpable among the witnesses who had turned state's evidence against them. One after another, they implored Price to make sure the Bowie Boys had been stripped of their assets. As Price recounted his conversations with potential witnesses, I felt a chill crawl up my spine: "Have you taken all their assets? If you haven't, I won't turn on them, because they will kill me. Even if they are in prison, they will hire somebody to kill me."

The bottom line? Unless their assets were seized, arresting the head honcho would have done nothing to prevent his replacement and a continuation of the business. "If you don't take their assets," concluded Price, "the business still operates."

In March 1986, Benito, his brothers, and six of their associates pleaded guilty to a variety of drug charges. U.S. District Judge Luther Eubanks characterized the defendants as powerful, wealthy, and dangerous, particularly because nobody wanted to testify against them. A memorandum filed by the U.S. Attorney's Office accused the Bowie Boys of complicity not only in drug trafficking, but also in at least two homicides and fencing stolen property. Price, who counted their conviction and lengthy prison sentences as milestones in his district, noted that the U.S. Department of Justice had been encouraging federal prosecutors to file similar memoranda for the benefit of judges who adjudicated and sentenced defendants in criminal enterprise cases.[5] Successful prosecutions of Richard Riley, Graham Kendall, and the Bowie Boys during Bill Price's tenure as U.S. Attorney contributed heavily to the district's renown for seizing more than $40 million in drug assets, a record rivaled by very few of the nation's judicial districts.[6]

A powerful tool in the crime-fighting arsenal was the Comprehensive Crime Control Act of 1984. Passed by the U.S. Congress and signed into law by President Ronald Reagan on October 12 of that year, the legislation was one of the largest and most sweeping reforms of the U.S. criminal justice system. The overhaul ran the gamut of crime-and-punishment issues: bail conditions, the insanity defense, crime victims, criminal and civil forfeiture, international money laundering, emergency wiretapping, trademarks, racketeering, U.S. Attorneys' salaries, and the misuse and counterfeiting of credit and debit cards. In an effort to put drug peddlers out of business, the act increased federal penalties for drug offenses and established a National Drug Enforcement Policy Board in the executive branch.

The act also created the U.S. Sentencing Commission, a bipartisan, independent agency located in the judicial branch of government. As one of seven U.S. Attorneys appointed to advise the commission, Price had the bully pulpit he craved to advocate against mandatory sentencing and promote proportionality in punishments. He was disappointed when sentencing guidelines were initially interpreted as mandatory; many years passed before they became advisory. "I had real problems with mandatory sentencing," explained Price about his commitment to fairness, which had crystalized in Okscam with Dorothy Griffin's and Guy Moore's sentencing. "Sometimes, under the sentencing guidelines, people who aren't that bad go away for twenty years without parole. It's just ridiculous! It doesn't do them or the public any good. We were trying to be fair. We weren't trying to get everybody into jail for the maximum amount of time." However, Price approved of a federal statute that allowed U.S. Attorneys to charge felons convicted of three crimes with a firearm to be charged and punished with a mandatory ten-year sentence without parole. As this statute was discretionary and tightly written, it was rarely abused and was a valuable tool in getting violent criminals off the street.[7]

Price described the sea change in law enforcement in an address to Rotary 29 in downtown Oklahoma City and numerous interviews that signaled his increasing stature in legal circles and prominence in the media. Criminals were certainly getting the message as mandatory sentencing guidelines for repeat offenders—the "three strikes and you're out" mandate—went into effect. Sometimes, their sentences seemed fair. But all too often, people found guilty of minor crimes, or who had played small roles in large conspiracies, were treated too harshly. Thanks largely to beefed-up provisions pertaining to asset seizure, his office was able to take down not just rank-and-file lawbreakers, but entire organizations whose methods were becoming ever more violent and whose operations extended far beyond American shores. "We're finding criminals who are much more violent and much more organized," said Price. "They also have more international connections." Price's aversion to overly harsh sentences did not extend to violent offenders, many of whom paid for their crimes with shockingly light sentences. "No wonder the public is disillusioned," said Price, who cited disturbing statistics on time served in prison: murder, 5.3 years, and rape, 2.8 years.

For evidence of his and other prosecutors' determination to reduce crime, Price cited Oklahoma's ranking number two in the nation in asset seizure. He characterized the crime bill's impact as nothing short of "tremendous," particularly as it dawned on scofflaws that their flashy cars were subject to seizure. The last thing young professionals with expensive cocaine habits wanted was to have their Porsches confiscated, much less incarceration.

To strengthen his office's track record in asset seizure, Price instructed his assistants to follow the money trail, with special attention to drug smugglers. "We're trying to take the money out of the dope trade," he said. "In the last year alone we have seized Ferraris, Jaguars, homes, airplanes, untold amounts of cash, farms—everything to try and take the money out of the dope trade."

With Okscam still on everybody's mind, Price felt obliged to comment on the state legislature's failure to introduce systemic reforms in county purchasing. "They did some superficial things that were beneficial to some degree—although they added to the cost of county government—but the fear factor is probably still there. That's why it hasn't returned to this day, but it will return some day." Not for the first time, Price blamed the system of county governance for spawning corruption. To back up his conviction, he cited other states (at least twenty, by his count) with similar systems of county governance that suffered from the same kind of corruption that had produced Okscam.

"It's amazing the difference in systems and what it yields in terms of corruption," said Price. His foremost recommendation to the legislature was to allow home rule, which would enable county residents to mold governance to the contours of their regional economies.

Hidden in plain sight was corruption in the tag agency system. "We found that this was a massive consumer fraud," said Price, "involving $2 billion a year throughout the country with people rolling back their odometers on used cars." Oklahoma's reputation as the title wash capital of the Southwest sprang from consumers' annual losses of $10–$20 million dollars from purchasing cars at artificially inflated prices. As with county commissioners, private tag agents with an entrepreneurial bent had the latitude to skim profits by processing titles with virtually no oversight from the state. Price called on the legislature to take over the tag agent system to protect citizens from getting ripped off.[8]

▶ ▶ ▶ ▶

Of all the crime and corruption that plagued Oklahoma, none was more vexing to Price than drug peddling. Enraged by the likes of Ramon D. Martinez (aka the Milkman), turkey dope kingpin Richard Riley, international drug smuggler Graham Kendall, and the Bowie Boys, Price founded the Oklahoma Alliance Against Drugs (OAAD), an organization committed to preventing drug and alcohol use among young people. Inspiration came from a U.S. Attorneys' conference at which experts were invited to speak about drug education and prevention. Price returned to Oklahoma City with a pile of books and a directive from the U.S. Attorney General to formulate and implement drug-demand strategies. The only thing Price did not get was money, leaving him and his colleagues to raise it themselves. When he was not fundraising, Price was on the hunt for educators, medical experts, law enforcement professionals, and drug and alcohol counselors to serve on the OAAD board of directors.

Price founded the Oklahoma Alliance Against Drugs in 1986 to combat the scourge of drug and alcohol abuse among youth. COURTESY BILL PRICE.

From its founding in 1986 to the decade's end, the OAAD mushroomed from a small, privately funded group of volunteers into a public-private coalition with hundreds of thousands of dollars in support from Governor Henry Bellmon's discretionary fund. Price did his part by raising almost a million dollars. With offices in five cities, hundreds of youth clubs carrying the no-nonsense moniker Teens Against Drugs, and community task forces across the state, the OAAD aimed to prevent the leaders of tomorrow from wrecking their lives.

OAAD was one of many antidrug organizations spawned by President Ronald Reagan's War on Drugs, including Teens Against Drugs, DARE (Drug Abuse Resistance Education), QUEST (Quality care, Universal access, Efficient utilization, Stabilizing costs, and Transforming health care delivery), Students Against Drugs (SAD), and Students Against Drunk Drivers (SADD). Famously, First Lady Nancy Reagan chimed in with her mantra, "Just say no to drugs." After conducting countless pretrial interviews with drug addicts who served as witnesses in his drug-gang prosecutions, Price was convinced that 70–80 percent of all crimes were drug related, and he had no illusions about the difficulty of actually winning the war. "But if we can instill the right kind of attitudes and behaviors in young people, we can keep them from wrecking their lives. So many people start using drugs when they are children. By intervening early, we stand a much better chance of being successful. Ultimately, it's the only way we're going to control the crime problem."[9]

Two initiatives differentiated OAAD from other antidrug organizations: enlisting peer pressure to influence youth behavior and sponsoring symposia and leadership training sessions. Sporting T-shirts and wrist bands emblazoned with the slogan "To know is to say no," about 2,500 young people gathered for OAAD's first symposium in the spring of 1987. Symposia with as many as ten thousand youth in attendance followed, in Oklahoma City and Tulsa, and gatherings of 1,000 youth in smaller communities. Rather than invite policemen and drug counselors to deliver all-too-familiar admonitions to stay away from drugs, OAAD trained older students to share their stories with younger ones. "It was so much better than a police officer, or anybody else, to have the high school kids that they look up to going down and talking to the middle school kids," explained Price. When adult speakers were invited, OAAD made sure they had the bona fides to influence young people. Actors, sports figures, and musicians were far more likely to get through to youth than stodgy professionals and officers in uniform.

OAAD also differentiated itself by providing young people with accurate data backed up by science and statistics to show the long-term effects of youthful drug use and the likelihood of addiction. "It was far more sophisticated than the image of Nancy Reagan saying, 'Just say no to drugs'," explained Price about OAAD's modus operandi. "We gave solid information, not exaggerated information. We would give it on alcohol too." Rather than recite Reagan's and others' familiar mantras, OAAD speakers explained that many people have a genetic tendency toward addiction. When used at an early age, even so-called soft drugs such as marijuana can produce quicker and more devasting consequences. As nobody knew if they were predisposed to addiction, youth needed to be encouraged to set positive examples for their peers.

To represent youth on the OAAD board of directors, Price knew where to turn: his teenage daughter, Anne, whose tenure on the board taught her a lifelong lesson in the importance of grassroots organization. "I was very impressed by how organized and fact-driven it was," said Anne. Later, as a student at her father's alma mater, the Georgetown University School of Foreign Service, where she graduated in 1996, she put those lessons to work in cofounding Students for an Energy Efficient Environment (S.E.E.E.), an international nonprofit aimed at promoting energy-efficient environments and programs such as the EPA's Green Lights Program. Equipped with an EPA grant, the organization won accolades for helping colleges and universities install energy-efficient lighting and, later, implement energy-efficient metallurgical processes in iron and steel factories in Russia and China. "It was more grassroots than some of the prior EPA programs," continued Anne. "A lot of that kind of structure was borrowed from how my dad had set up the Oklahoma Alliance Against Drugs."[10]

Price served as president of OAAD from 1986 to 1989. Always eager to give away credit, he singled out two associates, Executive Director Sherry Simmons ("a fabulous executive director!") and Oklahoma City Public Schools official Betty Mason ("she was just a dynamo!") for building OAAD into one of the nation's most successful antidrug programs. "We had a real philosophy of how to do it," continued Price. That philosophy was based on a simple progression: (1) prevention, beginning with so-called gateway drugs such as marijuana and alcohol, which was both the cheapest and most effective way to mitigate drug use; (2) if that didn't work, move on to treatment; and (3), if all else failed, prosecute. The aim of prosecution was not to deliver lengthy prison sentences, but to drive people into treatment. Absent a sword of

Damocles hanging over them, most people avoided treatment until it was too late or, in a worst-case scenario, were dead.

"I *really* felt like that was doing more good than all the prosecutions combined in turning around drug use among young people," concluded Price. "I kept thinking, if I am going to be involved in a nonprofit, I am going to be involved in drug prevention and treatment, because those things make a difference. You can't stop this thing otherwise."[11]

In recognition of his antidrug campaign, Price received awards from J. C. Penney, the Oklahoma State Association for Prevention of Alcoholism and Drug Abuse, and the Coalition of Civic Leadership that was composed mostly of African American pastors, all in 1989. Law enforcement joined the chorus when U.S. Attorneys nationwide, the FBI, and the DEA recognized OAAD as a model program in reducing demand for illicit drugs. In recognition of his growing expertise, Price was invited to speak at U.S. Attorneys' conferences about best practices in starting drug prevention programs.[12]

▶ ▶ ▶ ▶

Less than three years into his position as U.S. Attorney, rumors swirled that Price was planning a run for the governor's office in 1986. As noted by *Oklahoma Observer* editor and persistent gadfly in the state legislator Frosty Troy, Republicans were in for their usual uphill battle. With registered Republicans numbering 574,135 compared to 1,304,454 Democrats, Troy looked to the state's 50,049 registered Independents as a decisive factor in a close race. Likely Republican candidates represented a wide range of conservative ideologies, but they were on the same page when it came to replacing the two-term incumbent, Democratic Governor George Nigh, with a governor from their party. Although Price was not officially in the running, Troy included him in his roster of prominent Republicans who had a shot at Oklahoma's highest office: "Bill Price isn't a household name in Oklahoma, but it would become one very quickly in a race for governor. Price is the Oklahoma City Federal DA who put together the probe that put more than 230 county commissioners and vendors in jail. Price hasn't been an active Republican, something not possible in the DA's job; but he would probably be able to raise money and support on the basis of his work as a federal prosecutor of county commissioners and legislators—two of Oklahoma's least favorite political types. His politics: Conservative."[13]

Price's decision not to run enhanced the prospects for former Oklahoma governor and U.S. Senator Henry Bellmon, whose retirement from the Senate in 1980 did not mean that he had retired from public affairs. When he returned home to Noble County, in addition to farming, he served on corporate boards and taught at several state universities. A far more challenging opportunity came when Governor George Nigh asked him to serve as acting director of the Department of Human Services (DHS), a sprawling agency that consumed half of the state's revenue and had been mired in dysfunction under its longtime director, Lloyd Rader, who was stepping down after three-plus decades at the helm. "At first I thought the idea was completely ridiculous," wrote Bellmon in his autobiography. "The notion of a former Republican governor and former U.S. senator joining a Democratic administration in what was potentially the state's most explosive position was at first illogical."[14] Yet Rader had proven to be a valuable ally during his first term as governor, and with the blessing of the outgoing director, Bellmon accepted the position. Working side by side with Bob Fulton, former minority staff counsel for the Senate Budget Committee, Bellmon settled in for a two-month stint as the DHS's acting director.

Within hours, Bellmon realized that he had stepped into a hornet's nest of mismanagement, patronage, and outright corruption. The DHS's funding from an earmarked sales tax had given Rader ("a one-man empire," according to Bellmon) an ever-growing revenue stream that precluded legislative oversight.[15] The chaos was compounded by a blizzard of lawsuits, some with claims upward of $100 million, stemming from malfeasance at juvenile institutions and schools for the mentally disabled. A notorious micromanager with an aversion to budgets, whose political skills were slipping with age, Rader faced claims of personal liability for his agency's implosion, and he made a bad situation worse by dodging reporters and refusing to speak openly with his own staff.

Saddened by his friend's decline and the mess he had spawned, Bellmon exhibited a flair for understatement when he wrote, "Staying too long in office is a mistake public officials should try to avoid." In the prescient words of historian Will Durant, "It is impossible for a ruler to be omnipotent and sane."[16]

As he wrote budgets, closed facilities, and counseled demoralized employees against the backdrop of a deepening depression heralded by the FDIC's takeover of Penn Square Bank, Bellmon realized that he needed a general counsel, and what better place to go shopping than the U.S. Attorney's office? And who better to pick than his youth campaign coordinator in his first run for governor, guard at the governor's mansion, and legislative director of his U.S. Senate staff, Charlie Waters?

"He called me up one day and said he wanted to go to lunch," recalled Waters about the benign beginnings of what turned into a thirty-year career at DHS. "Bellmon wanted me to become general counsel and help him reorganize this department. I said, 'Senator, I don't know anything about this. Nothing!' He said, 'I don't either. But we can find out.'"

Waters was just coming off a series of prosecutions of nursing home operators, several of whom had earned prison sentences for filing fraudulent insurance claims. Those cases had left him with a distaste for Lloyd Rader, "the most powerful man in the state government," whose most loyal collaborator in the state legislature was the ubiquitous Gene Stipe, and who was notorious for setting insurance rates with nursing home directors over a fifth of whiskey. "There was no open process," continued Waters. "They weren't following the federal rules. It was just the way it was!" With plenty of experience in prosecuting corruption under his belt and encouragement from U.S. District Judge Ralph Thompson, Waters accepted Bellmon's offer and bade goodbye to Bill Price and his other colleagues in the U.S. Attorney's Office.

Waters quickly discovered that, like Bellmon, he had no idea what he was getting into.

"Did you enjoy that?" I asked a seemingly perturbed Charlie Waters.

"No, I didn't!" came the rather abrupt reply. "It was horrible! It was the absolute *opposite* of anything I ever wanted to do!"

What Senator Bellmon had dangled as "a green-eye-shade job" fit for an accountant turned out to be a daily battle against entrenched interests, both internal and external to the agency. Sadly, all too many of the DHS's twelve-thousand-plus staffers' allegiance to a dysfunctional system seemed to dwarf whatever commitment they once had to public service.

Waters went on to explain what it was like to unravel the snarl that Lloyd Rader had left at the DHS. "He bought up influence in the state of Oklahoma through money. He had a contract with every special-interest group in the state to provide some sort of service. Not only that, he had *patronage!*"

Waters found patronage to be particularly galling, and he winced to recall the rows of gunmetal-gray desks where legions of secretaries and attorneys with no responsibilities that he could discern whiled the time away, all with de facto tenure on the state payroll. A black-label filing system bulged with personnel files of employees with no apparent qualifications for their jobs, but who had the support of friends in high places.

After his bleak trip down memory lane, Waters returned to specific forms of corruption, including the child support enforcement program, which ranked dead last in the nation and its far-flung territories.

"I think we were number fifty-four!" railed Waters. "Rader was using this as a way to get money to the D.A.s!"

Waters concluded his diatribe with a description of his and other reformers' accomplishments at the DHS after Bellmon left to run for governor and Bob Fulton was named as full-time director. "A lot of good things happened," said Waters, almost wistful now about the things he had accomplished at Oklahoma's primary public-service agency. "We made a lot of changes. We restructured and re-did that agency numerous times, and I worked with a lot of nice people."[17]

As my interview with Charlie Waters wound toward its conclusion, I could not help but wonder if the corruption that he and Bellmon battled at the DHS was basically Okscam in another guise, where charismatic personalities and force of habit combined with structural flaws to foster an out-of-control system that was seemingly impervious to reform—until, that is, public servants like Henry Bellmon and Charlie Waters at the DHS and Bill Price in the U.S. Attorney's Office decided that enough was enough. Henry Bellmon came away (much sooner than Charlie Waters!) with a renewed commitment to reform, even in the face of stiff opposition. As Bellmon noted in his autobiography, "Public attitudes do change once the facts are understood."[18]

Bellmon's other immersion in corruption came when he was appointed as receiver for America's iconic repository of Western lore: the National Cowboy Hall of Fame and Western Heritage Center (later, the National Cowboy and Western Heritage Museum) in Oklahoma City. No sooner did he arrive at the museum than he discovered a dispiriting pattern of wealthy directors purchasing artworks at nominal prices, hiring friendly appraisers to inflate their values, and then loaning them back to the museum for display. Directors were rewarded for their perfidy with tax write-offs reflecting the inflated values. In equally devious transactions, the museum purchased artworks and sold them to directors at prices far below their real value to display in their homes and offices. One board member from California was proud to own a collection of works by Frederic Remington that he had purchased on the cheap. In a final indignity, Oklahomans were shocked to learn that board members from California (no doubt including the aforementioned Remington collector) were undermining the museum's viability in an effort to relocate it to their own state, a move that was stymied when a lawsuit was filed. Scrambling to pay bills, reduce costs, increase revenues, and placate creditors, Bellmon was fortunate to have *Daily Oklahoman* publisher Ed Gaylord in his corner. Through a deft combination of loans and influence peddling, Gaylord helped keep the museum afloat, safe from unscrupulous board members, and forever in Oklahoma.

Like Charlie Waters, Henry Bellmon relied on a positive attitude and a conviction that he was doing the right thing to alleviate the despair that might have engulfed him. "Overall, I enjoyed the role as troubleshooter at the Department of Human Services and at the Cowboy Hall of Fame and Western Heritage Center," he wrote in an upbeat assessment of his post-senatorial temp jobs. "I found the challenges stimulating and the results gratifying. These experiences would prove excellent preparations for a second term as Oklahoma's governor when the entire state faced troubled times."[19]

▶ ▶ ▶ ▶

Henry Bellmon won back his old job by defeating Democratic contender David Walters in the gubernatorial race of 1986. Resettled in the governor's mansion, he poured his energy into traditional conservative causes: ending pork spending, endorsing legislation to make the state more business friendly, promoting an ultimately successful effort to amend the state constitution by creating an ethics commission, laboring on behalf of turnpike construction, and advocating to limit the length of legislative sessions. The most notable achievement of Bellmon's second administration—and one destined to enrage staunch conservatives in his party—was passage of the Education Reform and Funding Act of 1990. Best known as House Bill 1017, the act called for a 27 percent increase in common school funding, compulsory kindergarten, smaller classes, teacher incentive pay, and tenure reform.[20]

Happy to remain on the sidelines in the race for governor, Bill Price spent his time playing whack-a-mole with an endless variety of self-serving schemes. In early 1985, a federal grand jury charged longtime Chickasaw governor Overton James with eleven counts of fraud and extortion. Specifically, he was accused of taking nearly $100,000 in kickbacks through phony invoices, billed over a three-year period, from James's Chief Pallet Company to Kraig Kendall and H. G. "Chuck" Thompson, contractors aiming to secure a $12 million contract from the Chickasaw Housing Authority in Ada. James's indictment alleged that he had "devised a scheme to defraud the citizens of the Chickasaw Nation of the right to have their business conducted impartially and free of corruption."[21]

The governor's indictment coincided with guilty pleas from two other tribal officials: former Chickasaw Housing Authority director and high school basketball coach Claudell Overton and former Absentee Shawnee Housing Authority director Duane Ellis. Both men admitted to receiving kickbacks from the same contractors. Suspicions had been confirmed when Overton and Ellis were spotted driving shiny new cars, paid for by Kendall and Thompson. The good news, according to Price, was that his office had uncovered no signs of corruption in the U.S. Department of Housing and Urban Development. He and Assistant U.S. Attorney Steve Korotash further explained that James's indictment was part of an ongoing investigation into alleged corruption in Native American housing. Assistance came from FBI Agent James Elroy, whose investigations into tribal corruption led to a number of prosecutions in Price's office.

Kendall and Thompson entered guilty pleas in early July 1985 and were duly punished. Overton and Ellis, who had entered guilty pleas in February 1985, were sentenced to two years in prison and fined $10,000 and $5,000, respectively. In imposing Overton's and Ellis's sentences and fines, U.S. District Judge Luther Eubanks berated them for taking funds from poverty-stricken Native Americans, making their crimes more egregious than those committed in Okscam. James's hearing was held in Judge Ralph Thompson's courtroom, where his former protestations of innocence fell flat. After finally admitting his complicity in kickback schemes, he was sentenced in January 1989 to nine months in a federal prison.[22]

Corruption of an entirely different sort went public after a three-and-a-half-year joint investigation by the FBI and the Air Force Office of Special Investigations uncovered sales of bogus airplane parts to the air force. Suspicions of wrongdoing dated back to March 1984, when the Air Logistics Command at Tinker Air Force Base realized that surplus parts dealers were delivering an "inordinate amount" of defective parts. At first glance, the parts appeared to be new. But a closer examination revealed used equipment (including parachutes!) that could prove dangerous, even deadly, to pilots who assumed they were flying with new parts.

The probe sent investigators from Oklahoma to Pennsylvania, Texas, California, Florida, Kansas, New York, and Ohio, and it ended with Price's announcement that his office had negotiated six guilty pleas with parts dealers nationwide and was expecting two indictments. As Price declared in a news conference, "We want to definitely give a message to the people in this industry that it's not going to be tolerated, and they will be prosecuted."[23]

The U.S. Attorney's Office also collaborated with investigators to discover cases of pharmaceutical diversion stemming from the enormous price deductions that pharmaceutical companies granted to charitable organizations, including clinics serving low-income patients. Such were the price reductions that employees succumbed to the temptation to sell their companies' products to wholesalers and pocket the profits. As the unintended consequences of their price reductions came to light, pharmaceutical executives were not surprised when law enforcement came calling. An FBI sting operation and the subsequent flurry of prosecutions in Price's office was a turning point in bringing a nationwide criminal network to justice.[24]

Trouble in the banking business did not end with Penn Square Bank. In 1985, former Cushing banker and Oklahoma National Guard Brigadier General James J. Wasson and his business partner, Melvin B.

Southeastern Oklahoma State University in Durant, represented here by the Administration Building, fell victim to fraud and misappropriation of funds during the freewheeling presidency of Eldon Leon Hibbs. COURTESY OKLAHOMA HISTORICAL SOCIETY

Pulliam, defrauded the Small Business Administration and a Cushing investment company, Investment Capital, out of $955,000 through improper loans. Price's office traced that sum to Wasson's private industrial bond account at the financial firm of Stifel Nicolaus. Six loans had been made to fictitious firms that Wasson operated using the names of unsuspecting national guardsmen under his command. Wasson and Pulliam, who owned loan companies specializing in loans up to $400, were also accused of committing bank fraud by forcing the First National Bank and Trust Company of Cushing and the Citizens Bank in Drumright to pay an unnecessary $379,000 premium on two Oklahoma Housing Finance Agency housing rehabilitation bonds.

Wasson's claims of innocence lost traction when, in August 1987, he was asked to resign his command of the National Guard's 45th Infantry Brigade. Although he and Pulliam continued to maintain their innocence, their trial, in late 1988, ended with convictions of conspiracy to commit bank fraud, embezzlement, and more than thirty other crimes.[25]

Anyone who assumed that higher education was immune to white-collar crime was dissuaded when Eldon Leon Hibbs, president of Southeastern Oklahoma State University in Durant, came under fire for wrongdoing ranging from patronage and fraud to outright thievery. Shortly after he succeeded Mike Turpen as Oklahoma's attorney general in 1986, Robert Henry launched a state investigation. But as federal crimes came to light, he pulled the U.S. Attorney's Office into the swamp. "The state auditor uncovered some corruption, and we began investigating it in the attorney general's office," explained Henry, an attorney in private practice in Oklahoma City at the time of our interview. When Henry ran into political pressure that threatened his state appropriation, he made a beeline to the FBI and then his friend, Bill Price, whose respect for academic achievement did not square with a university president with his hands in the till.

"Mr. Hibbs was a Democratic power broker," continued Henry. "He was very powerful in that Little Dixie part of the state. But he had a bad operation going!"[26]

A federal grand jury indicted Hibbs, in January 1989, on forty-two counts of using public and Southeastern Foundation funds for himself, his family, and his friends. Among his half-dozen schemes was submitting hundreds of thousands of dollars in false student payroll claims to orchestrate a $90,000 insurance scam involving a racehorse whose value was artificially inflated. Tragically, the horse died shortly after the second premium was due. Profits from the policy were allegedly distributed to participants in the scheme. Henry, who credited the *Daily Oklahoman*'s investigative reporting for exposing Hibbs's possible misuse of public money, said that nobody else was included in the grand-jury indictment. Yet the investigation was ongoing, and more indictments were expected. Joe F. Gary, then a member of the state Regents for Higher Education, was among those targeted in the probe.

At a joint press conference, Oklahoma Attorney General Henry and U.S. Attorney Price explained that the charges against Hibbs and a conspirator, Jefferson B. Kinney, Jr., of Florida, culminated a two-year investigation by their offices, the U.S. Attorney's office in Muskogee, the Oklahoma State Auditor and Inspector's office, the OSBI, the FBI, and the IRS. In one of the most noxious allegations, Hibbs was accused of using false student payroll claims to fund student scholarships. In Hibbs's calculation, that sleight of hand became necessary after he had depleted the foundation's scholarship funds by handing out money and granting low and no-interest loans to his family and friends. State Auditor Clifton Scott estimated that scheme alone cost the state more than $1 million. Equally noxious was putting his wife, Maxine, on the university payroll as a tennis instructor for $1,000 a month without the regents' approval. According to the indictment, "she had no position and performed no regular duties." Hibbs was further accused of arranging for $39,521 in false loans from the foundation to pay for furniture and the interior design of his home.[27]

Hibbs's case went to trial, in June 1989, in U.S. District Judge Ralph Thompson's courtroom. Assistant U.S. Attorney Arlene Joplin, together with a cadre of assistant attorneys general, formed the prosecution team. Facing a maximum penalty of 210 years in prison and a fine of $10.5 million, Hibbs endured a parade of angry employees who took to the witness stand to support the United States case. In one shocking testimony after another, Hibbs was accused of arranging for the school's scholarship foundation to pay rent for his son, Max, who operated a computer store; granting a low-interest loan to Max's friend Michael Harris to become a partner in the store; and forcing personnel to create minutes of directors' meetings that were never held. Some of those minutes falsely claimed that directors had approved of Hibbs's decisions. "We were trying to cover up past actions, or at least provide backup reports," explained Gayla Guillory, who prepared the fake minutes. When Max was not busy in his computer store, he was earning $2,480 a month to organize a national computer museum and $2,000 a month to maintain horse records at the college's equestrian center, all on the university payroll.

To be fair to the older generation, Hibbs moved a $1.2 million scholarship endowment to a bank in Beaver, Oklahoma, (a long day's drive from Durant!) to create a job for his father, P. O. Hibbs. Perhaps it was mere coincidence that the elder Hibbs was a former Beaver County commissioner. According to bank president John Lasater, he knew so little about banking that he often asked for help in calculating interest rates on loans he authorized from the scholarship account.[28]

"That was, I think, the first joint, major corruption prosecution that the state of Oklahoma and the feds ever did together," recalled Henry about a happy ending to Hibbs's ignominious career. "It was very successful. Mr. Hibbs was convicted, and Judge Ralph Thompson conducted the trial, and ran a superb trial. Mr. Hibbs got a ten-year sentence. That was a big victory!"[29]

For Henry, the case of the incredible Mr. Hibbs underscored the need to establish state control over college administrations and energize boards of regents to do their jobs—no small feat in a state whose tax-supported colleges and universities were governed by sixteen boards of regents and three boards of trustees. "And there should be plenty of outrage when something occurs," continued Henry, in an interview shortly after Hibbs's indictment. "There's not been enough of that." For the past several years, allegations of misconduct had roiled higher education. In addition to Southeastern State University, Northwestern State University, Rose State College, Central State University, and Northern Oklahoma College had been targeted for a variety of transgressions. About the time of Hibbs's indictment, the football programs at the University of Oklahoma and Oklahoma State University were placed on NCAA probation for rules violations.

Price wanted to put some muscle behind laws to allow the Oklahoma State Auditor and Inspector's Office full access to records of university-related foundations. Henry, then serving on the board of directors of St. Gregory's College in Shawnee, agreed with Price that steps needed to be taken to curb illegal and unethical practices on campus. In anticipation of his later career as dean of Oklahoma

City University's law school and, later still, president of the university, Henry aimed to use the power of the state attorney general's office to monitor university foundations for conflicts of interest and compliance with state laws. Higher Education Chancellor Hans Brisch weighed in to suggest that colleges and universities "must be accountable to the taxpayers" and "stand the test of public scrutiny."[30]

▶ ▶ ▶ ▶

Toward the end of his tenure as U.S. Attorney, Price heeded U.S. Attorney General Edwin Meese's directive to U.S. Attorneys nationwide to create law enforcement legislative committees. The purpose of these committees was to promote emulation of federal laws by encouraging state legislators to improve and modernize law enforcement. Cochaired by state Attorney General Robert Henry, Price's committee included representatives from a wide range of state and federal agencies that shared responsibility for fighting crime and corruption. As Price was a Republican and Henry was a Democrat, the committee cochairs demonstrated a spirit of bipartisanship that proved infectious in the normally partisan legislature. Between 1986 and 1989, their committee drafted and helped pass fifteen major pieces of legislation. None were more significant than antiracketeering laws and the creation of multicounty grand juries.[31]

At the federal level, antiracketeering laws dated back to 1970, when Congress passed the Racketeer Influenced and Corrupt Organizations Act (RICO), a law aimed specifically at putting ongoing criminal enterprises out of business. Such activity included illegal gambling, bribery, kidnapping, murder, money laundering, counterfeiting, embezzlement, drug trafficking, slavery, and a host of other unsavory business practices.[32] Whereas the federal RICO statue included civil and criminal provisions, Price was most interested in obtaining a criminal statute in Oklahoma, as a private litigant could rely on civil RICO charges to unfairly label an individual or business as a racketeer in an effort to force settlement of a civil lawsuit.

When legislators got around to debating RICO at the state level, in the spring of 1988, they ran afoul of opponents who fretted about the expansion of state criminal power. Price, who knew more than most about the growing influence of organized crime in Oklahoma, watched in dismay from the Senate gallery as Senator Gene Stipe railed against the proposed Senate Bill 127 (SB 127), better known as the Oklahoma Corrupt Organizations Prevention Act, as a red herring that would put every businessman who spent a few days frolicking in Las Vegas in danger of asset seizure when he came home. Such grandstanding aside, SB 127 actually targeted Price's nemesis—drug pushers, the backbone of organized crime. Support for the bill came from Oklahoma County District Attorney Bob Macy and Attorney General Robert Henry, who expressed confidence that SB 127 would deter gangs, most notably the Los Angeles–based Crips, from establishing outposts in Oklahoma.[33]

As the legislature was preparing to vote on SB 127, Price took his case to the House Judiciary Committee to explain that a state antiracketeering bill modeled on RICO would allow Oklahoma authorities to handle cases heretofore relegated to federal authorities and permit state law enforcement to seize assets that were linked to a "pattern of racketeering activity." Moreover, RICO would give authorities the latitude to go after entire organizations and include different crimes committed by the same people in the same indictment. Price's powers of persuasion helped win the day when, on March 14, 1988, the House of Representatives unanimously approved SB 127. In the Senate, Gary Gardenhire was especially articulate in rebutting Stipe's rhetoric and outlining the need for a criminal RICO statute. As a few senators were swayed by Gene Stipe's oratory, the Senate was a bit less enthusiastic and passed the bill by a vote of 39–8. Henry spoke for many in law enforcement when he praised legislators for their sound judgment. "The legislature has given law enforcement officials in Oklahoma a major tool to combat drug trafficking in our state by passing the RICO bill," he said. When SB 127 arrived on his desk, Governor Bellmon signed it with a flourish. "In my judgment this is a major step in the fight against crime, particularly organized crime."[34]

The other sea change in law enforcement came with passage of multicounty grand-jury legislation. Generally speaking, a grand jury's responsibilities are twofold: (1) to hear evidence of criminal accusations presented by the district attorney and decide whether the accused should be indicted and tried for a crime; and (2) to hear evidence of potential public wrongdoing by city and county officials, including acts which may not be crimes but are imprudent, ineffective, or inefficient, and make recommendations to county and city officials.[35] As the stymied grand-jury investigation of county commissioners in Stephens County had made all too clear back in 1978, restricting grand juries to a single county prevented effective prosecution of alleged crimes that crossed county lines.

Voters had approved a constitutional amendment authorizing multicounty grand juries in 1971, but lawmakers had never gotten around to drafting critical guidelines on how they would be conducted, how jurors would be selected, and where charges would be filed.[36] For the story of how that rather bizarre oversight was finally corrected, we turn to Bill Price, Robert Henry, and Frank Keating—friends and collaborators who combined the power of their offices to fight corruption in all its guises.

All three attorneys were keenly aware of the shortcomings of single-county grand juries. As Price explained, the magic of a grand jury is not in its power to charge, but in its investigative power, specifically its ability to subpoena documents and compel witnesses to testify. And in the absence of a statewide grand jury system, only the lowest-level criminals in an organization can be prosecuted, leaving their higher-ups to go free. "A county grand-jury system has limited jurisdiction and is full of loopholes," said Price. "Oklahoma needed a statewide grand-jury system authorized by an amendment to the state constitution and run by the state attorney general's office."[37]

Robert Henry agreed. "You might have been able to get somebody before a grand jury, but you couldn't even inquire of witnesses what goes on outside that county," he said. "And, as you know, criminals don't respect county boundaries." Henry attributed the problem to Oklahoma's founding fathers and their legendary suspicion of big government. As with so many vexing issues in Oklahoma history, their enthrallment to prairie populism had defied the passage of time to stymie law enforcement at the century's end.[38]

As Frank Keating put it, Oklahoma legislators needed "to muscle up" the Attorney General's Office. "There's no way to coordinate criminal prosecution," continued Keating. "We have three federal districts here, and you have a plethora of county grand juries and district attorneys here. So is there anybody who can bring everybody together to attack the problem? That would be the multicounty grand jury."[39]

Not long after he was named as state attorney general, Henry got a call from his father, Lloyd H. Henry, a former prosecutor and judge from Shawnee with a reputation as a crusader. He wanted to discuss an article that he had read about a speech Price had delivered on the need for multicounty grand juries.

"If you ever get a chance, you need to try to get this multicounty grand jury that Bill Price is talking about," said the elder Henry to his son.

Knowing that his father's convictions dovetailed with his own and determined to mitigate the scourge of drug trafficking, the younger Henry called his buddy in the U.S. Attorney's Office.

"I just read in the Shawnee paper that you're talking about multicounty grand jury," said Henry to Price. "I want to know more about that. Come on down!"

Price accepted Henry's invitation for a chat. With input from Frank Keating, they subsequently put their heads together and, as cochairmen of the newly created Law Enforcement Coordinating Committee, began a collaboration aimed at correcting one of the most egregious flaws in Oklahoma's system of law enforcement.

With assistance from the U.S. Attorney's Office, Henry's staff went to work to produce a document to introduce to the legislature. "I assigned a couple of people to it, and we worked really hard on it, and introduced it," explained Henry. "Bill supported it, and helped us, and came to press conferences. It took two years to get the legislature to expand the grand-jury investigative technique to replicate the federal system. It was a little difficult to get through the Senate, frankly, but we finally got it through and got it signed. It has been a very powerful tool!"[40]

CHAPTER FOURTEEN : *The Best Governor Oklahoma Never Had*

On May 23, 1989, Bill Price submitted his resignation as U.S. Attorney for the Western District of Oklahoma to President George H. W. Bush to launch his campaign for governor.[1]

Upon hearing of Price's resignation, FBI director William S. Sessions expressed his regret and congratulated him on his extraordinary tenure as U.S. Attorney. "You have every reason to look back with pride and satisfaction on your many accomplishments during the past eight years as United States Attorney and for many years prior to that as an Assistant in the Western District," wrote Sessions to Price on June 8. Sessions was particularly grateful for the close collaboration that Price had fostered between the U.S. Attorney's Office and the FBI during the heady days of Okscam. As Sessions put it, "The excellent spirit of cooperation between our offices has been considerably strengthened during your tenure, and your presence will be sorely missed."[2] President Bush chimed in at the end of June with his own assessment of Price's achievements: "You have served the Nation well, and in the years ahead you can look back with pride on the many accomplishments of your tenure. You have my best wishes for every future success and happiness."[3]

While Price was preparing to step down as U.S. Attorney, his friend since middle school at Casady and fellow Republican Bob Anthony was settling into his new job on the Oklahoma Corporation Commission. "I had never run for any state office before," explained Anthony about his 1988 campaign. "This was the first office that I ran for." As a former executive in his family's chain of clothing stores, C. R. Anthony, the newly elected corporation commissioner had a lot to learn in his transition from business to politics. "And lo and behold, there hadn't been a Republican elected to this agency since the Hoover landslide of 1928! For sixty years there had never been a Republican. Everybody assumed it was impossible. That wasn't going to happen!"

But it did happen and, in January 1989, Anthony made the switch from corporate executive to one of three elected officials responsible for regulating public utilities, oil and gas companies, and other economic sectors that constituted the engines of Oklahoma commerce.

Anthony's first inkling that something was amiss at the state's most powerful economic agency came even before he was elected. Trouble arrived in the person of Bill Anderson, an attorney saddled with the unfortunate nickname "Tater" for his resemblance to a potato.

"He wanted to support me," said Anthony about what appeared, at first glance, to be a welcome campaign overture. But when Anthony arrived at his office to discuss his candidacy for the Corporation Commission, Anderson handed him an envelope stuffed with ten hundred-dollar bills and a list of five names scrawled on a scrap of paper. Clearly, Anderson wanted Anthony to know that five people had contributed two hundred dollars each to his campaign, which was the legal limit for individual contributions to go unreported. Maybe so. But still, receiving a wad of cash and a list of what might have been bogus names put Anthony's radar on high alert.

Shortly after his election, Anthony ran into his old middle school buddy and recounted his first meeting and subsequent run-ins with an attorney whose name he chose not to mention. "Look, he's doing a full-court press on me!" said Anthony. "He's calling me at home! He offered to get me more money!"

"Are you talking about Bill Anderson?" asked Price.

Startled, Anthony replied that, yes, Anderson was indeed the attorney he was talking about.

"Bob," said Price, "we have been pursuing this attorney for a long period of time. He converts a lot of client checks to cash that isn't accounted for."

Oklahoma Corporation Commissioner Bob Anthony (left) and Bill Price (right), friends since middle school, bonded over their wars with corruption. COURTESY BILL PRICE.

Price proceeded to tell Anthony that he had been trying without success to build a tax case against Anderson, whose shady tactics were an open secret among the capitol cognoscenti. Now that Price was resigning as U.S. Attorney, maybe Anthony would have more luck in seeing justice prevail by going to the FBI.

"I did this recruiting of Bob Anthony," said Price, now sporting a mischievous smile. "Shortly thereafter, I left. My main involvement was in getting him recruited. Then I departed!"

Price wished his friend good luck and made his own career switch from U.S. Attorney to gubernatorial candidate, leaving a vexed Bob Anthony to figure out what to do about a crooked lawyer who had been tilting the scales at the state's most influential regulatory agency.[4]

▶ ▶ ▶ ▶

Price's first order of business was to win his party's nomination against three contenders: Vince Orza, Burns Hargis, and Jerry Brown. Early on, the smart money was on Orza, a former newscaster and a principal in Garfield's restaurant chain, whose business acumen, media savvy, and polished oratory made him a formidable candidate. "Orza would say totally opposite things," explained Price about his nemesis in the Republican primary. "We might appear in front of one group, and he would say he was for right-to-work legislation, and appear thirty minutes later in front of another group, and you'd swear he said he was against right-to-work legislation. He just spoke to fit the audience!" Cracks in Orza's façade appeared when his campaign manager up and quit in the middle of the campaign with no kind words for his former candidate. Orza later showed his true colors by running for governor as a Democrat on a platform that bore little resemblance to his Republican platform.[5]

Orza's polar opposite was Burns Hargis, a natural and congenial leader with degrees in accounting and law and whose resume included presidency of the Oklahoma County Bar Association. He practiced law for nearly three decades, most recently with McAfee & Taft. Hargis complemented his civic and philanthropic projects with regular appearances on *Flashpoint*, an award-winning television program aimed at illuminating the issues that roiled Oklahoma politics.[6] "Hargis may be the most likeable personality in the world," said Price about his much more affable opponent, who would one day be appointed as president of Oklahoma State University. But as an attorney who then specialized in bankruptcies, Hargis's after dinner speeches and wry sense of humor proved to be a thin basis for building a winning brand in politics.

"What label do you put on Burns Hargis?" asked Price rhetorically. That was a question for Hargis and his campaign staff to ponder as the Republican primary loomed ever closer.[7]

Dark-horse candidate and truck stop owner Jerry Brown rounded out the foursome. "He was a really nice guy—a good man with a heart of gold," said Price with his usual flair for kindness. Drawing from an über-conservative base that included evangelical Christians, Brown knew his prospects of actually winning the primary were slim to none. As the race heated up in 1990, his inexperience and inability to pay for TV advertising left the field to contenders more accustomed to the glare of public scrutiny.[8]

President George H. W. Bush visited Oklahoma City to support Price's 1990 gubernatorial campaign. Standing next to President Bush are Bill and Mary Price and their children (left to right), Eileen, Anne, and James. COURTESY BILL PRICE.

To assemble his campaign staff, Price knew where to start: with his wife, Mary, and their three children, Anne Katherine (16), James Edward (13), and Eileen Elizabeth (9). "Bill was just feeling the water, gathering together his kitchen cabinet, and talking to people and everything," recalled Mary about her husband's initial probing. For a campaign office, Price chose a space in Nichols Hills Shopping Center next to Mamasita's, a popular eatery whose aromas proved irresistible to campaigners after hours of stuffing envelopes and making cold calls. "It was right next to Mamasita's," recalled Eileen, "and so I remember eating at Mamasita's a lot." Campaign staff who might have dropped in for lunch included driver and notetaker Patrick Camaron; campaign manager Neva Hill; deputy campaign manager Randy Swanson; and

PR specialists Mike McCarvell, John Cox, and Larry Stein. Volunteers included state campaign cochairman Skip Healey; fundraiser and Oklahoma Habitat for Humanity founder Ann Felton; sign builders Dr. Gary Strebel and Malcolm Hall; and volunteer coordinators Sherry Strebel, Phyllis Stough, and Toni Wizenberg, whose campaign buttons blared, "Don't yell at me, I'm a volunteer!" As Price commented about his dream team, "They were the most dynamic, hardworking people anyone could hope for."

One of the family's first high-profile appearances was at an Eighty-Niners game when George W. Bush owned the team's MLB affiliate, the Texas Rangers. "We got to run out on the field. It was very exciting!" continued Mary as James smiled and nodded in agreement. Feasting on sub sandwiches and cookies (baked, of course, in Mary's kitchen) in a stadium suite festooned with homemade decorations, Bill and Mary told Bush how enthusiastic they were about his father's presidency. The only disappointment came when Eileen, not a fan of Babe Ruth candy bars, learned that there were no famous baseball players named Snickers.

Back in Oklahoma, Price experienced a wave of déjà vu from his days as G. T. Blankenship's bus driver when he packed his family into their red minivan and lit out on an odyssey to spread his message to as many as forty towns in a week. "We all piled in and went to every watermelon festival and parade across the state," said James with a laugh. Other venues included Okmulgee, where they sampled the world's largest pecan cookie (thirty-two feet in diameter, 7,500 pounds, and "a little doughy on the inside, but impressive," said Anne), threshing bees in the wheat country, and Republican women's luncheons for Mary and the girls throughout the patchwork of counties. While Bill delivered speeches—seemingly written, as Anne put it, in collaboration between movie icon Jimmy Stewart and a policy wonk—and glad-handed with dignitaries, Mary and the children passed out brochures while they devoured hamburgers, corndogs, and whatever else served as local favorites. Sporting activities included cow patty bingo—if the cow lets loose on your number, you win!

"It was so much fun, campaigning as a family," said Mary. In the diary that survives as a treasured keepsake from the gubernatorial campaign of 1990, Mary recorded the joy she experienced as the family crisscrossed the state and the pride she felt in her husband's bid for Oklahoma's highest office: "We are enjoying the campaign enormously. Mainly, I am convinced that this is Bill's destiny. He is so good and honest, and genuinely wanting to serve the state. His whole life so far has been dedicated to public service, and his dream has been to run for elective office."

For Anne, the campaign was nothing less than an immersion in political science that even her later education at Georgetown could not match, mainly because her father went out of his way to include his family. From crisscrossing the state in their red minivan to meeting President George Bush, Sr., as he descended from Air Force One and riding in Vice President Dan Quayle's motorcade, she and her siblings got an insider's view of American democracy at work. "I credit my dad with giving us lots of exposure," said Anne. "It was an education you couldn't receive from any political science book." Such was Anne's expertise that television reporters solicited her commentaries, knowing that her analyses of county voting were often more accurate than what seasoned pros had to say.

Anne was mature enough to perceive the downside of media saturation when her father was misquoted and inaccuracies were reported as facts. "It was disheartening and eye-opening when the media or an opposing campaign twisted the truth," she said, the disappointment in her voice still resonant some three decades later. Two misrepresentations stood out as particularly egregious: (1) that Price leveraged his position as U.S. Attorney to launch his gubernatorial campaign; and (2) that he pushed the limits of propriety by promoting the OAAD on U.S. Attorney stationery, even though the U.S. Attorney General had instructed him to use his office as a bully pulpit to endorse the government's antidrug campaign. "As always, he was following exactly what he was supposed to be doing," continued Anne. "He was

"We are enjoying the campaign enormously," wrote Mary Price in her campaign diary. "His whole life so far has been dedicated to public service, and his dream has been to run for elective office." COURTESY BILL PRICE.

always by the book, and he has lived a squeaky-clean life in a way that I don't think other people can claim. Many children become disillusioned with their parents when they grow up. Instead of becoming disillusioned with my dad, I was more disillusioned by the world because it sometimes lacked the integrity, fairness, and dedication that I saw in him. Unfortunately, the world isn't filled with enough Atticus Finch types."

Anne got a crash course in communications when her father sent her door-to-door to spread his message to skeptical voters. Grassroots politicking "definitely gets you over any sort of fear of public speaking," explained the future attorney. "You definitely feel empowered to talk to people about anything. You do learn a lot of debating skills. Thankfully, we were well prepared. On the long drives between campaign stops,

Dad educated all of us on the different policies, campaign issues, and the backgrounds of every county and city in Oklahoma. He could have been a professor in another life, and Oklahoma was one of his favorite subjects."[9]

Another member of Price's unofficial campaign staff was his nephew and media advisor, Steve Foerster. As a media professional with Griffin Communications in Oklahoma City, Foerster was obliged to tread carefully. "I had to separate myself at some level because I am in the media," explained Foerster. "But I did sit in on some of his planning of the production of the commercials, and I talked to him about buying media. That's a very important part of a political campaign—buying airtime. TV can make or break you!"[10]

To augment his campaign staff, Price turned to Tom Cole, a fifth-generation Oklahoman and member of the Chickasaw Nation. Cole came by his interest in politics honestly: his mother, Helen, a niece of the famed Chickasaw storyteller Te Ata, was elected not only as mayor of Moore, Oklahoma, but also to the state legislature, first in the House of Representatives and, later, the Senate. In recognition of her contributions to her tribe and state, Helen was inducted into the Chickasaw Hall of Fame, an honor that her son shared when his own political career went into overdrive.

Equipped with an MA from Yale University, a PhD in British history from the University of Oklahoma, and Thomas Watson and Fulbright fellowships at the University of London, Cole was poised for a career in academia, and he had, in fact, taught history and politics at the University of Oklahoma and Oklahoma Baptist University. But life had other plans, and he decided instead to follow in his mother's footsteps, serving as chair of the Oklahoma Republican Party from 1985 to 1989, state senator from District 45 (the same district that Helen had represented) from 1988 to 1991, and district director for U.S. Representative Mickey Edwards, who served in Congress from 1977 to 1993. Cole enhanced his political clout in 1989 when he teamed up with Sharon (Hargrave) Caldwell and Deby Snodgrass to form

Oklahoma City–based Cole Hargrave Snodgrass & Associates (later rebranded as CHS & Associates), a Republican-oriented consulting firm aimed at providing data and analysis to campaign managers, law firms, and corporate leaders in Oklahoma and, eventually, to clients nationwide.[11]

"Tom Cole did our polling and devised our campaign strategy," recalled Price. "He is not only one of the smartest people I know, he has great judgment and is a wonderful person to deal with. Everybody wanted Tom Cole and his associates to help run their campaigns. I am the one Tom chose. It was really more him choosing me, rather than me choosing him." Relying on daily tracking polls, Cole provided Price with the real-time data he needed to mount a credible campaign. "After two weeks, you had a tremendous sample!" continued Price. "You knew what the trends were. You knew *very precisely* where you were."[12]

"We were, collectively, very impressed with Bill," said Cole about the client who helped to transform his consulting company from a brash start-up into a powerhouse in Republican politics. "I got to know him, and of course knew his record, and was enormously flattered when he asked us to join his general consultants. Not too long after that, we became his pollster. We were setting up our first polling operation. We probably owe Bill, more than anybody else, for actually establishing our reputation during the course of his campaign."[13]

At the time of our interview, in April 2019, Tom Cole was serving his ninth term as Oklahoma's representative from the Fourth Congressional District and was ranking member of the House Rules Committee. Glancing at the photos and memorabilia scattered throughout his office in Norman, I tried to imagine the congressman at the dawn of his political career, conducting polls for a gubernatorial candidate who had never run for political office and, simultaneously, pondering how best to serve his constituents in south Oklahoma City.

"The campaign rocked along, and it was a very difficult year for Republicans."

Pulled back to the present, I made sure my recording device was capturing Cole's crystal-clear memory of Oklahoma's gubernatorial race of 1990.

Cole agreed with Price that Governor Henry Bellmon's tax increases, together with his support for substantial educational outlays in House Bill 1017, undermined his standing as a cost-conscious executive and had alienated the conservative wing of the Republican Party. The party's credibility dropped another notch when President Bush reneged on his pledge, at the 1988 Republican National Convention in New Orleans, not to raise taxes. (Remember "Read my lips: No new taxes"?) When Burns Hargis and Jerry Brown failed to ignite the electorate in the Republican primary, Price and Orza were the only two left standing, and they had only three weeks to gear up for a runoff fight to the finish.

"Come election time, Orza took off like a rocket," continued Cole. "All of a sudden, we found ourselves with a three-week, very different runoff, with a candidate that had both momentum and a thirteen-point lead on us. I think most people consigned Bill Price to the political ash heap of history at that point."

While pundits and reporters were predicting Orza's victory, Cole kept up his nightly tracking. Convinced that television stations' reliance on out-of-state pollsters and infrequent tracking skewed their results, Cole gathered the evidence he needed to show that Price, whose reputation as a no-nonsense prosecutor—appointed by the ever-popular Ronald Reagan—was certainly in his favor, was gaining on his over-confident opponent.

"That's why you never want to rely on television polling," declared Cole, "because they don't know what they're doing! We actually announced on Friday before the Tuesday election that we had caught up with Vince Orza, and that we thought we would pass him over the weekend, and edge him out on Tuesday night. And that's exactly what happened! Basically, we won, 51–49."

Asked to explain Price's upset victory, Cole put it this way: "Bill's record, Bill's personality, Bill's effort—honestly, to not quit when most other candidates would—were really, probably, the reason why we were able to pull it out. A lot of other candidates would have folded in the situation he was in."[14]

Price's elation over his upset win in the Republican primary was short-lived. A glance at the calendar revealed that the general election face-off against Democratic contender David Walters, who had orchestrated his own upset victory against State Senator Wes Watkins and House Speaker Steve Lewis to become his party's nominee, was weeks away.

None doubted that Walters would be a formidable opponent. Raised on a cotton and wheat farm near Canute in western Oklahoma, Walters held a degree in industrial engineering from OU and an MBA from Harvard. Still in his twenties, Walters exhibited a flair for management, first as a provost at the OU Health Sciences Center and, later, as president of the Burks Group, a commercial real estate company with $50 million in assets and 500 employees. Switching from private enterprise to public service, Walters served his community and state in a variety of positions, including cochairmanship of the one-hundred-member Commission on Government Reform under Governor George Nigh. After becoming his party's standard-bearer and then losing the gubernatorial election of 1986 to Henry Bellmon, in one of the narrowest margins in state history, Walters hung out his own shingle as president of the Walters Company, a real estate investment and property management company. But he was far from done with politics. Complementing his business experience with political savvy, Walters prepared for the gubernatorial race in 1990 on a platform of "no new taxes without public approval," a promise to run state government like a business, and support for term limits and educational reforms.[15]

Knowing what he was up against, Price was confounded by another challenge: his bruising campaign in the primary had left him desperately short of cash. Although he had vowed not to use his own resources for the campaign, Price woke up the morning after the primary to learn that unless he bought TV time for the runoff that day,

In addition to Mary and their children, Bill found support for his gubernatorial campaign in his extended family. Shown here are (left to right) Bill's brother-in-law and sister, Dr. Roland and Kelsey Walters (no relation to gubernatorial candidate David Walters); Bill and Mary Price; Bill's mother, Virginia; Bill's former sister-in-law Gudbjorg Chesnut, formerly married to his deceased brother, Bob, and her second husband, Dr. Dan Chesnut; and Bill's sister and brother-in-law, Montine and her second husband, Paul Sprehe. COURTESY BILL PRICE.

he would miss his opportunity. With three weeks left until the runoff, there was no time to raise enough money. After eighteen months of no earning and lots of spending, Price was running on empty, and he saw no alternative to selling a farm in northwest Oklahoma that he had inherited from his father for $450,000 to fund last-minute TV advertising.

"I had to do it," said Price, "or I'd lose."

To do their part, Price's sister and brother-in-law, Kelsey and Dr. Roland Walters (no relation to gubernatorial candidate David Walters), made their stand across the street from Penn Square Shopping Mall in northwest Oklahoma City. Sporting "Walters for Price" T-shirts, which might have confused motorists, the duo waved campaign posters and urged passers-by to vote for their candidate. More direct help came in the form of a $5,000 campaign contribution. Such generosity from his supportive family left Price speechless—until, that is, he gave the check a closer look. "Bill was thrilled until he saw that it was written on a Penn Square Bank check!" recalled Kelsey with a laugh. "However, we made good on it with a valid check shortly thereafter."[16]

Kelsey and Roland's generosity notwithstanding, Price's war chest was far smaller than his opponent's, and he spent frantic weeks following his campaign manager Neva Hill's directives to attend campaign rallies and rubber-chicken dinners and participate in televised debates with Walters, all the while scrambling—and failing! —to keep up with Walters's deluge of TV advertising. As Price pointed out, few people outside the political arena are aware of the behind-the-scenes effort, often spanning a year or more, that goes into a statewide campaign. Fundraising, press interviews, debates, advertising, and energizing staff and volunteers make for a grueling schedule that seeps into public awareness in the last few weeks of a campaign. And, of course, even the most skillfully orchestrated campaign can unravel at a moment's notice when something comes along that is beyond anyone's control. That happened when President Bush and Governor Bellmon arrived at the National Cowboy Hall of Fame and Western Heritage Center in support of Price's candidacy. By then Republicans had had enough of both of them. After reneging on his "no new taxes" pledge, Bush's popularity in Oklahoma had plummeted from 80 to 20 percent. Bellmon had undermined his base by supporting House Bill 1017, allocating more funding for education. As Price explained, "A huge number of people would say in the tracking polls, 'I don't like Bush, and I don't like Bellmon. I am going to vote for a Democrat!'"

Buoyed by piles of money and a torrent of TV advertising, Walters's victory seemed assured. The only part of the state that leaned toward Price was the Panhandle, an area chock-full of Republicans who were served by television stations from Amarillo rather than faraway Oklahoma City and Tulsa, leaving them relatively unaffected by nonstop advertising.[17]

"The general election effort was extremely difficult," recalled Cole. "We had to fight the general election with a divided party, with headwinds in our face, and with both a governor and a sitting Republican president who came out to help us, did a big event for us, and raised us some money when we really needed it. But probably being associated with him, at that point, was more damaging than helpful." Given their clear disadvantages vis à vis David Walters, neither Price nor Cole was surprised when voters in the Panhandle were about the only ones to cast their ballots for the Republican candidate.[18] As Price explained in a succinct postmortem for the gubernatorial campaign of 1990, "Walters's much bigger war chest, plus the political climate turning against the Republicans, were the two huge factors. I may have narrowly lost anyway, but it would have been close! It wouldn't have been a slaughter, which is what it was."[19]

As Cole described the play-by-play trouncing of one of his company's first clients, I could not help but wonder if he had any regrets about supporting Price's candidacy.

"Why did you choose Bill Price?" I asked.

"First of all, he was a conservative, and I was a conservative," began Cole. "Philosophically, I felt we were more closely aligned. Second, he had some people working with him that I really respected." Price's insiders included several of Oklahoma's most prominent opinion leaders: Neva Hill, his campaign manager; Herb Johnston, his longtime political mentor; and Tom Daxon, his former comrade in Teen Age Republicans, a successful auditor and inspector who had illuminated corruption in county spending, and whose 1982 gubernatorial campaign Cole had supported.

"My friends all seemed to be there," continued Cole. "He had a good collection of talent around him."

And then, there was this:

Honestly, I just like Bill Price. Nothing against the others. They are all wonderful people. But Bill and Mary Price are two of the finest people I have ever been associated with. You do think about that in politics. It's partly a matter of winning, but it's partly a matter of, are you going to be associated with somebody you're proud of? Somebody you think, if they can win, will do really great things for the state? And if they lose, you're never going to be embarrassed by them.

Bill is about the straightest arrow I have ever met in this business. Everybody that knew him respected him. Everybody liked his ability. Everybody liked him as a person. Everybody thought of him as somebody absolutely personable and professional, with integrity. He had established that reputation in the U.S. Attorney's office. He had established that he would take on the tough jobs; that he would fight to clean up the mess that was Oklahoma politics. We were a very corrupt state, politically, and Bill Price has been one of the people that helped turn that around, using federal office.[20]

For Cole, Oklahoma legislators' historic failure to confront corruption had once been a matter of embarrassment. Happily, Okscam had marked the beginning of the end of lawmakers' reliance on the feds to investigate and prosecute corruption. "I think we have gone through quite a metamorphosis as a state, where corruption isn't tolerated or accepted in the way that it was," he said. "But it was just part of Oklahoma politics. It just shows what a high degree of tolerance there was for corruption."

Cue United States Attorney Bill Price and Oklahoma Auditor and Inspector Tom Daxon, childhood friends and public servants who, as Cole put it, "were really critical figures in beginning to change that— changing the public, and then changing our reputation across the country. I thought, if we could get a guy like this into the governorship, he would make an enormous difference to us as a state. I still believe that. I always call him, the best governor Oklahoma never had."[21]

Mary agreed with Bill that a depleted war chest, coupled with the Republican Party's unpopularity at the state and national levels, spelled doom for her husband in the general election. But the first signs of trouble dated back to Price's runoff against Vince Orza. As a former newscaster and successful restaurateur, Orza's mastery of television had put Price on the defensive.[22] As Price's nephew and media advisor Steve Foerster put it, his uncle was "a squeaky-clean guy. You know what you're getting. There's no hidden agenda."[23]

That certainly counted for something in personal relationships and in front of a jury. But it was a feeble defense against a well-funded businessman with a winning smile and an eye for the camera. With the Republican primary behind him, no money left for an effective TV campaign, and a general election against a popular and well-funded Democrat right around the corner, Price's shot at the governor's mansion was looking like a lost cause. Orza added insult to injury when he failed to carry through on his promise to support his former opponent against Walters in the general election.

"I feel like God has a plan for everyone," said Mary, now on familiar turf as a deeply religious person whose admiration for her husband was clearly undiminished since their student days in Washington. "It just was not meant to be. On the other hand, Bill got his message out to the entire state. He became a prominent figure. Everyone knew and respected him, even though he didn't win." Equipped with notoriety as both a federal prosecutor and gubernatorial candidate, Price had the bona fides he needed to make things happen in both the public and private arenas.

"Bill is very idealistic and principled," continued Mary. "He just really wants to improve people's lives."

"Did he ever regret running for governor?" I asked, knowing that the campaign and lopsided defeat must have taken a toll on the entire family.

"No, not at all!" exclaimed Mary. "Bill was honored to be the Republican nominee for governor. Campaigning was great. We got to know lots of wonderful people and be part of something bigger than ourselves. It was the time of our lives."

James was quick to chime in: "Obviously, he wasn't happy about losing. But there was no bitterness."

But, of course, there was a letdown. For the candidate, there was the disappointment of not being able to accomplish his goals on behalf of his fellow Oklahomans. For the rest of the family, there was the need to figure out what came next, which included paying off substantial debts.

"It was a come down," said Mary, seeming to exhibit a flair for understatement. "We were both kind of blue." That sense of loss was not lost on Eileen, who learned at an early age the sadness that comes from unfulfilled ambitions. But she was also heartened to know that she and the rest of her family were not alone in their disappointment. "So many people were calling, and were saying, 'It should have been you. We wanted you to win!'"

While her husband was negotiating a return to private practice and trying to remember how to drum up clients, Mary dusted off her writing and marketing skills and went to work part-time at a television station and, later, a travel agency. To complement her jobs and give free rein to her creativity, she earned a master's degree in Fine Arts at the University of Central Oklahoma and taught aspiring creative writers at Rose State College.[24]

The last word on Bill Price's campaign for governor and the letdown when he lost goes to his nephew and media advisor, Steve Foerster: "He's just got a big heart. I have never seen him really angry. I have seen him frustrated, but never mad. I've never seen him lose his cool."[25]

▶ ▶ ▶ ▶

Less than a year had passed since Bob Anthony was elected to the Oklahoma Corporation Commission, in November 1988, and already he was wondering what he had gotten himself into. His immediate concern dated back to 1986, when the newly enacted Tax Reform Act had revealed that Southwestern Bell Telephone Company had overcharged customers to the tune of $52 million. When the case arrived at the Corporation Commission, commissioners Jim Townsend and Bob Hopkins ordered Bell to use about $30 million of its so-called surplus cash—that is, overcollections resulting from a drop in tax rates—to upgrade its phone network. As the lone dissenter, Anthony cited "serious irregularities" in the rates Bell was charging and insisted that the company refund a percentage of its overcharges to customers in Oklahoma.[26]

As the scion of a wealthy family with a pedigree that included Harvard, Yale, the Wharton School of Business, and the London School of Economics, Anthony was ill-prepared for the likes of Bill (aka Tater) Anderson, an attorney and former judge who had served as general counsel for the Oklahoma Corporation Commission in the 1960s. Forced to step down amidst charges that he was moonlighting for the utility companies he was supposed to regulate, Anderson compensated for his sullied reputation with a rise in popularity among corporate executives. Over drinks and copious plates of cheese and crackers, Anderson parlayed his insider status into brokering deals between businessmen, lawmakers, and lobbyists. Always generous with employees at the Corporation Commission, Oklahoma City's most notorious power broker hosted open houses during football games and, when the Christmas season rolled around, handed out gifts with abandon. As capitol gadfly and *Oklahoma Observer* editor Frosty Troy put it, "He's smart, clever and never underestimated the power of money. If you wanted anything done of large magnitude, you went to Bill Anderson or you didn't get it."[27]

Of course, Oklahoma City was not the only state capital with its version of Bill Anderson. What was unusual about him was that he fell into the crosshairs of an FBI probe, and his taped conversations with the state's rich and powerful opened a window into how business was conducted in the oil and gas patch. As Bob Anthony settled into his new job at the Corporation Commission, two of Anderson's high-profile clients were raising suspicions of undue influence: Southwestern

Bell, whose excessive rates were about to explode into a full-blown scandal; and Arkansas Louisiana Gas Company (ARKLA), a natural gas company headed by Thomas F. "Mack" McLarty, who would later become President Bill Clinton's chief of staff. Although no evidence surfaced that McLarty had done anything wrong, his association with Bill Anderson became a topic of some concern in the Clinton White House.[28]

At his first get-together with Anthony, in the fall of 1988, Anderson brushed over the cash-stuffed envelope he was proffering as a "campaign contribution" and insisted that all he wanted was access to the Corporation Commission, to have his phone calls returned, and an audience when he needed one— in influence-peddling vernacular, a "fair shake" on commissioners' votes that could mean millions of dollars for his clients.[29]

"When you work hand-in-hand on political corruption cases with the FBI, you know what's happening," explained Price. "You just can't prove it. And we knew Bill Anderson was getting enormous amounts of money from all the utility companies. He got retainers, like $5,000 or $10,000 a month. Not hourly fees, but monthly retainer fees. And then he was much freer to bribe the commissioners."[30]

Frustrated by his failure to build a tax case against Anderson, Price left the U.S. Attorney's Office to run for governor with full confidence that his successor, the FBI, and Bob Anthony would figure out what to do. Perhaps, like Wagoner County Commissioner Rufus Young of Okscam fame, Anthony could be tutored in the finer points of entrapment and persuaded to help the FBI get to the bottom of schemes that, once again, were undermining confidence in Oklahoma governance.

"You need to talk to the FBI!" declared Price as soon as Anthony told him about his meeting with Bill Anderson. "So I had him into the FBI that week."[31]

"I don't think Bill particularly did a sales job," said Anthony. "But I talked to him because I knew him and trusted him. I still trust him, and

I still think his reputation is that he's a no-nonsense person who is on the side of justice and honest government."

Whether or not Price did a sales job in enticing Anthony to cooperate in an FBI investigation, his advice certainly resonated with the newly elected commissioner, who took his oath of office seriously. As Anthony explained to me in an eerily silent hearing room that did not appear much different from a court of law, that oath was enshrined in the Oklahoma Constitution, and it called on elected officials to correct abuses, fight discrimination, and report extortion. I was caught off guard when a familiar name drifted into our conversation: G. T. Blankenship, whose lessons in public service dated back to his days as a Sunday School teacher, when Anthony was in grade school, and had continued when he had exposed the Oklahoma supreme court scandal in 1965. As Anthony reflected on Blankenship's courage in maintaining integrity and exposing corruption, I wondered if the former legislator and state attorney general ever realized the extent of his influence on young people, including his former campaign bus driver, Bill Price, who would one day inherit the mantle of leadership.

Anthony yanked me back to the subject at hand with an account of his service as an FBI informant, which began about the time of his election to the Oklahoma Corporation Commission: "I helped the FBI record—it's a challenge to even say it!—over *two hundred* recordings, some of which had thousands of dollars in hundred-dollar bills counted out in my office with the FBI's tape recorder going. I counted, photographed, and turned over the cash to them. At least one time, there were two agents with loaded guns in the car outside. And not only did they have a tape recorder; they had a transmitter, so they could listen in."

Not all of Anthony's taped conversations were with Bill Anderson. Others included lawyers, lobbyists, and executives, and although the Corporation Commission was responsible for regulating a wide range of economic sectors, "the heart of the corruption was on the public utilities side." According to Southwestern Bell's Paul Lane, his company had first gotten wind of the investigation in March 1991 and had been cooperating with both the FBI and the U.S. Attorney's office ever since.[32] Less forthcoming was Bob Hopkins, vice chairman of the Corporation Commission and a three-decade veteran of state government, who had represented Tulsa County in the House of Representatives and the Senate. His announcement that he would resign in early August 1991 coincided with Bob Anthony's undercover work for the FBI. Asked about funding for his recent campaign, Hopkins claimed that he had not filed a report with the State Ethics Commission in 1990 because he had received no contributions.

"I didn't take anything," said Hopkins. "I turned down some (contributions). I know the rules, and I play by the rules."[33]

Hopkins's protestations of innocence fell flat in the late spring of 1991 when subpoenas came raining down. Forced to resign from the Corporation Commission, Hopkins was replaced by Cody Graves, Governor Walters's pick to fill the remaining sixteen months of his six-year term. Graves had worked for Southwestern Bell before his appointment, and when it came time for the Corporation Commission to hear its case, he exercised his ethical responsibility to recuse himself. That left Anthony and his fellow commissioner, J. C. Watts, to decide whether to make Bell's rates subject to partial refund and, if so, under what terms. As the case wound its way through the system, Anthony and Watts went on record to seek a rate cut of more than $120 million and a refund of about $80 million to Oklahoma customers.[34]

As usual, *Oklahoma Observer* editor Frosty Troy was itching to comment on the toxic partisanship in state governance that, apparently, had infiltrated the Corporation Commission. "What would it take to turn Oklahoma into a true two-party state?" asked Troy rhetorically. "Elect more Bob Anthonys. What that single Republican has done since he was elected to the Corporation Commission is a major miracle in Oklahoma politics." Troy went on to castigate the Corporation Commission, "a bastion of Democratic Party power and patronage," as a wholly owned subsidiary of public utilities and the oil industry that it was expected to regulate. As a conservative businessman, Anthony was upending decades of influence peddling by exposing bribery and extortion. "If Oklahoma Republicans ever wake up and smell the opportunities," concluded Troy, "Bob Anthony would make an excellent GOP nominee for governor."[35]

On August 5, 1992, the Corporation Commission ordered Southwestern Bell's Oklahoma division to cut its rates by a record $92.8 million and refund $148.4 million to customers.[36] Later that month, the FBI confirmed that it was investigating the Corporation Commission for possible wrongdoing and had requested some of its "internal administrative documents." As an unnamed source quipped, "This is the tip of a big iceberg."

Now serving as chairman, Anthony would neither confirm nor deny that an FBI probe was underway. But he did acknowledge that the FBI was the only agency with the ability to clean up corruption in state government. He declined to elaborate.[37] Meanwhile, rumors swirled that Hopkins's resignation was a direct result of the FBI investigation, complete with wiretaps, that had been underway since 1990 and that Jim Townsend's relationship with utility companies had been less than transparent. The plot thickened when word hit the streets that several of the commission's top employees had resigned and gone to work for utility companies and energy firms.[38]

Then came the bombshell. On October 2, Anthony went public with the disclosure that he had been working undercover for the FBI ever since taking office in January 1989. "Instead of my mother hearing that her son had been taking thousands of dollars in bribes, or however that thing might break, I chose to make a *disclosure*," quipped Anthony about his decision to get ahead of the story.[39] In press announcements that grabbed headlines statewide, Anthony described improper communications in a case involving Oklahoma Natural Gas Company and its subsidiary, ONEOK, as well as envelopes stuffed with cash that Southwestern Bell had delivered to him to influence his and other commissioners' votes. Although he stopped short of using the word "bribe," he left no doubt about the impropriety of those transactions, and he insisted that he had turned over every dollar to the FBI.

Even as Southwestern Bell officials scrambled to deny misconduct, the *Tulsa World* was reporting that the FBI had placed wiretaps on phones belonging to Bill Anderson, "one of the Corporation Commission's most influential lawyers," whose association with Southwestern Bell dated back many years. Reportedly in poor health, Anderson declined to comment on the advice of counsel. In keeping with federal law, Corporation Commission employees and attorneys were notified that their phone conversations with Anderson's office had been intercepted.[40] Even though most of the activities Anthony described occurred before his colleagues, Cody Graves and J. C. Watts, took office, he refused to let them off the hook.

"I'm not able to give anybody a clean bill of health," said Anthony to reporters. "Why don't you go ask them?"[41]

Predictably, denials and accusations were quick to follow. According to Southwestern Bell spokesman Paul Lane, Anthony's pronouncement was politically motivated, to gain publicity for his District 6 congressional campaign against U.S. Representative Glenn English, a Democrat from Cordell. Former commissioners who weighed in included Jim Townsend, who denied improper conduct and agreed that Anthony was motivated by politics; Norma Eagleton, who was unaware of an investigation and had not been contacted by authorities; and Bob Hopkins, who could not be reached for comment. Sitting Commissioner Cody Graves questioned the timing of Anthony's announcement. "To me, it's pure politics," he said. "I hope he hasn't compromised a federal investigation by doing that." As tensions mounted, Anthony—now recognized as Oklahoma's version of Deep Throat from the bad old days of Watergate—remained resolute and insisted that he would continue to assist law enforcement in its ongoing investigation.[42]

"All heck broke loose," mused Anthony about his stunning revelations and the public's reaction to them. "People who were crooks, and people who thought that *I* was a crook because I was taking their money . . ."

Clearly pained to recount the allegations against him, Anthony rarely took time to breathe as he handed me one document after another from his collection of newspaper articles, correspondence, and even federal grand-jury indictments that constitute an impressive archive from yet another noxious chapter in Oklahoma history. "I was deposed for *two solid days*," declared Anthony as he stacked documents on the table. "There were sixteen attorneys sitting around a big table at one of the big law firms in Oklahoma, and they were all kind of horrified!"

As the pile of paper in front of me grew ever higher, I listened spellbound to Anthony's tale of corruption in the agency that he had served for three decades: "There were lots and lots of people that were being subpoenaed, and some of them would tell their friends at a party, and some of the people told the newspaper. It was just bigger and bigger and bigger! There were members of the legislature involved! There were members of the White House staff involved! This was getting to be a major thing!"

On June 17, 1993, a federal grand jury filed an indictment in the Western District of Oklahoma against Bill Anderson, Bob Hopkins, and a third alleged conspirator, Jewel B. Callaham, a Broken Bow businessman who was chairman of Pine Telephone, which served phone exchanges in southeastern Oklahoma, and was a longtime Democratic operative. According to the indictment, Hopkins "knowingly and corruptly agreed to accept something of value, intending to be influenced or rewarded in connection with the business of the Oklahoma Corporation Commission"—that is, he was being bribed to cast his vote in favor of Southwestern Bell's plan to reinvest approximately $30 million rather than reimburse its Oklahoma customers. The indictment, signed by U.S. Attorney John E. Green and his assistant, H. Lee Schmidt, went on to cite Bill Anderson as the one who had been doing the bribing.[43] As indictments wound their way to court, Hopkins continued to maintain his innocence.[44]

The Oklahoma Corporation Commission scandal was one of the largest corporate fraud cases in American history. To publicize and combat such blatant malfeasance, aggrieved citizens formed Oklahomans Against Bribery and set up a website, www. oklahomansagainstbribery.org/index.html.

With accusations and depositions and indictments raining down on the Corporation Commission and the companies that it regulated, Anthony found vindication for his crusade from two sources in the FBI: Agent Buck Revell, now based in Washington, D.C., who met him at the J. Edgar Hoover Building, at the height of the scandal, to offer his support and encouragement (and to advise Anthony to invest in a sawed-off shotgun); and Director Louis Freeh, who on October 5, 1995 presented Anthony with the agency's highest civilian honor—the Louis E. Peters Service Award, given to a citizen "who at great personal sacrifice, has unselfishly served his community and the nation."[45]

"Did you ever feel threatened?" I asked. I could not help but think of Price's harrowing story of coming home from an Okscam trial and discovering that someone had dumped ball bearings in his carburetor.

"The short answer is, yes," said Anthony. "But I have always refused to discuss it."[46]

I decided that would have to do and turned back to Price for his perspective on corruption at the Corporation Commission. Having delivered Bob Anthony into the FBI's embrace, Price took a keen interest in his friend's campaign to clean up his agency. "Anthony has been on this crusade, and justifiably so," he said. "This was at rate payers' expense. Rate payers, and particularly seniors and poor people who struggled to pay their utility bills, were the ones who were hurt." Anthony's challenge in standing up to powerful corporate interests was compounded by insufficient and even misleading coverage in the local press, often at Anthony's expense.

Always the thoughtful lawyer, Price refused to make accusations of misconduct without compelling evidence, and he declined to speculate on the media's reticence. "The full nature of the conspiracy was publicized in the Chicago papers, and it was publicized in *Newsweek*, but there was very little in-depth publicity in Oklahoma. It was mostly national publicity."[47]

The final word on the Corporation Commission scandal goes to Bob Anthony who, as of this writing in 2021, has remained as committed as ever to even-handed regulation of Oklahoma business and commerce.

"We did get a big refund out of Southwestern Bell, largely because I kept working on it," explained Anthony with a hint of well-deserved swagger. Found guilty of bribery, Commissioner Bob Hopkins appealed his conviction to the Tenth Circuit Court in Denver, where even his über-experienced attorney, Gene Stipe, was unable to secure a reversal. Other indictments and trials and convictions too numerous to mention put the Oklahoma Corporation Commission and the businesses under its purview on notice that corruption at the expense of taxpayers and ratepayers would no longer be tolerated. Anthony credited Bill Price for initiating what grew into one of the largest public utility scandals in American history: "None of that would have happened if Bill Price hadn't said, 'Bob, we need to do something about this!' When it comes to white-collar crime and corruption, they need the assistance of somebody in the public, or somebody inside, who is willing to be committed to justice."

Anthony's ongoing crusade against corruption continued with appearances on PBS's *Frontline* and, as the internet came roaring into history, creation of a website with the no-nonsense heading "Oklahomans against Bribery."[48] Back on more familiar turf, Anthony shared his experiences at Rotary 29 in downtown Oklahoma City. "And Bill was there. He was sitting there, and I made reference to him several times. I teased him a little bit. I said, yeah, let's see, I think Bill got me to do this, told me how important it was, and then he left to run for governor! And I was still sitting there, trying to work it all out!"[49]

▶ ▶ ▶ ▶

David Walters—young, articulate, and supremely intelligent—branded himself as a "New Democrat" with a laser-like focus on restoring faith in government and promoting economic development. The month after his inauguration, he launched his administration with Executive Order 91-3, a code of ethics calling on state employees to demonstrate "the highest standards of personal integrity, truthfulness, honesty and fortitude" as the prerequisite to inspiring people's confidence in their representatives and trust in their institutions.[50] Building on the broad-based mandate that voters had handed him in his lopsided victory over Bill Price, he poured his considerable energy into capital improvements on the state's higher education campuses and launched initiatives ranging from rural development and job creation to reforms in welfare programs and workers' compensation. A widely respected technology magazine recognized him as the nation's leading governor in enlisting high tech to improve government services.[51]

Yet from the day he assumed office in January 1991, Walters's promises and accomplishments were overshadowed by charges of campaign finance violations from the 1990 campaign, destined to dog him through his first and only term as governor. In mid-April 1991, headlines blared with the news that Walters had fired his director of state tourism, J. B. Bennett, a former state legislator and the governor's chief campaign fundraiser. Bennett countered with accusations that Walters had promised government jobs in exchange for campaign contributions exceeding the legal limit. Walters was indicted for accepting contributions from rank-and-file workers who got their money from their employers, special interests, and even their families. Funneling contributions through straw donors has always been a clear violation of campaign finance law, especially when it happens on a large scale.

A federal probe was launched, and a multicounty grand jury was summoned to consider an indictment against him. About the same time that former Corporation Commissioner Bob Hopkins was called to account, Walters received his subpoena and was ordered to surrender up to three thousand financial documents. His campaign treasurer, Sam Cole, seemed relieved at the opportunity to set the record straight. "The governor has always wanted everything brought out front, laid it out front," said Cole.[52]

Deeply in debt from his failed campaign and consumed with setting up a private law practice, Bill Price watched from the sidelines as his former opponent faced off against his accusers. Price was wounded to the core when the new governor took time from his increasingly complicated agenda to divert funding from the OAAD into a lackluster PR campaign admonishing youth not to drink or get pregnant. To Price, such advice was bound to fall on deaf ears, as there was no trace of the structure and scientific backing that made the OAAD a model for drug and alcohol abstinence programs nationwide. "It was extremely disappointing," said Price with more than a hint of sadness. "For children, the OAAD was a shining light that could change their future."[53]

In spite of the turmoil that marred his tenure, Walters remained optimistic that history would look favorably on his successes, especially increased spending on education and reduced waste in state agencies. Some called Walters a kamikaze pilot for his willingness to court trouble in the interest of sound fiscal policies. "It's amazing that he was able to accomplish what he accomplished," said Mike Turpen, chairman of the state Democratic Party and one of the governor's staunchest supporters. "Even his most severe critics, I think, give him now some credit for accomplishing amazing things in the face of having to play against all odds." Among those severe critics were pundits at the *Daily Oklahoman* who branded him as a poster child for political corruption. Legislators looked askance at his Harvard pedigree as proof that he had abandoned his Oklahoma roots and embraced East Coast liberalism.[54] Yet even after the tragic death of his and Rhonda's son, Shaun, from an overdose of prescription medications, Walters soldiered on through four years of bitter acrimony, knowing better than most the potential cost of high office. Asked if he would run for governor if he had it to do over again, Walters replied, "No, I would not. I lost my son because I ran for public office."[55]

A year and a half into his tenure, Governor Walters bristled at allegations that the Oklahoma National Guard Association had made improper contributions to his 1990 campaign. Other allegations followed, and Walters denied them all. "If there is a shred of evidence of a single fact that I have done something wrong, well then by all means let's tell me and let's tell the public," railed Walters. "If there are not any facts that suggest I've done something wrong, then for goodness sakes let's have the human decency to stop this unending, never-ending pain that's being caused for me and my family."[56] Although his pick to serve the balance of Robert Henry's term as attorney general, Susan Loving, and Oklahoma County District Attorney Robert Macy, both Democrats, were spearheading the ever-widening investigation, Walters credited the *Daily Oklahoman* for driving the probe with its incendiary reporting. Amid rumors that he had been indicted by the grand jury, TV crews set up a vigil outside the governor's mansion, as though Princess Di had taken refuge inside. As the beleaguered governor put it, in a December 1994 retrospective in the *Oklahoma Gazette*, "The Walters Watch was in full swing."[57]

Election Day 1994 was fast approaching. Walters signaled that he had had enough and asked prosecutors what they wanted to end the process. His options had narrowed considerably after a multicounty grand jury indicted him on eight felony counts. He ultimately agreed to plead guilty to a misdemeanor offense and pay a fine. In return, his record would be expunged after twelve months. But no sooner did he plead guilty to the misdemeanor than he issued a statement that he had done nothing wrong. Determined to have the last word, Attorney General Loving suggested that Walters's denial of wrongdoing after pleading guilty to a misdemeanor was bound to influence public opinion and jeopardize whatever political ambitions he might still have.

Denied the prospect of a second term as governor, Walters bowed out of politics and, armed with his degree in industrial engineering and a wealth of experience in the school of hard knocks, entered the independent power industry on an international scale.[58]

Asked if he might consider another go in the political arena, Walters smiled.

"I hope if I ever have another temptation," he said, "that somebody stops me before I sin again."[59]

CHAPTER FIFTEEN : *Private Practice, Public Citizen*

The year after his failed bid for the governor's office, Price went to work as a partner for Hastie and Kirschner, P.C., a private firm in Oklahoma City specializing in civil and criminal litigation. He later opted to limit his exposure to potential lawsuits by becoming of counsel, a term for an attorney who has a relationship with a law firm but chooses not to become an associate or partner. Restricting his upward mobility freed him from involvement in running the law firm. That turned out to be a wise choice when the firm became embroiled in a lawsuit.[1]

Any relief that Price felt in resigning from a stressful job in the U.S. Attorney's office and concluding a bruising political campaign was tempered by an emotional letdown. "He felt like he was on the side of the good guys," explained Mary, who was more forthcoming than her husband about his return to private practice. "He loved working with the FBI. He loved getting rid of crime and corruption. He's a crusader!" James agreed with his mother, and although he sensed that his father enjoyed some of his private practice cases, he knew that a major adjustment was in the works. Then, too, there were campaign debts that had to be paid, including one from his old friend from Teen Age Republicans Jack Edens. "He wouldn't want to show you his worry," said James. "We didn't really sense that. And he's such a hard worker that it wasn't an issue." Still, reimbursing people who had contributed to his campaign, drumming up clients, recording billable hours, and chasing legal fees to support his family were a far cry from rooting out corruption and running for the state's highest office.

"I think at first it was hard to make that transition," said Eileen. "When you're fighting corruption, and drugs, all these things . . ."

Eileen searched her youthful memory to describe her dad's career switch.

"My dad does have an ability to find the justice in things, the innocence in things," she said finally. "So he wasn't like your typical defense lawyer. I do remember that he would talk about a case, and he would say, 'This is unfair.' He wasn't just going through the motions."

No doubt true. Nevertheless, everyone knew that he was struggling. Practically in tandem, Mary and James cut to the chase: "It wasn't where his heart was."[2]

So what was a former anticorruption crusader and gubernatorial candidate supposed to do?

What else? Run for Congress.

▶ ▶ ▶ ▶

To signal his ongoing interest in politics, Price accepted chairmanship of the Republican Party's Fifth District, a swath of central Oklahoma that included most of the Oklahoma City metro area and Pottawatomie and Seminole Counties. Early on, Price played coy with supporters who wanted him to run for Congress. "I really wasn't even thinking about running," said Price. But then opportunity came knocking in the person of Mickey Edwards, a Republican who had represented the Fifth District in Congress since 1977, and who was now embroiled in yet another imbroglio in the nation's capital, known to history as the House banking scandal.[3]

Prior to his election to Congress, Edwards worked as a reporter and editor for the *Oklahoma City Times*, public relations director for Beals Advertising Agency, and editor of *Private Practice* magazine. In 1973, he put his law degree to work by launching a private practice in Oklahoma City and teaching law and journalism at his alma mater, Oklahoma City University. In his spare time, he served his party as a special legislative consultant for the Republican Steering Committee in Washington, D.C. His election to the U.S. House of Representatives marked the beginning of a twelve-year career that culminated in his appointment as

House Republican Policy Committee chair, the House's fourth-ranking Republican leadership position.[4]

And then came revelations in the House Committee on Ethics that several congressmen, including Edwards, had overdrawn their House bank accounts. Dubbed rather inelegantly as Rubbergate (a pastiche of rubber check and, of course, Watergate), what was basically a check-kiting scandal snared more than 450 representatives, 22 of whom were singled out as exceptionally inept in their handling of personal finances. With 386 bad checks totaling $54,000 and overdue for thirteen months, Edwards earned the dubious distinction of landing in the bottom half of the worst offenders list.[5]

"This was a big deal!" exclaimed Price, still dismayed that his friend and fellow Republican could be so careless with his checkbook. "Mickey was great on policy, but he was lousy on personal finance. He was always running hand-to-mouth financially. The Republicans, as well as the Democrats, were just outraged!"[6]

Tainted by scandal, Edwards could no longer count on a win in the 1992 primary against an increasingly less coy Bill Price and Ernest Istook, a former legal counsel for Governor David Boren and city councilman from Warr Acres, a western suburb of Oklahoma City. Istook had switched his political affiliation from Democrat to Republican in 1980 because, as he noted, his views were more in line with the GOP's "common sense and conservative principles." Like Edwards, Istook had earned his juris doctor from the Oklahoma City University School of Law. Based on a platform of eliminating waste and patronage in government, reforming welfare, and passing right-to-work legislation, Istook was elected to the Oklahoma House of Representatives in 1986, a position that he retained until he tossed his hat in the ring to run for Congress.[7]

As Price mentioned, regardless of their party affiliation, voters were indeed outraged by Edwards's complicity in Rubbergate, and they were looking for a fresh face and new ideas. "There were a whole bunch of people urging me to run," recalled Price. "They were citing the polling on Edwards, showing he was at 20 percent. He was going to get killed by any Republican in the primary. And if he survived the primary, he was going to get killed by a Democrat. It was just horrendous! This banking scandal had just torn him apart! I finally, very reluctantly, decided that he wasn't going to survive, so I decided to get in."[8]

One of the people enthused by Price's candidacy was Chip Carter. A native of Chickasha, Carter was working at the Republican National Committee when Price announced his candidacy. Predicting that Edwards's complicity in Rubbergate spelled doom for his reelection, Carter saw Price as a winner and, at the same time, a surefire ticket to reconnect with his Oklahoma roots. "This is a slam dunk!" exclaimed Carter. "I was able to contact his campaign, and they hired me." Carter returned to Oklahoma in the late spring of 1992 to begin a crash course in grassroots politicking.

Still in his early twenties, Carter joined Price in his travels throughout the state to organize county and precinct chairmen. Much as G. T. Blankenship had mentored him during their 1965 campaign odyssey, Price passed their windshield time by giving his young staffer an insider's view of policy and politics. "He would be making calls to donors throughout the drive," recalled Carter. "And then, on the way home, he would remember questions and comments from earlier in the day, and he could speak at length about what the policy ramifications would be if he were elected to Congress. I was just really struck, as a young professional, at his ability to develop policy, and the depth of knowledge that he had about public policy, and the nuances."

As Election Day approached, Carter gained ever more appreciation for Price's aptitude for public office and acumen in policy development. "He had a great mind for it, and an appreciation for it," continued Carter. "He was a good conservative, and was not timid in sharing his principled beliefs, but was also able to take that and use that as the proper basis for developing policy. I say that because there are a lot of people that have good opinions, but you drill down, and how do those opinions or beliefs affect policy A, or B, or C, or D. They kind of short circuit. But Bill was able to articulate that."[9]

Price's and Carter's prediction was borne out when Edwards garnered a paltry 26 percent of the vote in the August primary election. Deeming it "a brand-new race," Price figured that he and Istook were starting at dead even in the runoff election slated for September 15, 1992. He further expected his track record in the U.S. Attorney's office, recent gubernatorial campaign against David Walters, and experience in the energy industry, as a principal in Price Oil and Gas, to give him a leg up in a campaign against the lesser-known Ernest Istook. As Price explained in a *Daily Oklahoman* editorial just five days before the election, he was "a known commodity. There's not going to be surprises. Every conceivable attack that could ever be done has already been done." Touting the Republican Party as "the party of real change," Price campaigned on a platform of lower taxes, reduced spending, and business deregulation—all staples of Republican ideology, and all consistent with the values that he had promoted since his days in Teen Age Republicans.

Arguably, no issue loomed larger in the late 1980s and early 1990s than the nation's ballooning deficit. At the urging of President Ronald Reagan, the Private Sector Survey on Cost Control (PSSCC), commonly referred to as the Grace Commission for its chairman, J. Peter Grace, set about uncovering waste and inefficiency in federal spending. Grace admonished commission members to work like bloodhounds and leave no stone unturned in their crusade to root out needless spending. In his report to Congress in January 1984, Grace suggested ways to save $424 billion in three years and $1.9 trillion per year by 2000. Although Congress ignored recommendations that intruded on policy, some were considered, and a few were actually implemented.[10]

According to Price, voters ignored the cost-cutting imperative at their peril. "The deficit is one of the largest issues," declared Price. "If we don't cut spending . . . and really take the Grace Commission and dust it off and go after everything, we are in deep trouble, with a $4 trillion deficit. We're going to mortgage our country and mortgage our future."[11]

Against the urging of his staffers, Price was determined to run an ethical campaign, and he refused to court the Baptist vote by developing ads, no matter how subtle, that drew attention to Istook's Mormon faith. "I didn't want to do that," said Price matter-of-factly. "I would rather lose than use the man's religion against him." In addition to refusing to play dirty, Price's staff, with the notable exception of Chip Carter, never measured up to Tom Cole and his associates, who had managed his gubernatorial campaign. Now running campaigns for the Republican National Committee, Cole was unavailable to manage Price's run for Congress. "They were really good people," said Price with his usual bent toward fair-mindedness, "but I don't think they ran as good a campaign."

In his postgame analysis of the three-way primary and subsequent runoff election, Price singled out a key dynamic: Edwards branded Istook as a nonentity and focused like a laser on knocking Price out of the race. Price tried unsuccessfully to convince Edwards that his attack strategy was doomed to fail. In spite of ads contrasting Price's integrity with Edwards's complicity in Rubbergate (a favorite topic among speakers at the Republican National Convention!), polls showed that the former prosecutor's support was dropping, but not as steeply as his opponent's support. It seemed clear that Edwards would end up in third place, which is exactly what happened. With a scant three weeks before the runoff election, Istook remained above the fray and was in a perfect position to absorb Edwards's dwindling support. As Price explained, "Mickey Edwards viewed me as the only opponent. He did not view Istook as significant at all. His whole ad campaign was, *attack Bill Price*. In a three-person primary, when you have one person, Mickey Edwards, spending all his money attacking Bill Price, it always helps the third candidate. It's real hard to get Mickey Edwards' supporters in a three-week period of time, when they have just heard their candidate attacking him for three weeks."

Last-minute scrambling failed to save Price from defeat in the September runoff, leaving Istook to defeat Democrat Laurie Williams, an Oklahoma City attorney, in the general election. Istook's constituents returned him to five succeeding congresses. He did not stand for reelection when his term ended in 2007.

Deeply disappointed by his candidate's loss, Chip Carter offered three explanations. First, Ernest Istook's staff designed yard signs and a logo to resemble those used by U.S. Senator Don Nickles, arguably the most popular Republican in Oklahoma. "It was just smart—I tip my hat! —it was just a smart design," declared Carter about a wily campaign trick. Second, Price's opponents succeeded in branding him as mean and vindictive, a reflection of perceptions dating back to Okscam. "He doesn't have a mean bone in his body," insisted Carter. "But, in the county commissioner scandal, you heard people say, 'Commissioner Jones in my county is a good man. He took my momma to church every Sunday.' Well, Commissioner Jones was also getting kickbacks and committing crimes on a regular basis. 'Well, he took my momma to church.'" Finally, Price's campaign ads were probably too critical of Mickey Edwards. "They were a bit of a hit piece, at least in my memory, on Mickey Edwards," concluded Carter.

As the youngest member of Price's campaign staff, Carter was reluctant to speak up. I detected a whiff of regret as Carter described his reticence: "A lot of smart people, more mature than me, were making those decisions. I'm not to say that they were wrong, and I was right. But, at least in my twenty-two-year-old mind, I always thought, 'I don't think this was the right strategy.'"[12]

Of course, Price deserved the last word on his two failed bids for public office.

"You had two real high-profile races, back-to-back, for governor and Congress," I said as Price finished describing the second of his unsuccessful bids for high office. "Other than leaving you financially depleted, how did you feel about it?"

It came as no surprise to hear Price's upbeat postscript to what had surely been a deflating experience, coming on the heels of his loss to David Walters in the gubernatorial campaign: "I *really* enjoyed discussing the issues; I enjoyed meeting the tens of thousands of people throughout the state. The experience is invaluable. On the whole, it was wonderful, especially after the congressional race. But I was *really* in a bind. I'd have to get my law practice going. It was a rough time, economically. People think that I come from this family of unlimited resources. But that wasn't true."[13]

▸ ▸ ▸ ▸

With trouble brewing at Hastie and Kirschner, P.C., Price went on the hunt for a law firm that fit his three main criteria. First, it had to need a specialist in white-collar crime. Second, it needed to be big enough to generate cases that could return him to financial stability. Finally, it had to have a successful track record with of counsel attorneys. He found what he was looking for in Phillips McFall, P.C.— later, Phillips Murrah, P.C.—where he gave his interviewers an offer they could not refuse: if he failed to generate cases, the firm would not lose money; but if he performed well, the firm would benefit. Price's ploy worked, and he went to work for Phillips McFall, P.C. The firm rebranded as Phillips Murrah, P.C., when Judge Alfred P. Murrah's son, Paul, was added to the firm's name.

In addition to his civil litigation, Price represented clients whose alleged white-collar crimes remained under investigation. In contrast to most defense attorneys, Price hired former FBI agents with whom he had worked as a prosecutor before indictments were handed down. Those former agents often found evidence that his clients were innocent or their guilt would be difficult to prove. Equipped with FBI evidence, Price would try to persuade prosecutors not to hand down indictments. Price's technique precluded courtroom drama and diminished his visibility at trial, but if successful, it accrued to the benefit of his clients. All he lost was the element of surprise, which is arguably an overrated feature of courtroom procedure. Besides, even clients who had been exonerated left the courtroom with their reputations in tatters and their bank accounts depleted. Far better to leverage FBI evidence on his clients' behalf before they could be indicted than subject them to the trauma and long-term consequences of a trial.

To illustrate the effectiveness of his technique, Price told the story of an FBI agent who had heard two criminals discussing (on a clandestine wire, no less!) their preferences for a defense attorney.

"If I was guilty, I'd hire Gene Stipe," said one.

"And if you were innocent?" asked the other.

"Why, then I'd hire Bill Price!"[14]

Among Price's most significant cases at Phillips Murrah was not a white-collar crime case, but a congressional redistricting case pitting his client, Governor Frank Keating, against Democrats in the state legislature. Of paramount importance in drawing boundaries for congressional districts was what Price referred to as "communities of interest"—that is, regions whose residents were united by similar socioeconomic interests. Price aided his colleague and lead counsel, Fred Leibrock, in arguing that Keating's plan was superior to the Democrats' plan insofar as it acknowledged social and economic patterns that corresponded to geographic regions. In a classic case of gerrymandering, Democrats had based their plan solely on politics, and it was clearly aimed at ensuring their party's dominance at the polls.

What the Democrats wanted to do was combine sections of Oklahoma City and Tulsa with eastern Oklahoma to create two districts that could be counted on to vote in their favor. By contrast, the governor's plan left the two urban districts largely intact. Leveraging his Rolodex of opinion leaders statewide, Price summoned prominent black and Hispanic Democrats to lobby in favor of Keating's plan, as they preferred to have representatives from Oklahoma City or Tulsa, regardless of party, to being lumped into eastern Oklahoma, where their interests were likely to be downplayed or even ignored.

"They were trying to get the most Democrats in office," explained Price. "Ours was really a lot better."

When the case went to trial, Price was tasked with choosing about twenty witnesses who were best equipped to identify communities of interest. In what Price described as "the strangest trial in the world," they offered their opinions on what constituted a community of interest and where district lines, reflecting those interests, should be drawn to ensure effective representation in Congress. Ultimately, Governor Keating's plan won the day.

"Are those districts still in existence today?" I asked.

"With slight variations," said Price. "It's not exactly the same. Every ten years, you have a different one." Price went on to explain that his former rival for the Fifth District seat in Congress, Ernest Istook, would never have been elected under the Democrats' gerrymandered plan.

"Istook really liked what I was doing," concluded Price.

And so did Frank Keating.[15]

Taking on a completely different challenge, Price represented clients who had run afoul of immigration laws. A case that sent his commitment to fairness and aversion to mandatory sentencing into overdrive involved a Vietnamese woman who had immigrated to the U.S. at the age of three and had grown up as an English speaker, hopelessly lost in her native language. Fifteen years after she arrived on American shores, she was accused of stealing a sweater from a department store. She denied the theft, but no matter; she was convinced to plead guilty and accept a deferred sentence. Assured that her plea was meaningless, she forgot all about it and went on with her life.

A dozen years later, now married to a professor and pursuing a doctoral degree at Oklahoma State University, she applied for U.S. citizenship. Asked if she had ever been convicted of a crime, she responded honestly, which was a mistake, as she gave immigration officials no choice but to deport her to Vietnam.

Three days before she was due to board a plane, Price tracked down the assistant D.A., now serving on the pardon and parole board, who had denied her appeal for a pardon.

"I turned it down," shouted the attorney into his cell phone, struggling to be heard while hunting in South Texas. "She had a deferred sentence, so she didn't need a pardon."

And Price's response? "Under federal law, that is a conviction!"

"Oh," replied the attorney, "I didn't realize that. I will put that back on the docket."

He did, and Price's client was spared a one-way ticket to a land she never knew.[16]

A case that perhaps came closest to satisfying Price's desire to wage war on white-collar crime came in the form of syringes manufactured by Retractable Technologies, Inc., a Texas-based company that developed and marketed medical devices. Among the company's most marketable devices were its VanishPoint products, a new and improved line of safety needles designed to prevent needlestick injuries and prevent reuse. With multiple medical technology patents to his credit, company founder, president, and CEO Thomas J. Shaw sought nothing less than a revolution in how shots were administered.[17] As Price explained about his foray into medicine, "After you deliver the shot, the needle retracts into the syringe, so you cannot, as a nurse, accidentally stick yourself with a needle that might have hepatitis C, or B, or AIDS. That's a huge fear among nurses."[18]

Price was more impressed with Shaw's ingenuity than his personality. "He's a hard guy to work with," said Price simply. What lured Price's firm into Shaw's world was Retractable Technology's inability to sell its products to hospitals. Every time Shaw and his associates made their pitch to hospital purchasing agents, they got the same dispiriting runaround: due to long-term contracts, they were obligated to buy supplies through group purchasing organizations (GPOs), one-stop shops for equipment and supplies that kept hospitals in business. On the upside, these Goliaths of the medical supply industry offered clear advantages in bulk discounts, a simplified supply chain, and training sessions to acquaint medical personnel with their products. But as Dr. Marty Makary, a surgeon and professor of health policy at Johns Hopkins University, asserts in his bestselling book, *The Price We Pay* (2019), about the crisis in America's healthcare system, their business model undermined whatever benefits they provided to their customers.[19]

Among GPOs' most critical suppliers was Becton Dickinson, a medical technology company whose goal was to advance global health by improving medical discovery, diagnostics, and the delivery of care. More specifically, the company provided innovative solutions through medical research and genomics (the branch of molecular biology concerned with the structure, function, evolution, and mapping of genomes), diagnosis of infectious diseases and cancer, medication management, the prevention of infection, surgical and interventional procedures, and support for the management of diabetes. Customers ran the gamut from healthcare institutions, researchers, and laboratories to the pharmaceutical industry and general public. Becton Dickinson's vast array of products included syringes and hypodermic needles—exactly the devices that Retractable Technologies had made safer than ever and wanted to market to the world.[20]

As a primary supplier of medical products to GPOs, Becton Dickinson had positioned itself to limit and even cut off sales to hospitals if they tried to circumvent their group purchasing contracts. Not only did those contracts stymie Retractable Technology's ability to market life-saving syringes and needles; they also discouraged innovation.

To maintain its monopoly on hospital purchasing, Becton Dickinson relied on something called the safe harbor exemption, a 1987 law that exempted GPOs from anti-kickback regulations. With the stroke of a pen, Congress had given GPOs carte blanche to increase their profits by requiring manufacturers to pay fees for listings in their catalogs. Predictably, increased costs associated with those pay-to-play fees have been passed on to taxpayers, particularly those admitted to hospitals. "It's a federal law," explained Price. "The big manufacturers can afford to pay off the group purchasing organizations, which can control the hospitals. It is a demonstrative antitrust violation."[21] Price cited Dr. Makary's book to make two recommendations: Congress should repeal the safe harbor exemption, and hospitals should avoid purchasing supplies from GPOs whose pay-to-play business model conceded market dominance to manufacturing behemoths. Like Price in his multiple anticorruption crusades, Dr. Makary's solution was simple and straightforward: "It's time we banned all kickbacks in medicine."[22]

Relishing the prospect of an antitrust fight and certain that a private firm such as his could never succeed against a behemoth such as Becton Dickinson, Price took Retractable Technology's case to the Antitrust Division in the Department of Justice. "I spent almost a week presenting to the Antitrust Division in Washington," said Price about his David-versus-Goliath case. "They just loved the case! They were just as enthusiastic as can be."

As he delved deeper into the medical technology quagmire, Price discovered, to his horror, that some of the big hospitals were represented on GPOs' boards of directors. He further discovered that innovative companies, such as Retractable Technologies, often had no choice but to sell their products for as little as ten cents on the dollar. And who wound up owning those products? With alarming regularity, the owners turned out to be hospital administrators and GPO board members. To cite another example of the innovation that was being crushed, Price told the story of an inventor in Tulsa who came up with a device that alerted surgeons to remove towels and other paraphernalia from patients before they closed their incisions, an error that was shockingly common and often fatal.

"He was being kept out of every hospital," continued Price with undisguised disgust. "It was like the peasants versus the nobility. It was just incredible, how widespread this was!"

Price found support for repealing the safe harbor exemption from U.S. Representative, and later, U.S. Senator, Tom Coburn, a physician from Muskogee who had graduated from the University of Oklahoma Medical School in 1983. After an internship at St. Anthony Hospital in Oklahoma City and a residency at the University of Arkansas Area Health and Education Center in Fort Smith, Coburn returned to Muskogee to open his medical practice, specializing in family medicine and obstetrics. In 1994, he traded medicine for politics in a successful run for the Second District seat in the U.S. House of Representatives, an office that had been held by Mike Synar since 1979. Coburn won the Republican primary and defeated Democratic candidate Virgil Cooper to become only the second Republican in state history to represent the Second District. Coburn was reelected twice and, in keeping with his promise to serve only three terms, did not seek reelection in 2000.[23] In 2004, he returned to political life with a successful run for the U.S. Senate. Coburn was re-elected to a second term in 2010 and kept his pledge not to seek a third term in 2016. Not surprisingly for a former physician, Coburn took a keen interest in mitigating medical fraud, which he estimated was costing the U.S. government upwards of $40 billion annually.

Price found another confederate in Phil Zweig, the journalist who broke the Penn Square Bank story in the banking industry's flagship publication, *The American Banker*.[24] Such was Zweig's interest in Price's crusade that he wrote an article about corruption in the medical technology industry for *Business Week*. "This is the most important article I have ever written," said Zweig, who had written more than his share of important articles. Zweig became so committed to the cause that he left *Business Week* to accept Tom Shaw's offer of a job at Retractable Technologies, where he illuminated yet another arena that disadvantaged the powerless and, in this case, threatened lives worldwide. One has only to consider the danger posed by recycled needles during the AIDS crisis and among impoverished people across the globe to recognize the dire consequences of stifling the kind of innovation that Retractable Technologies had to offer.

Price and Zweig's campaign against Retractable Technologies was dramatized in *Puncture* (released in the United Kingdom as *Injustice*), a 2011 film starring Chris Evans and directed by Adam Kassen and

Mark Kassen that illuminated the tragic consequences of bribery in the healthcare and pharmaceutical industries. In recognition of their efforts, Price and Zweig were invited to the film's opening in Houston.

Price's and Zweig's war on medical corruption did not end with GPOs' control of hospital supply chains. Several years into their crusade on behalf of Tom Shaw and his fellow innovators, they met with Representative Coburn to discuss another swamp of malfeasance in the healthcare industry: Big Pharma's overpricing of prescription drugs. "It is an enormous issue!" declared Price. "A lot of pharmacists are being driven out of business." Ignoring Coburn's warning that they were challenging "the most powerful forces you can imagine," Zweig deployed his skills as a journalist to publicize their findings, while Price pressured the Antitrust Division of the Department of Justice to ramp up its investigations into drug pricing.

"This is a monster case," concluded Price, still seething with frustration at the unfairness of it all. As of this writing in 2021, Goliath has yet to stumble. But he certainly knows that his nemesis hasn't surrendered.

In the years since taking on Retractable Technology's case and launching his jeremiad against Big Pharma, first for pay and, after he retired from private practice, on a *pro bono* basis, Price has stayed in close touch with Zweig. Like Oklahoma Corporation Commission Chairman Bob Anthony, Zweig has never missed an opportunity to rib Price about his gift of persuasion.

"He emails me every week," said Price with a familiar, mischievous smile, "and he always says to me, 'Bill, you got me into this!'"[25]

▶ ▶ ▶ ▶

By the time his father, Joel, died on June 14, 1975, Price had been serving as managing partner and trustee of Price Oil and Gas and managing the family's trusts for about two years. As his schedule in the U.S. Attorney's Office precluded anything close to micromanagement, day-to-day responsibility fell to his mother, Virginia, who turned out to be an extraordinarily competent businesswoman. Presiding over weekly meetings to evaluate wells and make decisions with her son, her grandson Steve Foerster, and their bookkeeper, Virginia evolved into a de facto CEO. As Price learned during those meetings, which usually included dinner, "She really came into her own as a business lady." Foerster went so far as to dub his grandmother "the patriarch of the family." Virginia's immersion in the oil and gas business came just as Oklahoma's historic energy boom was hitting warp speed and making everybody's decisions a lot more consequential. But Virginia was careful not to let her responsibilities interfere with duplicate bridge, a game she enjoyed well into her seventies, and keeping up with her progeny. That included organizing the same kinds of trips that she and Joel had taken when their children were young, which had contributed so much to their youngest son's education.[26]

Virginia's death, on February 29, 2000, after an extended illness, left Price and Foerster to comanage their family's affairs. Over weekly dinner meetings (known to the family as Price Oil and Gas Night) at Price's home, which doubled as company headquarters, they and their bookkeeper, joined from time to time by other family members, enjoyed Mary's legendary feasts and made decisions on whether to participate in wells or to lease, analyzed massive amounts of data, and distributed royalties to family members.

"Bill was the patriarch now," explained Foerster about his grandmother's successor. "He was the glue that held the family together."[27]

As Price crossed the porous boundary from paid employment to volunteering, he took on projects that confirmed his long-standing interests in youth and education. As his daughter Eileen put it, "He's definitely not one of those people who say, 'Thank goodness I'm retired!' Retirement was just an opportunity to do other things, except you're not getting paid."[28]

Among those other things was the Children's Hospital Foundation. "That always struck me as a good, charitable cause," explained Price, who joined the organization shortly after its founding and remained on its board for two-plus decades. Turning to politics, as the vehicle most likely to spawn tangible results, he joined the foundation's Political Affairs Committee and met with congressmen, including his opponent in the 1992 Fifth District race, Ernest Istook, who was instrumental in securing a significant amount of federal money. "It has been really important in terms of improving the lives of kids in Oklahoma because of the research and clinical work that has been done," continued Price. "It has raised the chances of premature babies living, and children's health, period." Price was particularly proud of securing more endowed chairs than almost any children's hospital in the nation. As usual, he was happy to give credit away: "That board is just full of movers and shakers. It has been an enormous plus for Oklahoma City!"[29]

Price's bedrock conservatism led his good friend and fellow conservative, Jose Freede, to nominate him to become a trustee of the Oklahoma Council of Public Affairs (OCPA), a free-market think tank dedicated to public policy solutions. He also served as president of Town Hall, Oklahoma City's oldest and largest lecture series which, at the time of this writing, has brought six national speakers a year to an audience of up to a thousand people. Price's other positions included a two-year stint as president of the Men's Dinner Club and leadership roles in two downtown organizations: Kiwanis, a group that hosts speakers and works on behalf of disadvantaged youth; and the Fortune Club that enlists experts to address some of the metro area's most prominent opinion leaders. A career in public service prompted Price to join the Committee of One Hundred, an organization with chapters nationwide dedicated to honoring and rewarding law enforcement officers and fire fighters who risk their lives to keep their communities safe. Price was a master in the Holloway Inns of Court, which put on programs for young lawyers and law school students. Political responsibilities ranged from chairmanship of the Dewey Bartlett Center and the Republican County Convention to cochairmanship, with Ryan Leonard, of the finance committees for John McCain and Mitt

Romney's presidential races in Oklahoma. As active members of Christ the King Church, Bill and Mary attend Mass on a regular basis and participate in a book discussion group to enrich their spiritual lives.[30]

Price's commitment to education led to his appointment by Oklahoma Governor Mary Fallin to the Oklahoma State Board of Education. Two of his fellow board members, Superintendents of Public Instruction Janet Barresi and Joy Hofmeister, held views that were sometimes radically different from each other's, but Price worked with both of them to achieve his aims. To prioritize learning, Price promoted a comprehensive agenda: decrease funding for administration, decontrol state inputs on local schools, expand the teaching pool, cut waste by conducting performance reviews, promote peer coaching by videotaping teacher-leader evaluations, increase funding for classroom instruction, move school board elections to November, connect students with jobs at an early age, and raise the bar in terms of expectations that teachers have for their students. To honor teachers and students for excellence, he went so far as to suggest awarding trophies and cash prizes for academic achievement during halftime of sporting events, much as athletes are singled out for their prowess in sports. Their trophies would be displayed in hallways, across from trophy cases reserved for athletics. In keeping with his support for school choice, Price formed a board majority, which approved several charter schools that had the added benefit of making their communities attractive to newcomers: two for incarcerated children, another offering language immersion in Norman, and yet another geared toward the needs of Native Americans in Oklahoma City. His other school choice proposals included vouchers that parents could use to tutor their children to attain third-grade reading skills, vouchers for foster care and homeless children, statewide charter authority, equal funding for charters, and education savings accounts.[31]

Price's interest in education was not lost on his alma mater. Following seven years of service on Casady's board of trustees, from 1988 to 1995, he was recognized as the distinguished graduate in 2001.

No issue ranked higher on Price's list of priorities than education. COURTESY BILL PRICE.

Recognizing his commitment to education, Brandon Dutcher with the OCPA, in 2009, to serve as chairman of the newly formed Oklahoma School Choice Coalition (OSCC). The Friedman Foundation, represented by Leslie Hiner, was a staunch supporter of the OSCC. Thanks to the foundation's sponsorship, Oklahoma legislators had the opportunity to tour successful school choice programs around the country. In his capacity as chairman, Price was instrumental in convincing the state legislature to pass school choice bills, including two of major importance: the Lindsey Nicole Henry (LNH) Scholarship Act, authorizing parents or guardians of public school students with disabilities to request funding allowing them to attend private schools approved by the State Board of Education; and the Tax Credit Scholarship Program, an alternative to voucher programs that saves states money, because tuition at private schools is typically less than the per-pupil cost of public schools.[32] Price and other coalition members assisted the Attorney General's Office in establishing the LNH's constitutionality before the Oklahoma supreme court, where it was unanimously affirmed. To raise consciousness about the importance of giving parents a voice in their children's education, Price invited Florida Governor Jeb Bush to speak to the legislature and Rotary 29 in downtown Oklahoma City.[33]

Price's commitment to education led to a Man of the Year award from ChoiceMatters, an organization created to educate parents about educational choices available to their children. ChoiceMatters' executive director, and opinion leader in the Hispanic community, Robert M. Ruiz described a mission that dovetails perfectly with Price's nonprofit projects: "to help increase the health and well-being of Oklahomans through increased access to education, economic development, cultural development, and healthcare." Displayed prominently on ChoiceMatters' website is a catchy and deceptively simple slogan: "When it comes to selecting a school—parents have a voice in the choice."[34]

"Education is so important to him," explained Eileen. "And opportunities. It's about giving people the tools to be better."[35]

Like her husband, Mary Price has always been active in nonprofits. As a member of the Oklahoma City Junior League, she enjoyed all her volunteer placements, but none more than the Junior League magazine. Readers enjoyed her humor column about mothers' happy but frantic lives with young children. Mary doubled as a cartoonist for the magazine. Her passion for the arts carried over into a love for musicals, which she and Bill had shared ever since their college days. As a patron of the Lyric Theater, she was honored to join its board of directors. In 2003, she was named president.

Mary's interest in literature led her to join the Library Endowment Board. She was serving as president in 2011 when former First Lady Laura Bush attended the board's annual fundraiser, Literary Voices, to speak about her book *Spoken from the Heart*. "I was so impressed with Mrs. Bush," said Mary. "She was gracious, intelligent, and a tremendous advocate for reading and libraries."

Of course, nothing rated higher in the Prices' priorities than their extended family: Eileen Everett, her husband Josh, and their children, Isabelle and Asa; Anne O'Connor, her husband Josh, and their son, Jax; and James, his wife Victoria and, as of this writing in 2021, the newest addition to the Price family, William.[36]

▶ ▶ ▶ ▶

Realizing that outdoor education and Christ's teachings can be as vital to youth development as classroom instruction, Price was drawn into the orbit of Kids Across America, a boldly Christian organization aimed at turning urban youth and inner-city mentors and educators into leaders through camping and education. Headquartered in Branson, Missouri, Kids Across America was the brainchild of Joe White, a principal in Kanakuk Kamp, the nation's most prominent Christian sports camp. To serve what he perceived as an underserved population, White opened the first Kids Across America camp in 1991 and was gratified to see its popularity skyrocket.[37] Kids Across America's mission seemed perfectly suited to the kind of organization that Price wanted to create in Oklahoma City.

Through the OAAD, Price became acquainted with Eagle Ridge, a state-funded organization sponsoring drug and gang prevention and treatment programs, as well as drug and mental health courts, focusing on minorities. In keeping with his belief that drug prevention and treatment are more effective than prosecution in stopping the drug plague, Price agreed to join Eagle Ridge's board of directors. He was especially impressed with Eagle Ridge's Family Treatment Center in Guthrie, where mothers, instead of incarceration, receive the treatment they need without being separated from their children. Legislators and cabinet officials who accepted his invitations to tour the facility came away convinced that Eagle Ridge's programs offered a much-needed alternative in a state that led the nation in putting women behind bars.

"Instead of being incarcerated and their children going to foster care, they were able to go to this treatment center in Guthrie, and their children would stay with them in another part of the facility and go to school" said Price, whose experience with the OAAD made him an ideal spokesman for a cutting-edge program aimed at keeping people off drugs and out of prison. "They've got all the reason in the world to go straight, to keep their kids," continued the former prosecutor. "They get drug treatment, and they are much more likely to be successful." ReMerge in Oklahoma City adopted a similar model. In Price's view, the ReMerge and Family Treatment Center models could have been expanded across Oklahoma as part of criminal justice reform.

To emulate Kids Across America, and convinced that a Christian camp experience could change young people's lives, members of Eagle Ridge's board of directors, including Bruce Holmes and Father Patrick Bright from All Souls Episcopal Church, persuaded Eagle Ridge to devote forty-plus undeveloped acres that they owned north of 63rd Street and east of the Broadway Extension in northeast Oklahoma City to a camp. Under the leadership of John Mayfield, Eagle Ridge directors recruited Jason and Jill Mirikitani, a husband-wife team from Kids Across America, to serve as camp directors. Joining Price on news talk shows was George Young, a pastor and, later, a state senator who was equally determined to extol the benefits of a summer camp to the black community.

With a pond dug by the Army Corps of Engineers, the property began to look like a real summer camp, and it was poised to become a full-fledged Eagle Ridge program. By century's end, Eagle Ridge boasted everything that inner-city youth and their adult mentors needed for a transformative experience, including soccer fields, a ropes course, facilities for arts and crafts, and instructional venues, all infused with Christian values.

All was heading in the right direction when tragedy struck. On a trip through southeastern Texas, Jason Mirikitani swerved over a highway median and crashed into a semitruck in the oncoming lane. Jill died on impact, her brother and father suffered minor injuries, and her eighteen-month-old baby emerged from the horror with nary a scratch. Jason survived, but brain damage made continued service to the camp impossible.

The accident, commemorated with a simple marker outside the camp's headquarters, coincided with conflicts that nearly derailed the entire operation. "We went through some really rough times," explained Price, still saddened that his unique combination of a drug treatment program supported by federal and state funding and a camp for kids driven by a Christian mission proved to be incompatible. Yet Price and other visionaries refused to let go of their dream, and as tensions escalated, they separated from Eagle Ridge and rebranded their camp Shiloh, known in the Bible as "a place of peace." As noted on the camp's website, "for far too many in our inner-city communities, it is hard to find a peace amid turmoil, hurt, and anger in their daily lives. Our mission at Shiloh Camp is to transform our inner city with the love of Christ through sports, arts, and meaningful relationships." Leadership fell to Price, who became chairman of Shiloh Summer Camp's board of directors in 2000. Ten years later, Shiloh honored him with its Man of the Year award for his work on the camp's behalf. [38]

John Mayfield's departure and the Mirikitanis' accident left Shiloh in need of a camp director. The board of directors found what they were looking for in Andy Edwards. His resignation, after about two years on the job, left Shiloh once again adrift—that is, until the board's nationwide search led them back to Branson, the birthplace of Kanakuk Kamps and its innovative spinoff for disadvantaged youth, Kids Across America. And nobody was more qualified to take on Shiloh's challenges than the man responsible for recruiting Kids Across America's original campers, the Mirikitanis' former boss, Stephan Moore.

A native of Cushing, Oklahoma, and summertime counselor at Kanakuk Kamp, Moore earned notoriety as a member of Eddie Sutton's and, after he relocated to the University of Kentucky, Nolan Richardson's basketball team at the University of Arkansas. After graduating in 1988 with a degree in marketing, Moore spent a year playing basketball for Spirit Express, a team that combined collegiate exhibition games with a prison ministry. "So, we would go into prisons, and we would play the prison team," explained Moore, a towering man with infectious *joie de vivre* whose physique left no doubt as to his preferred sport. "I tell people I have been in jail a lot!"

I flinched when Moore let out a howl. After only a few minutes in his cramped office at the heart of Shiloh's bucolic acreage, I knew exactly why Price and his fellow directors had chosen him to head up their camp. Not for the first time, I checked my recording device to make sure it was catching all this. I did not want to miss a minute of what was sure to be an uplifting and inspiring story.

Moore left Spirit Express after a year. Following a foiled (and perhaps half-hearted) attempt to enter the corporate world, Moore answered Kanakuk Kamp Director Joe White's challenge to recruit youth for Kids Across America. "He kind of went Clint Eastwood on me, and he starts talking real low," said Moore about an interview that changed his life. "And his eyes get kind of squinty, and he basically told me, 'Have this camp full next year!'"

Moore took the bait and hit the road to find inner-city youth directors who might be interested in sending children to Branson. Moore's grueling trip through the South and Southwest eventually landed him at a Fairfield Marriott in Atlanta, where a call to the home office and quick calculations revealed that he had recruited an astonishing total of 1,500 youth. "I get choked up talking about this," said Moore. "It was one of the most tremendous feats I have ever been part of in my life. There was a big cheer on the other end of the phone." With that cheer echoing in his ears, Moore returned to Branson and was raring to go when Kids Across America made its debut in 1991.

Over the ensuing eighteen years, Moore served Kids Across America as director and assistant executive director. In his spare time, Moore participated in opening multimillion-dollar facilities nationwide and trained people to do what, as far as I could tell, came naturally to him.

Deeply saddened by the Mirikitanis' accident and always open to new challenges, Moore was receptive when Shiloh's board of directors invited him to Oklahoma City for an interview. Meeting with Price, Bruce Holmes, and Father Bright at All Soul's Episcopal Church in the fall of 2008, Moore was given no illusions about the challenges ahead. "They didn't even have a salary to pay me here," recalled Moore with a laugh. But there was a connection—what Moore recalled as a certain resonance—between him and his interviewers.

"People with good hearts, and good faith . . ."

Moore paused, searching for the right words to describe his and his wife's decision-making process.

"When God calls, you listen," he said finally. "We called them back not long after and said yes."

With seven children in a brood that eventually grew to ten (six boys and four girls), the Moores moved into a Holiday Inn at the intersection of Main and Dewey in downtown Oklahoma City. With only four full-time employees, Shiloh depended heavily on summertime recruits from area colleges and universities to make sessions rewarding and instructive. "We're trying to reach children and families who wouldn't normally have an opportunity to have a dynamic camp experience like this," said Moore. "Our hope is that we're going to have a deep impact on northeast Oklahoma City. What happens here is so cool, it is so significant. It is kingly. When I say kingly, I mean God's kingdom."

Moore's dream was for Shiloh to become the anchor of northeast Oklahoma City. He envisioned a day when people would introduce themselves as residents of the East Side— "You know, where Shiloh is."

"The support of our board, and Bill being a big part of that, has allowed us to develop a very unique program that reaches our inner city," continued Moore. "You can see where his heart is." Price showed his heart not only as a board member, but also on workdays when garden beds had to be dug and fences had to be erected. Moore recalled a blazing summer day when he looked over his shoulder to see Price striding into the garden, tools in hand, to dig postholes and string fences.

"He was out here and engaged in that," concluded Moore. "I am really grateful for his long-term commitment at Shiloh."

Shiloh's mission was particularly important in light of Oklahoma's abysmal record in child-rearing. As Moore was pained to point out, Oklahoma topped the national list in what psychologists refer to as "adverse childhood experiences"—that is, experiences that have a negative impact on mental and emotional health, whose effects linger well into adulthood to spawn health problems. To mitigate the effects of those experiences, Shiloh aimed to build young peoples' resilience through loving and caring relationships and opportunities to find a sympathetic ear.

"I believe, as a Christian, your success is going to be directly connected to your ability to really hear God," explained Moore. "What is God saying to you? How do you take something spiritual, and how can you take that in a way that accomplishes what is in the heart of God?"[39]

Without knocking, one of Moore's grown children, Stephan, Jr., entered the office through a side door. Introductions were made, and the two Stephans spoke briefly about a project they were working on. I took that as a signal to wrap things up, say my goodbyes, and be on my way.

Driving north from Shiloh's nondescript offices on a gravel road, I glanced in my rearview mirror to see skyscrapers some six miles to the south poking above the trees. To my left, horses grazed in a pasture belonging to a veterinary clinic.

As the sun cast its winter shadows across the land, I pulled over to stroll through the pavilions and beneath the ropes course. In my mind's eye, I imagined joyous youngsters playing volleyball and skipping stones along the pond's edge. Seemingly miles, and maybe years, removed from the throb of urban life, I reflected on what this place of peace has meant to children unaccustomed to the attention they so sadly lacked and so richly deserved.

Moments later, I reached the Broadway Extension and blended seamlessly into the northbound traffic.

During our interview, Moore mentioned another of Price's youth-oriented projects: Cristo Rey, a network of private schools launched on Chicago's southwest side in 1996. An extensive survey of underserved neighborhoods by the Chicago-Detroit Jesuit province indicated a desperate need for access to high-quality college-preparatory education. Realizing that private school tuition was out of reach for most residents, Father John Foley, SJ, gathered a team to develop a model for secondary education with a revolutionary twist. Rather than offering unpaid internships to the school, which Foley's team was establishing under the Cristo Rey moniker, participating companies would be required to pay students' tuition and tutor them in proper business comportment. Partnerships between Cristo Rey and corporate sponsors did more than keep the lights on; they helped students perceive the relevance of their education, grow in self-confidence, and prepare for success in college and their careers. The idea caught on, and by 2001, educators from Portland, Los Angeles, and Denver were collaborating with Fr. Foley to set up schools based on the Cristo Rey model. In 2003, the Cristo Rey Network was formed to replicate the model nationwide.[40]

Given his Catholic faith, participation in the Oklahoma School Choice Coalition, and membership on the Oklahoma State School Board, Price's interest in Cristo Rey was practically foreordained. At the urging of Damon Gardenhire, senior program officer for the Walton Family Foundation in Oklahoma City, Price agreed, in 2015, to head up a feasibility study and set off for a weeklong conference in Chicago to learn how to join the Cristo Rey Network.

Back at home, Cristo Rey Catholic High School's nascent board of directors, which Price chaired, hired Regina Birchum from the Oklahoma State Treasurer's office to handle the day-to-day responsibilities of creating a new school. "She's marvelous!" gushed Price. Next, the board needed to raise money through private donations, apply for grants from Inasmuch Foundation in Oklahoma City, and solicit companies as partners. "The business pays them the equivalency of an entry-level employee," continued Price. "They don't pay students; they pay the school. It pays sixty percent of the cost of the school. They are not bagging groceries or something at Love's Country Store. They work in the corporate office. They get a feeling of a career. They get a hundred percent college acceptance. They are about seventy percent Hispanic, about ten or fifteen percent African American, and then other, and maybe ten or fifteen percent white. They are almost all poor kids. If you can afford it, you can't go."[41]

Even though most Cristo Rey schools were in larger cities, a feasibility study left no doubt that Oklahoma City was ready to join the Cristo Rey Network. A key factor in Oklahoma City's selection was the state's Tax Credit Scholarship Program, which Price had helped to pass and that freed up funding for the new school. To head up the finance committee during the feasibility study, Price turned to Inasmuch Foundation chairman and CEO Bob Ross and Judy Love, co-founder with her husband, Tom, of Love's Travel Stops and Country Stores. "With Judy Love and Bob Ross heading the finance committee, how could it fail?" asked Price rhetorically. Love remained on the board as an honorary member while her company's multitasking officer, Carl Martincich, was appointed as the go-to person for financial matters. Mark Ruffin headed the facilities committee, and Dave Lopez helped students find jobs in the business community. Thanks to strong support from businesses, students were rarely turned down. Credit goes to Catholic Archbishop Paul Coakley, whose concern for underserved populations lay at the heart of Cristo Rey's mission. As plans were made to welcome the first freshman class in the fall of 2018, Cristo Rey's board of directors included Bill Price, Bob Ross, former Oklahoma Secretary of Commerce and Tourism Deby Snodgrass, former Oklahoma first lady Cathy Keating, and founding board chairman Gene Rainbolt, whose civic engagement set a high bar for citizenship. When Ross stepped down to become an honorary board member, his sister, Becky Roten, was invited to replace him.[42]

In his search for a president after the founding head, Renée Porter, resigned, Price turned to his former campaign staffer Chip Carter, whom he saw every Sunday at Christ the King Catholic Church. Several years before Cristo Rey prepared to open, Price invited Carter to a reception for Fr. Foley. Intrigued by Cristo Rey's educational model and looking for an exit ramp from six years at a public relations firm, Carter was receptive when the board of directors offered him the job.

When I caught up with Carter in August 2019, he had been on the job for all of two weeks. Nestled in an unpretentious building on Oklahoma State University's Oklahoma City campus, Cristo Rey was a beehive of activity as students flocked in for the school's second year of operation.

"I was just blown away by the whole concept of Cristo Rey," explained Carter about his career switch from public relations to heading up a high school. "We're going to have a college-preparatory school for low-income students, and in order for them to pay for the school, to receive this education, they are going to work five days a week at a local business. By working, not only are they helping to pay their tuition, but they are seeing a part of life that, in all likelihood, they would never see, or even imagine, otherwise." Carter was particularly impressed by Cristo Rey students' near-100-percent success rate in earning their diplomas and receiving offers from four-year colleges. "Any prep school of any kind would be envious of those numbers!"

Carter had no idea how Price had learned about Cristo Rey, but no matter: "He did, and he led the exploratory committee—the feasibility study—and then has been a great board member since."

"Two weeks' experience—that's not a whole lot to go on," I said, struggling to be heard over the hubbub outside Carter's modest conference room. "Do you have any vision for the future?"

"Sure," said Carter. "Two and a half years from now, our goal is that we have at least 75 percent go on to attend college. If we had 75 percent of our kids going on to four-year colleges, that means the other 25 percent are largely going to get associates' degrees, and maybe having a gap year, and maybe going into the military, all of which are fine opportunities. Even those that don't go on to college would have been academically prepared to go on, if they wanted."

Carter envisioned a day when Cristo Rey would close ranks with Oklahoma City's premier Catholic schools, Mount Saint Mary's and Bishop McGuiness. "Few people are familiar with Cristo Rey Oklahoma City. So, my job in the next several years is to raise our public image within not just the Catholic community, but the overall community. I want businesspeople to be able to say to one another, 'We've got a Cristo Rey team. Do you?' And have the other guy say, 'I need to call them.' There's a level of penetration that we need to get to. That's my priority."

Carter glanced at his watch and realized that he had a pressing phone call to tend to. But before he scurried back to his office, he wanted me to understand his debt to Bill Price who, as he had done several times before, in his law career and philanthropic endeavors, had lured a trusted friend into the adventure of a lifetime. "Oftentimes, how you know somebody is how you first come to know somebody. That's how I am with Bill. I will always think of him as the U.S. Attorney who ran for Congress. One of my great regrets is that I wasn't able to help him get elected. He has done so much for our community. I don't know—if he had gone to Congress, would he have done Cristo Rey? Probably not. So all things happen to work out for a good reason."[43]

Following his dual career in law and politics, Price continued to work on behalf of his fellow Oklahomans in nonprofit projects and policymaking organizations. COURTESY BILL PRICE.

EPILOGUE : *The Man in the Arena*

Titling chapters is a tricky business. In this effort to juxtapose Bill Price's biography with the story of corruption in Oklahoma, some chapter titles are definitely more descriptive than others in signaling what readers can expect when they turn the page. A few were shamelessly plagiarized when I couldn't come up with a better one. I tried unsuccessfully to avoid "Mr. Price Goes to Washington" as a too-obvious reference to *Mr. Smith Goes to Washington*, the 1939 classic, starring Jimmy Stewart, about a young man's trial by fire in the nation's capital. "The Rise and Fall of David Hall" has been used in countless iterations as shorthand for potential greatness turned to ashes when hubris trumps reason and its corollary in ethics. As former U.S. Attorney Bill Burkett shows, in his book under that title, it pretty much encapsulates what happened when the wily Oklahoma governor began his term in office with high hopes before making a descent to the dark side.

The county commissioner scandal that spawned this book merited two chapters, and I divided them into coequal parts: "Okscam: The Investigation" and "Okscam: Pleas and Convictions." Those are not very inspired, but they seem clear, and they definitely aren't plagiarized. "From Whom Much is Given, Much Is Expected" is a familiar trope of biblical provenance, and it had special meaning for Dr. Joel Scott Price, who played it forward, quite successfully, to his son. In his interview, U.S. Representative Tom Cole unwittingly gave me the title "The Best Governor Oklahoma Never Had," to underscore his disappointment that his candidate in the 1990 gubernatorial race never made it to the governor's mansion. I was going to use it as the title of this book until

Through his prosecutions of corrupt county commissioners, Bill Price earned a
reputation as the biggest corruption buster in Oklahoma history. COURTESY TULSA WORLD;
BILL PRICE.

Price pointed to a framed image hanging in his home. It was the cover
of the *Tulsa World*'s Sunday supplement, *OK Magazine*, from April
1984, featuring Price, arms folded and lacking his characteristic smile,
standing in front of an American flag. The title of the ensuing article,
definitely plagiarized on this book's cover, is "At War with Corruption:
Federal Prosecutor Bill Price." Was it coincidence that the article was
published on April 22, the day celebrated by generations of Oklahomans
to commemorate the fabled run of '89?

I saved the easiest chapter title for the epilogue. Although Mary Price mentioned it in her interview, credit goes to U.S. President Theodore Roosevelt, a real standout when it comes to speechmaking. A bit of online sleuthing revealed that the man who liked to walk softly but carry a big stick delivered "The Man in the Arena: Citizenship in a Republic" at the Sorbonne, in Paris, in 1910.

As someone weaned on notable speeches, Price knew lots of them. But, according to Mary, this was his favorite. It reads in part,

> It is not the critic who counts; not the man who points out how the strong man stumbles, or where the doer of deeds could have done them better. The credit belongs to the man who is actually in the arena, whose face is marred by dust and sweat and blood; who strives valiantly; who errs, who comes short again and again, because there is no effort without error and shortcoming; but who does actually strive to do the deeds; who knows great enthusiasms, the great devotions; who spends himself in a worthy cause; who at the best knows in the end the triumph of high achievement, and who at the worst, if he fails, at least fails while daring greatly, so that his place shall never be with those cold and timid souls who neither know victory nor defeat.[1]

▶ ▶ ▶ ▶

So what lessons did Bill Price learn from his life in the arena, and how did he apply them to his dual career in law and politics?

Perhaps the place to start is with the title that Price suggested for this book: *At War with Corruption*. As Price insisted again and again, fighting corruption is not so much a choice as an obligation—that is, if your goal is to maintain faith in public institutions and private businesses. As he noted in his postmortem of Governor David Hall's conviction on charges of extortion, a public official's willingness to sell offices to the highest bidder and run roughshod over rules and regulations to win political office is an invitation for others to join in the corruption. "That's the tragedy that I saw in this thing," mused Price with more than a hint of sadness. "It not only destroys the public's faith in our Republic, but if unprosecuted, it can persuade otherwise honest candidates and businesspeople to decide that corruption is the only way they can compete and be successful."[2]

On Corruption in America author Sarah Chayes agreed: "Systemic corruption, leaving no means of redress or civic appeal, drives citizens to extremes."[3]

To clarify why some people are drawn into corrupt practices and others are not, Price waxed sociological to cite two possible explanations—culture and structure—that cropped up repeatedly among Okscam's Monday-morning quarterbacks. For Price, blaming a culture of corruption dating back to Oklahoma's territorial days was nothing but an excuse for unethical behavior. Who was to say that Oklahomans were uniquely prone to, and accepting of, unethical behavior on the part of their elected officials? A theory of cultural corruption as the root cause of bribery and extortion in county governance failed the smell test on many levels. As with so many theories spouted by armchair sociologists, it comes perilously close to blaming the victim for circumstances beyond his or her control.

Far more culpable in spawning and perpetuating the largest case of public corruption in the FBI's history was the structure of county government. Thanks to a populist legacy of distrust for officialdom and reliance on so-called (and largely mythical) rugged individualism to get things done, county officials had the latitude to turn their jurisdictions into independent fiefdoms beyond the purview of watchdogs in Oklahoma City. Lacking a system of checks and balances that might have kept their darker angels at bay, county commissioners focused on keeping their constituents happy and their bookkeeping under wraps, never imagining that their under-the-table deals were really hurting anybody, least of all the state of Oklahoma. Over time, commissioners came to perceive their ten percents, 50-50s, and kickbacks on heavy-equipment purchases as part of their compensation. Pottawatomie County Commissioner Edward Leroy Strickland became the unwitting spokesman for legions of his fellow commissioners when he stormed into attorney Drew Neville's office to demand justice: "All I did was take my salary, *plus 10 percent!*"

Convinced that structure was the real culprit in sending corruption in Oklahoma off the charts, Price advocated successfully for two reforms aimed at tilting the balance toward honest government: legislation at the state level to allow multicounty grand juries to circumvent jurisdictional boundaries and broaden law enforcement's investigative powers, and reforms in county purchasing to discourage unethical behavior. For evidence that structural reforms would be effective, Price looked no further than the state of Kansas, where strict laws and competent commissioners fostered a system of county governance that bore nary a trace of Oklahoma's systemic thievery.

As Okscam faded from the headlines and into history, Price was invited to conferences nationwide to share his experiences with U.S. Attorneys and state officials as they waged their own wars with corruption. Price quickly learned that Oklahoma's systemic sleaze was rampant in states with similar governmental structures, most notably in Southern states where public officials stuck to an all-too-familiar playbook. Investigations in those states yielded dozens of convictions. Nowhere were corrupt officials more ubiquitous than Mississippi. Closer to home, prosecutors in northeastern Texas rivaled, and maybe even exceeded, their Oklahoma counterparts in bringing scofflaws to justice. According to Price, convictions in other states grabbed fewer headlines than in Oklahoma, not because there was less corruption. There are two reasons: investigators were extraordinarily skilled, and they benefitted from breaks on the way to cracking their cases.

In the absence of constant and vigorous prosecutions, Price doubted that corruption will ever be stamped out for good. Yet he wound toward the conclusion of this book on a note of optimism: "My experiences in Okscam showed state and federal prosecutors around the country how to replicate our methods, and they were able to mitigate the scourge of corruption in their counties. Hopefully, this book will serve as a guide to eliminating systemic corruption in county government."[4]

The effectiveness of post-Okscam reforms in county purchasing was apparent not only in the statistics that Price liked to cite, but also in the opinion of former U.S. Attorney for the Northern District of Oklahoma, Frank Keating, who went on to occupy the state's highest office from 1995 to 2003. I asked him about the reforms instigated during and after Price's tenure as U.S. Attorney and the prevalence of corruption during Keating's terms as governor. Keating's reply was unequivocal: "I think we gave it a diuretic. While I was governor, there just wasn't much discussion of county officials and corruption, because they had all been purged!"[5]

Tom Cole who, as of this writing in 2021, represents Oklahoma's Fourth Congressional District, said much the same thing: "I think we have gone through quite a metamorphosis as a state, where corruption isn't tolerated or accepted in the way that it was. But it was just part of Oklahoma politics."[6]

Price's war with corruption did not end with multicounty grand-jury legislation and new rules for county purchasing. Through what came to be known as the McNally fix, he and other U.S. Attorneys convinced U.S. Attorney General Edwin Meese to support two key reforms: broadening mail-fraud statutes to prosecute officials for violating citizens' intangible rights, including their right to good and faithful services from public servants; and enabling federal prosecutors to collaborate with state attorneys to enhance local law enforcement. Price was also instrumental in convincing Oklahoma legislators to adapt federal RICO statutes to state-level prosecutions. To paraphrase Frank Keating and Tom Cole, the reforms that Price instigated went a long way in tilting the balance toward honesty and away from criminality in a state whose moniker recalls its origins in land swindles and power grabs.[7]

Inseparable from Price's crusade against corruption has been his commitment to the Republican Party's bedrock principles: low taxes, an unfettered marketplace, and faith in people to build meaningful lives with a minimum of government meddling. Raised on tales of his grandparents' grit and ingenuity and his father's Horatio Alger story,

Price spent his teenage years absorbing conservative economics and debating at Casady School. He found kindred spirits in Oklahoma's chapter of Teen Age Republicans and, later, among like-minded students at Georgetown University, where antiwar protests pushed him ever deeper into a conviction that conservatism offered the best hope for American renewal. By the time he graduated from law school at the University of Oklahoma and launched his law career, his principles were set in stone, and they fueled his crusade against corruption and white-collar crime and gave him the bona fides he needed to assume leadership in the state's Republican Party.

Nobody was surprised when Price concluded his tenure in the U.S. Attorney's Office with a bid for governor. Nor was anyone surprised when he recovered from a bitter defeat and ran—once again, unsuccessfully—for Congress. Consolation over two failed political campaigns came from his gubernatorial campaign advisor, Tom Cole, who called him (at the risk of repetition) the best governor Oklahoma never had.

Corruption and white-collar crime were not the only brands of criminality Price fought against. Prosecutions of drug traffickers put the fire in his belly to form the Oklahoma Alliance Against Drugs, a grassroots organization based on science, powered by youth peer pressure, and aimed at wooing young people away from drugs and alcohol. "I have sought out causes that could mitigate social ills, mainly drug and alcohol abuse and the decline of family values," said Price. "I have always believed that families, strengthened by religious faith, are the foundation of a healthy society."

During and long after his law career, Price advocated for youth in Eagle Ridge, Shiloh Camp, Cristo Rey, the State School Board, the School Choice Coalition, the OCPA, and other organizations aimed at improving the life chances of underprivileged children, many of whom were black and brown and all of whom were unsuspecting beneficiaries of the mantra that Price learned from his father, Joel Scott Price: *from whom much is given, much is expected.*

As his daughter Anne put it, "I think he's probably the closest to really color-blind of anyone I know. I think he's just interested in other things."[8]

Anne knew something else about her father, and it accounts for his willingness to take on responsibilities that most would just as soon leave to somebody else: "My dad, of course, as you know, is always good about making sure that the buck stops with him, showing that you take ownership of something. You can't just let the corruption go on and imagine that there's somebody else who is going to do it for you. You have to be willing to do it yourself. A lot of times, there's nobody else who is going to go do it. When you take ownership, you can make things happen."[9]

Through all his prosecutions in the U.S. Attorney's office and defenses in private practice, the untimely deaths of a brother and sister, successful promotion of anticorruption rules and regulations, two hard-fought yet unsuccessful political campaigns, the ups and downs of a family oil and gas company, the nonprofit projects that turned his retirement into multiple episodes of re-careering, and family trips that included a heavy dose of education for his and Mary's children and grandchildren, Bill Price relied on his family to see him through the dark times and celebrate the bright ones. He and Mary, together with their extended family, celebrated their fiftieth wedding anniversary in 2020, the year before this book went to press—as clear a sign of a happy and fruitful union as you are likely to find.

I touched on those special bonds when I interviewed his then-eight-year-old granddaughter, Isabelle, in a venue that had become familiar in writing this book—Price's home office, where family photos, scrapbooks, boxes of videos and audiotapes, courtroom records, and bookshelves groaning under weighty tomes that he devoured at the rate of two or three per week always made me feel in the presence of something extraordinary.

I was not surprised when Isabelle started talking about family trips. Somewhere between the dragon rollercoaster and pirate ship at Legoland, I decided what I wanted to ask her.

"If you were going to have a whole page in this book that I am going to write about your Papa, what would I put in there?"

Isabelle's brow furrowed.

"Hmm..."

I glanced at my recording device, as I often did when I wanted to make sure it was lit up.

"He likes reading," came her reply. "He has lots of binders."[10]

Yes, Isabelle, he does—enough to fill a lifetime.

Endnotes

CHAPTER ONE: STAKING A CLAIM

1 Alvin O. Turner, "Cherokee Outlet Opening," *Encyclopedia of Oklahoma History and Culture*, Oklahoma Historical Society, https://www.okhistory.org/publications/enc/entry.php?entry=CH021.

2 James L. Brown, "Early and Important Litigations," *Sturm's Oklahoma* magazine 8, no. 2 (April 1909): 26–30.

3 Bill Price, email to author, December 28, 2020.

4 William S. "Bill" Price, interview by author, October 19, 2018, Michael J. Hightower Oral History Collection, Research Division, Oklahoma Historical Society, Oklahoma City (cited hereafter as Hightower Oral History Collection). Unless otherwise noted, the author conducted and transcribed all oral history interviews. *See also* William S. "Bill" Price, unpublished autobiography, William S. "Bill" Price Archives, Oklahoma City (cited hereafter as Price Archives).

5 Bill Price, interviews, October 19, 2018, April 19, 2019; Steve Foerster, interview by author, April 18, 2019, Oklahoma City, Hightower Oral History Collection; Price, unpublished autobiography. *See also* Richard L. Randolph, Jr., "The Golden Boy: William S. Price, United States Attorney, Western District of Oklahoma" (unpublished paper for 20th Century American Biography, University of Central Oklahoma, fall semester, 1991), Price Archives.

6 Virginia Price Giles, n.d., Price Archives; Price, unpublished autobiography; Bill Price, interviews, October 19, 2018, April 19, 2019; Randolph, "Golden Boy."

7 William S. "Bill" Price, curriculum vitae, Price Archives; Bill Price, interviews, October 19, 2018, April 19, 2019.

8 Bill Price, interview, October 25, 2018; Price, unpublished autobiography; Randolph, "Golden Boy"; Bill Price, email to author, June 15, 2020; Kelsey Walters, phone interview by author, June 19, 2020, Charlottesville and Oklahoma City, Hightower Oral History Collection.

9 Price, curriculum vitae; Price, unpublished autobiography; Bill Price, interview, October 25, 2018; Anne O'Connor, phone interview by author, June 12, 2020, Charlottesville and Las Vegas, Hightower Oral History Collection.

10 Bill Price, interview, October 19, 2018; Bill Price, email to author, June 15, 2020.

11 Richard Grant, "Rebellion in Seminole County," *Smithsonian* 50, no. 6 (October 2019): 54–65; Michael J. Hightower, *Banking in Oklahoma, 1907–2000* (Norman: University of Oklahoma Press, 2014), 48–49, 123. For thorough accounts of Oklahoma as a stronghold of socialism during the World War I era, *see* Garin Burbank, *When Farmers Voted Red: The Gospel of Socialism in the Oklahoma Countryside, 1910-1924* (Westport, Conn.: Greenwood Press, 1976) and James R. Green, *Grass-Roots Socialism: Radical Movements in the Southwest, 1895-1943* (Baton Rouge and London: Louisiana State University Press, 1978).

12 Price, unpublished autobiography; Bill Price, interview, October 19, 2018. For a revealing look at Oklahoma politics at midcentury, *see* Marshall Snipes and Bob Burke, *Al Snipes: Fighter, Founder, and Father* (Oklahoma City: Oklahoma Heritage Association, 2006), 114–15.

1 Bill Price, interviews, October 19, 2018, February 1, 2019; Bill Price, email to author, June 15, 2020. William S. "Bill" Price, video interview 1 by James Price, n.d., Oklahoma City, Price Archives (cited hereafter as James Price, video interviews). Video recordings are filed in Price Archives. Audio recordings and transcripts are filed in Hightower Oral History Collection.

2 National Teen Age Republicans, https://teenagerepublicans.org/about/; "Teen Age Republicans," Wikipedia, last modified December 5, 2020, https://en.wikipedia.org/wiki/Teen_Age_Republicans.

3 Tom Daxon, interview by author, April 16, 2019, Oklahoma City, Hightower Oral History Collection.

4 Bill Price, interview, October 19, 2018; Bill Price, James Price, video interview 2.

5 Price, curriculum vitae.

6 Bill Price, James Price, video interview 2.

7 Bill Price, interview, October 19, 2018; Bill Price, James Price, video interview 2; Bill Price, email to author, June 15, 2020.

8 Bill Price, interview, October 25, 2018; Bill Price, James Price, video interview 1.

9 Mickey Edwards, quoted in Snipes and Burke, *Al Snipes*, 11. Mary Fallin, quoted in Snipes and Burke, *Al Snipes*, 127.

10 Snipes and Burke, *Al Snipes*, 111–25.

11 Snipes and Burke, *Al Snipes*, 108–09. Snipes, quoted in Snipes and Burke, *Al Snipes*, 130.

12 Billy Joe Davis, "Edmondson, James Howard," *Encyclopedia of Oklahoma History and Culture*, Oklahoma Historical Society, https://www.okhistory.org/publications/enc/entry.php?entry=ED005.

13 Bill Price, James Price, video interview 1; Bill Price, email to author, June 15, 2020.

14 Carolyn G. Hanneman, "Bellmon, Henry Louis," *Encyclopedia of Oklahoma History and Culture*, Oklahoma Historical Society, https://www.okhistory.org/publications/enc.php?entry=BE012. For a complete biography of Henry Bellmon, *see* Henry Bellmon and Pat Bellmon, *The Life and Times of Henry Bellmon* (Tulsa: Council Oak Books, 1992).

15 Bellmon, quoted in Snipes and Burke, *Al Snipes*, 128.

16 Price, curriculum vitae.

17 Snipes and Burke, *Al Snipes*, 170–72; Bill Price, interview, October 19, 2018; Bill Price, James Price, video interview 1.

18 Bellmon and Bellmon, *Life and Times*, 202.

19 Snipes and Burke, *Al Snipes*, 134–35, 170–79.

20 Bill Price, interview, October 19, 2018; Bill Price, James Price, video interview 1.

21 Bill Price, interview, October 19, 2018; Bill Price, James Price, video interview 1.

22 Snipes and Burke, *Al Snipes*, 170–79.

23 Bellmon, quoted in Snipes and Burke, *Al Snipes*, 178; Bill Price, interview, October 19, 2018; Bill Price, James Price, video interview 1; Bellmon and Bellmon, *Life and Times*, 204–05. For more background on Al Snipes, *see*

Obituary for Al M. Snipes Jr., Vondel L. Smith, accessed January 3, 2021, https://vondelsmithmortuary.com/book-of-memories/3384586/snipes-al/obituary.php.

24 Bill Price, interview, October 25, 2018; Bill Price, James Price, video interview 3; Bill Price, email to author, June 15, 2020.

25 Bill Price, interview, October 25, 2018; Bill Price, James Price, video interview 3; Bill Price, email to author, June 15, 2020.; "Bud Wilkinson," Wikipedia, last modified December 16, 2020, https://en.wikipedia.org/wiki/Bud_Wilkinson.

26 Bill Price, interview, October 25, 2018.

27 Bill Price, interview, October 25, 2018; Bill Price, James Price, video interview 3.

28 "G. T. Blankenship," Wikipedia, last modified November 14, 2019, https://en.wikipedia.org/wiki/G._T._Blankenship.

29 Price, curriculum vitae.

30 Bill Price, interview, October 19, 2018; Bill Price, email to author, June 15, 2020.

31 Bill Price, interview, October 19, 2018; Bill Price, James Price, video interview 1.

CHAPTER THREE: TAINTED JUDGES

1 Bill Price, James Price, video interview 1.

2 Danney Goble, *Progressive Oklahoma* (Norman: University of Oklahoma Press, 1980), 78; Michael J. Hightower, *Banking in Oklahoma before Statehood* (Norman: University of Oklahoma Press, 2013), 311–15. For a deep dive into other crimes against Native Americans, *see* David Grann, *Killers of the Flower Moon: The Osage Murders and the Birth of the FBI* (New York: Doubleday, 2017). In shocking detail, Grann describes how Osages were routinely murdered for their headrights in northeastern Oklahoma's vast oil deposits. Perpetrators were duplicitous whites who did not think that Indian lives mattered, and they committed their atrocities with the complicity of local law enforcement.

3 Marc F. Conley, "History—Made in Oklahoma," *The Oklahoma Bar Journal* 65, no. 47 (December 10, 1994), 3999; Oklahoma Supreme Court, Vertical Files, Research Division, Oklahoma Historical Society, Oklahoma City (cited hereafter as OHS Vertical Files).

4 Orrin W. Johnson and Laura Johnson Urbis, "Judicial Selection in Texas: A Gathering Storm? Part 2, Historical Background" *Texas Tech Law Review* 23 (1992), 529–35; Oklahoma Supreme Court, OHS Vertical Files.

5 Bill Price, interview, October 19, 2018; Bill Price, James Price, video interview 1; Bill Price, email to author, June 15, 2020.

6 Harry Holloway with Frank S. Meyers, *Bad Times for Good Ol' Boys: The Oklahoma County Commissioner Scandal* (Norman: University of Oklahoma Press, 1993), 60.

7 James R. Scales and Danney Goble, *Oklahoma Politics: A History* (Norman: University of Oklahoma Press, 1982), 43.

8 Holloway, *Bad Times for Good Ol' Boys*, 60–61. *See also* Scales and Goble, *Oklahoma Politics*, 49; Michael J. Hightower, *Banking in Oklahoma, 1907–2000*, 26–29; Fred L. Wenner, "How the Capital was Moved from Guthrie," n.d., folder

5, box 4, in Fred L. Wenner Collection, University of Oklahoma Western History Collections, Norman; "Czar Charles Issues his Imperial Ukase at New State Capital," *Oklahoma State Capital*, June 14, 1910; Mrs. A. S. Heaney, interview by Harry M. Dreyer, March 5, 1937, vol. 41, in Indian-Pioneer Papers, in Western History Collections, University of Oklahoma, Norman, http://digital.libraries. ou.edu/whc/pioneer/, 15.

9 Larry O'Dell, "Robertson, James Brooks Ayers," *Encyclopedia of Oklahoma History and Culture*, Oklahoma Historical Society, https://www.okhistory.org/ publications/enc/entry.php?entry=RO006.

10 "Walton 'Makes Good' on Promise to Give People Great Party," *Daily Oklahoman*, January 10, 1923. Walton served as mayor of Oklahoma City from April 7, 1919, to January 9, 1923. *See* City of Oklahoma City Previous Mayors, http://www.okc.gov/council/mayor/previous.html.

11 Charles Francis Colcord, *The Autobiography of Charles Francis Colcord, 1859–1934* (Tulsa: privately printed, 1970), 217.

12 William Warren Rogers, "'I Want You All to Come': John C. Walton and America's Greatest Barbecue," *Chronicles of Oklahoma* 75, no. 1 (Spring 1997): 20–31.

13 Under the headline "Jack Walton's People's Party," the *New York Times* published an account of the great barbecue on January 10, 1923. The story was reproduced in its entirety by *Harlow's Weekly*, the *Tulsa Tribune*, and the *Okmulgee Times*. *See* "In the Trail of the Barbecue," *Harlow's Weekly*, January 20, 1923.

14 Colcord, *Autobiography*, 218; Rogers, "'I Want You All to Come'," 30; "Controversy Nothing New to Governor's Office," *Oklahoma Gazette*, July 10, 1991; Governors, Walters, David (Governor), OHS Vertical Files; Hightower, *Banking in Oklahoma, 1907–2000*, 65–67; Larry O'Dell, "Walton, John Calloway," *Encyclopedia of Oklahoma History and Culture*, Oklahoma Historical Society, https://www. okhistory.org/publications/enc/entry.php?entry=WA014.

15 "Controversy Nothing New to Governor's Office."

16 "Controversy Nothing New to Governor's Office"; Linda D. Wilson, "Trapp, Martin Edwin," *Encyclopedia of Oklahoma History and Culture*, Oklahoma Historical Society, https://www.okhistory.org/publications/enc/entry. php?entry=TR007.

17 "Controversy Nothing New to Governor's Office"; Bob Burke, "Johnston, Henry Simpson," *Encyclopedia of Oklahoma History and Culture*, Oklahoma Historical Society, https://www.okhistory.org/publications/enc/entry. php?entry=JO015.

18 Grann, *Killers of the Flower Moon*.

19 Perceptions of Oklahoma as a haven for outlaws, based in truth but distorted by sensational journalism, dates back to territorial days. *See* "Oklahoma Tired of It," unsourced newspaper article, April 17, 1905, Scrapbook, February 1–July 10, 1905, box 41, vol. 14, p. 59, Frederick Samuel Barde collection, 1890-1916, Research Division, Oklahoma Historical Society, Oklahoma City; Hightower, *Banking in Oklahoma before Statehood*, 197–219.

20 William A. Berry and James Edwin Alexander, *Justice for Sale: The Shocking Scandal of the Oklahoma Supreme Court* (Oklahoma City: Macedon Publishing Co.,

1996), 8; "Pierre Laval Led to Scandal," *Daily Oklahoman*, February 28, 1965.

21 Berry and Alexander, *Justice for Sale*, 10–11; "Two Justices Post Bond on Tax Evasion Charges," *Oklahoma City Times*, April 9, 1964; "Corn Gets 18 Months; Court Payoff Charged," *Oklahoma City Times*, July 1, 1964.

22 Berry and Alexander, *Justice for Sale*, 12; "Bellmon Seeks Probe of 'Court Corruption'," *Daily Oklahoman*, July 2, 1964.

23 Berry and Alexander, *Justice for Sale*, 12–17; Conley, "History—Made in Oklahoma"; "Corn Refuses to Answer Any Questions in Welch Trial," *Daily Oklahoman*, October 10, 1964; "Carroll Airs $150,000 Payoff to Justice Corn," *Oklahoma City Times*, October 12, 1964; "Welch Guilty of Tax Evasion," *Daily Oklahoman*, October 20, 1964.

24 Berry and Alexander, *Justice for Sale*, 17–19; "It's a Berry Boycott," *Oklahoma City Times*, January 4, 1965. In 1958, Berry ran for the Oklahoma supreme court in the third judicial district, comprising Alfalfa, Blaine, Canadian, Garfield, Grant, Kingfisher, Logan, and Oklahoma counties. He won the election and was sworn into office on January 12, 1959.

25 Carolyn Berry was the granddaughter of Dr. G. A. Nichols, developer of Nichols Hills, an upscale suburb northwest of Oklahoma City where Bill and Carolyn lived with their two children, Nick and Libby. Bill and Carolyn met in 1945 when he was recuperating at the naval hospital in Norman from ailments incurred when he was a prisoner of war in the Philippines during World War II. Carolyn was a Red Cross volunteer at the hospital. They married in 1946. For the complete story of Berry's naval career, imprisonment, and harrowing brushes with death, *see* William A. Berry and James Edwin Alexander, *Prisoner of the Rising Sun* (Norman: University of Oklahoma Press, 1993).

26 Berry and Alexander, *Justice for Sale*, 6.

27 Berry and Alexander, *Justice for Sale*, 24.

28 Berry and Alexander, *Justice for Sale*, 28–29; "Welch Ouster Probe Asked," *Oklahoma City Times*, January 6, 1965; "House Drags Welch Action," *Oklahoma City Times*, January 18, 1965.

29 Berry and Alexander, *Justice for Sale*, 29.

30 Berry and Alexander, *Justice for Sale*, 32–33; "Blankenship Text Tells 'Sordid, Sickening' Tale," *Oklahoma City Times*, January 21, 1965.

31 Berry and Alexander, *Justice for Sale*, 34; "Blankenship Text Tells 'Sordid, Sickening' Tale."

32 Berry and Alexander, *Justice for Sale*, 34–38; "Blankenship Forces House Committee Inquiry into Possible Bribery," *Daily Oklahoman*, January 22, 1965.

33 Albert McRill, *And Satan Came Also: An Inside Story of a City's Social and Political History*, revised and annotated by Larry Johnson (Oklahoma City: Full Circle Press, 2013), 183, 218–19. McRill served as city manager of Oklahoma City during its formative years. Originating in a series of newspaper columns and originally published in 1955, *And Satan Came Also* is a classic account of Oklahoma City governance from the run of 1889 through cycles of corruption that branded the young city as uniquely prone to dishonest politicians. Logan Billingsley's brother, Sherman, abandoned bootlegging to become the legendary king of New York's café society when he opened the Stork Club, the city's most famous

speakeasy. *See also* Albert McRill, *And Satan Came Also: An Inside Story of a City's Social and Political History* (Oklahoma City: Britton Publishing Co., 1955), 157.

34 Berry and Alexander, *Justice for Sale*, 39–51.

35 Berry and Alexander, *Justice for Sale*, 53, 58; "Justice Johnson Given Deadline on Lie Detector Test," *Daily Oklahoman*, March 10, 1965; "Corn Reaffirms Statement of Court Payoff," *Oklahoma Journal*, March 17, 1965.

36 Berry and Alexander, *Justice for Sale*, 58–65; "Text of Welch's Letter," *Tulsa Tribune*, March 22, 1965; "Confusion Clouds Bid to Impeach Johnson," *Oklahoma City Times*, March 24, 1965.

37 Berry and Alexander, *Justice for Sale*, 80–81; "Accused Justice's Record Tops," *Oklahoma City Times*, January 21, 1965.

38 Berry and Alexander, *Justice for Sale*, 81–87.

39 Berry and Alexander, *Justice for Sale*, 94.

40 "Seven Justices Get Subpoenas," *Daily Oklahoman*, May 29, 1965.

41 For a thorough account of the Senate trial, *see* Berry and Alexander, *Justice for Sale*, 99–112. *See also* "Justice Johnson Ousted," *Daily Oklahoman*, May 14, 1965.

42 Berry and Alexander, *Justice for Sale*, 66–78, 113–30.

CHAPTER FOUR: MR. PRICE GOES TO WASHINGTON

1 Bill Price, interview, October 25, 2018.

2 Bill Price, interview, October 25, 2018; Bill Price, James Price, video interview 2; Dianna Everett, "Keating, Francis Anthony II," *Encyclopedia of Oklahoma History and Culture*, Oklahoma Historical Society, https://www.okhistory.org/publications/enc/entry.php?entry=KE001.

3 Bill Price, interview, October 25, 2018.

4 Bill Price, interview, October 25, 2018; Bill Price, email to author, June 15, 2020; College Republican National Committee, http://www.crnc.org/about/history/; "Andrew Natsios," Wikipedia, last modified December 16, 2020, https://en.wikipedia.org/wiki/Andrew_Natsios; Bill Price, James Price, video interview 3; Price, curriculum vitae.

5 "Paul Manafort," Wikipedia, last modified January 1, 2021, https://en.wikipedia.org/wiki/Paul_Manafort; Bill Price, interview, October 25, 2018.

6 Foerster, interview; Bill Price, interviews, October 25, 2018, February 1, April 19, 2019; Bill Price, email to author, June 15, 2020.

7 Price, curriculum vitae.

8 "Young Republican National Federation," http://yrnf.gop/about/; "Young Republicans," Wikipedia, last modified December 27, 2020, https://en.wikipedia.org/wiki/Young_Republicans; Bill Price, interview, October 25, 2018.

9 Bill Price, interview, October 25, 2018; Bill Price, James Price, video interview 2; Price, curriculum vitae. Serbe was president of the College Democrats when Price was president of the College Republicans.

10 Bill Price, interview, October 25, 2018; "Carroll Quigley," Wikipedia, last modified December 25, 2020, https://en.wikipedia.org/wiki/Carroll_Quigley.

11 Bill Price, interview, October 25, 2018; Frank Keating, interview by author, February 5, 2019, Oklahoma City, Hightower Oral History Collection.

12 Bill Price, interview, October 25, 2018; Bill Price, James Price, video interviews 2, 4.

13 Bill Price, interview, October 25, 2018; Bill Price, email to author, June 15, 2020; Alexandra Clough, "Former Clinton Pal, Palm Beach Attorney, Convicted Felon Dies," *Palm Beach Post,* May 10, 2016, http://realtime.blog.palmbeachpost. com/2016/05/10/former-clinton-pal-convicted-felon-dies/.

14 Bill Price, interview, February 1, 2019; Bill Price, James Price, video interview 4; Bill Price, email to author, June 15, 2020.

15 Bill Price, interview, October 25, 2018; Bill Price, James Price, video interview 3.

16 Bill Price, interview, October 25, 2018; Bill Price, James Price, video interview 3; Bill Price, email to author, June 15, 2020; "Egil Krogh," Wikipedia, last modified August 18, 2020, https://en.wikipedia.org/wiki/Egil_Krogh.

17 Orrin and Urbis, "Judicial Selection in Texas: A Gathering Storm?"

18 Conley, "History—Made in Oklahoma."

19 Mary Price, email to author, October 19, 2020.

20 Mary Price, email to author, October 19, 2020; Bill Price, interviews, October 25, 2018, February 1, 2019; Mary and James Price, interview by author, February 5, 2019, Oklahoma City, Hightower Oral History Collection; Bill Price, emails to author, June 15, November 24, 2020; Immaculata University, https://www. immaculata.edu/about/ University.

21 Price, curriculum vitae.

22 Von R. Creel, "Murrah, Alfred Paul," *Encyclopedia of Oklahoma History and Culture,* Oklahoma Historical Society, https://www.okhistory.org/publications/enc. php?entry=MU010.

23 The Federal Judicial Center, https://www.fjc.gov/about.

24 Bill Price, interview, October 25, 2018; Bill Price, James Price, video interviews 3, 4; Bill Price, email to author, June 15, 2020; Mary Price, email to author, October 19, 2020.

25 Bill Price, interview, October 25, 2018; Bill Price, email to author, June 15, 2020.

CHAPTER FIVE: BEGINNINGS

1 Price, curriculum vitae; Bill Price, James Price, video interview 4.

2 Bill Price, emails to author, December 12, 28, 2020.

3 Bob Burke, "Bartlett, Dewey Follett," *Encyclopedia of Oklahoma History and Culture,* Oklahoma Historical Society, https://www.okhistory.org/publications/ enc.php?entry=BA029; Bob Burke and Eric Dabney, *Gentleman Jurist: The Life of Ralph G. Thompson* (Oklahoma City: Oklahoma Heritage Association, 2011), 90; Dianna Everett, "Inhofe, James Mountain," *Encyclopedia of Oklahoma History and Culture,* Oklahoma Historical Society, https://www.okhistory.org/publications/ enc.php?entry=IN024; Todd J. Kosmerick, "Edwards, Marvin Henry," *Encyclopedia of Oklahoma History and Culture,* Oklahoma Historical Society, https://www. okhistory.org/publications/enc.php?entry=ED010.

4 Bill Price, James Price, video interview 4; Price, curriculum vitae.

5 Cleta Deatherage was married for the second time in 1984 to Dale Mitchell, son of the all-star Brooklyn Dodgers left-fielder Dale Mitchell. After relocating to Washington, D.C. in 1991, Cleta Mitchell, rebranded as a Republican, became a partner in the Washington, D.C. office of Foley and Lardner, LLP, where she represented conservative organizations and politicians. In early 2021, the *Washington Post* identified Mitchell as "a prominent GOP lawyer whose involvement with [President Donald] Trump's efforts had not been previously known." *See* "In extraordinary hour-long phone call, Trump pressures Georgia secretary of state to recalculate the vote in his favor," "'I just want to find 11,780 votes': In extraordinary hour-long call, Trump pressures Georgia secretary of state to recalculate the vote in his favor," *Washington Post*, January 3, 2021. *See also* Cleta Mitchell, Foley & Lardner LLP, www.foley.com; "Cleta Mitchell," Wikipedia, last modified January 12, 2021, https://en.wikipedia.org/wiki/Cleta_Mitchell; Christine Pappas, "Mitchell, Cleta Deatherage," *Encyclopedia of Oklahoma History and Culture*, Oklahoma Historical Society, https://www.okhistory.org/publications/enc. php?entry=MI048. Many years after the debates, Bill Price and Eric Groves were cocounsels on a zoning dispute over an apartment building designed for tenants with mental illnesses. *See* Lawyer Central, https://www.lawyercentral.com/eric-j-groves-interactive-profile--20-543984.html. Price discussed Mitchell and Groves in Bill Price, interview, October 25, 2018; Bill Price, email to author, December 28, 2020.

6 Bill Price, interview, February 1, 2019; Price, curriculum vitae.

7 David Hall, "The Best Year of My Life," *Orbit* magazine, January 2, 1972; Governor David Hall, OHS Vertical Files. *See also* Burkett and McInnis, "Don't Talk about That," unpublished manuscript, n.d.; Governor David Hall, OHS Vertical Files; Bob Burke, "Hall, David," *Encyclopedia of Oklahoma History and Culture*, Oklahoma Historical Society, https://www.okhistory.org/publications/enc. php?entry=HA007.

8 "The Credit-Card Governor," *Time*, February 4, 1974; Governors, Hall, David, OHS Vertical Files. *See also* Burkett and McInnis, "Don't Talk about That"; Burke, "Hall, David"; Burke, "Bartlett, Dewey Follett." Price described Hall's memory aid in a phone interview with author, February 18, 2021.

9 "Rise and Fall of David Hall Top Political Story of 1970s," *Oklahoma City Journal Record*, January 5, 1980; Governors, Hall, David, OHS Vertical Files; Hanneman, "Bellmon, Henry Louis"; Burke, "Bartlett, Dewey Follett."

10 Price, curriculum vitae; Bill Price, interview, February 1, 2019.

11 Price, curriculum vitae; Bill Price, James Price, video interview 4.

12 "Inhofe Campaign Underway," *Oklahoma Republican News* 14, no. 9 (September 1974), Price Archives.

13 "Inhofe Campaign Underway"; "Campaign Ingredients: Coffee, Reform Ideas," *Tulsa World*, April 14, 1974, Price Archives. *See also* Bill Price, James Price, video interview 3; Bill Price, interview, February 1, 2019.

14 Dianna Everett, "McSpadden, Clem Rogers," *Encyclopedia of Oklahoma History and Culture*, Oklahoma Historical Society, https://www.okhistory.org/publications/enc/entry.php?entry=MC040; Bill Price, James Price, video interview 3.

15 Bob Burke, "Boren, David Lyle," *Encyclopedia of Oklahoma History and Culture*,

Oklahoma Historical Society, https://www.okhistory.org/publications/enc/entry.
php?entry=BO018; Bill Price, interview, February 1, 2019.

16 Bill Price, James Price, video interview 3; Bill Price, interview, February 1,
2019; Bill Price, email to author, June 15, 2020.

17 "Campaign Ingredients: Coffee, Reform Ideas."

18 Bill Price, James Price, video interview 3; Bill Price, interview, February 1,
2019.

19 Bill Price, interview, February 1, 2019; Bill Price, email to author, July 10, 2020.

20 Bill Price, James Price, video interview 3; Bill Price, interview, February 1, 2019.

21 "Rise and Fall of David Hall Top Political Story of 1970s."

22 Bill Price, James Price, video interviews 5, 6.

23 "Winters to Defend Himself in Hearing Opening Today," *Daily Oklahoman*,
December 7, 1967.

24 "Winters Probe to Wait Week," *Daily Oklahoman*, December 8, 1967.

25 William R. Burkett and James Edwin Alexander, *The Fall of David Hall*
(Oklahoma City: Macedon Publishing Co., 2000), 1.

26 "U.S. Investigates Leo Winters' Finances," *Daily Oklahoman*, February 9, 1972.

27 "Winters Subpoenas Former Gov. Gary," *Daily Oklahoman*, March 27, 1974;
"Winters, Smith Trial Opens Today," *Shawnee News-Star*, April 2, 1974; Gene
Stipe, interview by Rodger Harris and Larry O'Dell, March 1, 2007, McAlester,
Oklahoma, Oral History Collection, Research Division, Oklahoma Historical
Society, Oklahoma City.

28 "Indictment Against Rainbolt Dismissed, *Shawnee News-Star*, April 5, 1974.

29 "Rainbolt Sheds Indictment, May Testify in Winters Case," *Daily Oklahoman*,
April 5, 1974.

30 "U.S. Drops Case against Winters," *Daily Oklahoman*, June 26, 1974; "Winters
Freed of Charge of Bank Fund Misuse," *Shawnee News-Star*, June 26, 1974; Bill
Price, email to author, June 15, 2020.

31 Jim Bowles, interview by author, April 10, 2012, Shawnee, Oklahoma,
Hightower Oral History Collection.

32 Foerster, interview; Bill Price, interviews, October 19, 2018, April 19, 2019;
Eulogy for Montine Price Sprehe, delivered by Bill Price, dated by hand 2010, Price
Archives.

CHAPTER SIX: THE RISE AND FALL OF DAVID HALL

1 Hall, "The Best Year of My Life"; Burke, "Hall, David"; "Rise and Fall of David
Hall Top Political Story of 1970s"; Bill Price, email to author, June 15, 2020.

2 Burkett and McInnis, "Don't Talk."

3 "The Credit-Card Governor."

4 Burkett and McInnis, "Don't Talk"; Burkett and Alexander, *The Fall of David Hall*,
29.

5 "Prosecutor Recalls Rise, Fall of Former Governor Hall," *Daily Oklahoman*,
June 13, 1991; Governors, Hall, David, OHS Vertical Files; "Effort to Regain Hall
Trust Aired," *Daily Oklahoman*, March 1, 1975; Governor David Hall, OHS Vertical
Files; Burkett and Alexander, *The Fall of David Hall*, 1–6, 29; Burkett and McInnis,

"Don't Talk"; Bill Price, James Price, video interview 4.

6 "Prosecutor Recalls Rise, Fall of Former Governor Hall"; "Probe Discoveries Reportedly Involve Hall Aides," *Sunday Oklahoman*, April 7, 1974; Governor David Hall, OHS Vertical Files.

7 Burkett and McInnis, "Don't Talk"; Burkett and Alexander, *The Fall of David Hall*, 30–31.

8 Burkett and Alexander, *The Fall of David Hall*, 5.

9 Burkett and Alexander, *The Fall of David Hall*, 1–6, 23; "Chandler Bars Burkett, Aides from U.S. Court," *Daily Oklahoman*, March 12, 1974.

10 Bill Price, James Price, video interview 5; Burkett and Alexander, *The Fall of David Hall*, 7–18; Bill Price, email to author, June 15, 2020. *See also* Joseph C. Goulden, *The Benchwarmers: The Private World of the Powerful Federal Judges* (New York: Ballantine Books, 1976).

11 Burkett and McInnis, "Don't Talk"; Bill Price, email to author, June 15, 2020. For a detailed account of the disbarment, *see* Burkett and Alexander, *The Fall of David Hall*, 19–25.

12 "Probe Discoveries Reportedly Involve Hall Aides."

13 "The Governor Reacts," *Daily Oklahoman*, April 26, 1974; Governor David Hall, OHS Vertical Files; Burkett and Alexander, *The Fall of David Hall*, 26–27.

14 "Hall Rips Derryberry, Calls Him 'Turncoat'," *Daily Oklahoman*, April 25, 1974.

15 "Job First, Derryberry Says," *Daily Oklahoman*, April 26, 1974; Governor David Hall, OHS Vertical Files.

16 "Two Hall Probers' Cooperation Close," *Daily Oklahoman*, May 14, 1974; Bill Price, interview, February 1, 2019.

17 "Jobs First, Derryberry Says"; Bill Price, email to author, June 15, 2020.

18 "The Credit-Card Governor."

19 Michael J. Hightower, *Loyal to Oklahoma: The BancFirst Story* (Oklahoma City and Charlottesville: 2 Cities Press, 2015), 103.

20 Burkett and McInnis, "Don't Talk"; Burkett and Alexander, *The Fall of David Hall*, 34–35.

21 "Prosecutor Recalls Rise, Fall of Former Governor Hall"; "Effort to Regain Hall Trust Aired," *Daily Oklahoman*, March 1, 1975; "Extortion Trials of Hall, Winters Similar," *Sunday Oklahoman*, March 2, 1975; "Intrigue Marked End of Hall Inquiry," *Sunday Oklahoman*, January 26, 1975; "Hall, Taylor Convicted," *Daily Oklahoman*, March 15, 1975, all in Governor David Hall, OHS Vertical Files; Bill Price, James Price, video interview 4.

22 Bill Price, interview, April 19, 2019; Bill Price, email to author, June 15, 2020; *United States v. Hoffa* 307 F. Supp. 1129 (E.D. Tenn. 1970), Justia U.S. Law, https://law.justia.com/cases/federal/district-courts/FSupp/307/1129/1428421/. Price elaborated on the significance of *United States v. Hoffa* in a meeting with the author, December 12, 2019.

23 Burkett and Alexander, *The Fall of David Hall*, 52.

24 "Effort to Regain Hall Trust Aired"; "Extortion Trials of Hall, Winters Similar."

25 Bill Price, James Price, video interview 5; Burkett and Alexander, *The Fall of David Hall*, 58.

26 "Extortion Trials of Hall, Winters Similar"; "Intrigue Marked End of Hall Inquiry."

27 "Rise and Fall of David Hall Top Political Story of 1970s"; "Hall Conspiracy Case Goes to Jury Today," *Daily Oklahoman*, March 12, 1975; Governor David Hall, OHS Vertical Files; Burkett and Alexander, *The Fall of David Hall*, 53–61.

CHAPTER SEVEN: ASSISTANT U.S. ATTORNEY, PART ONE

1 Bill Price, interview, February 1, 2019; Bill Price, phone interview, January 15, 2021.

2 Drew Neville, interview by author, February 6, 2019, Oklahoma City; Charlie Waters, interview by author, December 10, 2019, Oklahoma City, both in Hightower Oral History Collection. *See also* Jack LeDrew (Drew) Neville, Jr., curriculum vitae, emailed to author February 7, 2019.

3 Price, curriculum vitae; Bill Price, interview, February 1, 2019; Bill Price, James Price, video interviews 4, 5, 6; Randolph, "Golden Boy."

4 "Effort to Regain Hall Trust Aired"; "Intrigue Marked End of Hall Inquiry."

5 Price curriculum vitae; Randolph, "Golden Boy."

6 Bill Price, interview, February 1, 2019; Bill Price, James Price, video interview 4; Bill Price, email to author, June 15, 2020.

7 Bill Price, interview, February 1, 2019; Bill Price, James Price, video interview 5; Bill Price, email to author, June 15, 2020.

8 Neville, interview; "Prosecutor Recalls Rise, Fall of Former Governor Hall." Price elaborated on Rogers's motivations for cooperating with Burkett's team in a meeting with the author, December 12, 2019.

9 For a thorough account of the summation, *see* Burkett and Alexander, *The Fall of David Hall*, 167–80.

10 James Linn, *Oklahoman*, October 28, 2009, http://legacy.newsok.com/obituaries/oklahoman/obituary.aspx?page=lifestory&pid=135106939; Randy Ellis and Nolan Clay, "After Success-Filled Life, Famed Lawyer James P. Linn Dies at 83," *The Oklahoman*, October 26, 2009, http://newsok.com/article/3412092.

11 "Effort to Regain Hall Trust Aired"; "Extortion Trials of Hall, Winters Similar"; "Hall Conspiracy Case Goes to Jury Today." *See also* "As He Waits, Hall Keeps Jovial, Confident Manner," *Daily Oklahoman*, March 13, 1975; "Jury in Hall Case Retires for Night," *Daily Oklahoman*, March 13, 1975, both in Governor David Hall, OHS Vertical Files; David Hall (Oklahoma Governor): Regarding charges against Hall, federal grand jury, and conviction, n.d., Governor's File, Hall, David, OHS Vertical Files. For a thorough account of the verdict, *see* Burkett and Alexander, *The Fall of David Hall*, 181–92. Price described Linn's and Daugherty's courtroom behavior in an email to the author, June 15, 2020.

12 Holloway, *Bad Times for Good Ol' Boys*, 67–68.

13 Bill Price, James Price, video interviews 5, 6; Bill Price, email to author, June 15, 2020.

14 Neville, interview; Neville, curriculum vitae; Bill Price, email to author, June 15, 2020.

15 Waters, interview.

16 "6-State Operation Alleged," unsourced newspaper article, n.d., Price Archives.

17 Bill Price, interviews, February 1, 5, 2019; Bill Price, emails to author, September 16, 2019, June 15, 2020; Randolph, "Golden Boy."

18 Ralph Thompson, interview by author, February 4, 2019, Oklahoma City, Hightower Oral History Collection. *See also* Burke and Dabney, *Gentleman Jurist*.

19 Thompson, interview.

20 Thompson, interview. *See* Chapter Four, "Mr. Price Goes to Washington," for a brief description of the constitutional amendments that Thompson helped frame.

21 Bill Price, interview, February 1, 2019.

22 Burke and Dabney, *Gentleman Jurist*, 121; Thompson, interview.

23 Keating, interview; Everett, "Keating, Francis Anthony II."

24 Daxon, interview.

25 Randolph, "Golden Boy"; Bill Price, email to author, June 15, 2020.

26 "6 Sooners Arrested in Steel Theft Case," unsourced newspaper article, n.d., Price Archives; Bill Price, interview, February 1, 2019; Randolph, "Golden Boy"; Bill Price, email to author, June 15, 2020.

27 Bill Price, interview, February 11, 2019; Department of Justice news release, November 6, 1975, Price Archives.

28 Bill Price, interview, February 11, 2019.

29 William Marvin Acree, Find a Grave; Obituaries, Acree—W. Marvin, World's Own Service, August 13, 1997, both in Price Archives; Bill Price, email to author, June 15, 2020.

30 Bill Price, interview, February 11, 2019; Bill Price, email to author, June 15, 2020.

31 "Auto Theft Ring Trial Hears Agent," *Daily Oklahoman*, June 17, 1976; United States of America, Plaintiff, v. William Marvin Acree, Robert Brown and Ida Brown, Defendants, No. CR-76-102-D, United States District Court, W. D. Oklahoma, June 16, 1976, both in Price Archives.

32 Bill Price, interview, February 11, 2019.

33 Bill Price, interview, February 5, 2019.

CHAPTER EIGHT: ASSISTANT U.S. ATTORNEY, PART TWO

1 "Rise and Fall of David Hall Top Political Story of 1970s." *See also* "Hall Hearty – And Smiling," *Daily Oklahoman*, May 22, 1978; "Ex-Gov. Hall's Ventures Failing, Deep in Debt," *Tulsa World*, May 21, 1995 (reprinted from the *San Diego Union-Tribune*), both in Governors File, Hall, David, OHS Vertical Files.

2 "Ex-Gov. Hall's Ventures Failing, Deep in Debt."

3 "Rise and Fall of David Hall Top Political Story of 1970s"; "Prosecutor Recalls Rise, Fall of Former Governor Hall."

4 Bill Price, James Price, video interview 5; Bill Price, interview, February 1, 2019; Bill Price, email to author, June 15, 2020; "Defendant in Tax Case Honest, Switzer Testifies," *Daily Oklahoman*, July 20, 1977, Price Archives.

5 Neville, interview.

6 Thompson, interview.

7 Keating, interview.

8 Daxon, interview; "Daxon Makes Enemies in Drive for Reform," *Tulsa Tribune*, October 9, 1981, Price Archives.

9 "Audit Report Uncovered Breeding Ground for State Corruption," *Sunday Oklahoman*, August 2, 1981, Price Archives.

10 Bill Price, interview, February 11, 2019.

11 "State Man Teaches How to Avoid Federal Income Taxes," *Norman Transcript*, June 1, 1977, Price Archives.

12 Bill Price, "County Commissioners Corruption Scandal" (PowerPoint presentation, William J. Holloway Inn of Court, October 17, 2012), Price Archives; Bill Price, interview, February 11, 2019.

13 "Appeals Court Upholds Tax Convictions of Anadarko Man, Wife," unsourced newspaper article, n.d., Price Archives; Bill Price, email to author, June 15, 2020.

14 Bill Price, Eulogy for Robert Allison Price, delivered August 25, 1979, Price Archives; Virginia Price Giles, n.d., Price Archives; Foerster, interview.

15 Price, curriculum vitae.

CHAPTER NINE: OKSCAM – THE INVESTIGATION

1 Daxon, interview. For an overview of the Association of County Commissioners of Oklahoma (ACCO), see the organization's website, https://www.okacco.com/about-acco.html. Daxon could not recall which Pittsburg County commissioner introduced him at the ACCO meeting. For a complete list of state and county officials at the outset of Okscam, *see* 1978 Roster of Oklahoma State and County Officers Elected at the General Election Held November 7, 1978. Together with Hold-over State Officials, Compiled by Lee Slater, Secretary of State Election Board, Oklahoma City, Oklahoma, Price Archives.

2 "Corruption Rocks Oklahoma," *Dallas Morning News*, August 16, 1981, Price Archives.

3 Holloway, *Bad Times for Good Ol' Boys*, 9–10; Johnston Murray, as told to Al Dewlen, "Oklahoma Is in a Mess!" *Saturday Evening Post* 227, No. 44 (April 30, 1955): 20. For a summary of Holloway's analysis of the county commissioner scandal, *see* Harry Holloway, with Frank S. Meyers, "The Oklahoma County Commissioner Scandal: Review, Reform, and the County Lobby," *Oklahoma Politics* (October 1992): 17-34, https://libraries.ok.gov/soonersearch.html, 1196-4415-1-PB.pdf.

4 Holloway, *Bad Times for Good Ol' Boys*, 9–14; "Bad Times Are Here for Good Old Boys Caught in a Dragnet," *Wall Street Journal*, September 22, 1981, Price Archives.

5 "Corruption Rocks Oklahoma."

6 Holloway, *Bad Times for Good Ol' Boys*, 14–15.

7 "Key Figure in County Commissioner Probe Sentenced to 3-Year Prison Term," *Daily Oklahoman*, December 10, 1981.

8 Holloway, *Bad Times for Good Ol' Boys*, 14–18.

9 "Abscam," Wikipedia, last modified December 25, 2020, https://en.wikipedia.org/wiki/Abscam.

10 "U.S. Attorney William S. Price: The Man Who Broke the County Commissioners Case," *Sooner Catholic*, March 13, 1983, Price Archives.

11   Bill Price, interviews, February 1, April 19, 2019, March 9, 2020; Bill Price, James Price, video interviews 6, 7, 8; Randolph, "Golden Boy." *See also* United States District Court for the Western District of Oklahoma: Proceedings before the Grand Jury, Transcript of Testimony of Dale McDaniel, March 5, 1981, Price Archives.

12   "Hogan's Alley (FBI)," Wikipedia, last modified December 25, 2020, https://en.wikipedia.org/wiki/Hogan%27s_Alley_%28FBI%29.

13   "Mapp v. Ohio," Wikipedia, last modified December 18, 2020, https://en.wikipedia.org/wiki/Mapp_v._Ohio.

14   "Miranda v. Arizona," Wikipedia, last modified January 1, 2021, https://en.wikipedia.org/wiki/Miranda_v._Arizona.

15   "Corrupt Crop Being Reaped," *Tulsa World*, July 24, 1981.

16   Hank Gibbons, interview by author, April 17, 2019, Oklahoma City, Hightower Oral History Collection. *See also* United States District Court for the Western District of Oklahoma: Proceedings before the Grand Jury, Transcript of Testimony of Henry Gibbons, February 5, 1981, Price Archives.

17   Hank Gibbons, interview by author, April 17, 2019, Oklahoma City, Hightower Oral History Collection. *See also* United States District Court for the Western District of Oklahoma: Proceedings before the Grand Jury, Transcript of Testimony of Henry Gibbons, February 5, 1981, Price Archives.

18   Bill Price, James Price, video interview 7.

19   Gibbons, interview.

20   Bill Price, James Price, video interview 7; Bill Price, interviews, April 19, 2019, March 9, 2020; Randolph, "Golden Boy."

21   Bill Price, James Price, video interviews 7A, 8; Bill Price, interviews, February 11, April 19, 2019; Randolph, "Golden Boy"; Holloway, *Bad Times for Good Ol' Boys,* 18–19.

22   Gibbons, interview; "Kickbacks Rife in Oklahoma, Probe Reveals," *Los Angeles Times*, October 11, 1981, Price Archives.

23   "Bad Times Are Here for Good Old Boys Caught in a Dragnet."

24   Bill Price, James Price, video interview 7; Bill Price interviews, February 5, April 19, 2019; Holloway, *Bad Times for Good Ol' Boys*, 22–27.

25   Holloway, *Bad Times for Good Ol' Boys*, 18.

26   Memorandum of interview, Dorothy J. Griffin, Principal; Paul M. Elledge, Special Agent; Howard Turner, Revenue Agent; R. Dale McDaniel, Special Agent, February 7, 1980, Farris, Oklahoma, Price Archives.

27   Memorandum of interview, Dorothy J. Griffin, Principal; Thomas C. Kemp, Special Agent; Paul M. Elledge, Special Agent; R. Dale McDaniel, Special Agent, February 8, 1980, Midwest City, Oklahoma; Memorandum of interview, Dorothy J. Griffin, Principal; Thomas C. Kemp, Special Agent; Paul M. Elledge, Special Agent; R. Dale McDaniel, Special Agent, February 9, 1980, Midwest City, Oklahoma. *See also* Dorothy Griffin, 1980 memoranda of interviews and reports by law enforcement, summaries of telephone conversations and handwritten notes, all in Price Archives.

28   Agreement between Dorothy Griffin, Farris, Oklahoma; hereinafter referred to as Griffin and the Federal Bureau of Investigation, of the United States

Department of Justice, United States of America, hereinafter referred to as FBI, April 2, 1980, Price Archives.

29 Bill Price, interviews, February 11, April 19, 2019; Bill Price, James Price, video interviews 7A, 8, 9; Bill Price, email to author, June 15, 2020; Randolph, "Golden Boy"; Holloway, *Bad Times for Good Ol' Boys*, 18. *See also* "Chance Remark Real Jewel in Commissioners Probe," *Tulsa World*, July 26, 1981; "County Corruption Scandal Largest in History," *Norman Transcript*, August 23, 1981; "FBI, IRS Find Key to State Scandal in Barn," *Tulsa Tribune*, October 7, 1981, all in Price Archives. For a list of Griffin's contacts in 1980 and transcripts of her conversations with Opal Hester, *see* Log of Contacts Made by Dorothy Griffin, OC 183-373, 2/20/80 – 9/18/80; Transcription of a recorded telephone conversation between Dorothy Griffin and Opal Hester, OC 183-381, February 20, 1980; Transcript of recorded conversation, Opal Hester – D. Griffin, February 20, 1980; Transcript of a recorded telephone conversation between Dorothy Griffin and Opal Hester, OC 183-381, February 27, 1980; Transcript of recorded conversation, Opal Hester – D. Griffin, March 5, 1980; Transcript of recorded conversation, Opal Hester – D. Griffin, May 15, 1980, all in Price Archives.

30 Holloway, *Bad Times for Good Ol' Boys*, 28; Bill Price, email to author, May 20, 2020.

31 Bill Price, James Price, video interview 6. For many years after Okscam, Price delivered lectures to business and community groups about his immersion in the scandal and the lessons he had learned. *See* "County Commissioners Corruption Scandal" (William J. Holloway Inn of Court, October 17th, 2012), Price Archives.

CHAPTER TEN: OKSCAM — PLEAS AND CONVICTIONS

1 Zephyr Teachout, *Corruption in America: From Benjamin Franklin's Snuff Box to Citizens United* (Cambridge: Harvard University Press, 2014), 196–99, 311.

2 Bill Price, interviews, February 1, April 19, 2019, March 9, 2020; Bill Price, James Price, video interviews 6, 8, 9; Bill Price, email to author, June 15, 2020; Gibbons, interview; Randolph, "Golden Boy"; "Chance Remark Real Jewel in Commissioners Probe," *Tulsa World*, July 26, 1981, Price Archives.

3 Bill Price, interviews, February 1, April 19, 2019, March 9, 2020; Bill Price, James Price, video interviews 6, 8, 9; Gibbons, interview; Bill Price, emails to author, June 15, December 28, 2020; Randolph, "Golden Boy." *See also* Larry D. Patton, United States Attorney, and William S. Price, Assistant U.S. Attorney, to Mr. Guy Moore, September 19, 1980; Guy Moore, 1980–81 contact list; United States District Court for the Western District of Oklahoma: Proceedings before the Grand Jury, Transcript of Testimony of Guy Roy Moore, May 6, 1981; United States District Court for the Western District of Oklahoma: Proceedings before the Grand Jury, Transcript of Testimony of Dorothy June Griffin, May 7, 1981; "Bribery Called Standard Procedure in Oklahoma," *Dallas Times Herald*, February 14, 1982; "Cleaning Up the Counties: Breaks and Bill Price's Persistence Toppled Corrupt Commissioners," *OK Magazine*, April 22, 1984, all in Price Archives.

4 "Daxon Says Only '2 or 3' of 77 Counties Untainted," unsourced newspaper article, n.d., Price Archives; Bill Price, interviews, April 16, 19, 2019; Bill Price, James Price, video interview 7; Bill Price, email to author, June 15, 2020; Daxon, interview.

5 "FBI, Federal Attorneys Honor Honest County Commissioner Young," *Oklahoma City Times*, July 2, 1982; "State's FBI Chief to Quit," *Daily Oklahoman*, December 14, 1983. *See also* Bill Price, interviews, February 5, April 16, 19, 2019; Bill Price, James Price, video interview 7; Randolph, "Golden Boy."

6 Bill Price, interview, March 9, 2020; Bill Price, email to author, June 15, 2020; Bill Price, phone interview with author, February 18, 2021; "County Kickback Scandal Grows," *Tulsa World*, August 1, 1981, Price Archives. U.S. Magistrate Ronald L. Howland issued arrest warrants based on charges filed by FBI agents on April 27, 1981. *See* Press Release, U.S. Department of Justice, Federal Bureau of Investigation, April 28, 1981, Oklahoma City, Oklahoma, Price Archives.

7 Bill Price, email to author, December 28, 2020.

8 Report by Internal Revenue Service special agents Paul M. Elledge, Jr., R. Dale McDaniel, and Joe M. Turner on Donald H. Skipworth, Title 26, U.S.C. 7206 (1); Title 18, U.S.C. 371; 1976, 1977, 1978, April 20, 1981, Price Archives.

9 United States District Court for the Western District of Oklahoma: United States of America v. Donald H. Skipworth, Magistrate's Docket No. 81-45-H, Complaint for Violation of U.S.C. Title 18, Section 1341, Filed April 27, 1981; United States District Court for the Western District of Oklahoma: United States of America, Plaintiff, vs. Donald H. Skipworth, Defendant, No. CR 81-82-E, Government's Response to Pre-Trial Motions, Motion to Dismiss Counts 1 through 23, June 8, 1981; United States District Court for the Western District of Oklahoma: United States of America, Plaintiff, vs. Donald H. Skipworth, Defendant, Case No. CR-81-82-E, Transcript of Proceedings of the Jury Trial Had before the Honorable Luther B. Eubanks, United States District Judge, June 22, 1981, in Oklahoma City, Oklahoma, all in Price Archives. See also Teachout, *Corruption in America*, 311, 199–200.

10 Bill Price, interview, April 19, 2019; Gibbons, interview; Randolph, "Golden Boy." *See also* United States District Court for the Western District of Oklahoma: United States of America, Plaintiff, vs. Donald H. Skipworth, Defendant, CR-81-82-E, Sentencing Had before the Honorable Luther B. Eubanks on July 2, 1981, in Oklahoma City, Oklahoma; "Many Admit Guilt, Resign in County Probes," *Tulsa World*, August 1, 1981; "Commissioner Probe: Guilty Pleas and Resignations," *Ponca City News*, August 2, 1981; "Skipworth's Conviction Upheld by 10th Circuit," *Oklahoma City Journal Record*, January 15, 1983, all in Price Archives. Enacted in 1946, the Hobbs Act criminalized both robbery and extortion. Whereas robbery is the taking of another's property without his or her consent, "traditional" extortion occurs when a person wrongfully uses force, the threat of force, or fear to obtain a recognized property right from another person with that person's consent. *See* Hobbs Act, http://dictionary.sensagent.com/hobbs%20act/en-en/; Interference with Commerce by Extortion, 18 U.S.C. 1951, Price Archives.

11 "Many Admit Guilt, Resign in County Probes"; "Commissioner Probe: Guilty Pleas and Resignations." *See also* "Corrupt Crop Being Reaped," *Tulsa World*, July 24, 1981; "Legacy of Waste," *Tulsa World*, September 6, 1981; "Prices for Counties' Supplies Dropping," *Tulsa World*, September 6, 1981; "County Commissioner Found Guilty," *Oklahoma City Times*, February 22, 1982; United States District Court for the Western District of Oklahoma: United States of America, Plaintiff,

vs. Orville L. Pratt, Defendant, CR-81-77-E, Excerpts of Testimony Had before the Honorable Luther B. Eubanks on June 4, 1981, in Oklahoma City, Oklahoma, all in Price Archives; Bill Price, interview, April 19, 2019. For a revealing look at a typical conversation between a county commissioner and a materials supplier, *see* Conversation between Guy Moore and Orville Pratt, OC 183-443 1B (8), February 16, 1981, Price Archives.

12 "Republicans Seize Initiative in Oklahoma Scandals," *New York Times*, October 29, 1981; "Richardson Begins Serving Sentence in Federal Prison," *Daily Oklahoman*, December 1, 1981, both in Price Archives; Bill Price, interview, April 19, 2019; Gibbons, interview.

13 "Daxon Makes Enemies in Drive for Reform"; "Audit Report Uncovered Breeding Ground for State Corruption." *See also* "Daxon Can't Vouch for Audit Reports," *Tulsa World*, August 8, 1981; "Counties Must Police Themselves, Daxon Advises," *Daily Oklahoman*, August 21, 1981, both in Price Archives.

14 "Audit Report Uncovered Breeding Ground for State Corruption"; "Commissioner Probe: Guilty Pleas and Resignations"; "Daxon Can't Vouch for Audit Reports."

15 "Probable Scandal Tally Now Put at Above 250," *Saturday Oklahoman & Times*, September 19, 1981, Price Archives.

16 "Pair Appointed to Nigh Panel," *Ponca City News*, August 2, 1981; "Nigh Vows Probe Support," *Tulsa World*, August 13, 1981; "Nigh Aides Meet County Probe Figures to Gather. . . ," *Tulsa World*, August 13, 1981; "Governor Calls Special Session of Legislature," *Daily Oklahoman*, August 27, 1981; "Counties Running Out of Control, Finis Smith Says," *Tulsa World*, September 12, 1981; "Panel Proposes County Changes," *Daily Oklahoman*, October 20, 1981; "Kickback Scandal Costly to Counties," *Tulsa Tribune*, n.d., all in Price Archives. *See also* "Special Elections for Commissioners Cost $117,980," *Daily Oklahoman*, January 3, 1982; Senator Finis W. Smith to Mr. William C. Douce and Mrs. Anna Belle Wiedemann, August 6, 1981, and Engrossed Senate Bill No. 100, March 18, 1981, both in Price Archives.

17 "Daxon Blasts Nigh," *Enid Morning News*, August 26, 1981; "Oklahoma Auditor Harbors Aspirations," *Dallas Morning News*, n.d., both in Price Archives.

18 "Legislators Pass Four Bills on County-Scandal Issue," *Tulsa World*, September 3, 1981, Price Archives.

19 "Prosecutor Says Probe to Net 200," *Oklahoma City Times*, August 27, 1981; "List Could Top 200," *Oklahoma City Times*, August 27, 1981, both in Price Archives.

20 "3 Counties Electing New Commissioners Today," *Daily Oklahoman*, December 1, 1981.

21 "Keating 'Ready to Go' on Commissioner Cases," *Tulsa World*, August 30, 1981, Price Archives.

22 "Key Figure in County Commissioner Probe Sentenced to 3-Year Prison Term"; United States District Court for the Western District of Oklahoma: United States of America v. Eston Ruel Fisher, Magistrate's Docket No. 81-39-H, Complaint for Violation of U.S.C. Title 18, Section 1951, Filed April 27, 1981, Price Archives.

23 "Where Graft Reached Epidemic Levels," *U.S. News & World Report*, January 11, 1982, Price Archives.

24 "Six Ex-Commissioners Due to Appear in Court," *Daily Oklahoman*, January

27, 1982; "Low Pay Not to Blame," *Daily Oklahoman*, February 26, 1982; "Federal Grand Jury Indicts 2 in State's Kickback Scandal," *Daily Oklahoman*, February 12, 1982; "County Commissioner Found Guilty"; Bill Price, email to author, June 15, 2020.

25 "Corruption Rocks Oklahoma," *Dallas Morning News*, August 16, 1981, Price Archives.

26 "County Government Makes Graft Easy, Critics Say," *Tulsa World*, July 13, 1981, Price Archives.

27 "Citizens, Law Enforcement on Losing Side of Crime War, Top FBI Man Says," *Daily Oklahoman*, March 3, 1982.

28 "Doonesbury Strip Hits Home," *Saturday Oklahoman & Times*, October 31, 1981; "A Bit of Comic Relief Creeping into Scandal," *Saturday Oklahoman & Times*, October 31, 1981, both in Price Archives.

29 "Price Nominated for Attorney Post," *El Reno Daily Tribune*, April 7, 1982, Price Archives.

30 "Price Nominated for Attorney Post"; Todd J. Kosmerick, "Edwards, Marvin Henry," *Encyclopedia of Oklahoma History and Culture*, Oklahoma Historical Society, https://www.okhistory.org/publications/enc.php?entry=ED010.

31 Mickey Edwards, Member of Congress, to Mr. Bill Price, Assistant U.S. Attorney, November 17, 1981, Price Archives.

32 The White House, Office of the Press Secretary, press releases, April 8, 12, 1982; Fred F. Fielding, Counsel to the President, to Mr. William S. Price, April 26, 1982; U.S. Senator Strom Thurmond to U.S. Senator David Boren, April 13, 1982, all in Price Archives.

33 "Good-Natured Asst. U.S. Attorney Excited about his Role as Prosecutor," *Sunday Oklahoman*, April 11, 1982, Price Archives.

34 "New U.S. Attorney for Oklahoma's Western District to Be Sworn in Today," *Daily Oklahoman*, May 7, 1982; Bill Price, email to author, June 15, 2020.

35 William S. Price acceptance speech for the office of U.S. Attorney for the Western District of Oklahoma (May 7, 1982), Price Archives; O'Connor, interview.

CHAPTER ELEVEN: TOP JOB, PART ONE

1 "Payoffs as High as an Elephant's Eye," *Newsweek*, September 21, 1981, Price Archives.

2 "Oklahoma!" *Time*, October 12, 1981; "Bad Times Are Here for Good Old Boys Caught in a Dragnet," *Wall Street Journal*, September 22, 1981, both in Price Archives.

3 "Kickbacks Rife in Oklahoma, Probe Reveals," *Los Angeles Times*, October 11, 1981; "Oklahoma—The State that Came Unglued," *San Francisco Chronicle*, October 25, 1981, both in Price Archives. Gibson, quoted in "Oklahoma Scandal," *Washington Post*, October 22, 1981, Price Archives.

4 "Ex-Official Talks of Regret, Justification," *Los Angeles Times*, October 11, 1981, Price Archives.

5 "Pittsburg County Commissioner Resigns," *Daily Oklahoman*, August 20, 1981, Price Archives.

6 "Honest Commissioner to Write Book," *Tulsa Tribune*, October 26, 1981; "Crooks Agree Grant County Man One of Few Totally Honest Commissioners," *Tulsa World*, October 27, 1981; "It's Lonely on the Honesty Limb," *Tulsa World*, October 27, 1981, all in Price Archives.

7 "Bad Times Are Here for Good Old Boys Caught in a Dragnet."

8 "Republicans Seize Initiative in Oklahoma Scandals"; "Oklahoma Scandal"; Bill Price, email to author, June 15, 2020; United States District Court for the Western District of Oklahoma: United States of America v. Billie R. Pool, Magistrate's Docket No. 81-41-H, Complaint for Violation of U.S.C. Title 18, Section 1951, Filed April 27, 1981, Price Archives.

9 Bill Price, phone interview with author, February 2, 2021.

10 Waters, interview; Bill Price, interview, April 16, 2019; Bill Price, James Price, interview 9; Bill Price, phone interview, February 6, 2021; Randolph, "Golden Boy."

11 Keating, interview; Everett, "Keating, Francis Anthony II."

12 Neville, interview; "Federal Agents Called Key to Probe," unsourced newspaper article, October 15, 1982; "Kickback Cases Called Too Much for County Level," *Tulsa World*, October 15, 1982, both in Price Archives.

13 Thompson, interview.

14 "A Clear Choice," *Sunday Oklahoman*, October 10, 1982. *See also* "Daxon a Conservative and 'Proud of It'," *Daily Oklahoman*, August 25, 1982; "Daxon Wants Reagan's Help in Race for Governor," *Daily Oklahoman*, September 3, 1982; "Gov. Nigh, Daxon Spar in Tulsa on Economic Philosophies," *Daily Oklahoman*, October 1, 1982; "'David' Daxon Attempting to Catch Up with 'Goliath' Nigh in Governor's Race," *Sunday Oklahoman*, October 24, 1982.

15 "Daxon Builds Campaign Based on Conservatism," *Sunday Oklahoman*, October 3, 1982; "'David' Daxon Attempting to Catch Up with 'Goliath' Nigh in Governor's Race."

16 Steven A. Schneider, *The Oil Price Revolution* (Baltimore: Johns Hopkins University Press, 1983), 103. To understand how policies in the 1970s sowed the seeds of America's economic decline, see Judith Stein, *Pivotal Decade: How the United States Traded Factories for Financing in the Seventies* (New Haven: Yale University Press, 2010).

17 Darrell Delamaide, *Debt Shock: The Full Story of the World Debt Crisis* (New York: Doubleday, 1984), 34.

18 Bobby D. Weaver, "Anadarko Basin," *Encyclopedia of Oklahoma History & Culture*, Oklahoma Historical Society, http://digital.library.okstate.edu/encyclopedia/entries/A/AN003.html.

19 Bill Price, interview, April 16, 2019.

20 "The History of Regulation: The Natural Gas Policy Act of 1978," http://www.naturalgas.org/regulation/history.asp#gasact1978.

21 Bill Price, email to author, December 28, 2020.

22 Phillip L. Zweig, *Belly Up: The Collapse of the Penn Square Bank* (New York: Crown Publishers, Inc., 1985), 91. Price further explained that the NGPA left natural gas above 15,000 feet under price controls. To sway Democrats in Congress, proponents of the NGPA assured them that very little natural gas was

produced below 15,000 feet. The compromise created a perverse incentive insofar as natural gas that was relatively easy to extract, at shallow depths, was stuck at low prices while natural gas that was the hardest to extract would rise to whatever prices the market would bear. Bill Price, email to author, June 15, 2020.

23 For an expanded account of the rise and fall of Penn Square Bank and Robert A. Hefner III's key role in unleashing the potential of deep gas in the Anadarko Basin, *see* Michael J. Hightower, *Banking in Oklahoma, 1907–2000*, 191–253. *See also* Hightower, *Loyal to Oklahoma: The BancFirst Story*, 56–58, 63–70, 73, 76–78, 162. Articles by the same author include "Penn Square: The Shopping Center Bank that Shook the World, Part 1 – Boom," *Chronicles of Oklahoma* 90, no. 1 (Spring 2012): 68–99; "Penn Square: The Shopping Center Bank that Shook the World, Part 2 – Bust," *Chronicles of Oklahoma* 90, no. 2 (Summer 2012): 204–36. *See also* "The Rise and Fall of Oklahoma City's Penn Square Bank," *Daily Oklahoman*, August 1, 1982, box 10, Phillip L. Zweig Penn Square Bank Collection, Research Division, Oklahoma Historical Society, Oklahoma City (cited hereafter as Zweig Collection); Jack T. Conn, *One Man in his Time*, ed. by Odie B. Faulk (Oklahoma City: Western Heritage Books, Inc., 1979), 481.

24 Mark Singer, *Funny Money* (New York: Alfred A. Knopf, 1985), 13–20.

25 "The Rise and Fall of Oklahoma City's Penn Square Bank."

26 Singer, *Funny Money*, 59–53; Roy Rowan, "The Swinger Who Broke Penn Square Bank," *Fortune*, August 1982, 122–23, box 4, Zweig Collection.

27 Bill Price, interview, April 16, 2019.

28 Bill Price, interview, April 16, 2019.

29 Carlisle Mabrey III, interview by author, October 24, 2011, Bixby, Oklahoma, Hightower Oral History Collection.

30 Bob McCormack, interview by author, June 22, 2011, Duncan, Oklahoma, Hightower Oral History Collection.

31 Bill Price, interview, April 16, 2019.

32 Zweig, *Belly Up*, 118–22.

33 Zweig, *Belly Up*, 268–69; Hightower, *Banking in Oklahoma, 1907–2000*, 226.

34 Steve Plunk, interview by author, August 3, 2012, Oklahoma City, Hightower Oral History Collection; "Penn Bank Was Victim of Oil Boom It Created," *Sunday Oklahoman*, July 3, 1983.

35 Plunk, interview; Zweig, *Belly Up*, 404. For decades thereafter, Steve Plunk carried a transcript of the closing script in his briefcase as a talisman of an event that shook Oklahoma banking to its core.

36 "More than 340 Possible Violations Involving Penn Square Bank Discovered," *Daily Oklahoman*, July 1, 1983; Bill Price, email to author, June 15, 2020.

37 Bill Price, interview, April 16, 2019.

38 "Ex-Bank Official Conducted More than 'Horse-Tradin'," Investigators Say," *Sunday Oklahoman*, June 12, 1983.

39 "Penn Bank Exec Guilty," *Oklahoma City Times*, January 12, 1984, box 8, Zweig Collection; Hightower, *Banking in Oklahoma, 1907–2000*, 247.

40 "Penn Square Bank Official Indicted," *Daily Oklahoman*, July 18, 1984, box 12, Zweig Collection.

41 "Jury to Decide if Former Penn Banker 'Master of Deceit' or Victim of Plot,'"
Daily Oklahoman, September 11, 1984, Banks and Banking, OHS Vertical Files.

42 Bill Price, interview, April 16, 2019; Gibbons, interview.

43 Bill Price, interview, April 16, 2019; Bill Price, email to author, June 15, 2020;
"Patterson Acquitted; Chicago Charges Filed," *Daily Oklahoman*, September 28,
1984, Banks and Banking, OHS Vertical Files.

44 "Other States Follow Oklahoma Lead in Probing Corruption," *Sunday
Oklahoman*, October 25, 1981, Price Archives.

CHAPTER TWELVE: TOP JOB, PART TWO

1 "State Senator Accused Again," *Daily Oklahoman*, May 8, 1982.

2 "10,000 Payoffs Made, Salesman Says in Murray County Commissioner's Trial,"
Daily Oklahoman, June 11, 1982. *See also* Transcript of a Telephone Conversation
between Gary Ledford and Cotton Irwin, OC 183D-352 1B (22), April 3, 1981, Lawton,
Oklahoma; Transcription of a Conversation between Franklin Shaw and E. L. Irwin,
OC 183D-357 1B (9), December 21, 1979, Meeker, Oklahoma, both in Price Archives.

3 "Suppliers, Former Commissioner to Be Arraigned," *Daily Oklahoman*, July 20,
1982.

4 "Corruption Investigation Heats Up Again," *Ponca City News*, August 29, 1982,
Price Archives; Bill Price, email to author, June 15, 2020.

5 "6 County Commissioners Given Prison Sentences," *Daily Oklahoman*, September
3, 1982.

6 "Skipworth's Conviction Upheld by 10th Circuit." For a revealing look at a typical
conversation between materials suppliers, *see* Conversation between Guy Moore and
Dick Irwin, OC 183-509 1B (3), January 14, 1981, Price Archives.

7 "Ending Kickbacks Brought Huge Taxpayer Savings," *Sunday Oklahoman*, January
12, 1986.

8 Randolph, "Golden Boy"; O'Connor, interview.

9 "New Purchasing Rules Cause Confusion for Commissioners," *Daily Oklahoman*,
January 14, 1983. *See also* "County Reforms Saving Millions, Director Says,"
unsourced newspaper article, n.d.; House of Representatives, House Bill No. 1518,
January 14, 1982; State of Oklahoma, 38th Legislature (1981-1982), House Bill No.
1578, January 6, 1982; State of Oklahoma, 38th Legislature (1981-1982), Conference
Committee Substitute for Engrossed House Bill No. 1578, April 23, 1982, all in Price
Archives. Price discussed his aversion to paperwork and insistence on structural
reform in a phone interview, February 6, 2021.

10 "U.S. Attorney William S. Price: The Man Who Broke the County Commissioners
Case," *Sooner Catholic*, March 13, 1983, Price Archives.

11 "Ending Kickbacks Brought Huge Taxpayer Savings."

12 "County Reforms Saving Millions, Director Says."

13 "Toll 230 as Book Closes on County Commissioner Scandal," *Oklahoma
City Times*, February 3, 1984. *See also* "Toll 230 as Book Closes on County
Commissioner Scandal," *Sunday Oklahoman*, February 19, 1984; "Kickback
Scandal Investigation Finished, Official Says," *Tulsa World*, February 3, 1984, both
in Price Archives.

14 O'Connor, interview.

15 Bill Price, interview, February 11, April 19, 2019; Bill Price, email to author, June 15, 2020; Waters, interview; O'Connor, interview.

16 "Charges Signal End to Probe of County Kickback Scandal," *Daily Oklahoman*, November 9, 1984, Price Archives; Price, curriculum vitae.

17 "Oklahoma's Continuing Shame," *Sunday Oklahoman*, December 18, 1983, Price Archives. *See also* "Denman Case Proves Point," unsourced newspaper article, June 17, 1984, Price Archives.

18 "Cleaning Up the Counties"; "Recovering Kickback Loot," *Sunday Oklahoman*, June 24, 1984, Price Archives. *See also* "Players in the Kickback Scandal Now Picking Up the Pieces," *Sunday Oklahoman*, January 12, 1986; Bill Price, email to author, December 28, 2020; Bill Price, phone interview with author, February 18, 2021.

19 "Recovering Kickback Loot"; "Pushing Kickback Cases," unsourced newspaper article, May __, 1984, Price Archives; Bill Price, email to author, June 15, 2020.

20 Bill Price, interviews, February 5, 11, April 16, 19, 2019; Bill Price, James Price, video interviews 7, 9.

21 "Kickback Witness Still Gets Threats," unsourced newspaper article, n.d., Price Archives.

22 Bill Price interviews, February 5, 11, April 16, 19, 2019; Bill Price, James Price, video interviews 7, 9.

23 Bill Price, email to author, December 13, 2020.

24 Bill Price, interviews, February 5, 11, April 16, 19, 2019; Bill Price, James Price, video interviews 7, 9.

25 Teachout, *Corruption in America*, 46–47.

26 Sarah Chayes, *On Corruption in America: And What Is at Stake* (New York: Alfred A. Knopf, 2020), 22.

27 Holloway, *Bad Times for Good Ol' Boys*, xiii. For a colorful account of Okscam, see Martin Hauan, *Legal Graft, Illegal Graft & Just Plain Stealin'* (Oklahoma City: Midwest Political Publications, 1992). In a multi-faceted career that took him from Oklahoma to Washington, D.C., Hauan reported for newspapers, radio, and television. He was appointed as press secretary for Oklahoma governors Johnston Murray and Raymond Gary and served in a variety of positions for local and national political campaigns.

28 "Horse-and-Buggy County Government Languishes," *Tulsa World*, June 30, 1991.

29 "Some Commissioners Still Serving Time," "Let Us Out Now, Jailed Ex-Commissioner Says," "Doing Time Tough for Former Commissioners," *Sunday Oklahoman*, January 12, 1986; United States Court of Appeals, Tenth Circuit: United States of America, Plaintiff-Appellee, v. Bird Lance, Jr., Defendant-Appellant, No. 82-1843, Appeal from the United States District Court for the Eastern District of Oklahoma (D.C. No. 82-4-CR), Filed September 30, 1983, Price Archives.

30 William "Bill" Price, "The Penn Square Bank" (PowerPoint presentation, n.d.), Price Archives.

31 James P. McCollom, *The Continental Affair: The Rise and Fall of the Continental Illinois Bank* (New York: Dodd, Mead & Company, 1987), 282.

32 "U.S. Attorney Welcomed Patterson Guilty Plea," *Daily Oklahoman*, July 1, 1988, Price Archives; Bill Price, email to author, December 28, 2020.

33 "Patterson Sentenced in Penn Bank Fraud," *Daily Oklahoman*, August 31, 1988; "Plea of Guilty Averts Second Penn Bank Trial," *Daily Oklahoman*, July 1, 1988, both in Price Archives.

34 Bill Price, interview, April 16, 2019.

35 Bill Price, interview, April 16, 2019.

36 "Commercial bribery," Wikipedia. Last modified May 3, 2020, https://en.wikipedia.org/wiki/Commercial_bribery.

37 Bill Price, interview, February 5, 2019; Bill Price, James Price, video interview 6.

38 Bill Price, interview, February 5, 11, 2019.

39 Bill Price, interviews, February 5, 11, April 16, 2019; Bill Price, email to author, June 15, 2020; "Payoffs, Kickbacks Common in Oil Field, U.S. Official Says," *Daily Oklahoman*, May 22, 1985.

40 "Testimony Starts in Commercial Kickback Scandal," *Daily Oklahoman*, October 14, 1983; "Former Enid Drilling Firm Executive Convicted of Fraud," *Daily Oklahoman*, October 18, 1983; "Former Drilling Firm Executive Guilty of Accepting Kickbacks," *Daily Oklahoman*, November 18, 1983, all in Price Archives.

41 Linda D. Wilson, "T.G.&Y. Stores," *Encyclopedia of Oklahoma History and Culture*, Oklahoma Historical Society, https://www.okhistory.org/publications/enc/entry.php?entry=TG001.

42 "TG&Y Follows Unusual Course in Filing Bribery Lawsuits," *Sunday Oklahoman*, December 11, 1982, Price Archives; Bill Price, email to author, December 28, 2020.

43 "TG&Y Follows Unusual Course in Filing Bribery Lawsuits." *See also* "Kickback Scandal Hits TG&Y Stores," *Daily Oklahoman*, November 18, 1983; "TG&Y Charts Unusual Course in Lawsuits, Observers Say," unsourced newspaper article, n.d., both in Price Archives.

44 Bill Price, interviews, February 5, 11, 2019; Bill Price, James Price, video interview 6.

45 "Ardmore Firm, Official Charged in Bid-Rigging Indictment," *Daily Oklahoman*, August 22, 1984; "More Construction Firms Named in Bid-Rigging Indictment," *Daily Oklahoman*, August 23, 1984, both in Price Archives.

46 "Ride 'em Cowboys! Get 'em, Federalists! New Anti-Corruption Proposal Has Got 'em Feuding," *Boston Sunday Globe*, March 27, 1988, Price Archives.

47 New Testament, Luke 12:48.

CHAPTER THIRTEEN: FROM WHOM MUCH IS GIVEN, MUCH IS EXPECTED

1 "Others Sucked in as Kingpin's Empire Crumbles," *Sunday Oklahoman*, January 22, 1984; "Turkey-Dope Kingpin Takes Prominent Figures with Him when He Falls," unsourced newspaper article, n.d., both in Price Archives; Bill Price, email to author, September 26, 2019.

2 "City Plane Broker Charged in Scheme to Smuggle Drugs," *NewsOK*, April 8, 1983. *See also* "Drug Smuggler Called to Testify in Conspiracy Trial," *Daily Oklahoman*, May 24, 1983; "Drug Trial Jury Told of Intrigue," *Daily Oklahoman*, May 24, 1983, both in Price Archives.

3   Bill Price, interviews, February 1, 5, April 23, 2019; Thompson, interview.

4   Bill Price, email to author, May 20, 2020.

5   Bill Price, interviews, February 5, April 19, 23, 2019; "Prosecutors Say that a 'Cycle of Fear' Ends with Bowies' Demise," *Black Chronicle*, April 17, 1986, Price Archives.

6   Price, curriculum vitae.

7   Bill Price, interviews, February 5, 11, April 16, 19, 2019; Bill Price, James Price, video interview 7; Bill Price, email to author, June 15, 2020; Comprehensive Crime Control Act, http://criminal-justice.iresearchnet.com/crime/school-violence/the-comprehensive-crime-control-act/; United States Sentencing Commission, https://www.ussc.gov/.

8   "Payoffs, Kickbacks Common in Oil Field, U.S. Official Says"; "Price: 'Top to Bottom' Attack Working," *Oklahoma City Journal Record*, May 22, 1985; "Crime Cost Getting Higher," *Oklahoma Gazette*, June 19, 1985, all in Price Archives. *See also* "Change in Prosecution Cited," *Shawnee News-Star*, January 8, 1986; "Whys of Official Corruption," unsourced newspaper article, n.d., both in Price Archives.

9   "State Alliance Fighting War against Drugs," *Sunday Oklahoman*, January 8, 1989; "William S. Price, President, Oklahoma Alliance against Drugs," *OKC Rotary News*, July 24, 1989, both in Price Archives; Bill Price, email to author, May 20, 2020.

10   O'Connor, interview; O'Connor, email to author, November 27, 2020.

11   Bill Price, interviews, February 5, 8, April 23, 2019.

12   Price, curriculum vitae; Bill Price, email to author, May 20, 2020.

13   "The Race for Governor: See How They Run," *Oklahoma Observer*, February 10, 1985, Price Archives.

14   Bellmon and Bellmon, *Life and Times*, 318.

15   Bellmon and Bellmon, *Life and Times*, 320.

16   Bellmon and Bellmon, *Life and Times*, 322.

17   Waters, interview.

18   Bellmon and Bellmon, *Life and Times*, 323. For Henry Bellmon's account of his brief tenure as acting DHS director, see Bellmon and Bellmon, *Life and Times*, 318–23.

19   Bellmon and Bellmon, *Life and Times*, 323–24.

20   Bellmon and Bellmon, *Life and Times*, 333–75; Hanneman, "Bellmon, Henry Louis."

21   "Grand Jury Indicts Chickasaw Governor," unsourced newspaper article, n.d., Price Archives.

22   "Grand Jury Indicts Chickasaw Governor"; "Chickasaw Governor Indicted by Grand Jury," *Daily Oklahoman*, February 15, 1985; "Ex-Indian Housing Directors Plead Guilty to Mail Fraud," unsourced newspaper article, n.d.; "Tribal Officials Admit Guilt in Kickbacks," *Oklahoma City Journal Record*, n.d.; "Six Plead Guilty to Federal Kickback Charges," unsourced newspaper article, July 4, 1985; "James Enters Innocent Plea to Kickbacks," unsourced newspaper article, n.d.; "Tribe Officials Draw 2-Year Prison Terms," unsourced newspaper article, n.d., all in Price Archives. *See also* "Builder Tells of Indians Taking Bribes," *NewsOK*, February 2, 1989.

23 "Price Hopes Guilty Pleas Send Message to Bogus Parts Dealers," unsourced newspaper article, n.d., Price Archives.

24 Bill Price, email to author, May 20, 2020.

25 "Wasson Guilty of Bank Fraud, Embezzlement," *Daily Oklahoman*, December 16, 1988, Price Archives.

26 Robert Henry, interview by author, August 12, 2019, Oklahoma City, Hightower Oral History Collection.

27 United States of America vs Elvin Leon Hibbs, Jefferson B. Kinney, Jr.; United States District Court for the Western District of Oklahoma; "Southeastern's Former President Indicted," *Daily Oklahoman*, January 13, 1989, both in Price Archives. *See also* Thompson, interview.

28 "Southeastern's Former President Indicted"; "Prosecutors Building Case against Hibbs," *Daily Oklahoman*, June 22, 1989, Price Archives.

29 Henry, interview.

30 "Attorney General Blames Leadership," unsourced newspaper article, n.d., Price Archives.

31 Price, curriculum vitae; Bill Price, interviews, February 8, April 23, 2019; Bill Price, email to author, May 20, 2020.

32 Bill Price, interview, February 5, 2019; Racketeer Influenced and Corrupt Organizations Act (RICO), https://www.nolo.com/legal-encyclopedia/content/rico-act.html; RICO Law and Legal Definition, https://definitions.uslegal.com/r/rico/.

33 "Anti-Racketeer Bill Designed to Reduce State Drug Traffic by Confiscating Proceeds," *Daily Oklahoman*, April 12, 1988; "Senate Oks Racketeer Crackdown," unsourced newspaper article, n.d., both in Price Archives.

34 "Senate Oks Racketeer Crackdown"; "Anti-Racketeering Bill OK'd in House," unsourced newspaper article, March 15, 1988; "Bellmon Signs Bill to Help Fight Organized Crime," unsourced newspaper article, n.d., all in Price Archives; Bill Price, email to author, June 15, 2020.

35 "Grand Jury," Wikipedia, last modified December 20, 2020, https://en.wikipedia.org/wiki/Grand_jury; Grand jury, https://legal-dictionary.thefreedictionary.com/grand+jury. For grand jury guidelines and regulations in Oklahoma, *see* Wyatt Law Office, Oklahoma Criminal Lawyers, https://wyattlaw.com/practice-areas/grand-jury-practice-oklahoma/.

36 "Counties Must Police Themselves, Daxon Advises."

37 Bill Price, email to author, May 20, 2020.

38 "Henry Assembles Task Force to Stem State Drug Traffic," unsourced newspaper article, October 31, 1988, Price Archives.

39 Keating, interview.

40 Henry, interview; Bill Price, interview, October 19, 2018; Bill Price, emails to author, September 16, 2019, December 28, 2020; "Henry Assembles Task Force to Stem State Drug Traffic."

1 George Bush to William S. Price, June 28, 1989, Price Archives; Price, curriculum vitae.

2 William S. Sessions to William S. Price, June 8, 1989, Price Archives.

3 Bush to Price.

4 Bob Anthony, interview by author, February 4, 2019, Oklahoma City, Hightower Oral History Collection; Bill Price, interview, February 5, 2019.

5 Bill Price, interview, February 8, 2019; Bill Price, phone interview with author, February 18, 2021.

6 V. Burns Hargis, President, Oklahoma State University, https://president.okstate. edu/.

7 Bill Price, interview, February 8, 2019.

8 Mary and James Price, interview; Bill Price, interview, February 8, 2019.

9 Mary and James Price, interview; Bill Price, email to author, December 28, 2020; O'Connor, interview; Eileen and Isabelle Everett, interview by author, August 5, 2019, Oklahoma City, Hightower Oral History Collection. The children's birthdates are as follows: Anne Katherine, May 20, 1973; James Edward, March 27, 1976; and Eileen Elizabeth, July 24, 1980. *See* Bill Price, email to author, July 10, 2020.

10 Foerster, interview.

11 Congressman Tom Cole, Serving the 4th District of Oklahoma, https://cole.house. gov/about/full-biography;
Linda D. Wilson, "Cole, Thomas Jeffery," *Encyclopedia of Oklahoma History and Culture*, Oklahoma Historical Society, https://www.okhistory.org/publications/ enc/entry.php?entry=CO084; CHS & Associates, https://chs-inc.com/about/; Kosmerick, "Edwards, Marvin Henry."

12 Bill Price, interview, February 8, 2019.

13 Tom Cole, interview by author, April 24, 2019, Norman, Oklahoma, Hightower Oral History Collection.

14 Cole, interview; Bill Price, interview, February 8, 2019.

15 Bob Burke, "Walters, David Lee," *Encyclopedia of Oklahoma History and Culture*, Oklahoma Historical Society, https://www.okhistory.org/publications/enc/entry. php?entry=WA012. *See also* "The Honorable David Walters, Governor of Oklahoma," *State Almanac, Directory of Oklahoma, 1991-1992*, Oklahoma Department of Libraries; Governors File, Walters, David (Governor); "Controversy and Conflict: Gov. Walters Reflects on the Past Four Years," *Oklahoma Gazette*, December 8, 1994; Governors File, Walters, David (Governor), both in OHS Vertical Files.

16 Walters, interview.

17 Bill Price, interview, February 8, 2019.

18 Cole, interview.

19 Bill Price, interview, February 8, 2019.

20 Cole, interview.

21 Cole, interview.

22 Mary and James Price, interview.

23 Foerster, interview.

24 Mary and James Price, interview; Everett, interview.

25 Foerster, interview.

26 "Anthony Claims Bell Officials Paid Cash Inducement," *Oklahoma City Journal Record*, October 3, 1992; "Anthony Tells of FBI Query, Cash Deals," *Saturday Oklahoman & Times*, October 3, 1992; "Ex-Commissioner Indicted," *Edmond Evening Sun*, June 18, 1993; "Hopkins, Two Others Named in Indictments," *Tulsa World*, June 18, 1993, all in Bob Anthony Archives, Oklahoma City (cited hereafter as Anthony Archives).

27 "Tapes Open Up Closed-Door Deals: Big Utility Firms Caught in Web of Oklahoma Scandal," *Chicago Tribune*, November 25, 1993, Price Archives.

28 "Ex-Executive Denies Illegality by Arkla," *Daily Oklahoman*, June 23, 1993, Anthony Archives.

29 "Lobbyist, Utilities Caught in Scandal," *Amarillo Daily News*, November 27, 1993, Price Archives.

30 Bill Price, interview, February 5, 2019.

31 Bill Price, interview, February 5, 2019.

32 "Anthony Tells of FBI Query, Cash Deals."

33 "Commissioner Retiring Amid Inquiry," *Tulsa World*, May 31, 1991, Anthony Archives.

34 "Oklahoma Official Tells of Inquiry," *Dallas Morning News*, October 3, 1992; "Corporation Commissioner, Cody Graves, Worked for SW Bell as recently as May 1991," *Capitol Hill Beacon*, November 21, 1991; "Graves Won't Hear Part of Bell Case," *Daily Oklahoman*, December 11, 1991, all in Anthony Archives.

35 "Bob Anthony & Co.," *Oklahoma Observer*, August 10, 1991, Anthony Archives.

36 "Anthony Claims Bell Officials Paid Cash Inducement." *See also* "Ellis to Retire from Bell; Roy Set to Take Post," *Oklahoma City Journal Record*, September 16, 1992, Anthony Archives.

37 "Utility Dealings under FBI Scrutiny," *Daily Oklahoman*, August 21, 1992, Anthony Archives.

38 "FBI – Corp. Comm. Probe Includes Wiretaps on Homes," *Oklahoma Political Report*, September 14, 1992; "FBI Taps Phones in Probe Involving Southwestern Bell," *Shawnee News-Star*, September 19, 1992, both in Anthony Archives.

39 Anthony, interview.

40 "FBI Phone Taps Part of Bell Probe," *Tulsa World*, October 14, 1992, Anthony Archives.

41 "Anthony Says FBI Info Bigger than He Said," *Tulsa World*, October 7, 1992. *See also* "B. Anthony, Secret Agent," *Tulsa World*, October 6, 1992, both in Anthony Archives.

42 "Anthony Claims Bell Officials Paid Cash Inducement"; "Oklahoma Official Tells of Inquiry"; "Anthony Tells of FBI Query, Cash Deals." *See also* "Anthony Says He Worked for FBI Corruption Probe," *Tulsa World*, October 3, 1992.

43 United States of America, plaintiff, vs William L. Anderson, Jewel B. Callaham and Robert H. "Bob" Hopkins, Defendants, filed in the United States District Court for the Western District of Oklahoma, June 17, 1993, CR 93-137A, Anthony Archives. *See also* "Ex-Regulator, 2 Others Face Bell Indictments," *Daily*

Oklahoman, June 18, 1993; "Grand Jury Indicts Anderson, Hopkins on Bribery Charges," *Oklahoma City Journal Record*, June 18, 1993; "Utility Scandals Nothing New at Commission," *Sunday Oklahoman*, June 20, 1993, all in Anthony Archives.

44 "Hopkins Enters Not Guilty Plea in Bell Bribery Case," *Oklahoma City Journal Record*, June 22, 1983; "Hopkins Enters Not Guilty Plea at Arraignment," *Tulsa World*, June 22, 1993; "Hopkins Denies Guilt in Bell Bribery Case," *Daily Oklahoman*, June 22, 1993, all in Anthony Archives.

45 Anthony, interview; FBI Presents Bob Anthony with Bureau's Highest Civilian Honor, http://www.bobanthony.com/bob/awards.htm.

46 Anthony, interview.

47 Bill Price, interview, February 5, 2019.

48 Oklahomans against Bribery, http://www.oklahomansagainstbribery.org/.

49 Anthony, interview.

50 State of Oklahoma – Executive Department, Executive Order 91-3, February 4, 1991, Governors File, Walters, David (Governor), OHS Vertical Files.

51 Bob Burke, "Walters, David Lee"; "The Honorable David Walters, Governor of Oklahoma"; "Controversy and Conflict: Gov. Walters Reflects on the Past Four Years."

52 "Controversy and Conflict: Gov. Walters Reflects on the Past Four Years"; "Walters Pleads Guilty: Charges against Governor Listed," *NewsOk*, October 22, 1993. *See also* "Walters, Hopkins Date Subpoenaed," *Tulsa Tribune*, June 5, 1991, Anthony Archives. Price explained straw donors in a phone interview, February 6, 2021.

53 Bill Price, interview, February 8, 2019.

54 "Controversy and Conflict: Gov. Walters Reflects on the Past Four Years."

55 Burke, "Walters, David Lee."

56 "Walters Rips Reports of Fund Investigation," *Tulsa World*, June 9, 1992, Governors File, Walters, David (Governor), OHS Vertical Files.

57 "Controversy and Conflict: Gov. Walters Reflects on the Past Four Years."

58 Burke, "Walters, David Lee"; "Walters' Actions Swayed Political Fate, Loving Says," *Daily Oklahoman*, October 26, 1994, Governors File, Walters, David (Governor), OHS Vertical Files. *See also* "Walters Accuses Loving of Politics in Bell Case," *Tulsa World*, July 23, 1992, Governors File, Walters, David (Governor), OHS Vertical Files; "Oklahoma Has Share of Scandal," *Dallas Morning News*, October 19, 1992, Anthony Archives; "Cleaning House," *Daily Oklahoman*, June 24, 1993, Anthony Archives; "Walters Denies He Broke Law," *Daily Oklahoman*, May 13, 1994, Governors File, Walters, David (Governor), OHS Vertical Files.

59 "Controversy and Conflict: Gov. Walters Reflects on the Past Four Years."

CHAPTER FIFTEEN: PRIVATE PRACTICE, PUBLIC CITIZEN

1 Price, curriculum vitae; Bill Price interview, February 8, 2019.

2 Mary and James Price, interview; Everett, interview.

3 Price, curriculum vitae; Bill Price, interview, February 8, 2019.

4 Kosmerick, "Edwards, Marvin Henry."

5   "House Banking Scandal," Wikipedia, last modified November 3, 2020, https://en.wikipedia.org/wiki/House_banking_scandal; "Mickey Edwards," Wikipedia, last modified November 3, 2020, https://en.wikipedia.org/wiki/Mickey_Edwards.

6   Bill Price interview, February 8, 2019.

7   Dianna Everett, "Istook, Ernest James, Jr.," *Encyclopedia of Oklahoma History and Culture*, Oklahoma Historical Society, https://www.okhistory.org/publications/enc/entry.php?entry=IS001.

8   Bill Price, interview, February 8, 2019.

9   Chip Carter, interview by author, August 8, 2019, Oklahoma City, Hightower Oral History Collection.

10   "The Grace Commission," Wikipedia, last modified April 8, 2020, https://en.wikipedia.org/wiki/The_Grace_Commission.

11   "Bill Price Stresses Unity, Change," *Daily Oklahoman*, September 10, 1992, OHS Section X – Biographies, Price, Bill, OHS Vertical Files.

12   Carter, interview.

13   Bill Price, interview, February 8, 2019.

14   Bill Price, email to author, September 23, 2020.

15   Bill Price, interviews, February 1, 8, 2019.

16   Bill Price, interview, February 11, 2019.

17   Retractable Technologies Inc., https://www.bloomberg.com/profile/company/RVP: US, https://www.bloomberg.com/research/stocks/people/person.asp?personId= 1504318&privcapId=747507; Thomas J. Shaw, Chairman/Pres/CEO/Founder, Retractable Technologies, Inc, https://www.bloomberg.com/profile/person/4148901.

18   Bill Price, interview, February 11, 2019.

19   Marty Makary, *The Price We Pay: What Broke American Health Care—and How to Fix It* (New York: Bloomsbury Publishing, 2019), 205–13.

20   Becton Dickinson, https://www.bd.com/en-us/company; "Becton Dickinson," Wikipedia, last modified December 30, 2020, https://en.wikipedia.org/wiki/Becton_Dickinson.

21   Bill Price, interview, February 11, 2019; "Safe Harbor (law)," Wikipedia, last modified December 28, 2020, https://en.wikipedia.org/wiki/Safe_harbor_(law).

22   Makary, *The Price We Pay*, 213.

23   Matthew Rex Cox, "Coburn, Thomas Allen," *Encyclopedia of Oklahoma History and Culture*, Oklahoma Historical Society, https://www.okhistory.org/publications/enc/entry.php?entry=CO011.

24   Zweig, *Belly Up*; Phillip L. Zweig, "Oklahoma's Penn Square Bank, Maverick Oil Patch Lender: Some Say It's Bet Too Heavily on Energy," *American Banker*, April 26, 1982. See also Hightower, *Banking in Oklahoma, 1907–2000*, 217–53; Hightower, "Penn Square: The Shopping Center Bank that Shook the World, Part 2 – Bust."

25   Phillip L. Zweig and Wendy Zellner, "Locked out of the Hospital: Are Medical Buying Consortiums Squelching Innovation?" *Business Week*, March 16, 1998, Price Archives; Bill Price, interview, February 11, 2019; Bill Price, email to author, December 28, 2020.

26 Bill Price, interviews, October 19, 2018, April 19, 2019; Foerster, interview; Virginia Price Giles, Price Archives.

27 Foerster, interview.

28 Everett, interview.

29 Bill Price, interview, April 23, 2019.

30 Bill Price, emails to author, September 23, 2020, January 26, 2021.

31 Bob Ross, email to author, August 17, 2020; Bill Price, email to author, September 23, 2020.

32 Oklahoma State Department of Education, https://sde.ok.gov/lindsey-nicole-henry-lnh-scholarship-program-children-disabilities; National Conference of State Legislators, https://www.ncsl.org/research/education/school-choice-scholarship-tax-credits.aspx#; Bill Price, email to author, December 28, 2020; Price, curriculum vitae.

33 Price, curriculum vitae; Bill Price, interview, February 11, 2019; Mary and James Price, interview.

34 ChoiceMatters, https://www.edchoicematters.org/.

35 Everett, interview.

36 Mary Price, email to author, October 20, 2020; Bill Price, email to author, December 13, 2020. At the time this book was published in 2021, the children's ages were as follows: Isabelle, 10; Asa, 6; Jax, 7; and William, 1.

37 Kids Across America, https://www.kaakamps.org/mission; Kids Across America, https://www.kaakamps.org/history.

38 Bill Price, interviews, February 5, 11, April 23, 2019; Price, curriculum vitae; Bill Price, email to author, December 28, 2020; Shiloh Camp, http://shilohcamp.org/about/.

39 Stephan Moore, interview by author, December 10, 2019, Oklahoma City, Hightower Oral History Collection; Price, email to author, September 27, 2020.

40 Cristo Rey Oklahoma City, The Inasmuch Foundation Grant Request, Start-Up Costs and Operating Expenses, April 11, 2016.

41 Bill Price, interview, April 23, 2019; Price curriculum vitae.

42 Bill Price, email to author, December 28, 2020; Cristo Rey OKC, https://www.cristoreyokc.org.

43 Carter, interview.

EPILOGUE: THE MAN IN THE ARENA

1 Roosevelt, Theodore, "The Man in the Arena: Citizenship in a Republic," (speech at the Sorbonne, Paris, France, April 23, 1910), http://www.theodore-roosevelt.com/images/research/speeches/maninthearena.pdf.

2 Bill Price, James Price, video interview 5; Bill Price, email to author, June 15, 2020.

3 Chayes, *On Corruption in America*, 18.

4 Bill Price, email to author, December 10, 2020; Bill Price, phone interview, February 6, 2021.

5 Keating, interview.

6 Cole, interview.

7 For the complete story of central Oklahoma's foundation story, see Michael J. Hightower, *1889: The Boomer Movement, the Land Run, and Early Oklahoma City* (Norman: University of Oklahoma Press, 2018).

8 O'Connor, interview.

9 O'Connor, interview.

10 Eileen and Isabelle Everett, interview.

Bibliography

ARCHIVAL, CORPORATE, PERSONAL, AND VERTICAL FILE COLLECTIONS

Bob Anthony Archives, Oklahoma City.

Banks and Banking Vertical Files, Research Division, Oklahoma Historical Society, Oklahoma City.

Frederick Samuel Barde Collection, 1890-1916, Research Division, Oklahoma Historical Society, Oklahoma City.

Governors Vertical Files, Research Division, Oklahoma Historical Society, Oklahoma City.

Governor David Hall Vertical Files, Research Division, Oklahoma Historical Society, Oklahoma City.

Michael J. Hightower Oral History Collection, Research Division, Oklahoma Historical Society, Oklahoma City.

Indian-Pioneer Papers, Western History Collections, University of Oklahoma, Norman, Oklahoma, http://digital.libraries.ou.edu/whc/pioneer/.

Oklahoma Oral History Collection, Research Division, Oklahoma Historical Society, Oklahoma City.

Oklahoma Supreme Court Vertical Files, Research Division, Oklahoma Historical Society, Oklahoma City.

William S. "Bill" Price Archives, Oklahoma City.

Fred L. Wenner Collection, University of Oklahoma Western History Collections, Norman, Oklahoma.

Phillip L. Zweig Penn Square Bank Collection, Research Division, Oklahoma Historical Society, Oklahoma City.

NEWSPAPERS AND MAGAZINES

American Banker	*Daily Oklahoman*
Harlow's Weekly	*NewsOk*
Oklahoma City Times	*Oklahoma Journal*
Oklahoma State Capital	*Shawnee News-Star*
Sunday Oklahoman	*Tulsa Tribune*
Tulsa World	*Washington Post*

BOOKS

Bellmon, Henry, and Pat Bellmon. *The Life and Times of Henry Bellmon*. Tulsa: Council Oak Books, 1992.

Berry, William A., and James Edwin Alexander. *Prisoner of the Rising Sun*. Norman: University of Oklahoma Press, 1993.

_____. *Justice for Sale: The Shocking Scandal of the Oklahoma Supreme Court*. Oklahoma City: Macedon Publishing Co., 1996.

Burbank, Garin. *When Farmers Voted Red: The Gospel of Socialism in the Oklahoma Countryside, 1910–1924*. Westport, Conn.: Greenwood Press, 1976.

Burke, Bob, and Eric Dabney. *Gentleman Jurist: The Life of Ralph G. Thompson*. Oklahoma City: Oklahoma Heritage Association, 2011.

Burkett, William R., and James Edwin Alexander. *The Fall of David Hall*. Oklahoma City: Macedon Publishing Co., 2000.

Chayes, Sarah. *On Corruption in America: And What is At Stake*. New York: Alfred A. Knopf, 2020.

Colcord, Charles Francis. *The Autobiography of Charles Francis Colcord, 1859–1934*. Tulsa: privately printed, 1970.

Conn, Jack T. *One Man in his Time*, ed. by Odie B. Faulk. Oklahoma City: Western Heritage Books, 1979.

Delamaide, Darrell. *Debt Shock: The Full Story of the World Debt Crisis*. New York: Doubleday, 1984.

Goble, Danney. *Progressive Oklahoma*. Norman: University of Oklahoma Press, 1980.

Goulden, Joseph C. *The Benchwarmers: The Private World of the Powerful Federal Judges*. New York: Ballantine Books, 1976.

Grann, David. *Killers of the Flower Moon: The Osage Murders and the Birth of the FBI*. New York: Doubleday, 2017.

Green, James R. *Grass-Roots Socialism: Radical Movements in the Southwest, 1895–1943*. Baton Rouge and London: Louisiana State University Press, 1978.

Hauan, Martin. *Legal Graft, Illegal Graft & Just Plain Stealin'*. Oklahoma City: Midwest Political Publications, 1992.

Hightower, Michael J. *Banking in Oklahoma before Statehood*. Norman: University of Oklahoma Press, 2013.

_____. *Banking in Oklahoma, 1907–2000*. Norman: University of Oklahoma Press, 2014.

_____. *Loyal to Oklahoma: The BancFirst Story*. Oklahoma City and Charlottesville: 2 Cities Press, 2015.

_____. *1889: The Boomer Movement, the Land Run, and Early Oklahoma City*. Norman: University of Oklahoma Press, 2018.

Holloway, Harry, with Frank S. Meyers. *Bad Times for Good Ol' Boys: The Oklahoma County Commissioner Scandal*. Norman: University of Oklahoma Press, 1993.

Makary, Marty. *The Price We Pay: What Broke American Health Care—and How to Fix It*. New York: Bloomsbury Publishing, 2019.

McCollom, James P. *The Continental Affair: The Rise and Fall of the Continental Illinois Bank*. New York: Dodd, Mead & Company, 1987.

McRill, Albert. *And Satan Came Also: An Inside Story of a City's Social and Political History*. Oklahoma City: Britton Publishing Company, 1955.

_____. *And Satan Came Also: An Inside Story of a City's Social and Political History*. Revised and annotated by Larry Johnson. Oklahoma City: Full Circle Press, 2013.

Scales, James R., and Danney Goble. *Oklahoma Politics: A History*. Norman: University of Oklahoma Press, 1982.

Schneider, Steven A. *The Oil Price Revolution*. Baltimore: Johns Hopkins University Press, 1983.

Singer, Mark. *Funny Money*. New York: Alfred A. Knopf, 1985.

Snipes, Marshall, and Bob Burke. *Al Snipes: Fighter, Founder, and Father*. Oklahoma City: Oklahoma Heritage Association, 2006.

Stein, Judith. *Pivotal Decade: How the United States Traded Factories for Financing in the Seventies*. New Haven: Yale University Press, 2010.

Teachout, Zephyr. *Corruption in America: From Benjamin Franklin's Snuff Box to Citizens United*. Cambridge: Harvard University Press, 2014.

Zweig, Phillip L. *Belly Up: The Collapse of the Penn Square Bank*. New York: Crown Publishers, 1985.

"Abscam." Wikipedia. Last modified December 25, 2020. https:// en.wikipedia.org/wiki/Abscam.

"Andrew Natsios." Wikipedia. Last modified December 16, 2020. https://en.wikipedia.org/wiki/Andrew_Natsios.

"Becton Dickinson." Wikipedia. Last modified December 30, 2020. https://en.wikipedia.org/wiki/Becton_Dickinson.

Brown, James L. "Early and Important Litigations." *Sturm's Oklahoma* magazine 8, no. 2 (April 1909): 26-30.

"Bud Wilkinson." Wikipedia. Last modified December 16, 2020. https://en.wikipedia.org/wiki/Bud_Wilkinson.

Burke, Bob. "Bartlett, Dewey Follett." *Encyclopedia of Oklahoma History and Culture.* Oklahoma Historical Society. https://www.okhistory. org/publications/enc.php?entry=BA029.

————. "Boren, David Lyle." *Encyclopedia of Oklahoma History and Culture.* Oklahoma Historical Society. https://www.okhistory.org/ publications/enc/entry.php?entry=BO018.

————. "Hall, David." *Encyclopedia of Oklahoma History and Culture.* Oklahoma Historical Society. https://www.okhistory.org/ publications/enc.php?entry=HA007.

————. "Johnston, Henry Simpson." *Encyclopedia of Oklahoma History and Culture.* Oklahoma Historical Society. https://www. okhistory.org/publications/enc/entry.php?entry=JO015.

————. "Walters, David Lee." *Encyclopedia of Oklahoma History and Culture.* Oklahoma Historical Society. https://www.okhistory. org/publications/enc/entry.php?entry=WA012.

"Carroll Quigley." Wikipedia. Last modified December 25, 2020. https://en.wikipedia.org/wiki/Carroll_Quigley.

"Cleta Mitchell." Wikipedia. Last modified January 12, 2021. https:// en.wikipedia.org/wiki/Cleta_Mitchell.

Clough, Alexandra. "Former Clinton Pal, Palm Beach Attorney, Convicted Felon Dies.*" Palm Beach Post,* May 10, 2016. http:// realtime.blog.palmbeachpost.com/2016/05/10/former-clinton-pal-convicted-felon-dies/.

"Commercial bribery." Wikipedia. Last modified May 3, 2020. https:// en.wikipedia.org/wiki/Commercial_bribery.

Cox, Matthew Rex. "Coburn, Thomas Allen." *Encyclopedia of Oklahoma*

History and Culture. Oklahoma Historical Society. https://www. okhistory.org/publications/enc/entry.php?entry=CO011.

Creel, Von R. "Murrah, Alfred Paul." *Encyclopedia of Oklahoma History and Culture.* Oklahoma Historical Society. https://www.okhistory. org/publications/enc.php?entry=MU010.

Cristo Rey Oklahoma City, The Inasmuch Foundation Grant Request, Start-Up Costs and Operating Expenses, April 11, 2016.

Davis, Billy Joe. "Edmondson, James Howard." *Encyclopedia of Oklahoma History and Culture.* Oklahoma Historical Society. https://www.okhistory.org/publications/enc/entry. php?entry=ED005.

"Egil Krogh." Wikipedia. Last modified August 18, 2020. https:// en.wikipedia.org/wiki/Egil_Krogh.

Ellis, Randy, and Nolan Clay. "After Success-Filled Life, Famed Lawyer James P. Linn Dies at 83." *The Oklahoman,* October 26, 2009. http://newsok.com/article/3412092.

Everett, Dianna. "Inhofe, James Mountain." *Encyclopedia of Oklahoma History and Culture.* Oklahoma Historical Society. https://www. okhistory.org/publications/enc.php?entry=IN024.

_____. "Istook, Ernest James, Jr.," *Encyclopedia of Oklahoma History and Culture.* Oklahoma Historical Society. https://www. okhistory.org/publications/enc/entry.php?entry=IS001.

_____. "Keating, Francis Anthony II." *Encyclopedia of Oklahoma History and Culture.* Oklahoma Historical Society. https://www.okhistory.org/publications/enc/entry. php?entry=KE001.

_____. "McSpadden, Clem Rogers." *Encyclopedia of Oklahoma History and Culture.* Oklahoma Historical Society. https://www.okhistory.org/publications/enc/entry. php?entry=MC040.

"G. T. Blankenship." Wikipedia. Last modified November 14, 2019. https://en.wikipedia.org/wiki/G._T._Blankenship.

"Grace Commission." Wikipedia. Last modified April 8, 2020. https:// en.wikipedia.org/wiki/The_Grace_Commission.

"Grand Jury." Wikipedia. Last modified December 20, 2020. https:// en.wikipedia.org/wiki/Grand_jury.

Grant, Richard. "Rebellion in Seminole County." *Smithsonian* 50, no. 6 (October 2019): 54-65.

Hanneman, Carolyn G. "Bellmon, Henry Louis." *Encyclopedia of Oklahoma History and Culture*. Oklahoma Historical Society. https://www.okhistory.org/publications/enc.php?entry=BE012.

Hightower, Michael J. "Penn Square: The Shopping Center Bank that Shook the World, Part 1 – Boom." *Chronicles of Oklahoma* 90, no. 1 (Spring 2012): 68–99.

—————————. "Penn Square: The Shopping Center Bank that Shook the World, Part 2 – Bust." *Chronicles of Oklahoma* 90, no. 2 (Summer 2012): 204 –36.

"Hogan's Alley (FBI)." Wikipedia. Last modified October 20, 2020. https://en.wikipedia.org/wiki/Hogan%27s_Alley_%28FBI%29.

Holloway, Harry with Frank S. Meyers. "The Oklahoma County Commissioner Scandal: Review, Reform, and the County Lobby." *Oklahoma Politics* (October 1992): 17–34. https://libraries.ok.gov/soonersearch.html, 1196-4415-1-PB.pdf.

"House Banking Scandal." Wikipedia. Last modified November 3, 2020. https://en.wikipedia.org/wiki/House_banking_scandal.

Kosmerick, Todd J. "Edwards, Marvin Henry." *Encyclopedia of Oklahoma History and Culture*. Oklahoma Historical Society. https://www.okhistory.org/publications/enc.php?entry=ED010.

"James Linn." *Oklahoman*, October 28, 2009. http://legacy.newsok.com/obituaries/oklahoman/obituary.aspx?page=lifestory&pid=135106939.

"Mapp v. Ohio." Wikipedia. Last modified December 18, 2020. https://en.wikipedia.org/wiki/Mapp_v._Ohio.

"Mickey Edwards." Wikipedia. Last modified December 31, 2020. https://en.wikipedia.org/wiki/Mickey_Edwards.

"Miranda v. Arizona." Wikipedia. Last modified January 1, 2021. https://en.wikipedia.org/wiki/Miranda_v._Arizona.

Murray, Johnston as told to Al Dewlen. "Oklahoma Is in a Mess!" *Saturday Evening Post* 227, No. 44 (April 30, 1955): 20, 96.

"Obituary for Al M. Snipes Jr." Vondel L. Smith. Accessed January 3, 2021, https://vondelsmithmortuary.com/book-of-memories/3384586/snipes-al/obituary.php.

O'Dell, Larry. "Walton, John Calloway." *Encyclopedia of Oklahoma History and Culture*. Oklahoma Historical Society. https://www.okhistory.org/publications/enc/entry.php?entry=WA014.

_____. "Robertson, James Brooks Ayers." *Encyclopedia of Oklahoma History and Culture*. Oklahoma Historical Society. https://www.okhistory.org/publications/enc/entry.php?entry=RO006.

Pappas, Christine. "Mitchell, Cleta Deatherage." *Encyclopedia of Oklahoma History and Culture*. Oklahoma Historical Society. https://www.okhistory.org/publications/enc.php?entry=MI048.

"Paul Manafort." Wikipedia. Last modified January 1, 2021. https://en.wikipedia.org/wiki/Paul_Manafort.

Rogers, William Warren. "'I Want You All to Come': John C. Walton and America's Greatest Barbecue." *Chronicles of Oklahoma* 75, no. 1 (Spring 1997): 20–31.

"Safe Harbor (law)." Wikipedia. Last modified December 28, 2020. https://en.wikipedia.org/wiki/Safe_harbor_(law).

"Teen Age Republicans." Wikipedia. Last modified December 5, 2020. https://en.wikipedia.org/wiki/Teen_Age_Republicans.

Turner, Alvin O. "Cherokee Outlet Opening." *Encyclopedia of Oklahoma History and Culture*. Oklahoma Historical Society. https://www.okhistory.org/publications/enc/entry.php?entry=CH021.

Weaver, Bobby D. "Anadarko Basin." *Encyclopedia of Oklahoma History & Culture*. Oklahoma Historical Society. http://digital.library.okstate.edu/encyclopedia/entries/A/AN003.html.

Wilson, Linda D. "T.G.&Y. Stores." *Encyclopedia of Oklahoma History and Culture*. Oklahoma Historical Society. https://www.okhistory.org/publications/enc/entry.php?entry=TG001.

_____. "Trapp, Martin Edwin." *Encyclopedia of Oklahoma History and Culture*. Oklahoma Historical Society. https://www.okhistory.org/publications/enc/entry.php?entry=TR007.

_____. "Cole, Thomas Jeffery." *Encyclopedia of Oklahoma History and Culture*. Oklahoma Historical Society. https://www.okhistory.org/publications/enc/entry.php?entry=CO084.

"Young Republicans." Wikipedia. Last modified December 27, 2020. https://en.wikipedia.org/wiki/Young_Republicans.

Zweig, Phillip L. "Oklahoma's Penn Square Bank, Maverick Oil Patch Lender: Some Say It's Bet Too Heavily on Energy." *American Banker*, April 26, 1982.

INTERVIEWS

Bob Anthony, February 4, 2019, Oklahoma City.

Jim Bowles, April 10, 2012, Shawnee, Oklahoma.

Chip Carter, August 8, 2019, Oklahoma City.

Tom Cole, April 24, 2019, Norman, Oklahoma.

Tom Daxon, April 16, 2019, Oklahoma City.

Eileen Everett, August 5, 2019, Oklahoma City.

Isabelle Everett, August 5, 2019, Oklahoma City.

Steve Foerster, April 18, 2019, Oklahoma City.

Hank Gibbons, April 17, 2019, Oklahoma City.

Robert Henry, August 12, 2019, Oklahoma City.

Frank Keating, February 5, 2019, Oklahoma City.

Carlisle Mabrey III, October 24, 2011, Bixby, Oklahoma.

Bob McCormack, June 22, 2011, Duncan, Oklahoma.

Stephan Moore, December 10, 2019, Oklahoma City.

Drew Neville, February 6, 2019, Oklahoma City.

Anne O'Connor, June 12, 2020, Las Vegas and Charlottesville.

Steve Plunk, August 3, 2012, Oklahoma City.

James Price, February 5, 2019, Oklahoma City.

Mary Price, February 5, 2019, Oklahoma City.

William S. "Bill" Price, October 19, 25, 2018; February 1, 5, 8, 11, April 16, 19, 23, 2019; March 9, 2020, Oklahoma City.

William S. "Bill" Price, James Price video interviews, n.d., Oklahoma City.

Bob Ross, email to author, August 17, 2020.

Ralph Thompson, February 4, 2019, Oklahoma City.

Kelsey Walters, June 19, 2020, Oklahoma City and Charlottesville.

Charlie Waters, December 10, 2019, Oklahoma City.

Index

50 Penn Place, 188, 191, 218
50-50s, 196, 208, 400. *See also* Blue-sky deals

A

Abscam (Arab scam), 187, 191, 243
Absentee-ballot fraud, 101-02, 106-07, 279
Absentee Shawnee Housing Authority, 322
Acree, Marvin, 158-60
Act dumb subpoenas, 211
Adair County, Okla., 101-02
Adams, Givens, 121
Adverse childhood experience, 390
AIDS, 375, 378
Air Force, Logistics Command, 323; Office of Special Investigations, 323; One, 339
Albert, Carl, 94
Alfalfa County, Okla., 273, 419n24
Alfred P. Murrah Federal Building, 87
Alito, Joseph, 72
All Souls Episcopal Church, 386
Allard, Lou, 64
Allred, Darwin L. "Bill," 271; Supply Co., 271
Altus, Okla., 225
Amarillo, Tex., 347
American Banker, 378
American Indian Movement, 173
American Party, 95
American-Arab Relations Committee, 187. *See also* Abscam (Arab scam)
Anadarko, Basin, 257-58, 261, 272, 288, 434n23; Okla., 175-76, 193, 220
Anderson, Bill, 334-35, 351-53, 356-58
Anderson, Jack, 174
Andrews Air Force Base, 106
Annunciation Catholic Church, 88-89
Anthony, Billy Ray, 296

Anthony, Bob, 333-35, 350-60, 379
Antitrust, Division of the Dept. of Justice, 296, 377-79; violations, 295, 376-77
Arab oil embargo, 128, 257-59
Ardmore, Okla., 155, 296
Arizona State University, 177
Arkansas Louisiana Gas Company (ARKLA), 352
Army War College, 141
Arnold, Benedict, 125
Articles of Confederation, 3
Asset seizure, 307-08, 311, 329
Assn. of County Commissioners of Oklahoma, 181, 186, 225, 427n1
Atkinson, William P., 35
Atoka County, Okla., 195, 200-01, 248, 283
Atwater, Lee, 73
Atwell, Gordon G., 293
Ayatollah Khomeini, 258-59

B

Bahamas, 88, 91
Baker, Bobby, 26
Baker, W. C., 275
Ballew, Carl, 115-19, 124-27
BancFirst, 129
Bar Harbor, Me., 29
Baresel, Paul, 130
Barresi, Janet, 382
Bartlesville, Okla., 95
Bartlett, Dewey, 92-96, 99, 103-04, 135, 145, 149-51, 174, 381
Beals Advertising Agency, 92, 366
Beaux Arts Ball, 15
Beaver, County, Okla., 25, 327; Okla., 327
Beckerdite, Diana, 147-48; Ernest, 147-48
Becton Dickinson, 376-77

247-48, 273, 276-78, 281-83, 310;
Lumber Co., 195, 211
Group purchasing organizations
(GPOs), 375-79
Groves, Eric, 93, 422n5
Guaranteed Investors Corp., 129, 132
Guevara, Che, 71, 80
Guillory, Gayla, 326
Guthrie, Okla., 48, 51, 385-86

H

Habana Inn, 117-18
Habitat for Humanity, 81, 338
Haldeman, H. R., 93
Hall, David, 98-99, 101, 151;
administration of, 111-20, 122-28; early
career of, 94; gubernatorial campaign
of, 94-95; indictment, trial, conviction,
and imprisonment of, 108, 133, 137-
43, 153, 163-71, 186-90, 236-37, 278,
298, 397-99; investigation of, 128-33;
San Diego, activities in, 163-65, 244;
Jo (David Hall's wife), 94, 141-42, 163;
William "Red" (David Hall's father), 94
Hall, Hugh, 57
Hall, Malcolm, 337-38
Hamilton, Victor, 203-04
Hammons, Mamie, 52
Hanson, Peterson & Tompkins, 135
Harding Junior High School, 149
Hardy, Ed, 126-27
Hargis, Burns, 335-36, 343
Harney, Phil, 122
Harper, Roy W., 55
Harris, Curtis, 58-59
Harris, Michael, 326
Harrison, Mrs., 21-22
Harrod, Jim, 58-59
Hartford Insurance Co., 75
Harvard University, 94, 344, 351, 362
Haskell, Charles N., 47-48, 138
Hastie and Kirschner, P.C., 365, 372
Hayek, Friedrich (author, *The Road to*

Serfdom), 20
Healey, Skip, 337-38
Hearst, newspapers, 48; Patty, 173
Hefner, Robert A. III, 258, 434n23
Heggy, Tom, 148
Helm, Jim, 28
Henkoff, Ronald, 243
Henry, Lloyd H. (Robert Henry's father),
331; Robert H., Law Enforcement
Coordinating Committee,
participation on, 331-32; Law
Enforcement Legislative Committee,
participation on, 328; Leon Eldon
Hibbs investigation, trial, and
conviction, participation in, 325-28;
multicounty grand jury legislation,
support for, 330-32; Oklahoma State
Attorney General, tenure as, 362; SB
127, support for, 329
Hester, Opal, 194, 213, 230
Hibbs, Eldon Leon, 324-27; Max (Eldon
Leon Hibbs's son), 326; Maxine (Eldon
Leon Hibbs's wife), 326; P. O. (Eldon
Leon Hibbs's father), 327
Hightower, Frank, 33
Hill, Neva, 337-38; 346-47
Hiner, Leslie, 383
Hoar, Keith, 246-47, 273
Hobart, Okla., 286
Hobbs Act of 1946, 220-21, 269, 297,
430n10
Hodgins, Champ, 246
Hoffa, Jimmy, 168. See also *United
States v. Hoffa*
Hofmeister, Joy, 382
Hogan's Alley, 188-89
Holden, John "Jack," 293
Holloway & Dobson, 96-97, 108, 135,
154
Holloway Inns of Court, 381
Holloway, Harry (co-author, *Bad Times
for Good Ol' Boys*), 284-85
Holmes, Bruce, 386, 389

Russell, David, 145, 222-23, 226-27, 230, 233-34, 238
Rystrom, Tom, 256

S

S&J Materials Co., 191-95
Safe harbor exemption, 376-77
San Diego Union-Tribune, 164
San Diego, Calif., 163; Senior Olympics, 164-65; Senior Sports Festival, 165
San Francisco Chronicle, 244
San Francisco, Calif., 32-33, 39, 72, 152
Sand Springs, Okla., 172
Sandlin Report, 182-85
Sapulpa, Okla., 66
Saturday Evening Post, 182, 188-89
Schlesinger, Jim, 258
Schmidt, H. Lee, 357-58
Scott Lawn, Tenn., 10, 14
Scott, Clifton, 275, 326
Seattle First National Bank, 262
Seattle, Wash., 152
Seay, Frank, 249-52, 271, 286
Sebring, Carl, 102-03
Second Congressional District of Oklahoma, 378
Selected Investments Corp., 54-58, 63-67
Selected Investments Corp. v. Oklahoma Tax Commission, 58, 61
Seminole County, Okla., 24, 99, 273, 366
Serbe, Steve, 76-79, 420n9
Sessions, William S., 333
Shaw, Thomas J., 375, 378-79
Shawnee Okla., 117-18, 124, 209, 322, 327, 331
Sherman Antitrust Act, 296
Shiloh Summer Camp, 386-90, 403, 410
Siegel, Barry, 245
Simmons, Sherry, 315
Simon, William, 175
Sixth Congressional District of Oklahoma, 356

Skiatook, Okla., 136
Skipworth, Donald, 185, 220-22, 230, 273-74
Slattery, Edward J. (Mary Lynn Price's father), 85-86; Evelyn Alber (Mary Lynn Price's mother), 85-86; Jo Ann (Mary Lynn Price's sister), 85-86; Mary Lynn, *see* Price, Mary Lynn (née Slattery; Bill Price's wife)
Smith, Coy, 231
Smith, Don, 230
Smith, Finis, 226
Smith, Vondel L., 37-39
Smithsonian, 84
Sneed, Earl, 46, 83
Snipes, Al, 28, 31-41, 171; Grace (Al Snipes's sister), *see* Moore, Grace; Marshall (Al Snipes's son), 28; Rebecca Davis (née Burril; Al Snipes's wife), 31
Snodgrass, Deby, 341-42, 392
Sooner Catholic, 276
Soonerism, 46, 53, 105, 199
South Oklahoma City Women's Republican Club, 37
Southeastern, Foundation, 325; Oklahoma State University, 324-27
Southwest Bank, 116
Southwestern Bell Telephone Co., 351-56, 359
Spirit Express, 387-88
Sprehe, Montine (née Price; Bill Price's sister), 15, 75, 107-08, 177-78, 345; Paul (Montine Sprehe's second husband, 108, 345; Bill Price's brother-in-law), 108, 345; Tia (Paul and Montine Sprehe's daughter), 108
Spring Valley, 85
Springfield, Mo., 55, 61, 64
St. Anthony Hospital, 377-78
St. Bonaventure University, 85
St. Gregory's College, 327
Standard Oil Co., 48